Informers in
20th Century Ireland

Informers in 20th Century Ireland
The Costs of Betrayal

ANGELA DUFFY

McFarland & Company, Inc., Publishers
Jefferson, North Carolina

LIBRARY OF CONGRESS CATALOGUING-IN-PUBLICATION DATA

Names: Duffy, Angela, 1939– author.
Title: Informers in 20th century Ireland : the costs of betrayal / Angela Duffy.
Other titles: Informers in twentieth century Ireland
Description: Jefferson, North Carolina : McFarland & Company, Inc., Publishers, 2018 | Includes bibliographical references and index.
Identifiers: LCCN 2018021519 | ISBN 9781476673295 (softcover : acid free paper) ∞
Subjects: LCSH: Informers—Ireland—History—20th century. | Ireland—History—20th century.
Classification: LCC HV8198.A2 D84 2018 | DDC 363.25/2—dc23
LC record available at https://lccn.loc.gov/2018021519

BRITISH LIBRARY CATALOGUING DATA ARE AVAILABLE

ISBN (print) 978-1-4766-7329-5
ISBN (ebook) 978-1-4766-3202-5

© 2018 Angela Duffy. All rights reserved

No part of this book may be reproduced or transmitted in any form or by any means, electronic or mechanical, including photocopying or recording, or by any information storage and retrieval system, without permission in writing from the publisher.

Front cover photograph by Ysbrand Cosijn (iStock)

Printed in the United States of America

McFarland & Company, Inc., Publishers
  Box 611, Jefferson, North Carolina 28640
  www.mcfarlandpub.com

For Nino,
and for Ray.
God rest them both.

Acknowledgments

This book could not have been written without the help of the following:

Dr. Diane Urquhart, dear Supervisor with the eagle eye for mistakes, and Professor Marianne Elliott and the rest of the staff of the Institute of Irish Studies, University of Liverpool;

Des Long, who sent me countless documents, and was never too tired to answer my questions or to engage in long arguments about Irish history;

Sean Spellissey, who introduced me to Des and was kind enough to read and comment on the Stakeknife section;

Nicky Furlong, the Wexford historian, who generously read the whole Stephen Hayes chapter and sent me his very useful comments.

Eileen Hayes, for years of help and friendship. God rest her, I miss her a great deal.

Larry Browne, for sharing his memories, and will understand why I'm prouder of finding him than of anything else;

And all the librarians and archivists in Ireland, who were always interested and answered so many questions, especially Gráinne Doran, Wexford archivist, who let me read documents not yet catalogued and is still answering my questions.

My thanks to all of you, and also to Dr. Nicola Morris, for the countless hours she spent listening to my various historical obsessions.

Table of Contents

Acknowledgments   vi

Preface   1

   • "Kate Maloney" 3 •

Introduction   5

   • "Dripsey Ambush" 21 •

1. The Evolutionary Years   22

   • "Let Erin Remember" 56 •

2. The Emergency and After (1939–1974)   58

   • "The Crime of Castlereagh" 86 •

3. Persuasion in Castlereagh   87

   • "The Informer" 119 •

4. British Intelligence and the Army   120

   • "Daddy, who was Judas?" 158 •

5. The Supergrasses   159

Conclusion   191

Appendix: Principal Methods of Torture Used in Holywood and Girdwood Barracks   197

Chapter Notes   199

Bibliography   220

Index   227

Preface

Some twenty years ago I went blind and was invalided out of my teaching job. It seemed as though there was nothing left, but I was one of the lucky ones. Although it took a long time, eventually my sight returned, so did my health, and I searched for something to do. Thus I found the Flexible Degree course at the University of Liverpool and started reading Irish history.

I first encountered the Irish informer when reading about the Battle of Kinsale, which took place on Christmas Eve, 1601 (Julian calendar), or 3 January 1602 (new Gregorian calendar). The Irish forces were mainly those of Hugh O'Neill, Earl of Tyrone, and Red Hugh O'Donnell of Ulster, the English were commanded by Lord Mountjoy, O'Neill lost the battle (which he should probably have won) because of an informer. Though this proved to be untrue it set me thinking: why would people risk their lives to do this? As my reading expanded I found more and more of them throughout the years; mostly they were unnamed, as if this had no relevance, and my curiosity grew, as did my realization of the Irish loathing of the informer. So by the time that I was looking for a research topic it was already in my head. Who were they? Why did they do it? Where could I find out about them?

I began my research with the Northern Ireland Political Collection, begun in 1969, of a quarter of a million items of printed material relating to "The Troubles" available in many volumes of microfiches in academic libraries. It took me a year to go through them all. Then I began writing this book backwards, and as I wrote the whole format of the book started to take shape. At the same time I searched for other books on informers: they exist, of course, but most of them concentrate on the political or legal impact of their activities and the authors are not historians. Notable exceptions to this are the work done by historians such as Thomas Bartlett on Francis Higgins, dubbed the Sham Squire, and that of John Borgonovo in his *Spies, Informers and the "Anti-Sinn Féin Society."* But Bartlett deals with eighteenth-century Dublin, Borgonovo only with Cork. I wanted to cover both the twentieth century and as much of Ireland as possible, as well as finding out who the informers were, how they were recruited, and, above all, why they risked so much. This book is an attempt to fulfill all that. It does not cover politics, nor the uses to which their information was put, and their assorted paymasters are only considered in the light of their recruitment and handling of the informers. The only other aspect of the phenomenon, over and above the questions noted above, is the ways in which all these things changed during the course of the century, so that we can see a progression from the lone activities of Mrs. Lindsay and William Joyce during the early years to the organized recruitment of the Supergrasses and Brian Nelson much later on.

Later my research methods changed. Each time I went to Ireland I visited libraries, bookshops, tourist and heritage centers, and talked to people about what I was doing. Invariably the response was: "That's really interesting! You should talk to so-and-so." So-and-so would mention another name, and I would pass from person to person until I found the one who really did have valuable information. I found local historians, bought their books, talked to them, and gradually amassed many contacts, a great deal of knowledge, and much material. The traditional way, visits to county and national archives, added to the mix and thus I found the marvelous resource of the Witness Statements which had only just been released (they are now online).

Despite the years I have been engaged on the whole topic of informers in Ireland I am still interested, still looking for others, still adding to my knowledge of them. For me they are important precisely because they are the little people, the pinpricks in the tapestry of history, whose betrayal of friends and comrades can cause the grand narrative to move in a completely different direction, and who invariably suffer, in return, betrayal by the very organization they served.

"Kate Maloney"

In the Winter when the snowdrift stood against the cabin door
Kate Maloney, wife of Patrick lay nigh dying on the floor
Lay on rags and tattered garments, moaning out with feeble breath
"Kneel beside me Pat my darlin', pray the Lord to give me death"

Patrick kneeled him down beside her, took her thin and wasted hand
Saying something to her softly that she scarce could understand
"Let me save ye O Mavourneen, only speak a single word
And I'll sell the golden secret where its wanted to be heard"

"Sure it cuts my heart to see you lying dying day by day
When its food and warmth you're wanting just to drive your pains away
There's a hundred golden guineas at my mercy if ye will
Do you know that Mickey Regan's in the hut upon the hill?"

Kate Maloney gripped her husband then she looked him through and through
"Pat Maloney am I dreaming did I hear these words of you
Have I lived an honest woman loving Ireland, God and you
That now upon my deathbed ye should speak those words to me

Come ye here ye tremblin' traitor stand beside me now and swear
By your soul and your hereafter while he lives you will not dare
Whisper even a single letter of brave Mickey Regans name
Can't I die of cold and hunger, would you have me die of shame?

Let the Saxon bloodhounds hunt him let them show their filthy gold
What's the poor boy done to hurt them, killed a rascal rich and old
Shot an English thief who robbed us grinding Irish peasants down
Raising rents to pay his wantons and his lackeys up in town

Are we beasts we Irish peasants whom these Saxon tyrants spurn
If ye hunt a beast too closely and ye wound him won't he turn?
Wasn't Regans sister ruined by the scoundrel lying dead
Who was paid his rent last Monday, not in silver but in lead?"

Pat Maloney stood and listened then he knelt and kissed his wife
"Kiss me darlin' and forgive me sure I thought to save your life
And it's hard to see you dying when the gold's within my reach
I'll be lonely when you're gone dear" here the sobbing stopped his speech

Late that night when Kate was dozing Pat crept cautiously away
From his cabin to the house where the hunted Regan lay
He was there, he heard him breathing, something whispered to him, Go
Go and claim the hundred guineas, Kate will never need to know

He would plan some little story when he brought her food to eat
He would say the Priest had met him and had sent her wine and meat
No one passed their lonely cabin, Kate would lie and fancy still
Mick had slipped away in secret from the hut upon the hill

Kate Maloney woke and missed him guessed his errand there and then
Raised her feeble voice to him with the voice of God and men
From her rags she slowly staggered, took her husbands loaded gun
Crying "God, I pray thee help me ere the traitor's work is done"

All her limbs were weak with fever as she crawled across the floor
But she writhed and struggled bravely till she reached the cabin door
Then she scanned the open country for the moon was in its prime
Then she saw her husband running and she thought, there yet is time

He had come from Regan's hiding past the door and now he went
By the pathway from the mountain on his evil errand bent
Once she called him but he stopped not, neither give he glance behind
For her voice was weak and feeble and it melted in the wind

Then a sudden strength came to her and she rose and followed fast
Though her naked limbs were frozen by the bitter winter blast
She had reached him very nearly when her new born spirit fled
"God has willed it" said the woman, then she shot the traitor dead

From her bloodless lips half frozen rose a whisper to the sky
"I have saved his soul from treason, here O heaven let me die
Now no babe unborn shall curse him nor his country loathe his name
I have saved you O my husband from a deed of deathless shame"

No one yet has guessed their story, Mickey Regan got away
And across the kind Atlantic lives an honest man today
While in Galway still, the peasants show the lonely mountainside
Where an Irishman was murdered and an Irishwoman died.

Source: G.R. Sims, The Dagonet ballads *(London, 1879).*

Introduction

"Il n'est point de secrets que le temps ne révèle."¹

A great deal of violence runs through this study, much of it implicit, some otherwise; it also includes intelligence matters and politics to a certain degree, as applied to the security forces and official reports on their activities. However, this study is not a consideration of any of these things: violence is a symptom of a nation's malaise: an initial reaction to perceived injustice; or to fear; or a by-product of treachery; or else it is a clumsy method of attaining a specific goal by force. Another thread, common to most of the chapters as also to the verses interspersed between each chapter, is that of the money or other rewards to be earned by informing. It is present too in the cartoon of the small boy bribed by the soldiers.² This last, however, bears an even more cogent symbolic meaning: thirty pieces of silver is the price of treachery and the very words evoke the story of Judas, the arch-traitor who informed on Christ.

Brief History

Informing in these islands was not an organized phenomenon until Elizabeth I came to the throne in 1558. Then the adoption of espionage, from Italy, and the need for accurate information was so widespread that it became an integral part of English state thinking, to the point where Elizabeth, in the Rainbow portrait at Hatfield House, wears a cloak symbolically scattered with lips, eyes, and ears.³

Initially much of the information came from travelers, merchants and traders as gossip, and was a by-product of their occupations. Later it became essential when the queen's unacknowledged fears for her life and her throne gave rise to the triumvirate of Cecil, Walsingham and Dudley as spy masters each running his own secret service to gather and filter information for her from "intelligencers."[4] When Walsingham employed a Captain Thomas in 1570, "an Irish intelligencer who had served under the French king"[5] to encompass the political ruin of the Archbishop of Cashel, it is possible that Thomas thus became the first documented Irish government informer.

In 1568, during the Reformation, the seminary at Douai was established. English government surveillance began there in 1571, and by the mid-1570s Walsingham had a secretary responsible for "the capture and examination of Jesuits and seminary priests … as well as for Irish matters,"[6] but the system declined in the final decade of the sixteenth century until priest-hunting began again under Cromwell. Later, following the bill of 1704 to prevent the further growth of Popery, a corps of informers was organized as pursuivants (England) and priest catchers (Ireland), who gained sizeable rewards for the apprehension of priests.

Lecky's theory that the unforeseen aftermath of the Penal Code was its corrupting effect on the people of Ireland is still persuasive[7]: "The mass of the people gradually acquired the vices of slaves."[8] They saw the country filled with spies and informers and the "creation by law of a gigantic system of bribery."[9] For Lecky, this breakdown of the moral law serves as an explanation for the great numbers of informers before, during and after the 1798 rebellion, though Miles Byrne of Monaseed, Co. Wexford, a United Irishman prominent in the Wexford Rising and in Emmet's conspiracy in 1803, insists frequently in his *Memoirs* that there were no informers at all: "Towards the end of the year 1797, the Orange magistrates used all their influence … [to] discover what the United Irishmen were bent on doing; but in vain. They could not for any sum of money find any to turn informer and betray the sacred cause."[10]

Fitzpatrick bears this out to a certain extent: "There were informers from the first, but not to the extent suggested; nor can it be fairly said that they were men deepest in the secret."[11] Madden is less sanguine: "A regular system of espionage was adopted so early as 1795; and in 1796 there were few secrets of the United Irishmen which were not in the hands of the government."[12]

Leonard MacNally was a popular barrister, playwright, United Irishman and the most successful informer of his time. Even after his death, when his treachery became known, there were still those who refused to believe it. Notable during the same period was Francis Higgins, "The Sham Squire," though his secret life was no secret at all[13]; and as for women, James Connolly wrote "Think of all the slimy roll of informers in Erin, and wonder when you remember how seldom even tradition places woman's name upon the list."[14] Nevertheless, in 1798, Belfast had Bella Martin; in Wicklow, Rachael Valentine of Manger as well as Mrs. White and Mrs. McGrath of Athdown; and in Wexford Bridget Dolan, better known as Croppy Biddy.

That the culture of informing had become endemic in Ireland can be seen clearly in reactions to the *poitín* industry, particularly during the period of 1735–1855 in Donegal, where more *poitín* was produced than in any other area.[15] The revenue officers made extensive use of informers: in 1786, for example, the Rev. Thomas Bedford, rector of a parish worth £800 per year, was tried and fined £440 on the word of an informer who said he "had sold beer and *poitín* in his house after service on Sundays."[16] The period also led to a hardening of attitudes towards the informer, where suspicion was sufficient proof: in 1815 "suspicious neighbors burned Daniel Gillespie's house and outhouses containing 12 sheep"; and in October 1817 "*poitín* makers had burned the house of suspected informer Lindsay of Carndonagh."[17] While towards the end of the century Michael Davitt's Land League (1879) and the agrarian disturbances, together with the IRB and the Fenians, caused much government worry which might have affected their intelligence network, but the Register of Informants held in Dublin Castle indicates that this was not the case.[18]

The information provided in the register is sparse, but useful as an indication of (mainly) minor informer activity. It records the years 1880–c. 1891 and reveals the presence of 105 informers spread across most of the counties, including some 56 sworn IRB men. For each informer there is a brief note of the type of information provided, his trustworthiness and, sometimes, his reward. The majority of these sums range between £1 and £4, though "Nero" received £205 and the accolade: "The informant 'Nero' is worth any amount and being in a good position he has really received very little."[19] All are listed under codenames and the register contains only one woman: "Mary Sullivan" who "enabled us to break up a Boycotting conspiracy … [and] to check the 'Cattle Manifesto' Conspiracy and arrest 3 of Conspirators." Mary was rewarded with £60, one of the most highly paid on the register, and the use of financial reward for information continued in the twentieth century.

This work is an attempt to set the informer within the context of the grand narrative of the twentieth century, and within his own society. A primary aim is to identify the informers themselves and, through the case studies which make up the majority of the text, to look in some detail at their lives, to seek an understanding of why they became traitors and of how this affected their lives. Also included are some who may not have been guilty of the accusations they faced: this category includes Stephen Hayes (Chapter 2) and Fred Scappaticci (Chapter 4).

By focusing on micro-historical research several matters have emerged. The most important of these is the theme, the factor which unites every case study whether the accused is guilty or innocent, of betrayal. Nor is this simplistic: it is not just the obvious betrayal of comrades, friends or The Cause. Instead the evidence points clearly and repeatedly to treachery on all sides. Secondly, the evidence shows a strong contrast between the informers of the first part of the century (and earlier) and those in Northern Ireland after 1969. This contrast is not merely numerical. Sources reveal that a culture of informing was fostered in Northern Ireland by the security forces during the twentieth century,[20] and has produced a definite hierarchy: from the children stopped by soldiers and bribed with sweets; the women watching their neighbors and passing on gossip; to the supergrasses willing to accuse anybody at all at the behest of the RUC.[21] Thirdly, surprisingly little has been written about the Irish government informer; in terms of modern writing there is only Bartlett,[22] who has done interesting work on those of 1798 and, more recently, an upsurge of interest in intelligence spearheaded by O'Halpin,[23] which throws the researcher back onto media accounts and those books written by lawyers and journalists.

Implicit within the concept of the informer in Ireland is the powerful idea that to betray a comrade is a betrayal of our Fenian dead, of all those Irishmen whose lives and deaths have been made holy in the Irish mind: of Emmet, Pearse and the rest, stretching back in a long long line of heroes to Cuchulain in his chains. Homi Bhabha uses a striking illustration of this when he writes:

> Nations ... only fully realize their horizons in the mind's eye ... it is from ... traditions of political thought and literary language that the nation emerges as a powerful historical idea in the west. An idea whose cultural compulsion lies in the impossible unity of the nation as a symbolic force ... the origins of national traditions turn out to be as much acts of affiliation and establishment as they are moments of disavowal, displacement, exclusion, and cultural contestation.[24]

Benedict Anderson adds to this explanation noting: "Nationalism has to be understood, by aligning it not with self-consciously held political ideologies, but with large cultural systems that preceded it, out of which (as well as against which) it came into being."[25]

Thus the nationalist concept of the Irish informer is completely negative, as can readily be seen in the verses, especially "I am Judas Stephen Hayes" which names a wide assortment of those he was alleged to have betrayed as well as his putative paymaster, de Valera. Verse is always more memorable than prose, indeed under the Brehon law it was a much-feared way to traduce an enemy, leaving him with the realization that this poem would remain to tarnish his reputation long after he was dead.[26]

In direct contrast to this outlook, and underpinning it, is the endurance esteemed by nationalist opinion and enshrined in Bobby Sands's "The Crime of Castlereagh," as well as in the clever but grim cartoon published in the *Belfast Bulletin* of the judicial death's head whose eyes are formed by two hands gripping prison bars.[27] This perspective is shared equally by the Northern loyalists, but they take it further: much information in these pages was gleaned from the republican press, but very little, until the supergrass trials, was to be found in loyalist publications such as *Loyalist News* and *Ulster*.

Finally, case studies of informers provide some answers to the question which I find most interesting: what motivated the informer himself? In the quest to understand this, Braudel's *Ecrits sur l'Histoire* has broadened the scope of my thinking: "History seems to us to be like life itself, a spectacle which is fleeting, moving, made up of an intricate interlacing of problems which can take on a hundred different and contradictory faces.... There is no unilateral history."[28]

Braudel urges both a breaking down of the artificial frontiers between specialists and a greater focus on the individual, who is too often seen as an abstraction.[29] He also argues that historiographers should use illness, death, suicide, desertion of children, illegitimate birth, concubinage, hospitals, treatment of the old, and so on, as a social panoply rich in evidence, so that they can explain history in such a way that the societies and individuals of the past will again take on the charm and warmth of life.[30] Nevertheless, it is noticeable that Braudel prefers the disciplines which look at man from the outside and misses out those which look at man the individual, such as art, literature, religion, and psychology.

Betrayal

Dante places informers among the traitors in the last circle of Hell, with Judas condemned to spend eternity in a place of utter darkness at the bottom of the universe, where the worst of the damned are caught in a frozen lake. There they are surrounded by a thick veil of ice symbolizing the secrecy within which they had operated. Worse still, he says that betrayal kills the soul, which goes immediately to its place in Hell, while a demon takes over the still living body until the appointed end of its life.[31] Dante writes of all traitors when he says: "Oh worst of all created people who dwell in this unspeakable place, better for you if you had been born beasts."[32]

The example of Judas rests on events of two millennia ago, but there is another instance long before that. The serpent brought disobedience into the garden of Eden, but he also brought betrayal. When God taxed Adam with having eaten the forbidden fruit the latter informed on Eve: "It was the woman you put with me; she gave me the fruit and I ate it."[33] Just as with the Judas story, though to a lesser extent, this accusation has echoed down the centuries and reaches its apotheosis in the anonymous 11th-century Irish poem where Eve holds herself responsible for all the ills that she and Adam brought on the human race: "I am Eve, great Adam's wife / It is I that outraged Jesus of old / It is I that stole Heaven from my children / By rights it is I that should have gone upon the tree."[34]

Thus betrayal is one of the world's great themes, present not only since the beginning of history, but also in a wide range of literature: Shakespeare provides a prime example of the attempted recruitment of an informer when a minor character in *All's Well That Ends Well* is speaking of the scoundrel Parolles: "Be but your lordship present at his examination: if he do not, for the promise of his life and in the highest compulsion of base fear, offer to betray you and deliver all the intelligence in his power against you, and that with the divine forfeit of his soul upon oath, never trust my judgment in any thing."[35]

In more recent times betrayal seems to have become the province of psychologists, but their thinking is predicated almost exclusively on marital infidelity and child abuse, nevertheless some of their findings are useful despite the ponderous language exemplified by a definition of treachery as "a voluntary violation of mutually known pivotal expectations of the trustor by the trusted party (trustee), which has the potential to threaten the well-being of the trustor."[36] A better, and more comprehensible, definition is supplied by Rachman:

> Betrayal is the sense of being harmed by the intentional actions or omissions of a trusted person. The most common forms of betrayal are harmful disclosures of confidential information, disloyalty, infidelity, dishonesty.... The effects of betrayal include shock, loss and grief, morbid pre-occupation, damaged self-esteem, self-doubting, anger. Not infrequently they produce life-altering changes.[37]

Chan lists the different kinds of betrayal, some of which have obvious connections to this work: in egoistic betrayal "the perpetrator is so consumed with his ... goal that whoever stands in his ... way will be betrayed"; in ideological betrayal "employees may blow the whistle on their employers when their superordinate value of ethics is breached"; in personalistic betrayal "the perpetrator deliberately chooses the course of action that is detrimentally relevant to the victim"; in reciprocal betrayal "the perpetrator is reciprocating a previous betrayal that was committed by the victim" (children know this as "tit for tat").[38] Germane to this study, "research has shown that the perpetrator may engage in account-giving after a betrayal.... There are four types of social accounts—(i) pure confession, (ii) denial, (iii) excuse, and (iv) justification.... In pure confession the perpetrator assumes full responsibility for the betrayal act."[39] This can plainly be applied to the books written by the informers and their handlers, of which only Eamon Collins's *Killing Rage* (London, 1997) could come under the heading of pure confession, while the rest are all simultaneously denial, excuse, and justification.

Sources

Sources include archival material, parliamentary records, oral history, and printed material (such as newspapers, memoirs, and secondary sources). Their quality must always be variable but, as Bloch writes, "the historian does not put all the good evidence on the right, the bad on the left. In his eyes, there is no good evidence which he trusts once and for all, giving up all control. To be exact on certain points, a testimony is not perforce free of all error. There is hardly any bad evidence. A very imperfect narrative can contain useful information."[40]

A caveat is necessary at this point: many of the sources used here are, or might be, unreliable and this is especially true of those memoirs which are self-justifying, or which legitimize the actions of the army and the police. Worse still, there is frequently only one source of information, so great care is necessary. Nevertheless, that need not prevent the researcher mining them for what is useful.[41]

In the first half of the twentieth century the main suppliers of news were the newspapers and even the very poor had access to them, because they were passed from hand to hand. Such newspapers, many of them local, are among the most significant of the documents used here. The principal reason for this is summed up by Jackson: "Provincial readerships are … seen as a rigorous check on the accuracy of news reports and features where these concern the local scene. For collectively readers have a detailed knowledge of all the local material. They act as a check not only on factual accuracy but also on any distortion or exaggeration that may result from the mode of selection or the manner or presentation."[42]

The researcher's approach to newspaper articles should be the same as to any other historical document, while bearing in mind such matters pertaining to journalism as copying from other newspapers and speed of writing leading to factual errors, as well as the possible bias of the writer, the editor or the proprietors or, alternatively, pressure from advertisers. It seems strange that the local press can be more accurate than powerful national newspapers, but the local readership factor is cogent. The letter to Máire Comerford in Chapter 2 serves as an example: the Hayes trial was held in Dublin in June 1942; that *The Enniscorthy Guardian* sent their own journalist to Dublin can be inferred from the more complete copy of Hayes's letter which appeared in the Wexford newspaper. This leaves possible bias and interference from advertisers. Of the former Jackson says, "the factor of prejudice may … act as a conscious or unconscious influence on what to include and what to omit, or on the degree of prominence judged to be appropriate," but goes on to point out the external checks which again arise from the readership: such prejudice might offend readers and "their resulting attitude to the local Press may ... influence the attitude of others."⁴³ Finally, of attempts by advertisers to influence the press, Jackson notes:

> there is a widely held belief that advertisers can and do exert an influence on editorial policy ... [that] Commercial concerns can ... withhold their advertising.... In practice, editors know that retributive strategies of this sort will, in the long run, hurt the institutions more than the Press ... the commercial institution that withholds advertising is cutting its own financial throat.... Its revenue will often largely depend on advertising in the local Press.... When provincial newspapers comment on the subject ... they invariably put forward two propositions: first, that extremely few attempts to influence content occur, and, second, that when they do occur they are firmly resisted.⁴⁴

It might seem that the Northern Ireland local weekly newspapers could fall into a different category given that "the local Press adjusts its content, in terms of subject matter and depth of presentation, in accordance with a continuing assessment of its readers."⁴⁵ The implication here is that, for instance, readers of the *Andersonstown News* want to know about the supergrasses and informer recruitment attempts by the RUC as well as local news. It is worth noting that the circulation of the *Andersonstown News* is far greater than its name would suggest, as its coverage is reproduced not only in *An Phoblacht/Republican News* (though this may well be a two-way factor), but also in Irish-American newspapers such as *The Irish People*.

This gives rise to the question of propaganda. It would seem, however, that this was far more a problem for the British in earlier years than it has been for anyone in Northern Ireland since 1969, largely because of the D-notices preventing media use of adverse information emanating from the province.⁴⁶ In 1921, though, British concerns about adverse propaganda abroad escalated, clearly to be seen in such Dublin Castle documents as the Minute Sheet for 1921 which notes "foreign propaganda is becoming more important than home. I am not satisfied that F/O [Foreign Office] and Colonial Office do as much as might be done."⁴⁷ A despatch from the Consul General in New Orleans resulted in action: "An official summary of events in Ireland ... will be put at the disposal of the United States press correspondents so that they may transmit the information to the United States before ... publishing distorted versions in the absence of authentic news."⁴⁸

Furthermore, none of the articles in *An Phoblacht/Republican News* or the *Andersonstown News* reproduced in (mainly) the Irish-American newspapers show signs of the overt and sentimental propaganda which appeared on the front page of a Toronto paper in 1921. This claimed to be a letter from a Cork Gentleman to His Brother in Ontario, Portraying Vividly the State of Ireland and included such anecdotes as the following: "I have known the case of a young family which had to go to bed supperless, as their mother had been driven from the town by a British officer, for venturing to sell a few dozen of eggs. Their father was dying of cancer and their mother had to depend on the sale of those eggs in order to buy bread for the children."[49]

Two other sources proved to be significant here: archival documents and the informers' memoirs. The former include the Billy Quirke typescript on Hayes, the accuracy of which was vouched for by Nicholas Furlong, the Wexford historian, who had known Quirke; and the Witness Statements, held in the Bureau of Military History, Dublin. The statements were the result of an organized attempt, beginning in 1947, to ensure that the memories of those who had participated in these events would not die with them, and the witnesses were guaranteed that none of the documents would be released until the last witness died. These two facts inspire confidence. The statements cover the period from the formation of the Irish Volunteers in 1913 to the Truce in July 1921 and are of varying length: Florrie O'Donoghue, Brigade Intelligence Officer in Cork City, wrote very little, but he wrote extensively elsewhere; while others (Eamon Broy, one of Michael Collins's agents in the Castle, wrote two statements amounting to around 200 pages) are very much longer.[50] Of particular value here are the two statements made by Joseph Togher of Galway, because in his role as Intelligence Officer he discovered much about William Joyce, used as a case study in the first chapter.[51]

With the informers' memoirs caution is necessary: these texts are not written to tell the truth, but to bolster the agent as hero, so are plentifully supplied with euphemism and inaccuracy and can present their past as they would like it to have been. Thus Bloch's advice is wise: "Lies are perhaps more easily discovered than inaccuracy, because their cause is more obvious and better known generally. Most people do not realize how rarely evidence is completely and utterly exact in every way. Two kinds of fault are to be feared: those of memory and those of awareness."[52]

Therefore the informers' published memoirs form another significant source, principally Raymond Gilmour's *Dead Ground* (London, 1999), Kevin Fulton's *Unsung Hero* (London, 2006) and Eamon Collins's *Killing Rage*. One of the greatest differences between the modern informer and his counterpart in previous times is his tendency (at least after the fact) to seek rather than avoid publicity. While this is a boon for the chronicler and those who seek to understand his actions, it is puzzling. Arguably these memoirs are both self-justifying and confessional. Gilmour, Barker and Collins provide evidence for a tentative theory about IRA[53] informers, that however weakened the religious aspect of their lives it still affects them all: confession is important to the IRA where informers are concerned and few are executed without it, though it may be obtained by force. It may be a ritual like Catholic confession, or a useful expedient in that it tells the commanders what information has been given and when, but these two explanations are not mutually exclusive. In the same tradition Collins records Scappaticci's question: was there any chance of my "going down the Damascus road?"⁵⁴ Collins explains his dilemma at this time: "I had come to ditch almost everything and everybody not connected in some way to the IRA ... I felt myself to be part of a large family whose members had powerful emotional links to each other. The idea of turning my back on the IRA had become as repugnant to me as turning my back on my own children."⁵⁵

Collins is rightly ashamed of the first part of his life yet needs to justify his later status as a tout and one of the many questions raised by his experiences, first under interrogation, later under constant pressure from the RUC, and finally under the psychological effects of applied gentleness, is whether those who have been brainwashed in one aspect of their lives can be more easily influenced a second time? "Once I started talking, I crossed over into the enemy camp. Effectively I had become a hesitant convert to the forces of the Crown. Looking back, I realize that the interrogator must ensure that in the prisoner's mind loyalty to his new friends replaces loyalty to his old ones. This smooth operator certainly knew how to create and cement such loyalty."⁵⁶

Killing Rage contains detailed accounts of informer recruitment procedures and IRA debriefing, so it is valuable as a source, and Eamon Collins is interesting, partly because he is at pains to lay bare his motivation, disillusion, and self-disgust, partly because he is of a higher degree of intelligence than most of his peers.⁵⁷ Yet *Killing Rage* is as much apologia as autobiography, and it was ghost-written, thus setting up between Collins and the reader a screen behind which much can be hidden.⁵⁸ This book was in part the cause of his death, because it was such a critical account of life inside the IRA, and the resultant publicity led to many television appearances for Collins, then he testified against Thomas "Slab" Murphy in a libel case against the *Sunday Times*. This may have been the step too far, because nine months later, on 27 January 1999, he was killed.⁵⁹

Dead Ground was written when Raymond Gilmour was in his late thirties, some twenty years after he became a supergrass. It is an attempt to rationalize his actions, mainly by way of the oft-quoted mantra of "saving lives," and to excuse them by pointing to a deprived childhood. Yet he does not mention his mother's mental health problems, nor her absences from home when she was hospitalized, neither does he use the only valid reason for his treachery: that he was groomed and flattered by Special Branch when he was far too young to understand what he was doing.⁶⁰ It is therefore noteworthy that the evidence given in his book for deprivation—the single fire in the living room as a source of heat, having to share bedrooms, no holidays, broken glass where the children might play—were all fairly common elsewhere in the UK at this time. Nastier are comments about others scattered through the book: of his older brother, Gerry, he says, "he eventually went south to

Dublin ... which was no loss at all"; and of his father: "I suppose he didn't know any better."[61] Yet he lays emphasis on his own sensitivity and that "uniquely among the kids on the Creggan, I grew up with friendly feelings towards the RUC."[62] He attributes this to his mother's refusal to treat either the army or the police as enemies, and to individual RUC men who were kind to the small boy of the house each time they arrested his brothers.[63]

Peter Keeley, better known as "Kevin Fulton," also wrote about his informing activities. In his foreword to Fulton's book *Unsung Hero*, Martin Ingram attempts to justify Kevin Fulton's actions by throwing blame back onto British military intelligence and the Force Research Unit (FRU). Despite Ingram's intentions this attempt fails: it has been an accepted principle since the Nuremberg trials that "following orders" is not a defense. Kevin Fulton chose for his own (mostly mercenary) reasons to engage in immoral and illegal operations, some of which resulted in murder, and *Unsung Hero* clearly depicts the downward path followed by this man.

He constantly claims to be a secret agent, but agent, spy, informant or informer—the word used for such activities depends entirely on the standpoint of the writer. In Fulton's case he *was* a British soldier, however briefly; it is highly unlikely that he would ever have joined the IRA if not pushed by his handlers, but his first betrayal was the identification of an old school friend, and many other such identifications followed.[64] He inveigled two close friends in Newry into becoming informers[65]; there was his betrayal of "Johnny" to the FBI[66]; and finally he offered his services as an "agent" to whichever organization would pay him the most.[67]

Two secondary sources merit attention because both are by academic authors and add to the perspective on the supergrasses: the first, *Supergrasses*, is by Steven Greer, who is a lawyer, so his focus is on the show trials and their impact on the law[68]; in the second, *Informers*, Andrew Boyd has written an excellent account of the informers themselves.[69] Greer is exceptionally impartial in his writing. He can see the advantages of the supergrasses from the law's point of view: "Their unique contribution is to allow the carefully cultivated results of sophisticated police intelligence-gathering systems to be presented in court for the purpose of convicting large numbers of suspected terrorists or organized criminals."[70] Yet at the same time he is aware of the drawbacks:

> Each supergrass has been involved in serious, and mostly violent, crime and is therefore regarded by the law as of unusually bad character.... The pressure to tell a story sufficiently appealing to attract the various rewards on offer is also likely to be more intense than with most other accomplices turning Queen's evidence. There is, in addition, ample time and opportunity during the many months spent in protective police custody for false evidence to be rehearsed in preparation for a convincing court-room performance.[71]

The second part of the book concerns the individual supergrasses, the trials (and the appeals) with which each was involved and their rewards. He includes different aspects of the phenomenon: the anti-supergrass campaign; views across the sectarian divide; the Gifford Report of 1984; and a useful series of appendices which list the numbers convicted and those found guilty after appeal. His conclusions are not in favor of the system, but it is difficult to resist the idea that this is because it is a legal experiment which failed, rather than because of any injustice inherent in it.

Boyd, on the other hand, looks at individual lives: "At all places and in all times informers are the most despised of the human race. If they do not meet with quick and violent execution they live out their fugitive lives in constant fear of the assassin's fist, shunned even by those for whose benefit they betrayed the cause they once upheld."[72]

Even this brisk summary of the precarious nature of the informers' lives is indicative of the confidence with which Boyd approaches his subject. *The Informers* covers only the major supergrass trials (approximately those from 1981–82), nevertheless he gives us a detailed exposition of these to set usefully against the same trials as covered by Greer. He considers the informers, their employers, and the opinions of the Gifford inquiry, but never loses sight of the humanity of these men. He accepts fully that they are despicable, yet can still write with empathy of the lifelong nightmare which awaits them and their families when the trial ends: a new identity means that "they will ... cease to be the persons they were.... One breach in ... [the] protective arrangements and the informer is doomed."[73]

Oral evidence has made a small but significant contribution to this work, most particularly in that the information obtained is entirely original and provides additional understanding of the subjects. As with every other research method, oral history brings advantages and dangers in its train. Nevertheless, and perhaps because there has been no sense of information being withheld by any of the interviewees, from the standpoint of this study other problems (such as the fallibility of memory) can be largely discounted. The principal reasons for this are that firstly each interviewee was recalling just one person, at a time when that person's life was so traumatic that it seriously affected the lives of an entire family. Thus the events in question, and the reactions of outsiders, remain sharply delineated in the memory. Secondly, the interviewer was seeking to round out the character depicted in the case study so most of the questions were fairly specific, though the interviews were unstructured; this has also made for briefer and more accurate transcripts.

Seldon and Pappworth make the point that "oral evidence cannot be verified by others,"[74] but this has not been the case here. Characteristics observed over a period of time can remain in the mind until long after such details as precise dates have been forgotten: thus, Eileen Hayes, widow of Hayes's nephew, whose knowledge was based on the years when Hayes lodged with her mother, spoke about Stephen Hayes's laughter that would fill a room and set everyone else laughing, and Larry Browne, Hayes's son, confirmed that his mother often remarked on this as well.

The most significant interviews were with Eileen Hayes, because her recollections led to the discovery of Stephen Hayes's son, whose own memories, though based entirely on his mother's reminiscences, provided much useful information: especially the episode during the early days of Hayes's captivity when the conspirators abducted her to add to the pressure exerted on Hayes. Though some minor questions remained unanswered, the information revealed by these interviews, though fragmentary, has proved very worthwhile.

The importance of poetry in Ireland, well-attested from Celtic times, cannot be overestimated. In fact it is notable that during the Elizabethan conquest, in a pragmatic move which argues a far greater understanding of the Irish than is usually acknowledged, not only the Irish language but also the poets were targeted, and this continued during the Penal days. Daly writes of Seán Clárach Mac Dómhnaill,[75] that he was "hunted in his early day by the squirearchy, who took to the chase of the priest and the poet with as keen a zest as did their descendants of later times to the less exciting pastime of fox hunting."[76] Moreover, centuries later, it was no coincidence that 1916 has often been described as the poets' rebellion. In addition, as Kinsella writes: "The Irish tradition has always presented an intimate fusion of literature and history. At certain times the literature and the history are functions of one another,"[77] while Corkery says that it was the "intimate expression of the hidden life of the people among whom it flourished."[78] Both of these things are still so to a degree.

Thus the final source could be variously labeled poetry, verse, doggerel: but, with the exception of Bobby Sands's work, poetry is too lofty a word; verse can be clever but is seldom either inspiring or informative; and doggerel smacks too much of nursery rhymes. So I have chosen the old Irish word amhrán [plural—amhráin]: literally "song" but frequently used also to mean poem, and this seems to cover all the pieces I have used. The amhráin have certain characteristics in common, not only with each other but with all amhráin stretching back to the first recorded verse warning of the arrival of Christianity in Ireland.[79] Later a stream of what might be termed folk poetry (*Amhráin na nDaoine*) began. Many of the examples which have survived are anonymous, typical also of their twentieth-century counterparts, but the most valuable quality they all have is a sense of history. Each one is about events which had great importance both to those immediately involved and (though maybe to a lesser extent) to the country itself.

So the amhráin chosen to illustrate this study, like the Táin (once dismissed as a legend, now valued for its background knowledge),[80] show us a world that is gone, and it is important to the historian for what it cannot help revealing: a picture of the feelings and beliefs of the past. "Kate Maloney" gives us the traditional portrait of the informer himself. His motive is good but it involves the betrayal of another man and is, therefore, irrelevant even to his wife who appoints herself his judge and his executioner. "Dripsey Ambush" tells a different story: the results of informing with the capture and deaths of several men. The amhrán itself is simplistic, but the episode is far more complicated as we shall see. Chapter 2 is introduced by "Let Erin Remember," an old title borrowed from Thomas Moore which would be well-known to all those who read it. This version is a diatribe of accusations against Stephen Hayes, its contents reflecting so much of the notorious "Confession" as to force the reader to think the two are one and the same. This also is anonymous, but a certain amount of internal evidence and a knowledge of Hayes's tendency to irony lead to a supposition that it might have been written by Hayes himself.

The other three, each one introducing a chapter, deal with the situation in Northern Ireland. Castlereagh, feared and loathed, comes alive in the poetry of Bobby Sands MP, the most famous of the hunger strikers of 1981[81]; the British army efforts to recruit informers are explained briefly by a warning verse "The Informer," published in *The Volunteer*, which echoes an *Andersonstown News* cartoon also titled "The Informer" depicting a pub table complete with bottles and glasses; and finally "Daddy, who was Judas?" which was originally published in *Combat*,[82] is both more sophisticated and more scathing than "The Informer," and points out only Joe Bennett, the first loyalist supergrass.

While appreciating the above, it might be useful to have a way of differentiating between poetry and verse. Most poetry in any language is poor, and some is execrable. As posterity we are protected from many of the vapid outpourings of other times—though we have no such protection against modern poetry—for the simple reason that, like the cream rising to the top of the milk, only the best survives. Those poets who spent their career in obscurity, relative or otherwise, probably deserved it. The best poetry is a kind of shorthand. It is life reduced to its essence by much thought and skill, with the meaning (as with sculpture and all good writing) lying as much in what is left out as in the words. Perhaps the best definition comes from the words of the old Galway farmer questioned by Mac Réamoinn: "How do you tell a great poet?"

"Better words," he said, "better placed ... the way you'd be building a wall and you'd know where to put the bricks."[83]

Introduction   19

Chronology and Structure

This study reconsiders the phenomenon of informing by looking primarily at the whole of the twentieth century and at several counties across Ireland. Thus the evolution of the informer is traced from the amateurish and opportunistic traitors of the earlier years, to the full-scale networks which gradually emerged in end-of-the-century Northern Ireland. Moreover, it discusses the evidence which suggests that both Special Branch and the British army, the main paymasters, ultimately learned that the subtle approach to recruitment was far more effective than the brutality used during the 1970s.

The format of the work is designed to provide a brief overview of each significant period of the century, against which are set the lives and activities of certain informers (or alleged informers). The overall intention is to draw a picture of the twentieth century from an unfamiliar viewpoint: to depict the havoc wrought by betrayal in those years; to set out the gamut of informers: men, women, children; the innocent as well as the guilty; the effects of their actions on their lives; their recruitment; and to demonstrate that, despite their utter lack of importance as characters in the grand narrative, these people have all had a disproportionate effect on the history of their time: the Stephen Hayes affair, for example, almost finished the IRA, and the supergrasses brought about internment without trial as well as focusing the disapproving eyes of the world on events in Belfast. The chapters are in chronological order, though in the final three, dealing with Northern Ireland, this is interpreted loosely.

Thus, Chapter 1 covers the period from the Easter Rising to the Civil War, with the emphasis on the Anglo-Irish War and the numbers of informers at that time. Chapter 2 covers the Emergency and Irish neutrality, the consequent difficulties besetting the IRA, their attempts to enlist German aid without a German presence in Ireland and the later years until Operation Harvest, the fifties Border Campaign of 1956–62. The other three chapters investigate the Northern Ireland situation (1969–c.2000) from the viewpoint of the lives of those living there and the profusion of informers involved with the security forces. The chapters overlap to a certain extent, but each concentrates on a different aspect of the whole, and the theme of betrayal continues throughout: Chapter 3 deals with RUC Special Branch and their recruitment of informers in Castlereagh Interrogation Center, a place ruled by fear. Chapter Four considers the British army involvement with informers and the connection, via Stakeknife, with MI5, and the final chapter concerns the supergrasses, the RUC attempt to provide Hermon with converted terrorists, and the ignominy of the show-trials which brought down the opprobrium of both Europe and America on Northern Ireland.

In general, a picture emerges from this multifaceted approach of a group of people who, though despised, nevertheless have their place in the history of the last century and, surprisingly, that certain individuals in the group might even arouse our sympathy and understanding. This idea, though, is highly contentious, above all because of the traditional Irish view of the informer, illustrated by "Kate Maloney" and by the words of the secretary who suggested that Sir Matthew Nathan, under-secretary for Ireland, when referring to Dublin informers in 1916, should use a neutral word instead because: "the word informer ... sounds so badly in an Irish ear that there is sure to be a howl about it. I always remember an old ballad which, referring to such an informer, breaks out—'May the hearthstone of Hell be his rest bed forever.'"[84]

"Dripsey Ambush"

One Friday in January,
As the boys from far and near,
assembled down at Godfreys' Cross,
An ambush to prepare,
There were boys from Dripsey Valley,
And famed old Donoughmore,
All going to fight for Ireland,
Where the Dripsey River flows.

II
Long and patiently they waited,
Though the day was bitter cold,
They little knew that behind their back,
The ambush had been sold,
For a traitor dwelt amongst them,
And this they did not know,
And the soldiers found their hiding place,
Where the Dripsey River flows.

III
At four o'clock the soldiers came,
And they were well prepared,
With rifles and machine-guns,
They surrounded the volunteers,
The lads were brave and daring,
And they made a gallant show,
They bravely faced the foe that day,
Where the Dripsey River flows.

IV
God's Angels must have guarded them,
For bullets fell like hail,
The bravest of them waited,
To let their comrades go,
And they were shot and captured,
Where the Dripsey River flows.

V
Their parents went to see them,
Into the prison cell,
They first asked for their comrades,
Were they alive and well,
And when they the boys escaped,
'Tis glad they were to know,
That God had their comrades brave,
To strike another blow.

Source: Volume 344, Page 49, The Schools' Collection, National Folklore Collection, University College Dublin, www.duchas.ie. Used with permission.

1

The Evolutionary Years

"a traitor dwelt amongst them"

A great deal of this book is made up of micro-history and this first chapter is deeply indebted to the documents written by those who took an active part in the 1916 Rising and the Anglo-Irish war, stored in the Bureau of Military History, and generally known simply as the Witness Statements. There are, of course, other personal accounts of the period, such as Margaret Skinnider's *Doing My Bit for Ireland*, published in the wake of 1916, where she wrote with pride about the impossibility of informers: "there was no traitor in our ranks. No one had whispered a word of our plans to the British authorities ... the temptation to betray the rising must have been just as strong ... as heretofore. Yet no one yielded to this temptation."[1]

Though Margaret Skinnider attributes the lack of informers to the implied nobility of the men who took part in the 1916 Rising, there was a more pragmatic explanation: Britain was at war and so the RIC[2] were searching primarily for signs of German involvement with the Volunteers.[3] Eamon Broy in his Witness Statement, however, could still say of that time: "The people felt that the local R.I.C. knew all about them and there was no use doing anything illegal and secret because the police were certain to find out."[4] It seems that the RIC shared these sentiments, and in Dublin Castle the Executive (Augustine Birrell, Chief Secretary; Matthew Nathan, Under-Secretary; and Lord Wimborne, Lord Lieutenant of Ireland) was focused on the problems of making conscription acceptable to the Irish. As late as April 1916 Nathan wrote, "Though the Irish Volunteer element has been active of late ... especially in Dublin, *I do not believe that its leaders mean insurrection*."[5] Equally there is the possibility that the methods of recruitment into the Volunteers, as recounted by David Daly, worked well: "Our country had such a legend of informers and betrayers over the centuries of its occupation that ... every recruit's background and upbringing was gone into carefully before he was accepted."[6] In addition, the Easter Rising was planned by the seven-man IRB Military Council whose activities were concealed even from the IRB Supreme Council, so few people knew the Rising was imminent until the middle of Holy Week 1916. There was, however, at least one informer, Quinlisk (discussed below) and there were the spotters, moving among the GPO garrison as they waited outside the Rotunda Hospital, who pointed out notable prisoners for the British officers.

The interim period following the Rising was first a time of confusion, then bereavement, then of small acts of indignation rather than insurrection. At the same time the execution of the leaders had taught their successors that a small poorly armed force could not confront the British Army in battle with any hope of winning. The alternative was a war of attrition which needed excellent intelligence to counter that available to the Castle from the RIC and from what was, according to Frank Gallagher, an extensive network of petty informers.[7] Both ideas took time to reach the forefront of the Volunteers' thinking, neither came from any one man but rather evolved gradually from the Rising itself. Count Plunkett's success in the Roscommon by-election brought a heavy-handed reply from Dublin Castle in the early months of 1917 when men were arrested and charged with trivial offences. The consequent fines and prison sentences did nothing to quell the rising tide of nationalism and Easter 1917 was celebrated with, among other things, the tricolor flying at half-mast over the remains of the GPO. This scenario adds weight to Máire Comerford's summation of this time: "Most of the historians seem to accept that we reacted to the Rising in the way we did because of the executions. But it wasn't death, it was the call to freedom which captivated us."[8]

The prospect of partition fuelled more anger, but there were small victories, defiance grew, and Sinn Féin won another by-election in Longford.[9] The prisoners had come home in time for Christmas 1916, and the welcome they received was made manifest in De Valera's election victory of July 1917 in East Clare. Prison in Frongoch had provided both a nascent organization and a spreading of knowledge among these young men which had reinvigorated them all. The end result was a new confidence in themselves which translated into a successful recruitment drive for the republican movement. Yet the secret service vote spending on information actually decreased in the financial year following the Easter Rising.[10]

As O'Halpin explains: the secret service vote was an annual amount provided by parliament to buy secret information, so, given the widespread rise in poverty of these years, it is surprising that "Despite the substantial rewards available, very little intelligence was obtained from within the I.R.A. by these means, perhaps because informers could not be guaranteed protection in Ireland.... In 1922 the army concluded that, overall, rewards or bribes had been of little use in the fight against the I.R.A."[11]

Complacent though the RIC had been earlier, however, police confidence had been shaken by the Rising and they became far more active. As Eamon Broy explained in his Witness Statement:

> A particular menace to the Volunteers was the small area, policed by one sergeant and five constables. The police ... knew almost everything about every native of the area, and when a prominent Volunteer officer from Dublin came ... [he] was soon noted by the R.I.C ... [and] his being in the company of local Sinn Féiners gave a clue to his business ... when the Volunteer left by train ... his description ... was sent immediately ... to G. Division ... [who] met the train and shadowed the suspect.[12]

Hence one of the first acts of Dáil Eireann in early 1919, following Broy's suggestions to Collins that local RIC men should be neutralized, was to recognize and deal with the threat posed by the RIC's knowledge of local affairs.[13] The proposal that they be ostracized was carried by the Dáil and was the first implicit acceptance that intelligence would play a key role in the future.[14] Nevertheless, by October 1920 IRA General Headquarters in Dublin (GHQ) was still sufficiently concerned to write, "From being the eyes and ears of the Army the old R.I.C. man has now become the pointer for the Black and Tans."[15] But the words of a British Intelligence report give more credit to the later "systematic murder campaign [of RIC men], with the result that ... the police source of information ... was dried up and the intelligence services paralyzed."[16]

The British civil administration was disintegrating but Dublin Castle's espionage resources were still intact, and Michael Collins, now IRA Director of Intelligence, had begun to counter this with a network of contacts. From March 1917 this network included representatives in the Castle itself, whence Eamon Broy had been passing on confidential documents and police codes, and David Neligan, Joseph Kavanagh, and James McNamara also reported to Collins. There were agents of the network in the British Army and the police, and, above all, there were innumerable post office clerks who proved their value frequently by passing on codes and ciphers. Collins's men also investigated and, if the facts were proven, executed spies and informers.

A typical example of these executions occurs in the statements of William Stapleton,[17] Joseph Dolan,[18] and Vincent Byrne.[19] William Doran, the night porter at the Wicklow Hotel, Dublin, was shot dead on 28 January 1921. Several newspapers (*Irish Times, Independent, Times, Observer,* and *Manchester Guardian*) carried the story to some extent, with one fact mentioned in all of them: "He had, according to an official statement, been on friendly terms with the police."[20] Doran had been warned several times by the IRA to stop his activities. Confusingly, in their Witness Statements, both Dolan and Stapleton claim to have done the shooting. As there seems to be no clear motive for these claims, this is possibly the result of faulty memory, or, as Stapleton also gets his name wrong (Peter instead of William) the inference may be that Doran, as an informer, was of scant importance. This lack of importance is borne out by Dalton who writes, "Subsequently Doran's widow communicated to Michael Collins that her husband had been shot by Crown forces and that she was in dire straits financially. Rather than tell her the true facts, Collins instructed that she receive financial assistance."[21] Doran can be compared to his detriment with Christopher Harte, porter in Vaughan's Hotel, who was arrested on New Year's Eve, 1920, and "ill-treated" in Dublin Castle. When questioned about Collins he denied all knowledge of him "but was confronted with the statement that he had frequently been seen carrying Michael Collins's bicycle down the steps of Vaughan's Hotel. He was told the authorities would pay up to £10,000 'for information ready to the capture of Collins,' and that when Collins was in the hotel he had only to ring the Castle, extension 28, and say: 'Brennan: The portmanteau is now ready.'" He did not do it.[22]

Frank Thornton, on the other hand, relates an anecdote which reveals the quality of British agents to be less than ideal. He was asked by Neligan, member of DMP's G Division, and Collins's agent in Dublin Castle, to meet some friends and found himself:

> with three of these touts sitting round a table having fish and chips. A general discussion was taking place when one of these fellows, who was an English man, turned round to me and said "Gor blimey how did you learn the Irish brogue! We're here in Dublin for the last twelve months and we can't pick up any of it, yet you fellows seem to have perfected it" ... we told them that there was an art in these matters.[23]

At the same time "Collins's ... insistence that all lines of communication ran through him ... diminished the risk of leaks to British Intelligence and limited the scale of any leaks that occurred."[24] However, most of the efforts to recruit informers in Dublin were made by the police G Division, who were the principal paymasters, though O'Halpin notes that there was "a huge increase [in secret service expenditure] in 1920–21. The last three years of British rule in Ireland accounted for [over £100,000]."[25] Some of this may have been spent on imported British agents, such as "Jameson"[26] and Brian Fergus Molloy, a private in British Army GHQ, who volunteered to help Collins but was found to be a spy. On 24 March 1920 his execution was thus dismissed: "he ceased to be our headache."[27]

David Neligan described Jameson as the "most dangerous man the British sent over here,"[28] and to Basil Thomson of British intelligence he was "one of the best and cleverest Secret Service men that England ever had."[29] The only part of his story to bear out such summations is that he actually met Collins several times while posing as an arms salesman. The main importance of Jameson and Molloy seems to have been that both had met, and so could identify, Michael Collins and other members of the Squad but, though initially successful, they were so clumsy in their approach that they did not last very long. Their failure and death, however, became instrumental in the arrival of Colonel Ormonde Winter in May 1920 to take over Castle Intelligence, and his importation of the experienced men who later died on Bloody Sunday.

The initial effect of Ormonde Winter's work to build an efficient system was that in summer 1920, "paranoia ... gripped the population, had neighbor suspecting neighbor of informing.... A witch-hunt for spies and traitors gathered pace, first enveloping and then sweeping away many innocent people."[30] Nevertheless Jameson and Molloy are the best known of the Dublin agents and informers; most others only figure anonymously. The exception is Harry Timothy Quinlisk, initially helped financially and found a job by Collins. Quinlisk wrote to Dublin Castle offering his services when Collins refused to give him more money and may have intended to claim the reward offered for his capture. Broy found out, warned Collins, and Quinlisk was sent to Cork. There he was kidnapped and shot by the IRA on 20 February 1920, the first civilian to be executed by the Cork city IRA. Florence O'Donoghue commented, "Out of the Quinlisk case ... there arose a comparing of notes [with Collins] and a mutual co-operation and close contact that proved valuable."[31]

Perhaps it may be adduced from this that the whole situation in the city was so well under control because of Collins's intelligence network that spies and informers were not a great problem.[32] This probability is underlined by Sergeant Mannix' brief comment: "I also attended a number of meetings ... which were convened for the purpose of passing the death sentence on a number of spies. The death sentence was passed on 9 or 10 informers for a date not fixed."[33] Thornton also wrote "Information was gleaned in a lot of instances through the carelessness or idle talk of individuals, but I am rather proud to say not from informers on our side, because there is one thing we can boast of in the Movement from 1916 to 1921 and that is that we bred no informers."[34] This was not true.

Erskine Childers

The year 1921 brought first the truce, then the Treaty negotiations. At the start of the Anglo-Irish War there had been no organized national IRA intelligence system and it became the responsibility of provincial brigade leaders to develop and organize their own practical system with the help of GHQ in Dublin, the undoubted experts. However, no intelligence system, however good, is proof against an attack from within, and so, among all the informers of this time, perhaps the crown should be awarded to Erskine Childers. E.M. Forster famously said: "if I had to choose between betraying my country and betraying my friend, I hope I should have the guts to betray my country."³⁵ The implication, that treachery to a friend is the worst betrayal, might not have been lost on Collins. During the Treaty negotiations Barton and Childers suddenly found themselves ignored by Collins, Hart suggests a reason for this estrangement: "It has been suggested that Childers was actually a spy, but his much-speculated-upon secret letters to de Valera were actually straightforward reports on the negotiations."³⁶

However, *were* these the only letters? On 26 October 1961 Marie Kelly, de Valera's Personal Secretary, gave N.S. Ó Nualláin some of the President's papers to be placed in the official files. The following day Ó Nualláin wrote to her querying the presence of two almost identical telegrams:

> As you will see, both telegrams are essentially identical—they were both sent on the 17th October 1921 from London, by someone signing himself as "Secretary," to Dr. Hayden, of 20 Fitzwilliam Square, Dublin, and the texts are identical—except that
> (1) the first telegram was dispatched from Sloane Street Post Office in London at 6.42 p.m., whereas the second was dispatched from the Central Telegraph Office in London at 6.52 p.m. (10 Minutes later); and
> (2) as regards the texts, "Edwards" in the first telegram appears as "Edward" in the second...
> The telegrams were apparently intended to convey to the President, through an intermediary, a message from Mr. Erskine Childers, who was the senior of the Secretaries attached to the Irish Delegation which was, at that time, carrying out the Treaty negotiations with the British Government in London.³⁷

An essential element of the work of the delegation was to keep the President and Cabinet fully informed on a daily basis of all that transpired at the talks. This was obviously necessary. Less obvious was that the President had so little trust in the delegation that, in addition to the official reports and letters to the President (signed "E.C for Delegation") sent from Hans Place, which retailed the minutiae of the meetings with the British delegates, he seems to have set up a secret accommodation address for Childers to keep him informed, also on a daily basis, with a Dr. Hayden, of 20 Fitzwilliam Square, Dublin. Given that the official letters are so detailed and so numerous, could these others have been reports on the behavior and loyalty of the Irish delegation? The two almost identical telegrams signed "Secretary" bear the hallmark of Childers' fussiness: the name "Edwards" in the first becomes "Edward" in the second, sent ten minutes later.

Childers must have realized that ultimately neither side in the negotiations trusted him, even Collins, who had also admired him, had doubts ("Who should one trust—even on my own side of the fence? Griffith. Beyond Griffith no one. As for C [Childers]... He is sharp to realize how things will have due effect in Dublin and acts accordingly"³⁸), while Lloyd George summed him up savagely where he sat outside the room where the Treaty was finally signed: "a man who had used all the resources of an ingenious and well-trained mind, backed by a tenacious will, to wreck every endeavor to reach agreement, Mr. Erskine Childers. At every crucial point in the negotiations he played a sinister part."[39]

So *did* Major Erskine Childers, D.S.C., late of the British Naval Air Service and famous author, become the Irish Republican who also spied on his friends and became in a sense that loathsome figure of Irish history—the informer?

There were others. Vincent Fouvargue was a member of the IRA who was captured and gave information. He was shot in London on 3 April 1921.[40] While Frank Gallagher's description of the Castle in the days after Bloody Sunday adds credence to this idea: "From all corners of the capital there began a trek of minor spies and spotters and touts into the Castle.... They crowded in behind those high walls in full admission that their day was done ... undesirables of all kinds ... who had looked for blood-money, and in this day of doom wanted nothing so much as protection ... corrupt, furtive, down-at-heel."[41]

Elsewhere in the country there were also informers. Charles Pinkman, (Second Lieutenant in Kiltubrid South Company, South Leitrim Brigade), for instance, gives a detailed account of incidents in Mohill, Co. Leitrim, involving Mr. Lattimer and Dr. Pentland, both discovered to have laid information resulting in the shooting of some IRA men at Gorva, South Leitrim, though the date is unclear (internal evidence suggests after April 1921).[42] Many of the Statements include the phrase "There were no spies shot in the area," and most of the others go into very little detail (in Co. Meath, for instance, just the names Blagriff and Johnston surface, with no details), and even names can be missing: Patrick Lennon of Co. Westmeath, tells the brief story of the death of "Slickfoot" whose real name he did not know. "Slickfoot," shot near Carrickbrien, was so-called because he had a cork leg. After the shooting he was thrown in the river, "but the cork leg made him float, so he had to be weighted down with sandbags."[43] In Cork, however, the entire situation was different.

Since 1919 the Volunteers in Cork had comprised three brigades, of which the biggest was the Cork No.1 Brigade, covering Cork city and the area from Youghal to the Kerry border, led by Seán O'Hegarty. Mindful of Cork's failure to come out in 1916, the brigade was determined to fight in the Anglo-Irish conflict and O'Hegarty had a reputation for ruthlessness and even savagery. Ernie O'Malley said of him: "East Cork had shot many spies. Hegarty had the name of not being very particular about evidence, but that might be talk."[44] In Cork in 1920, for example, the killing of Tomás MacCurtain and Terence MacSwiney's hunger strike exacerbated an already tense situation, where every IRA setback was examined for the possibility of informers. This was aided by "G," the link between Dublin and Cork, much mentioned in the

Witness Statements and assumed to be in the Castle. "G" was actually Mrs. Josephine Brown (later Mrs. Florrie O'Donoghue) who worked at Victoria Barracks and was the source of much information.

Then came rumors about and threats of reprisals from the "Anti-Sinn Féin Society," which may have been a Crown force ruse rather than the organization of local unionists it claimed to be.[45] From then until the Truce the history of Cork provides many instances of suspected informers: some held and interrogated by the IRA before either being shot or given an expulsion order, others shot at the first opportunity.[46] Only two Volunteers are known to have been shot as informers, "Cruxy" Connors[47] and Din Din Riordan (executed possibly in December 1920), though at least one source said of Seán O'Hegarty, "It would have been better for him and his command if he had looked more closely at his own men for they needed looking after, and some of them were giving information as well as Connors."[48] This is borne out by the many ambushes in Co. Cork, such as Nadd (March 1921), Mourneabbey (February 1921), and Clonmult (20 February 1921), where betrayal came from IRA men who were either angered by their comrades or trapped by British Intelligence. Between 1919 and 1923 tension in Cork was so high that suspicion often became the equivalent of guilt.

Given the high incidence of informers in Cork, the first case study is Mrs. Lindsay of Cork; the second is well known, though William Joyce's notoriety occurred years later. Both he and Mary Lindsay claimed a strong connection with Britain which could lead to the idea that neither is a typical informer. Nevertheless they are both included because each shows the informer and the action of betrayal in a different light.

Mrs. Lindsay of Cork

Mary Georgina Rawson was born in Co. Mayo to a family with social status and married John Lindsay, a successful linen merchant from Co. Down, while still in her early twenties. The couple settled at a country residence outside Banbridge and Mary attempted to replicate the position her family had held in Mayo but failed to achieve her ambitions and this, together with her childlessness, led to discontent and bitterness.

On holiday with her husband's relations in Cork they went to see Leemount House, which stood beside the River Lee near Coachford. She persuaded her husband to retire and they moved there in 1901, when Mary was 41 and John was 53. Their butler, James Clarke, who had been in the service of the Lindsay family since he was a boy, came with them from County Down, but other Leemount servants were from the locality. Mrs. Lindsay, as she had done in Banbridge, began her campaign to become the leader of Coachford society only to meet with her first setback almost immediately.[49] However, the couple were welcomed by their Protestant neighbors, they began to receive invitations and the men of Coachford raised their caps to her when they met. Such things mattered to Mary Lindsay, and her response was to throw lavish parties, unaware that this amused her Protestant neighbors.

There was quite a high proportion of Protestants in Cork, and Coachford was no exception. The 1911 census reveals these statistics: Cork City had a gross population of 315,000, of whom 22,992 were Church of Ireland, 2047 Methodists, 1038 Presbyterian, and 899 were of other Protestant denominations; Cork County had a gross population of 76,500, of whom 6576 were Church of Ireland, 643 Methodists, 912 Presbyterian, and 728 other Protestants.[50] These large numbers can be correlated with the fact that Cork was a garrison city, though the Anglo-Irish War reduced the Protestant minority in Cork to about half its pre-revolutionary size, so the majority of those claiming allegiance to the Church of Ireland were either officers or owners of the large estates, and this was Mary Lindsay's preferred *milieu*.

John Lindsay died in 1918 and his widow horrified the neighborhood by burying him in the back garden at Leemount beside her dog. Mary Lindsay had already ruffled ascendancy sensibilities in Coachford, first with her pro-conscription activities after the outbreak of the Great War in August 1914, then with her vehement condemnation of those who took part in the 1916 Rising.[51] Most Southern Protestants, no matter how they felt privately, prudently ignored anything to do with rebellion, and the threat of conscription was contentious. Moreover the relationship between Protestants and Catholics was mainly one of tolerance: there was "no significant religious or political persecution of Protestant Unionists in Cork City."[52] Peter Hart, in *The IRA and Its Enemies*, insists on a theory of sectarianism, but Borgonovo is convinced (and convincing) that the unionists, like the ex-soldier victims, were shot because the IRA thought they were informers and for no other reason.[53] At the same time Lindsay's attitude to Catholics was that at best they were idolaters, at worst Fenians, and she could not understand the more tolerant attitude of her loyalist neighbors. On the surface, then, her cultivation of Fr. Edward Shinnick, the curate in Coachford, was surprising. However, Mrs. Lindsay had noticed that Fr. Shinnick shared her views, preaching openly in favor of the Conscription Bill and against the activities of the IRA.

The Dripsey Ambush

Tom Barry's November 1920 victory at Kilmichael against the Auxiliaries brought new hope to the Cork republicans, inspiring them to fresh action against a force which many Irish had come to consider all but invincible. As Eamon Broy noted, the impact of Kilmichael was increased because British propaganda in Ireland had "lauded the new force [Black and Tans] to the skies ... and [suggested] the I.R.A. would never dare to attack or even face such redoubtable adversaries."[54] At the same time republican anger was augmented first by the death on hunger strike of Terence MacSwiney in October of the same year, then by the burning of Cork City on the following 11 December. Sean O'Hegarty, who had succeeded MacSwiney as Officer Commanding (O/C) of Cork No.1 Brigade, was particularly bitter because, the day after the burning of Cork, Bishop Cohalan pronounced a decree of excommunication on IRA members who killed any Crown forces. This was an attempt to protect his diocese from further reprisals, but it was also a serious blow to the Volunteers and O'Hegarty was one of those affected. Thus, among others, the 6th Battalion, commanded by Jackie O'Leary, stepped up activities with a good deal of success.

This was the situation when O'Hegarty encouraged O'Leary to ambush the Manchester Regiment, stationed at Ballincollig, which regularly patrolled the main road from Iniscarra to Macroom. The lorries traveled from Coachford to Dripsey through Godfrey's Cross every Friday morning at a time varying from 9 a.m. to midday, so the ambush was to take place on Friday 28 January 1921. The chosen spot had certain strategic advantages: "It was the end of a bend of the road, the lorry driver would not be able to see a road block at that point.... There was a good ditch cover for the men and a sloping hill directly behind it which meant that a few rifle men placed at the top would dominate over the ambush site.... There was a minor link road ... nearby joining up with Peak ... which would allow them to get away quickly."[55]

From the start the ambush was beset by difficulties. Seasoned British Intelligence officers had been drafted to the Manchester Regiment and they had already assembled a large volume of information. This may have been the cause of their persistent question during a raid on Tower village, near Blarney, on 27 January 1921: "Where is the ambush to take place?"[56] Reports of this were sent to the IRA at Dripsey and Donoughmore, but the plans went ahead and that night the lookouts were in place.[57]

At first light the McSweeney and O'Sullivan families, who lived in two houses close to the ambush site, were warned by the IRA men to leave for their own safety. Jack O'Sullivan arrived for work at Tim Sheehan's grocery in Coachford earlier than usual, and, when his employer commented on this, told him exactly where the ambush was to take place. The local gossip continued with Tim O'Mahony, the postman, who spotted men under cover, though they warned him to say nothing, and Mrs. Godfrey of Broomhill House, near the site, also heard about the ambush early that morning. "Throughout the day, the fact that an ambush was being planned was becoming common knowledge in the area. People were discussing it in the shops.

Local businessmen, sympathetic to the Volunteers, sent word to the ambushers alerting them to the fact that the location was common knowledge in the surrounding villages."[58]

Some hours later Mrs. Lindsay was on her way to Ballincollig Barracks to submit her car for military inspection in accordance with new government regulations, but stopped at the grocery with a list of provisions to be delivered to Leemount House. Tim Sheehan advised her not to take the Dripsey road because of a rumored ambush. She immediately paid a visit to Mrs. Gillman of Clonteadmore, Coachford, to ask her opinion. On her way she picked up Fr. Shinnick and asked him to warn the men at Godfrey's Cross. Mrs. Gillman's advice was to let matters take their course and hope for the best because any interference would be dangerous. This was both wise and in keeping with the Southern Protestants' attitude, but Lindsay's motivation was possibly connected with General Strickland's letters to Barry Egan (Acting Lord Mayor of Cork) and to the *Manchester Guardian*, on 17 and 24 January respectively, urging the people of Cork to further the cause of peace by assisting the army. So Mrs. Lindsay went on to Ballincollig, left the information for Strickland, then took her car for inspection.

Under IRA regulations the Battalion Commandant (in this case O'Leary) did not control the Active Service Unit (A.S.U. or Flying Column) during an ambush. Frank Busteed commanded the A.S.U. but was also Vice-Commandant of the 6th Battalion, and *Execution*, published in 1974, was written almost entirely from Busteed's viewpoint. According to O'Callaghan, when interrogated by Busteed, James Clarke claimed that Fr. Shinnick told Mrs. Lindsay about the ambush. So Shinnick's supposed guilt rests entirely on the words of a very frightened man who would have been likely to agree with anything suggested to him by his captors. Sheehan's version is more convincing, both because it is a natural extension of the gossip about the ambush and because Busteed was anti-clerical so might have preferred the priest to be the culprit.[59] This point is important because republican opinion, based on O'Callaghan's book and thus on Busteed's words, still holds the priest to have been the source of Mrs. Lindsay's information.[60]

Fr. Shinnick sent a warning to the men at Godfrey's Cross via a man he trusted. Frank Busteed, knowing that the curate was pro–British, assumed it was a trick. Only Jim Barrett, the Quartermaster, raised serious doubts. Jackie O'Leary, fearful for his leadership and anticipating a victory like that at Kilmichael, decided not only that they would stay, but that any man who left would face a firing squad.[61]

Mrs. Lindsay's car inspection was more important to the outcome than she ever realized. In order to maintain security at Ballincollig Barracks while vehicles were being inspected no patrols were sent out that day, thus the ambush would not have taken place. However the news from General Strickland changed this, so at 3:30 p.m. a company of officers and about sixty men set off for Godfrey's Cross.⁶² O'Leary's men were still waiting, though it was long after the expected time, until at about 3 p.m. certain of the lookout men began to drift away from their positions in search of warmth and food, so the arrival of the soldiers was not signaled to those at the ambush site until a local gardener saw them.

With soldiers approaching from both sides O'Leary ordered the retreat, leaving six men to cover them. All six were captured. The column halted at Aghabullogue and each man of the Dripsey section, threatened with court-martial, had a similar explanation: no one had contacted them from half past seven that morning until three o'clock. They assumed that the column had pulled out as had happened at other ambushes. They also talked at length about the failed ambush, coming to the obvious conclusion that information had been received. Their search for the informer began with Fr. Shinnick, who had been seen that day in Coachford getting into Mrs. Lindsay's car and being dropped at the school where, highly unusually, he gave the children the rest of the day off. A late night visit to the elderly priest revealed that Mrs. Lindsay had told him about the ambush. O'Leary and Busteed's authority was challenged by the near-mutiny of the Dripsey men, understandably determined not to be the scapegoats when the death penalty could result from "grave insubordination on active operation duty, involving danger to others and to the success of the operation."⁶³ The two senior men decided to restore their authority by taking Mrs. Lindsay hostage against the release of the prisoners whose trial had opened at Victoria Barracks.⁶⁴

The Abduction

Grace Conway, Mrs. Lindsay's maid, heard in Coachford that Mrs. Lindsay was the suspected informer and advised her mistress to go away for a while. She wrote to Mrs. Lindsay's sisters that same night, urging them to second her advice, but Mrs. Lindsay refused. Meanwhile O'Leary was making detailed plans for her abduction, and late on 17 February a group of the men of the 6th Battalion came for her.⁶⁵ Thus began many weeks of endurance for both prisoners and men, worsened by a sudden decision by Jackie O'Leary to abduct James Clarke, found hiding under a bed.

The army searched for her, though they had waited for some days expecting to find her body with the usual warning to spies attached. They only began the search as a result of political pressure from Westminster, probably sparked off by articles in British newspapers extolling her bravery. Nevertheless, once begun, the search was thorough and included a low-flying plane over the mountain areas. This, however, was not just (or even primarily) for Mrs. Lindsay: "Large convoys moved through the more isolated areas.

They were trying to hunt down Flying columns but also moving through safe areas trying to capture Volunteers who were on the run."[66]

Twice the party was almost spotted, once by the plane, once by soldiers, but three days later they finally reached their objective: Jer Mickey Murphy's house at Goulane in Donoughmore, accessible only by a long narrow mountain road to the south.[67] Then Jackie O'Leary arrived with the news that five of their men had been sentenced to death.[68] Previously, under duress from Busteed, Mary Lindsay had refused to write a personal letter to General Strickland asking for leniency in the treatment of these men, now she did so, stressing that her own fate was interconnected with theirs, but neither Strickland nor Macready was in favor of canceling the arrangements and on Monday 28 February the executions took place. Later there was plainly some uneasiness about the decision because Macready felt the need to justify himself: "The rebels endeavored to bargain her life against the lives of men who had been condemned to death after trial … such a proposal … would have resulted in the kidnapping of loyal or influential persons every time the death sentence was passed on a rebel"[69]; and Foulkes, the propaganda director, wrote, "It looks as though Mrs. Lindsay's first letter was intended to reach General Strickland too late to prevent the executions of 28.2.21. from being canceled."[70] Now Jim Barrett and Denis Murphy, who had both been too seriously wounded at Dripsey to stand trial with the other men, were due in court. Therefore O'Leary asked Mrs. Lindsay to write to Strickland once more, in the hope that the two would be spared. Again she did so.

Meanwhile Jer Mickey Murphy was beginning to be concerned by the length of his visitors' stay. He wrote later, "Myself and my house was kept drawing turf from the bog and they burned one load of turf every 24 hours … and the anguish of mind they caused us for 3 weeks and 3 days of terror was worse than all to me."[71] The men on guard had strict orders to shoot the prisoners if soldiers were seen in the vicinity, and if this happened Murphy and his wife would be burned out and possibly shot. At the same time, keeping up a twenty-four hour guard in Goulane was a strain on the battalion's manpower, and the men were becoming bored and restive. Florrie O'Donoghue said of the situation "The absence of any facilities for the detention of prisoners over a long period made it impossible to deal effectively with the doubtful cases. In practice there was no alternative between execution and complete immunity … this was never an easy matter."[72] At a battalion council meeting it was decided to burn Leemount House on the night of 12 March 1921.[73]

O'Leary had gambled with Lindsay's life in wagering it against the lives of his men but had never intended to kill her. Now he was being forced to come to terms with the consequences of his own lack of forethought, but told Frank Busteed that it was the refusal to heed Fr. Shinnick's warning which had caused all the problems they faced. Busteed was in no doubt that the prisoners must be shot. Sean O'Hegarty had been in touch with GHQ in Dublin, they were not in favor of this solution (it was not IRA policy to execute women) but offered no alternative suggestions. Collins said "they should have referred it to me for decision, but did not do so.... I don't think I'd have shot her on account of her age,"[74] but the Cork battalions had a tendency to act unilaterally. If GHQ *was* contacted they could have relied on this to disclaim responsibility to the press if the decision were left to O'Hegarty. In the event this was what happened.[75] The choice was plain: the *status quo* involved not only a drain on their resources but also danger to the men guarding two prisoners who were now valueless, particularly since it was very doubtful that Jim Barrett, about to stand trial with Denis Murphy, was going to survive a surgical operation to remove his leg; and both Lindsay and Clarke, if released, could identify far too many of the men guarding them. Execution was ultimately deemed the simplest and most effective method of bringing the whole situation to an end.

Expediency ruled, and the prisoners again walked a mountain track, this time to Flagmount in the next parish, where a grave had been dug. The last action of the squad was to place an identification mark a short distance from the grave.[76] "I told her she was going to die. She never blinked an eye. I will say this for her—for bravery she was excellent. I sent a report to Sean O'Hegarty and got a confirmation. The report said Execution completed."[77]

Michael Collins summed up the whole situation with a simplicity which many have since seen as cold-blooded:

> I was sorry about that ... but she wasn't murdered in cold blood, she was executed. She lived in County Cork in the martial law area ... she acted as an informer ... she warned the police of an ambush and was the cause of military reprisals.... Strickland tried five men and was going to shoot them and did so. My fellows sent word if he did they'd shoot Mrs. Lindsay whom they'd tried and found guilty as a spy and informer. The men were shot, so was Mrs. Lindsay.[78]

The problem of allegiance had long been solved pragmatically by Mrs. Lindsay's peers, but this was no solution for her. She was ruled not only by the certainty of being right, by obstinacy, and a strong tendency to interfere with all those around her, but also by her determination to be seen as the leader of her small community's society and her attempts to lionize the military, particularly General Strickland, to that end. As these characteristics must have been obvious to her captors, the inescapable conclusion is that they were the ultimate reason for her execution.

When Mary Lindsay and James Clarke were abducted the propaganda war between the British government and Sinn Féin was already at its height. No opportunity was lost (on either side) to use every event in pursuit of the prize: influencing public opinion, not just in Ireland and Britain, but especially in America. This facet of the conflict had been seen principally in the press, where the republicans, via the IRA's official organ, the *Irish Bulletin*, enlarged every encounter with the Crown forces to heroic status, and the British government, with far greater resources at its disposal, dismissed the whole Anglo-Irish war as a matter of a hard-pressed police force trying to control a gang of terrorists.

In August 1921, after Mrs. Lindsay's death, the Earl of Selborne waxed lyrical about her heroism. A great deal of noise had been made in the newspapers and in parliament, but it signified nothing other than a concerted effort to propagandize the whole Lindsay affair, and it is highly probable that, had she not been kidnapped, far less interest would have been paid in Britain. Selborne said:

> all that can be alleged against Mrs. Lindsay by her murderers is that in the normal experience of daily life she obtained some information which she passed on to the police.... If that is the story ... throughout the whole of the English-speaking world Mrs. Lindsay's case will run on parallel lines with that of Nurse Cavell, and she will be nothing less than a martyr in the eyes of the whole Empire.[79]

Mary Lindsay is one of the most publicized informers in Irish history. Her name appears not only in many newspapers, both of the time and later, but also in general histories of the period and opinion is still divided, particularly in view of the "spy" epithet applied to her actions. From the republican viewpoint she was undoubtedly an informer and thus, in the terminology in use at the time, a spy. The British view, shorn of its rhetoric, was simply outrage that an old woman was shot for saving British lives. The attempts to equate her with Edith Cavell could never have held water, but seem to have been part of a British effort to disguise the fact that, for the two generals, Strickland and Macready, she was expendable.[80]

Some five months before the death of Mrs. Lindsay (Clarke was largely ignored by everyone, the death of an elderly woman had far more propaganda value for the British) the press on both sides of the water had seized on the hanging of Kevin Barry. Sinn Féin (and Erskine Childers, the master propagandist) brought the details into the public domain, despite the fact that the last days of MacSwiney's hunger strike were preoccupying the newspapers; both the Westminster politicians and General Macready intended to use his hanging as an instrument of propaganda in itself, countering emotional arguments about his youth with the information that the three soldiers killed in Dublin's Upper Church Street raid (20 September 1920) were also very young. At this distance from the event it is easy to see who was victorious in this particular propaganda battle, though it was won by a mournful ballad, not the newspapers:

> In Mountjoy Jail one Monday morning,
> High upon the gallows tree,

1. The Evolutionary Years 37

> Kevin Barry gave his young life
> For the cause of liberty.
> Just a lad of eighteen summers,
> Yet no one can deny,
> As he walked to death that morning
> He proudly held his head on high.[81]

In comparison, Mrs. Lindsay, a provincial widow, provided little in the way of romantic headlines until the inspired, if inaccurate, coupling of her name with that of Edith Cavell, thus giving rise to such emotive epithets as noble, dutiful, and courageous. It is doubtful if even her sisters would have subscribed to this description, (in fact Mrs. Benson's letters are distinguished for their lack of hyperbole and drama), nevertheless such references spread and this onslaught of words could well be the explanation behind O'Leary's efforts to ensure that her body was never found. Such an event would only have renewed and redoubled the outcry and might have acted as a reminder of the IRA policy of not shooting women. This may also be the reasoning behind Patrick Mannix' anecdote about Maud Walsh, the Dublin informer: Mannix was a DMP constable and agent for Michael Collins, who asked him to identify the woman who, in 1921, gave information about Austin Stack to Captain James Walsh, RIC, "then [Collins] sent word not to pursue the matter as it would be too bad to have a woman shot at that particular period."[82] She rang Walsh at the Shelbourne one day to say she had just seen Stack, and "asked Captain Walsh would she share the reward if they were successful in getting Stack. She was assured she would be rewarded and the figure of two thousand pounds was mentioned."[83] Such anecdotes highlight the financial motive for some informers and underline the differences between them and misguided British patriots like Mary Lindsay.

The press, however, continued to speculate frequently about Mrs. Lindsay's fate, and the comparison with Edith Cavell made for enormous propaganda value in Britain; her two sisters continued their search for her and made a futile appeal to de Valera; GHQ repeatedly requested information about her; locally the Dripsey Ambush was still a subject of conversation and, worst of all, the firing squad had been noticed coming down the mountain. Gossip was rife. Barry's Field in Flagmount was mentioned, and the curious went there to look for the grave. The military search went on, particularly in the Donoughmore area during April 1921[84] and Jackie O'Leary worried in case the grave was discovered and used as anti–IRA propaganda. Matters came to a head in July with the Truce. Lloyd George asked de Valera about her during their discussions and, on his return to Dublin, his enquiries caused an immediate demand for information from Sean O'Hegarty. This time the reply confirmed the execution of Mrs. Lindsay and Cathal Brugha notified Mrs. Benson of the reason for her death[85]: "The charge against her was that she was directly responsible for conveying to the enemy information which led to the execution of five of our men by the British authorities, to the death of a sixth from wounds received in action, and to a sentence of 25 years' penal servitude passed upon a seventh."[86]

There are two possible reasons that the letter was published in the newspapers: the continuing public interest in Mary Lindsay's fate; and it was newsworthy that her sisters were so tenacious in their efforts. Apart from this, a scapegoat was needed, and the pressure eventually caused O'Leary and Busteed to exhume the bodies and rebury them in the bogland where they remained until April 1924. But peace in Ireland brought none for O'Leary. The families of soldiers and police shot during the Anglo-Irish War began to make requests for the repatriation of their bodies, and so did Mrs. Lindsay's sisters. In his determination to forestall British propaganda O'Leary again exhumed the bodies. This time they were left forever in a deep pool somewhere between Donoughmore and Blarney.

Though Mary Lindsay's fate soon ceased to preoccupy the British (the last newspaper reference is in the *Manchester Guardian* of 20 August 1921), in Ireland the after-effects continued to linger: Both of Mary Lindsay's sisters had to leave Ireland, though their demands for answers continued until at least June 1926.[87] They co-opted Fr. O'Connor of Ballinasloe,[88] then Professor Alton, T.D. for Trinity College, Dublin, who raised questions in the Dáil on 19 November 1923,[89] and finally Jeremiah Murphy. Presumably this last resulted from his writing to the Post Master General, J.J. Walsh, in December 1923 seeking compensation for the cost of keeping Mrs. Lindsay in his house. It might be thought that Jer Mickey would have been thoroughly alarmed on receiving Mrs. Benson's letter, especially in view of her demands for "complete information of those that brought her to your house,"[90] but not so, because the expected compensation did not materialize and, as he says in another letter: "I was going to give them up to the Representatives of the late Mrs. Lyndsay [sic] but the priest wouldn't allow me, fearing I'd bring back the enemy."[91]

A consideration of the actions of the 6th Battalion reveals that the responsibility for the deaths of the Volunteers left to cover their comrades' retreat does not rest entirely on Mary Lindsay's shoulders. The officers had been told about the Auxiliaries' questioning in Tower village on the night before the ambush; they had been alerted by local businessmen to the fact that the ambush was common knowledge; the patrol's arrival time at Godfrey's Cross was variable, but it was always before noon. Here again lay the shadow of Kilmichael: the patrol on that occasion had varied their time unexpectedly. "Constant vigilance and sound security measures were vital both in action and billets. Clonmult, Mourne Abbey, Dripsey and Nadd were bitter lessons.... To retain the initiative ... our blows should combine the elements of speed, surprise and success. When evasion was essential to survival, evasion was the correct policy."[92]

In addition, no attempt was made to communicate with the outlying scouts; the priest's warning should have been heeded, if only because he knew enough to choose a messenger who could identify the ambush site; and there was an intelligence failure about the military inspection of private cars. Any one of these things should have given Busteed and O'Leary pause for serious thought. All of them together should have made them cancel the ambush, but here again character is important: these two men were seeking to emulate Tom Barry's success at Kilmichael, but they allowed the fact that patrols had been late in other places to override their local knowledge; Busteed's anti-clericalism was key to his refusal to heed Fr. Shinnick's warning; both men subsequently showed, in the long drawn out weeks of the kidnapping which involved the whole battalion, an obstinacy at least the equal of that shown by Mary Lindsay; and a certain rivalry between them may be adduced from the accounts of the ambush where neither seems to have been in overall control. Busteed "like all Volunteers, was subject to the authority of his Battalion Commandant [O'Leary] (when the Flying Column was not in action)."[93] The ASU had only been established in early January 1921, followed by two weeks of intensive training, thus by 28 January neither Busteed nor O'Leary was used to the new system of authority.

A General Order from GHQ for dealing with women spies had been laid down the previous November. It read as follows:

> Where there is evidence that a woman is a spy ... the Brigade Commandant whose area is involved will set up a Court of Inquiry to examine the evidence against her.
> If the Court finds her guilty of the charge, she shall then be advised accordingly and, except in the case of an Irishwoman, be ordered to leave the country within seven days.[94] It shall be intimated to her that only consideration of her sex prevents the infliction of the statutory punishment of death.
> A formal statement of the conviction shall be issued in poster or leaflet form or both, according to the local circumstances, as a warning and preventative.[95]

This had already been pre-empted by a directive, dated 9 November 1920, from the adjutant general of the Cork No.2 Brigade:

> Where there is evidence that a woman is a spy ... the brigade commander whose area is involved will set up a Court of Inquiry to examine the evidence against her. If the court finds her guilty ... she shall then be advised accordingly, and except in the case of an Irishwoman, be ordered to leave the country within 7 days. It shall be intimated to her that only consideration of her sex prevents the infliction of the statutory punishment of death.

This was followed by "a formal public statement ... in the form of a poster or leaflet warning women that if they were caught spying they would be neutralized."[96]

General Orders, issued by the Adjutant General from GHQ in Dublin, applied to all Volunteers across the whole country. Orders of the Fermanagh Brigade, dated the following month, included the instruction "if women spies (enemy) are detected in your area full particulars must be reported to Battalion H.Q. before taking any action."[97] Taken together, these two instances imply that, while women informers might not be a new phenomenon, the situation was worsening to the point where all the brigades needed to be told how to deal with it. Possibly the whole problem of informers was becoming more serious given two General Orders of April 1921: one listed four offences for which the death penalty could be inflicted on members of the IRA, of which the first two were: "Knowingly conveying information to the enemy" and "Disclosing to unauthorized persons particulars of plans of operations"[98]; the second consisted of brief general instructions for dealing with informers:

> A convicted spy shall not be executed until his conviction and sentence have been ratified by the Brigade Commandant concerned.
> All cases of execution of spies shall be notified at once to the Adjutant-General.
> All cases of persons killed by the British, and marked by them as spies "executed by the I.R.A.," shall be speedily investigated and reported on.
> In all cases of alleged spying, in which, while the evidence obtainable is suggestive of guilt, it is considered to be inconclusive, it is, before the arrest of the suspected person, to be placed before a Court of Enquiry, and notes of the evidence, together with a full report in the matter, shall be submitted without delay to the Adjutant-General.[99]

The General Order dealing with women informers concludes "Ordinarily it is not proposed to deport Irishwomen, it being hoped that the bringing of publicity on the actions of such will neutralize them. In dangerous and insistent cases of this kind, however, full particulars should be placed before G.H.Q. and instructions sought."[100]

This leads inevitably to the question: Was Mrs. Lindsay *not* an Irishwoman? Was she not *seen* as Irish? Born in Mayo, living in Ireland all her life, did this not make her Irish? Yet it is doubtful that Mary Lindsay saw herself as Irish: she was of the ascendancy class; her social life revolved around her wealthy neighbors and officers of the British Army; to her the Irish were the lower orders, servants or the men of Coachford who doffed their caps as she passed by. Frank Busteed is, perhaps, typical of the Irish who saw the British soldiers as the occupying force, and the war as being against British rule in its entirety. His scornful words when questioning Mrs. Lindsay after the abduction put her firmly among the enemy:

> we're no bunch of down-trodden tame Catholics. My grandfather was a Protestant, and my bloody cousins are Protestants.... I don't give a damn for any religion. I'd shoot Father Shinnick just as soon as I'd shoot you. We are fighting to get rid of you

and your kind, to sweep your British Government and your British army out of Ireland for ever...

I am an Irishman first and foremost. That is more than can be said for your so-called upper crust Protestant.[101]

The most serious deficiency at Dripsey, however, was in the area of security. As Feeney writes, "Scouts and lookouts should have been checked regularly.... The lookouts after nearly ten hours on the jobs should have been relieved, fed and kept up to date on any developments on a regular basis ... [also] the possibility of a change of plans on the part of the British, or indeed that they had been informed of the ambush, should have been foreseen."[102]

In addition to the five men who were executed, the military captured sixteen shotguns and 109 rounds of ammunition, four rifles and 33 rounds, three revolvers and 86 rounds, and six Mills bombs. It is well-documented that the IRA was always short of arms at this time, so it is hardly surprising to learn that the 6th Battalion Flying Column was stood down after the Dripsey ambush.

Mary Lindsay, however, did not consider herself to be an informer, she saw it as her duty, though her social pursuit of Strickland was probably a strong motivating force. Thus it becomes a question of allegiance, and whether she owed this to the government in power or to the country where she was born, though this does not impact on her death at the hands of her abductors because, as Mrs. Benson claimed in a letter to the *Irish Times*: her sister was the only woman to be treated like this.[103] The case of Mary Lindsay reveals without any doubt that the contributory factors in her fate were the mismanagement of both the ambush and her kidnapping, as well as the certainty that, if released, she would relate everything to Strickland or his representatives; in addition, once she could identify so many of the members of the Cork IRA 6th Battalion, her captors were left with a simple choice between her death and the deaths of their men.

William Joyce

Writing about the young Willie Joyce some twenty years after he had known him at school during the 1920s, E.L. Kineen remembered facets of his personality which prefigured later events: "Emotionally he never seemed to grow up. He was a morose and lonely little fellow at all times ... in his way Willie was a clevery [*sic*] sort of lad.... Still, for all his brightness, there was something missing in Willie ... he was not the normal sort of healthy schoolboy ... [he] made impromptu speeches in the playground. Even then he had the gift of the gab."[104]

William Joyce, better known subsequently as Lord Haw Haw, the last man to be hanged for treason (in 1945), was born on 24 April 1906 in Brooklyn, the first child of Michael and Queenie (Gertrude Emily) Joyce. Michael had emigrated from Mayo in 1888, became a U.S. citizen in 1894 and, when he met Queenie in 1904, was prospering as a builder. This prosperity was, presumably, the reason why Catholic Michael was an acceptable husband for the daughter of a Protestant doctor from Lancashire. Quentin Brooke, Queenie's brother, was to state some 35 years later that "Both retained their original Faith and this has produced a most unhappy married life,"[105] but this possibly reflects Brooke's anxiety to separate himself from his nephew's notoriety at the time as no other evidence suggests this.

William Joyce was an only child until June 1912. In 1909 his parents left the U.S. and moved back to Mayo, where his father bought a pub near Westport and three year-old Willie honed his conversational skills and his self-confidence in the bar.[106] In 1913 the family moved to Galway, William was sent to the Sisters of Mercy primary school and their rolls show the first concrete evidence of a tendency, marked in Michael, but which William was to exhibit throughout his life: lying.[107] Though some of his biographers comment on the effects of his parents' marriage and the family's early years in Ireland on his character,[108] none mentions the influence of his father's lies, told for convenience (when he later sought to hide his American citizenship) or to enhance his status (as in this instance).

William's lies were told for much the same reasons and had a slight base in reality: that he had been a boy scout when there were no scout groups in Galway, but he did acquire and wear part of their uniform; that he had learned to speak German from German neighbors in New York at three and a half years old, but he would not have remembered the language once he was in Ireland; that he had "left school at about the age of fourteen or fifteen and more or less ran away from home to join the Black and Tans."[109] Arguably, his most spectacular lie was to cover up the rejection by the Foreign Office of his application to the diplomatic service in April 1928: "He told a story of having first taken the examinations and done brilliantly. Only then did the selection board turn him down. He was not rich enough, they informed him. Such posts as these were intended for the sons of the well-heeled or at least the well-connected. There was no place for a young man of humbler origins who had shown ... energy and determination."[110]

Worst of all was the lie about his nationality when applying for a British passport, ultimately to be a hanging offence. The reality behind this claim can only be found in his letter of application to join the Officer Training Corps of London University, where he wrote "I was born in America, but of British parents. I left America when two years of age, have not returned since, and do not propose to return. I was informed, at the Brigade Headquarters of the district in which I was stationed in Ireland, that I possessed the same rights and privileges as I would if of natural British birth."[111]

The MI5 report setting out the case against him in preparation for his trial for treason in 1945 states: "In all three documents [passport application and two renewal applications] ... JOYCE describes himself as a British subject by birth though born in Galway, Ireland."[112] In reality he was an American citizen by birth. A later application to the Foreign Office in April 1928 included an apology that he had not fought in the Great War, when he would have been eight years old. He was rejected.[113]

Michael's affairs prospered and he bought a house in Salthill.[114] Of these years William was to say later: "I was brought up by my parents ... in a creed of fanatical patriotism.... From my earliest days, I was taught to love England and her Empire. Patriotism was the highest virtue that I knew."[115] His transfer to St. Ignatius College, the Jesuit secondary school, proved to be a turning point in his life as well as proof positive of his mother's influence in religious matters.[116] Equally affecting his later life, his nose was broken during a fight with another boy,[117] leaving him with the distinctive voice which identified him to the British soldiers he met by chance in Germany after the war and they arrested him immediately. Nevertheless his gratitude to his Jesuit teachers still remained many years later when, in 1940 in his anti-semitic book *Twilight Over England*, he wrote: "I went to school in Ireland where the Jesuits, with whom I had differences, gave me the benefit of their splendid educational system.... I have good reason to be grateful to them for what they did for me. Nor do I know any better motto in the world than *Ad Majorem Dei Gloriam*."[118]

He was not, however, grateful enough to speak kindly of Catholicism, in fact he later wrote: "I can imagine no greater handicap upon any universal creed than that the Son of God should come upon earth as a Jew and His Church be left to the tender mercies of the Wops."[119]

Though certain characteristics, amply demonstrated in his later life, became apparent from his schooldays, the present concern is mainly limited to the two years before he left Ireland permanently in December 1921, when he was fifteen. Many years later Miles Webb was to write of William at this time: "He was one of my closest acquaintances ... [because] I was an English lad and Joyce at that time was very pro–British ... we had certain things in common, particularly a great interest in literature. He taught me too to play chess and we spent hours together at this pastime.... He always spoke in an exaggerated fashion and bubbled over with self-importance."[120]

There was nothing unusual in a young boy's fascination with soldiers, even in Galway at this time, in fact any procession at all would frequently be followed by a cohort of children. For William Joyce, however, following in the wake of marching soldiers was not enough, he had to become one of them. Even in adult life he kept up the fiction that he had been stationed in Galway; that he had joined the Black and Tans. It is a mystery why MI5, in the shape of agent "M," does not seem to have wondered how a lad of fourteen who was quite small for his age could possibly have done this, when his home was in the same area as the regiment.[121] Douglas Duff, an RIC sailor, said of him "He was one of our greatest embarrassments in Galway City. His trouble was fanatical patriotism to England and a burning wish to fight against the Irish rebels, as he always called them. He often tried to smuggle himself into our lorries ... we used to chase him fairly fiercely for, if he had been killed or wounded, his ending would have caused the man in charge of the patrol a lot of trouble."[122]

Perhaps this was what turned him towards the Black and Tans and the Auxiliaries, for Miles Webb wrote that this was indeed what he had done: "He spent a considerable amount of time in the barracks of the Black and Tans and at Lenaboy Castle ... the headquarters of the R.I.C. Auxiliary Cadets. The townspeople ... used to say that he was a Police spy and that he swore away the lives of Irishman [sic] to the Auxiliaries ... he was heartily detested by, not only the ordinary local Irish townspeople but even by the average loyalist too."[123]

Nobody had given much thought to Willie Joyce and the other boys when they followed the soldiers, but heightened tensions and suspicions during the Anglo-Irish War made open association with the Black and Tans a different matter. Selwyn refers to this episode as "a schoolboy game,"[124] but many of the Galway people who saw him at this time sitting on Crossley-Tenders believed that he pointed out houses and individuals with republican connections.[125] While Tom McDonough said that when they were both at school: "Willie Joyce organized a group of the RIC men's children.... I was looking in a window, and he came up to me, and he had all these youngsters with him ... he said 'If anything happens any of my men ... your house will go up!'"[126] Then, in 1920, Patrick Joyce (a common surname in the region, the two were not related) disappeared and William Joyce's name became associated with the murder of Fr. Michael Griffin. "Patrick Joyce, a National Teacher from Barna, County Galway, 'disappeared' on 15 October 1920 after the IRA discovered that he was sending a list of Sinn Féiners' names and addresses to police and Dublin Castle authorities."[127] The teacher underwent a court-martial by the Volunteers and was executed. There followed a protracted but fruitless search for him by the Black and Tans.[128] Reprisals were expected, and among those who suffered was Laurence Tallon, the manager of Moycullen Co-operative Stores, who was shot and injured by the Crown Forces.[129]

In his Witness Statement Joe Togher wrote: "In November, 1920, at about 2:00 a.m., a person called to Father Griffin's house. He answered the door himself, and after a conversation with the caller in Irish,[130] he departed with him on an alleged sick call. We were convinced that the caller (a tout for the Auxiliaries) was none other than William Joyce, later executed by the British after World War 2."[131]

Fr. Griffin, the junior curate for the parishes of Bushy Park and Barna, Galway, was called out shortly after midnight on 14 November. At first this was assumed to be a sick call, but he did not take the Blessed Sacrament with him. The priest did not return and search parties found him, late on the following Saturday night, shot through the head, and buried in bogland beyond Barna. A local newspaper wrote: "Mr. Cruise, Divisional Commissioner R.I.C., declares he is confident that no member of the Crown forces had anything to do with the abduction."[132]

A military inquiry found that Fr. Griffin died on or about 15 November 1920, and that he had other injuries as well as the bullet wound. Two years later the *Galway Observer* wrote: "Recent disclosures ... have established that he was captured by Crown forces in the vain hope of extracting from him information which he would not or could not give. As Father Griffin did not turn informer he was brutally murdered."[133]

Joe Togher, IRA Staff Captain and Intelligence Officer in the Galway Brigade, was arrested in November 1920 and noticed during his interrogation that the Crown forces had a great deal of information about the Galway Volunteers.[134] His work in the Post Office meant that he "dealt personally with all mails for both the military and the RIC at Renmore and Eglinton Barracks,"[135] and thus he identified letters from Patrick Joyce addressed to the RIC. Though Togher does not claim that Fr. Griffin's murder was a result of Patrick Joyce's disappearance, he wrote: "Joyce and Father Griffin were not on friendly terms"[136] and that "local rumor had him [Fr. Griffin] a prisoner of the Auxies in Lenaboy."[137]

There was also a considerable amount of local speculation that the Black and Tans believed Joyce had last been to confession to Fr. Griffin, but this seems a less likely reason for his murder than does the killing of a popular priest in reprisal. There were a few other instances where the Crown forces made such efforts to find an abducted informer, as in the case of Tom Downing in Cork, but it did not normally happen.[138] Even in the case of Mrs. Lindsay the search was not solely for her. Perhaps informers in Galway were in short supply, and thus the services of William Joyce, despite his age, would have been appreciated by the Auxiliaries.

Could William Joyce have had any connection with the murder? Local speculation would have it that he had. Kenny insists that there is absolutely no evidence that young William Joyce was involved in any collaboration with the Tans over this killing, but in a small community rumor can be as powerful as fact. While this is true, does it not seem extraordinary that such a rumor could be attached to the name of a boy of fourteen? Or that local dislike, even if based mainly on his habit of riding in lorries with the Black and Tans, could possibly translate itself into accusations of complicity in the murder of a priest without there being good reason for such ideas?

Moreover, in October 1920, the month before Togher's arrest and discovery of the information held by the troops, as he relates in his second statement: "the British set up a centralized Intelligence depot and took over a house in Dominick St. Capt. Keating, a British army officer, was in complete charge, the object being to pool all the information there, have it assessed and dealt with immediately.... This depot had a complete over-riding authority over all branches of the British forces—army, R.I.C., Black and Tans, Auxiliaries, and navy."[139]

This can be compared with William Joyce's own words in a letter relating to his application to join London University Officer Training Corps: "I served with the irregular forces of the Crown in an Intelligence capacity, against the Irish guerillas. In command of a squad of sub-agents I was subordinate to the late Captain P.W. Keating, 2nd R.U.R."[140] Moreover, had his presence in the barracks and the lorries not been useful, they, too, would have sent him away. Miles Webb's opinion adds further weight: "Certainly he reviled in no uncertain fashion everyone who held anti–British views. There is no one more pro–British than your extreme Irish loyalist, he is almost a fanatic as Joyce certainly was.... I doubt if Joyce was 'officially' a police spy but I have no doubt on the other hand that he interested the Auxiliaries and they may have made use of him."[141]

In addition, when Joyce was passing on information about the British Union of Fascists, Maxwell Knight wrote a report on him for MI5 which states: "Under favorable circumstances or where he thought his own cause would benefit he would certainly not shrink from violence, but it would not be unthinking, senseless, spectacular violence."[142]

Arguably, then, not only was Joyce's value to the Crown forces under Keating that of an informer, but he could have both disliked and despised a Catholic priest whose anti–British affinities were widely known. Thus he could very well have been involved, if only peripherally, with Fr. Griffin's murder. Moreover, Togher reveals that in 1921 the Galway Volunteers were instructed by Collins to investigate various murders. Prominent among the list of names is that of Fr. Griffin, together with the results of the investigations: "it was an inside job, concocted and carried out by the local company of Auxies stationed at Lenaboy, Taylors Hill."[143] A little further on Togher writes a damning summary of the culprits: "Auxiliaries, one of whom was named Nichols, and William Joyce."[144] He also notes:

> We did not succeed in actually pinning anything on him [William Joyce] until the following incident which occurred during the Truce. I intercepted a letter from Joyce

to an Auxie, which, after being broken down, revealed that Joyce had the R.I.C. cypher which was in use that particular month. Michael Staines, our Liaison Officer, confronted Divisional Commander Cruise of the R.I.C. with this information, as Cruise had continually denied Joyce's association with the R.I.C. Had we had this information earlier, Joyce would have been executed.[145]

This claim is all the more credible in the light of the IRA's pursuit and occasional execution of Boy Scouts and junior YMCA members in the early 1920s, especially in Cork, because it was believed that they acted as spies for the military.[146]

Togher's statements are thematic rather than sequential, contain few exact dates and, while more concerned with the murder of Fr. Griffin, it is slightly odd that he terminates his account of William Joyce's activities with the information that he joined the 4th Worcester Regiment soon after his connection with the RIC came to light, and went to England with them. In fact he joined the Royal Worcester Regiment on 8 December 1921, and his career as a soldier ended on 20 March 1922, after his lie about his age was discovered. Kenny's account of his sudden departure seems more probable. She relates the story of a young IRA man waiting to shoot William on the road between his school and Salthill one evening in the first week of December 1921. The boy escaped execution because the family had moved house. However, a message transmitted from the IRA ensured that William was immediately sent to England alone. The rest of William's family followed a year later: "My people, being Loyalists ... were given a week's notice to clear out of the country or be shot.... We had to leave the country and lose all our property and most of the money that my people had, in 1922."[147]

Cole alone mounts a defense of Willie Joyce as an informer: "I cannot see that there was anything discreditable in providing information for his own side. He had been brought up pro–British, ... and he served ... in the only way he was able. Although young, he could have been useful ... a boy could have been better than an adult at eavesdropping and trailing suspects."[148]

This account of William Joyce's early career leaves certain questions unanswered, above all those concerned with the discipline of a teenaged boy: his lies; his freedom to ride through the town in lorries with the Auxiliaries and to spend so much time with them at Lenaboy; and why did his parents not see that these things were dangerous?

Queenie Joyce's attitude to her eldest son may be relevant in this context. The mother who can not only say to her young son: "I shall never in my life forget how lonely I have felt in America. Even before you were born you were my only comfort in this atmosphere of strangeness, lack of interest, and hostility,"[149] but say it so often that he still quoted her words twenty-four years later, is illustrative of a careless woman whose own comfort comes before that of her child. The mother who was so neglectful that, when his nose was broken in the playground fight, she did nothing, might allow him to run wild outside the home as long as it did not impinge on her. As for the townspeople, for whom it would have been second nature to restrain an unruly boy: William had friends in the Crown forces, and those friends had guns. If he was capable of threatening Tom McDonough, he might have done the same with adults attempting to check him.

It is unlikely that William was sufficiently introspective to dwell on these episodes later in his life, or even to realize how much his adolescent behavior foreshadowed his future. His adult life in England, following his studies at Birkbeck College, was dominated by his work for the British Union of Fascists (BUF), and he was largely responsible for their later focus on antisemitism. His association with Maxwell Knight, the agent for MI5, bears the same stamp as his relationship with the forces in Galway: the agent seems to have known him well, to judge from the report already cited, and, according to the *New Statesman*, Knight was the source of the warning which sent Joyce fleeing to Germany in late August 1939.[150]

On the surface one would not expect an elderly woman from Cork and a schoolboy from Galway to have much in common, but their respective stories show many similarities. Both Mary Lindsay and William Joyce shared an inability to empathize with other people, to the extent that neither appears to have accepted the dangers inherent in their stance. Their openly held conviction that British rights were paramount; their lack of understanding that they were living in the midst of a war zone; their stubbornness and arrogance born of the certainty that only their attitudes were right; all these things were a recipe for disaster, both for themselves and others.

Neither is a stereotypical Irish informer. There was no money involved in Mary Lindsay's betrayal of the Dripsey ambush, in fact, though she and the British press indulged in much talk of duty, it is probable that it was a part of her social climbing. Nor is there evidence to suggest that William Joyce received any financial incentives. His reward was to feel that he was important to those he perceived as powerful friends. In this thinking he resembled later boys in Northern Ireland, groomed and flattered into treachery by adults, imagining themselves invincible and indispensable to a great power.[151] Both sought a form of social importance, and there is nothing in either story to show that they ever accepted that they were wrong.

Yet even those whom they would both have thought beneath their notice thought more clearly about their actions and about the opposition. Other spies in Cork, for instance, were fully cognizant of their position: how could it be otherwise when every corpse found on the road wearing the notice "Spies and informers beware" was so widely reported that everyone understood the message? This was the traditional fate of the informer throughout Ireland at the hands of the IRA and the resultant publicity, serving as discouragement over a wide area of the country, is the intention behind the action.¹⁵² Presumably, when it came to the killing of an elderly woman, O'Leary's worries about the adverse effects on the IRA of such publicity were the cause of his obsessional attempts to hide the two bodies. It is also entirely possible that the seeming omnipotence of the British Empire and the constant presence throughout Ireland of her armed forces, particularly during the Anglo-Irish War, encouraged a sense of superiority in those like Mrs. Lindsay and William Joyce who were overtly partisan in their view of Britain. This showed itself not only in their conscious desire to demonstrate how different they were from the Irish, but also in Mrs. Lindsay's confidence in the British army and in Joyce's boastfulness.

The Civil War

The Civil War of 1922–23 still casts a long secretive shadow over Irish history. Two incidents of this time illustrate both the widespread confusion of loyalties engendered by civil war and its barbarity. The first, which occurred during the Truce, involved Lady Albina Brodrick (better known throughout Kerry as Gobnait Ní Bhruadair), a loyal Protestant, and republican sympathizer, who did a great deal to help the poor of Kerry and sheltered IRA men on the run during the Anglo-Irish War. When the Truce was declared: "Albina warned the Republicans against her own brother, the Earl of Midleton, and his colleagues in the Southern Unionist organisation… [Later] an English lady asked her one day… "Are you related to Lord Midleton?" Gobnait said: "He used to be my brother."¹⁵³

The second took place in Cork, in March 1923. Mrs. Powell had just put her three small daughters to bed when four young men with guns came into the house. They poured petrol everywhere, including over the three little girls in their beds, and told her that her house was to be burned as a reprisal for the arrest of the girls of the Cumann na mBan. Though terrified, she said: "I am not responsible for the arrest of anybody, and I belonged to the Cumann na mBan before these people." Two shots were heard, she rushed the children from the house and threw them to the ground during the ensuing gun battle, expecting the house to blaze at any minute. Then she realized thankfully that her family had been rescued by the Free State army. Mrs. Powell was the sister of Michael Collins.¹⁵⁴

Neither incident could possibly be a cause for boasting by either side in the conflict, hence, perhaps, the secrecy was a necessary component. This is particularly the case in the areas which contribute to this study and, where the activities of Cumann na mBan are concerned, the difficulties faced by the historian are multiplied. Information about the women with a higher profile, such as Mary MacSwiney and Máire Comerford, is readily available in the contemporary press, but details of the many anonymous members who hid guns in their skirts after a shooting or carried messages in hats and bicycle handlebars are sparse. Moreover, questions remain about how they spent the rest of their time. While it is perfectly true that this was an era when women were treated very differently from their male counterparts, some seven years of fighting must have had a hardening effect on the women too. So can we really believe that they only succored wounds and never inflicted them? Or that there were no informers, not even through carelessness or accident, in the ranks of the Cumann na mBan? Were none of them ever involved in such incidents as happened in Kenmare in April 1921, when a young woman seen talking to constables in the village was dragged into the street and had her hair cut off?[155] Such questions are unanswerable, but not unthinkable. It could be discounted as propaganda that *The Sunday Graphic* published "Irish Gunwoman Menace" which describes them as "trigger happy harpies"[156]; but the Irish Catholic hierarchy had to be taken more seriously. A pastoral letter, dated October 1922, reminds all the anti-treaty forces that "killing in an unjust war is as much murder before God as if there were no war," speaks scathingly of their claim to be good Catholics and warns: "No one is justified in rebelling against the legitimate government ... set up by the nation and acting within its rights.... A Republic without popular recognition behind it is a contradiction in terms."[157] The following January, the Free State government banned Cumann na mBan and Kevin O'Higgins, Minister for Home Affairs, described them as "hysterical young women who ought to be playing five-fingered exercises or helping their mothers with the brasses."[158]

Nevertheless, an appreciative letter from IRA intelligence states, "Girls can get any amount of information from most men.... Don't think there is anything ignoble about army intelligence work.... No army can ... win the slightest victory without it.... Realize your own importance—we realize it and rely on you."[159]

In January 1922, before the occupation of the Four Courts (30 April 1922) signaled the civil war to come, Jim Larkin wrote an inflammatory message from the United States about the Anglo-Irish treaty. The *Southern Star* reprinted this, without comment, in May 1923 after the conflict had ended: "We demand the rejection of this foul and destructive bargain (the Treaty); we demand that the creatures who discussed and agreed to such an unholy bargain be dismissed from the ranks ... that the fate that was meted out to the mean-spirited traitors, spies and informers during the past struggle [the Anglo-Irish War] is too holy a death for these six helots; that the fate of Judas is the only fate they merit."[160] Almost fifty years later Seán Irwin, a former Free State soldier, wrote about that same war: "I cursed the fates, the frailty of the leaders, the stupidity of men, or whatever it was that brought the country to this pitch of barbarity."[161]

These two quotations encapsulate the whole gamut of feeling about the Civil War. Larkin's intemperate outburst places the plenipotentiaries even lower than the worst traitors he can imagine—the informers, while Irwin reveals the problems facing the historian attempting to chronicle any part of the struggle or the feelings of shame surrounding the subject so that few will discuss it. As Anne Dolan writes: "There was a shame in civil war, shame in winning. There could be nothing 'glorious' or 'holy' in celebrating the victory."[162] Dolan's work echoes the mourning of those who took part, which also militates against the historian who stands outside the conflict. She notes that "The monuments are few, the graves unmarked, ignored, grudgingly adorned."[163] Fewer still are the official documents released so far. Yet some, like Michael Hopkinson in *Green Against Green*, have tried to write the Civil War's history. We cannot, then, agree timorously with F.S.L. Lyons who wrote in 1971: "it is not yet possible for the historian to approach it with the detailed knowledge or the objectivity which it deserves."[164]

Sources, then, are rare, and even rarer are those dealing with intelligence, though McMahon's work indicates the availability of documentation on the situation prevailing between Ireland and the UK.[165] Even the Witness Statements were designed to ignore the civil war, yet more evidence of residual shame. Therefore, for the purposes of this necessarily brief study of informers active during those eleven months, the main sources used are newspaper accounts of shootings and inquests and Ernie O'Malley's (Assistant Chief of Staff of the anti-treaty IRA,) civil war papers.[166] It does, however, seem that none of the informers executed made much of an impact on the progress of the war, nor is it clear from the available accounts which side killed them, though the balance of probability indicates that they were spying for the Free State army. This is borne out by the lengthy plea to all divisions of the Irregulars in April 1922 from D/Intelligence GHQ for the establishment of an information network,[167] and by Ernie O'Malley's constant complaints and excuses to Liam Lynch (IRA Chief of Staff) about lack of intelligence.[168]

There is much in the O'Malley papers which leads to wonderment that the conflict continued for as long as it did. O'Malley, on the evidence of his memoranda, spends too much time issuing complaints, especially about propaganda.[169] Dangerously, he puts in writing details, including addresses, of those who can be trusted,[170] and loses papers.[171] The editors of his papers see this as "a perpetual fight against the apathy of men who have no will to organize, against the officers who have no resolve to write the continuous reports that he demands."[172] It could also be seen as ineptitude, and in either case augurs badly for the progress of the war. Liam Lynch, seemingly more organized, sent General Order No.6: Spies to all Officers Commanding on 4 September 1922. This order differs from that applicable during the Anglo-Irish war (the Treaty had given a general amnesty to everyone on both sides, including informers) in allowing fines to be exacted, as well as temporary deportation from the Divisional area, where information given led to the wounding or capture of the anti-treaty soldiers.[173] Yet it is unclear whether or not this more lenient treatment was followed, given that some two weeks earlier the *Nenagh Guardian* had reported the opposite:

> A notice headed "Oglaigh na hEireann," ... has been extensively posted in Dublin. The notice states that the "Army Executive" orders that all citizens of the Irish Republic found conveying information to the enemy which leads to the death, wounding, or capture of Irish Republican Soldiers will be regarded as spies and will be liable to the same penalties as those inflicted on spies and informers previous to the Truce of July, 1921. The notice is signed "By Order, Army Executive."[174]

Moreover, on 24 November 1922, less than three months later, General Order No.6 was cancelled by General Order no. 12 from Liam Lynch clarifying that "Boys under 18 years and women spies shall not be executed" but does not state how they should be treated.[175]

The O'Malley papers contain little of value to this study, though a memorandum from the Adjutant of the 3rd Eastern Division, dated 30 September 1922, refers to some Free State soldiers: "We find them a fruitful source of information and our ammunition is being supplied through this channel,"[176] and another from the Assistant Officer Commanding Dublin 2 Brigade recommending James Anderson of Dublin who "is desirous of joining our Intelligence Service as he could do some good work."[177] The British newspapers had little interest in events in Ireland during the Civil War: the *Times*, for example, only mentions it in passing when reporting parliamentary debates. Certain provincial newspapers, however, provide something more in that they record the finding of six dead men in 1922-23 labeled "Spies and informers beware," with variations in the wording. The men, in chronological order, were: Israel Sagarsky (23), of Manchester, in Ireland to sell cutlery, was found murdered at Gortin, Co. Tyrone. His father said that he "had no connection with any secret society"[178]; John Powell, of Shallee Upper, Co. Tipperary, was taken from his home by armed men and found the next day lying on Shallee Cross by people going to Mass[179]; James Cleary, of Derrycloney, Co. Tipperary, went from his home with a visitor and was found the next day by his brother. The wording on his label read: "Convicted Spy. Spies and traitors beware. The first of many. I.R.A." He was described in the *Irish Independent* as "an honest, hardworking man who took no part in politics.... The military authorities stated that deceased had never given them any information"[180]; Michael Barry, the local postman, was fatally wounded while delivering letters one morning around Carrigtwohill, Co. Cork, and the usual warning was found in his postbag. He died that afternoon in Midleton Hospital. He had a British Army pension of twelve shillings per week, which might have sealed his fate[181]; John Melvin (24), of Ballina, Co. Mayo, was also found dead on the road on a Sunday morning. His label read "Convicted spy. All spies beware. Sooner or later we will get them. Your brother and sister will get the same fate if they don't quit."[182]

Mr. W. Cooley, a New Ross District Councillor, was more fortunate, or perhaps his was a lesser crime. In October 1923 he was found chained to the church railings at Campile, Co. Wexford, and after his release by the Civic Guard he had to leave the district. In a flash of humor unusual for the time the newspaper commented "It is quite on the cards that District Councils are to be abolished, but to endeavor to abolish District Councillors in this manner deserves more than a passing reference."[183] Whether or not these men had been passing information is unclear, but plainly somebody thought they had. Paradoxically, a definite suspicion rests on Mr. Cooley since he had to leave Wexford.

As with other aspects of the Civil War, information is sparse. There are many accounts, particularly in the provincial newspapers, of bodies left on the roads but only those bearing the warning have been used here. There is also a strong possibility that many of the bodies, with or without warnings, were the result of old grievances being settled. It is also indubitably true that it was a deliberate policy to target ex-soldiers throughout the years of violence. As Florrie O'Donoghue stated "Numbers of ex-soldiers and others have been murdered ... not so much because they were ever discovered in active espionage ... but ... partly because there was a possibility that they might become informers and partly in order to keep alive the terrorism which it was considered important to impose. The outside public knew not whether ... the man who had been foully done to death was an agent or not."[184]

On the whole it is highly unlikely that anyone will ever produce credible numbers for informers during this time. Furthermore, it is quite possible that the Civil War was a conflict where informers were not only few but also largely unnecessary, especially for the Free Staters who would still have had much of Collins's network. Only about six months earlier the combatants had all been on the same side, shared the same help from the same people and used the same safe houses. They had fought together, been on the run together, and so had an intimate knowledge of each other. Now, suddenly, there was hatred between them—and, if hatred seems too strong a word, look again at Larkin's message or at the verses about the tricolor beginning: Take it down from the mast Irish traitors / It's the flag we Republicans claim, / It can never be owned by Free-Staters, / Who brought nothing upon it—but SHAME![185]

Conclusion

A comparison of Michael Collins's unpaid intelligence network and that of Dublin Castle and the Crown forces shows that those who enter such dangerous waters to repel the enemy occupation of their country proved themselves efficient and effective, as well as likely to survive the experience. Those for whom it was a means of financial gain or of winning the respect of their perceived superiors often ended up looking like amateurs. The Anglo-Irish war, apart from the important role played by propaganda, was essentially an intelligence war (for most republicans even the most notable ambushes were primarily attempts to secure arms), and both sides needed information about the enemy. It is even conceivable that the British forces needed that information far more than did the IRA who were on their own ground and among their own people.

Informers' actions had repercussions far in excess of the information they supplied during Ireland's revolutionary years. So William Joyce, the schoolboy at whom so many fingers were pointed, probably did pass on much gossip to the Auxiliaries in return for his visits to Lenaboy, and it is probable that he knew what he was doing. The evidence also points quite strongly towards his involvement in the death of Fr. Griffin. Mary Lindsay, on the other hand, caused the deaths of six young men because she was in single-minded pursuit of what she saw as her rightful position in society, and was executed because she was blind to the dangers of her actions. The incompetence evident at Dripsey is a contributory factor, but without her actions the ambush would not have taken place. Moreover, her attempt to warn the men misfired too, in that it had the unforeseen consequence of causing much undeserved republican blame to be levied at Fr. Shinnick over the years. Peter Hart promulgates this same idea: "The man who originally 'gave the show away' was ... Father Shinnick."[186]

No matter how we play about with words—spies, informers, agents, touts, informants—what characterizes the deed and the informer is a readiness to betray others in return for the gratification of one's own needs, whatever they may be. For those such as Quinlisk and Maud Walsh the motivation was financial, and these people often know and accept the concomitant dangers, but more interesting and also more pitiful are the Mary Lindsays and William Joyces, more complex characters, though equally as egocentric as the others, vainly seeking acceptance and even friendship from the powerful. The time of the Anglo-Irish war was a period when the need for intelligence was great, but the lives of those providing that information were precarious and none of them, not even those like Mary Lindsay and William Joyce who attributed the noblest of motives to their actions, could rely on their powerful friends for protection once those actions were discovered.

Just as the presence of informers varied between areas, so did the fighting. The link here is obvious, in that the opposing forces needed reliable information on an almost daily basis in Cork and Dublin where violence was endemic and they made great efforts to secure it. It is not, however, obvious why, during both the Anglo-Irish and Civil Wars, areas such as Westmeath, for example, should have been relatively quiet and this is a topic which could repay investigation.

Ostensibly, after 1922 British intelligence showed little or no interest in the Free State until 1939 and the beginning of World War II; in fact, McMahon provides a detailed account of the sources available to the UK government. These ranged from the still-anonymous British agent in Dublin who thought anti–Treaty plans to take over the Four Courts were preparations for a full-scale attack on the capital, to the unreliable and highly emotive letters passed on to them: "invariably Protestant, loyalist, and unionist—and prone to exaggeration." Eventually British government focus changed and, with Cosgrave's government, began to encourage full collaboration with Ireland on intelligence matters. Sources included, in particular, the British Navy which patrolled Irish waters and attempted to intercept Irregular gun-runners. The co-operation became more efficient until 1923, when "the Free State and Britain were working together closely, if secretly, to starve the Irregulars of arms, ammunition and financial support from abroad."[187] It is, therefore, interesting and thought-provoking that the most lasting legacy of those years was the Crime Investigation Department (CID), set up on Collins's orders in 1921, which became G2, the intelligence agency discussed in the next chapter, which collaborated freely with Britain throughout the emergency years.

"Let Erin Remember"
(To the memory of Stephen Hayes)

1
My name is Judas Stephen Hayes, a traitor to my land,
At selling out or murdering, sure none with me could stand,
I've made myself a pile of cash as plainly can be seen,
For there's pots of dough and gold galore for the selling of the green.

2
The first thing that I had to do was clear the lads away,
So I split the gaff on Flaherty and Grogan one fine day,
Then when the G-men came around I skipped from off the scene,
And I drew my pay without delay for the selling of the green.

3
I betrayed the boys in England when the bombing they did start,
I sold McCormack to the foe and murdered Peter Barnes,
And Churchill sent a message, just you and me between,
The Empire's funds will see you right for the selling of the green.

4
I met with Dr. Ryan and he brought me word from Dev,
He called for drinks around the house and this to me he said:
Sure you're the best informer that ever yet has been,
So we'll make of you our President for the selling of the green.

5
When Dr. Ryan came to me his face was pale with fright,
Says he this wireless broadcasting keeps me awake at night,
For if the people hear the truth, our State aint [sic] worth a bean,
They'll kick us out, no more we'll get, for the selling of the green.

6
So I split on Jack McNeela, and sent him to the Joy,
And dined with McEntee, the Saxon's white-haired boy,
Says he that was good business, for you and me I mean,
For we'll get each a thousand quid for the selling of the green.

7
When Sean Russel [sic] left for Germany, a message came from Dev,
To say I cannot rest or sleep until that man is dead,

2. The Emergency and After (1939–1974)

So we'll send the word to London and they'll meet him on the sea,
And Russel gone we'll all be safe for the selling of the green.

8
From Dublin to Kerry and from Howth to Galway bay,
I betrayed the boys in hundreds and sat back and drew my pay,
And then I got my bottles, the whisky ones I mean,
And we'll strike a blow for Erin and the selling of the green.

9
Then they started on the hunger-strike, bold Lar de Lacy said:
'Tis well to let them carry on till some of them are dead,
For certain men are dangerous, you know the ones I mean,
And we'll strike a blow for Erin and the selling of the green.

10
In August 1940, I sold McGrath and Harte,
And Butcher Boland murdered them in Mountjoy Prison yard,
For if we let them carry on the teachings of sixteen,
It would interfere with business and the selling of the green.

11
But Ireland still had fighting men, despite the blood and loss,
So I conspired with Dr. Ryan to murder Richard Goss,
And when he faced the firing squad, so brave and so serene,
I drank a toast with Boland to the selling of the green.

12
So I issued proclamations and statements to the Press,
I strutted and I pouted and I wore my fancy dress,
I stabbed my country in the back, a traitor vile and mean,
So I worked in league with Fianna Fail for the selling of the green.

13
I've seen the ghosts of murdered men around my bedside stand,
I've raised my arms to ward them off and seen my bloodstained hands,
And when I cried for mercy, the answer came to me,
With your vile blood you must repay for the selling of the green.

14
So now despised by all the world, to Mountjoy jail I'm bound,
When my good friend, old Dev, will see that I am safe and sound,
But Dev, I fear is falling fast and soon we'll se [sic] seeing,
Two gashed and bloody corpses for the selling of the green.

Source: private collection. The author has endeavored to find the original copyright owner of "Let Erin Remember," but has been unable to do so. If anyone can assist in establishing the copyright holder, the author will be pleased to acknowledge the owner.

2

The Emergency and After (1939–1974)

"My name is Judas Stephen Hayes"[1]

Before the civil war began in 1922, Michael Collins had warned that the people of Ireland were exhausted and weary of fighting. By the time that conflict was over in 1923 poverty exacerbated the problems facing the country after six years of war[2]: trade, commerce, and the administration had collapsed; crime was rife, despite the efforts of the Garda Siochána who had replaced the RIC[3]; the Free State Army was cut from 60,000 to under 25,000; and partition removed the bulk of industry. At the same time the IRA in the North was underground, with most republicans in prison or internment camps. Subsequently:

> Republicans were ... released into a very different society from the one they had fought for and many left the country in disgust. A mini-diaspora occurred between 1924 and 1927, with about 100,000 emigrating to the United States and elsewhere. Those who remained found that earning a living was a struggle. They were victimized by employers and deliberately barred from employment by loyalty oaths to the new regime.[4]

Then the fruitless outcome of the Boundary Commission in 1925, while not entirely unexpected, hastened the eventual defeat of the Cosgrave government in 1932. Meanwhile republicanism was at a low ebb but Moss Twomey[5] began to reorganize and reactivate the IRA in 1926, though with few tangible results, and de Valera's attempts to lead his Fianna Fáil party into the Dáil failed because of their refusal to take the oath of allegiance. At the same time, because the IRA claimed to be upholders of the Republic of 1916 and that the Free State government was invalid, the Gardaí began a crackdown against them, with constant surveillance, raids, arrests, interrogations, and beatings deterring recruits while making normal life an impossibility for the members of the organization.

2. The Emergency and After (1939–1974)

The New York stock market crash of 1929 had a devastating effect on the already impoverished Free State. Agricultural exports more than halved (from £35.8 million to under £14 million) and the traditional escape route of emigration was barred by rising unemployment in Britain and America. Cosgrave's Constitution (Amendment No. 17) Act (1931) ensured extensions to police powers, courts replaced by military tribunals, and many organizations (notably the IRA and Cumann na mBan) proscribed, and, as coercion became the norm, it led inevitably to unrest. Though this attitude strengthened the IRA, de Valera's popularity also grew as support for Cosgrave's government weakened. Even the most moderate nationalists on both sides of the border had been outraged by the Free State agreement of 1926 to pay certain RIC pensions and the British land annuities as the poverty-stricken nation faced the facts of the settlement: a payment of £150,000, plus an annuity of £250,000 for the next sixty years. There was a noticeable overlap in membership of Fianna Fáil and the IRA. This situation was underlined after the majority of de Valera's new ministers in 1932 were IRA veterans, many of whom had been imprisoned only eight years earlier, and the first action of the new government was to release the political prisoners from the military prison at Arbour Hill, Dublin. This move disarmed the rank-and-file IRA members, though their leaders were more cautious. Nevertheless they all welcomed the bill to remove the hated oath of allegiance and the rumor that de Valera would declare a republic after the Eucharistic Congress of July 1932. For Britain, however, these were danger signs and, following the Free State failure to pay the land annuity, an economic war between the two countries began.

The year 1933 brought the appointment of Eamon Broy, already head of the Special Branch, as chief of police, and this led to the creation of the armed auxiliary Special Branch group, later known as the Broy Harriers, as part of the Free State government's crack-down on the Blueshirts. Despite this, the 1930s saw the rise of communism and fascism in the South, and the IRA's attempts to distance itself from the subsequent disturbances and to stress their hostility to atheism. De Valera's popularity in the country continued, and in 1934 he instituted a pension for those IRA men who had fought in the War of Independence and had not applied for the first pension in the 1920s. However, applying for the pension meant dismissal from the IRA, and in the following year de Valera began a low-key campaign against the organization which resulted in imprisonment for a number of the members. Nevertheless, as MacEoin notes, "Almost everyone believed that sometime very soon he [Dev] would produce a plan that would unify Ireland once again. Therefore it was thought that the harassment of the I.R.A. in the South ... was just a ploy ... to fool the British."[6]

Meanwhile in Belfast there was an upsurge in sectarian violence prompted by parades to celebrate George V's jubilee which resulted in widespread rioting and the destruction of Catholic houses.[7] At the same time veteran IRA men were switching their allegiance to Fianna Fáil; Catholic Church leaders condemned the IRA; and the republicans stepped up their efforts on behalf of strikers, particularly the Dublin bus and tram workers, resulting in yet more republicans in prison and the first post–1932 references to the IRA as an illegal organization.[8] IRA man Harry White noted that "De Valera was as bad to Republicans as the Northern junta. I had been brought up in Belfast to regard Dublin as the promised land, and. .. De Valera the heart and soul of republicanism. But ... when I was arrested ... in 1935 and condemned to Arbour Hill ... I learned very young what it was like being in solitary custody in the Free State. That soon changed my opinion."[9]

The Spanish Civil War (1936–1939), with its stories of the slaughter of priests and nuns, induced some young Irishmen to join the International Brigade causing a loss of potential IRA recruits. Seán MacBride replaced Moss Twomey as Chief of Staff but was not popular, and, in the following month, Sean McCaughey and Stephen Hayes took their first steps to prominence. Hayes became the IRA candidate who failed to win the Wexford by-election of 1935, while McCaughey, in Belfast, was engaged in the hunt for an informer following the abortive Campbell College raid (in Belmont, East Belfast) of December in that year. The raid was an attempt to seize rifles from the Officers' Training Corps, but the rifles had been removed previously, the RUC were waiting for the raiding party and four of the eight Volunteers were arrested. Among those who escaped was Sean McCaughey. The Belfast Commandant, Tony Lavery, gave his permission for the arrested men to recognize the court at their trial and so was called to an IRA court-martial at Crown Entry in Belfast. This proved to be a mistake. The RUC arrived, thirteen IRA officers were arrested and jailed, and, following IRA investigations two men were identified as informers and shot: Dan Turley in December 1936 and Joe Hanna in January 1937.

The new 26-county state had achieved a partial freedom, but the endemic poverty and unemployment led to considerable disillusion. In Northern Ireland nearly one in three workers was unemployed, and the mortality rate from tuberculosis was 20 percent higher than in the rest of the UK, caused by "Lack of hygiene, poverty and utterly inadequate medical care ... [and] cramped and poor-quality housing."[10] The popularity of the IRA diminished, recruits were in short supply, and morale among the active members was low because so many of the leaders had either been killed in the Spanish Civil War or retired from active service. With tensions growing between MacBride's political stance and Sean Russell's followers who favored action, the mood of the majority of the members was made clear at the 1936 convention, when Tom Barry's proposal to invade the North and resume the war with Britain in six months was carried enthusiastically. The first contact was also made, in 1937, between the Abwehr (the German Intelligence Organization, under Admiral Canaris) and the IRA. Barry became Chief of Staff and MacBride was appointed Information Officer, but Barry called off the offensive when he discovered that his detailed plans were known by republicans on both sides of the border. Shortly afterwards Barry resigned, then Peadar O'Flaherty promoted Russell's bombing campaign so that at the next convention in April 1938 the idea had taken hold and the IRA executive was swept away. Russell was appointed Chief of Staff at the head of a largely unknown Army Council, one of whom was the Commanding Officer of the Wexford Brigade, Stephen Hayes. Most of the old guard resigned from GHQ in protest, but euphoria created by the prospect of action blinded Russell's supporters into imagining that the British government could be forced to concede control of Northern Ireland.

The most pragmatic description of the time and of the bombing campaign comes from Stephen Hayes, writing long after the event, but as one who had been at the center of it: "None of us looked around to ask where was the experienced personnel, what state of organisation we had set up in England, and above all what intelligence system we could depend on. The fact was we had no organisation in England, and could do nothing more than arrange lodgings for the men going there on jobs: this in hostile England where at the first bang every English landlady would be nosing after her Irish lodgers."[11]

The English campaign began on 16 January 1939 and, by the winter, had already failed. The most noteworthy result was that de Valera's insistence on Irish neutrality, and his fear that Britain might use the campaign as a pretext to seize the treaty ports, led to an unprecedented cooperation between the gardaí and the British police. In addition, 1939 and 1940 saw the enactment of emergency legislation, in particular the Irish Emergency Powers Act of July 1940 which set up the Special Military Court to try certain offences specified in a Government Order before three military officers, with the only possible sentence being death.

It is possible that the Free State government's insistence on neutrality and the consequent ever-increasing Special Branch activity led also to the raid on a house in Dublin which brought about the arrest of all the members of GHQ, with the exception of Stephen Hayes, by this time Acting Chief of Staff, and Matty Tuite, as well as the seizure of more than $8,000, thus sealing the fate of the English campaign both organizationally and financially.[12] England's declaration of war against Germany in September 1939 was also instrumental in bringing the IRA campaign to an end because the whole country became highly security conscious: throughout World War II special passes were needed for military areas, and the constant checks meant that the slightest hint of an Irish accent could lead to attention from the police.

Patrick Stephen Hayes

Stephen Hayes was born in Enniscorthy in 1902, educated by the Christian Brothers, the ninth of eleven children. He grew up with two constant influences on his life, republicanism and Catholicism, and, like many others, found no difficulty in reconciling the two. His father, Thomas, was a publican (Hayes Bar and Lounge still exists at 7–8 Court Street, Enniscorthy); his mother, Ellen, took in lodgers: all were republicans and one, Larry de Lacy who later married Stephen's sister, Mary, became his lifelong friend, and was named as a "trusted Fianna Fáil agent" in the document of August 1941, later known as "The confession of Stephen Hayes."[13] Through these men Stephen met Liam Mellowes, who became his hero, and Eamonn Ceannt, and in 1916 the fourteen-year-old became a messenger for the republican forces. By the end of World War I, when all arms in private hands throughout Ireland were called in, he was a *sluagh* [troop] leader with the Fianna, raided houses throughout County Wexford at gunpoint, and took all the revolvers and ammunition brought home by British army officers. When he left school in 1920 he had led raids on the mails and trains and reported to the Volunteers on British troop and supply movements until, in April 1921, he became OC of the Wexford Fianna Brigade. Years later, in his Mountjoy diary, Hayes was to reflect wistfully on those days: "What memories come crowding round of glorious and spirited days from 1915. How elated I felt marching in 1917 in Fianna uniform. Thought the whole town belonged to me. That spirit + enthusiasm for things National and idealistic is dying hard but certainly dying."[14]

Hayes wanted to be an engineer when he left school, but instead became a clerk for Wexford County Council.[15] This was at a time when the vast majority of pupils left school at fourteen, or even earlier, in order to earn money, but Stephen Hayes stayed at school for another four years and, presumably, sat both levels of the School Certificate.[16] He was interned as an IRA man in Hare Park camp, in the Curragh, from the summer of 1922 until the end of 1923, then, once the British had left, the need for a new fully functioning Civil Service became apparent.

The qualifications necessary for the new Irish Civil Service were high, included Irish (Hayes was fluent), and he found himself the holder of what many, including his own family, regarded as a very desirable post with the County Council. Later, however, to qualify for annual pay increments, civil servants had to sign an oath of allegiance to the Free State government and Hayes refused to do this.[17] He began to reactivate the IRA in County Wexford, under the pretense of reorganizing the GAA clubs and, at the same time, he realized that all that Michael Collins had taught them about putting intelligence first was forgotten and attempted to put that right, though his efforts were discounted later. For the rest of his career in the IRA Stephen Hayes was obsessively secretive, even to the point of not telling any of his IRA colleagues that he was an Irish speaker. He spoke of this to Tarlach Ó hUid, editor of *Republican News*, in a 1962 interview: "I never saw any reason to let my I.R.A. colleagues know this. It was part of my natural caution and many's the time it proved valuable, for people talked freely, if rudely, in front of the ignorant."[18]

At thirty he was the Commandant in Wexford and, because of the constant attrition of the more experienced men, he was also the oldest of the prominent IRA men in the east and south of the country. Sean Russell asked him to come to Dublin as his Adjutant General and Hayes accepted. It meant giving up his post at Wexford County Council, which caused a number of his family to cut him off: they had expected his ultimate promotion to a fairly high level and regarded this decision as feckless, especially as the pay offered by the IRA was very much lower than his salary.[19] Hayes said of this time that "Russell was the most single purposed person I have ever known and his attitude towards foreign intervention, as apart from foreign aid in the way of supplies, made a deep impression on me, and perhaps played a great part in what happened to me."[20]

Initially, he was happy in Dublin working with Russell, who must have been pleased with the arrangement since he had no hesitation in going to America in April 1939, leaving Hayes as Acting Chief of Staff during his absence. There were, as it subsequently transpired, others who were not so pleased, and these included Hayes himself, though his written admission of this came many years later:

> My term of office as Acting Chief of Staff was to be very short, just the few weeks of Russell's absence. I was really more unfitted for the job than anyone could imagine. It was entirely beyond my experience and ability. I looked on myself merely as a recording caretaker clerk. Russell did not take my appointment very seriously, I fancy, for he told me nothing of what our resources were, but simply to whom I should address requisitions when my department needed money.[21]

This was the point of no return, when Stephen Hayes's whole life began to unravel in such a grave fashion that it was to affect him until the day he died.

In December 1938 the RUC had raided known republican houses in Belfast, searching for IRA members. Prior to this all personnel of the Belfast Battalion were ordered not to sleep in their homes. Finally they were informed that the alert was over. All those who returned home were arrested that night and almost all the battalion staff were detained.[22] Those who escaped formed a new staff, and this included Charlie McGlade and Liam Rice, both recently released from Crumlin jail, and Sean McCaughey. Liam Rice told Quinn: "it was later learned that the R.U.C. received information from Dublin to carry out that Belfast round up."[23] It would be naïve not to expect the main topic of conversation among this new staff to be the raids. Did Liam Rice plant the suspicion in McCaughey's mind that all was not well at GHQ in Dublin? If so, since this was before Russell went to America, could he have been the original target? Was the whole idea to mount a Northern takeover of the IRA in the South in order to carry out their plans together with help from Germany? Certainly Hayes thought so years later, when he wrote that "It was to win control of the I.R.A. and place it entirely at the disposal of the friends of Germany in Ireland that I was arrested."[24]

In both North and South the majority of the Volunteers wanted action, but the war made communication between Dublin and Belfast very difficult, hence the creation of the Northern Command.[25] In Belfast Sean McCaughey had surrounded himself with a like-minded group to carry out operations "without the authority of their Brigade leadership."[26] The Northern Command also had contacts "in every British Army barracks in Northern Ireland, [and] a radio code was intercepted, allowing the IRA to listen to British communications, and regular intelligence reports were sent to Dublin."[27] However, McCaughey's arrest in the autumn of 1939 at a training camp in the Dublin mountains had more repercussions than the short prison sentence he received. He returned to Belfast concerned about security in the South and with a poor impression of Hayes as Chief of Staff.

That autumn thirty-six republicans were arrested and jailed in Belfast, and a number of other men from the North were caught and interned in the South. McCaughey had been brought into the Northern Command by Charlie McGlade in the summer, and now the arrest of so many leaders resulted in McCaughey's promotion, aged twenty three, to Commanding Officer of the Northern Command, with McGlade as his Adjutant General. In view of McCaughey's youth this promotion seems unwarranted, but according to Des Long: "Most Volunteers do not last five years. If he had been active at officer level for that length of time he would be a very experienced officer."[28]

McCaughey added to his growing reputation in 1940 by capturing thirty Lee Enfield rifles from Ballykinlar Army base. This feat was far surpassed by the Magazine Fort raid of December 1939, organized by Hayes, but the ensuing jubilation over that did not last long. The IRA took 1,084,000 rounds of ammunition in thirteen lorries. This caused chaos because the ammunition dumps were not big enough to store them, and most of it was eventually given back (though the circumstances of its return were ambiguous).[29] Nevertheless, initially, the raid had great psychological and propaganda value.

Subsequently McCaughey and McGlade started making regular visits to Dublin and the former devoted a great deal of thought to the IRA in the South. Hayes had frequently said that IRA intelligence was inadequate but both Annual Conventions and the Army Council, placed intelligence low in the order of priorities: they relied instead on veteran IRA men in the police, so that throughout the 1930s the IRA had informants among the detectives at Dublin Castle who provided photographs of every plainclothes officer in Dublin.[30]

This ended when Sergeant Michael Gill joined the reorganized Special Branch at the beginning of World War II: he became expert at finding IRA men and was rapidly promoted to Chief Superintendent. However, mistakes were still made. In summer 1940 Stephen Hayes was in a house in Victoria Avenue, Donnybrook, on the run like the rest of the IRA, when he heard that a German was walking unscathed around Dublin asking where he could find Stephen Hayes, the Chief of Staff of the IRA. The German was Captain Hermann Goertz.

The German Spies and Operation Mainau[31]

The common perception of the German war machine during World War II, exemplified by innumerable books and films, is one of complete efficiency. This image is at variance with the ludicrous sequence of events surrounding the arrival in Ireland of the agents sent by the Abwehr and many of their subsequent activities. Throughout this period neither the Germans nor the IRA seem to have revealed to each other what was required from this contact: Germany thought at first that the IRA was the Irish army and wanted an intelligence gathering force in the North, and later they wished to control the IRA; the IRA wanted money, arms, and wireless transmitters from the Germans, not their presence. Mark Hull writes "Germany failed in almost every aspect of intelligence planning as it pertained to Ireland: from hazy military intelligence objectives, flawed local and political information, questionable personnel selection, to sloppy execution."[32]

Altogether, and at varying intervals, the German intelligence sent twelve agents to Ireland during the war years until 1944. They were intended to form a base for wartime espionage against Britain but, apart from their own failings, they came up against "a brilliantly effective Irish army counterintelligence system [which] mathematically eliminated any chance of German success."[33] The Irish secret weapon in intelligence matters was Dr. Richard Hayes,[34] Director of the National Library and linguist with a talent for cryptography, who, aided by the capture of Abwehr code books, recreated the German cyphers. These became of huge importance to G2 (Irish Military Intelligence), because they were used to great effect when tracking Hermann Goertz's movements and contacts. This information was also valuable to MI5.[35]

Shortly before the outbreak of war the IRA transmitter and basic coding system for messages arrived, but not all the intellectual failings were on the German side, as a memorandum to G2 in early 1940 demonstrates:

Once operational, the IRA used the radio for internal propaganda broadcasts, not realizing that the transmission source could be detected by the Irish police ... and Irish Military Intelligence.... This process was made considerably easier since the IRA announced their broadcast times in advance. The result was predictable: the transmitter and four IRA men were seized on 24 December 1939, cutting the only link between the Abwehr and its new Irish affiliate.[36]

Dr. Hermann Goertz, a failed lawyer and World War I veteran, the third German agent to be sent during World War II, is most relevant to this study because his involvement with the IRA was significant in the accusations against Stephen Hayes.[37] Goertz's career with the Abwehr began in 1935 when he was sent to England to gather RAF intelligence. This mission ended in August of the same year when he was arrested; his trial at the Old Bailey achieved international notoriety because of the incredible incompetence revealed and he was given a four-year prison sentence.

The Abwehr was not deterred. In May 1940, Goertz (now 50 years old) was parachuted into Ireland in full Luftwaffe dress uniform, with World War I decorations, and riding boots. His destination was Francis Stuart's house in Laragh, Co. Wicklow, but he landed near Ballivor, Co. Meath, some 70 miles away, late at night.[38] He had brought another wireless transmitter, but this was on a separate parachute and he failed to find it in the dark. Among other incidents on his subsequent night-march south the secret ink in his shoulder pads dissolved when he swam the River Boyne, and he stopped at the police station at Poulaphouca to ask for directions. "For reasons not entirely clear, the police did not notice anything suspicious about the person dressed in riding boots speaking with a German accent, and made no report of the incident."[39]

Though Goertz has been described as the most successful of the German agents in Ireland, this is difficult to substantiate.[40] Certainly he remained at liberty longer than the others, but this was with the connivance of G2 to whom (unknown to himself) he was exceedingly useful. His presence was discovered on 22 May 1940, when the gardaí and detectives raided Stephen Held's house in Dublin where Goertz was living and found and confiscated a great deal of evidence, in addition to Goertz's belongings[41] :

> [a] file which contained military details about Irish harbors, airfields, bridges, roads, and landing places and about the distribution of the Irish defence forces. Other documents included a code and details concerned with cyphered wireless traffic.
> The detectives also found a parachute, a wireless transmitter and receiver and a locked safe containing about twenty thousand American dollars.[42]

Goertz, who had been out on the day of the raid, fled to Laragh, found that Iseult Stuart had also been arrested, and eventually lay low in Dublin, convinced that the IRA was unreliable. He had, however, been brought to the attention of G2, and from then until his arrest on 27 November 1941 he was

2. The Emergency and After (1939–1974) 67

followed and watched. "Irish G2 ... used him as a convenient lightning rod for extreme republican elements—arresting and interning IRA elements as Goertz moved from place to place."[43]

Goertz's own writings are self-serving, in that they are couched in terms which show his activities in the best possible light.[44] Thus his early demands of Hayes: for a cease-fire in the south; to direct IRA activities against the six counties; to consult the Irish Army with a view to their collaboration with the IRA; to make peace with de Valera; eventually give way to scathing denunciations of the IRA, this last probably to rationalize an abortive series of attempts to return to Germany. Both attitudes need to be read in conjunction with the fact that several times Stephan has occasion to remark that Goertz's accounts of his adventures are unreliable or even pure fantasy.[45]

Goertz was equally dismissive of Stephen Hayes: "I do not think it is necessary for me to describe the disappointment which I felt when I met Stephen Hayes, although I had already been warned.... At first he showed himself as a man of good personal qualities but that is not enough for the leader of nationalist extremists. Later his character deteriorated. I think from alcohol and fear."[46] For Hayes, on the other hand, Goertz was a foreigner who refused to understand the basic facts of the Irish situation, and an irritant who interrupted IRA meetings at his house in Dalkey, by playing the grand piano for lengthy periods. Hayes's colleagues sometimes left the meeting early, thoroughly angry, because they had traveled all day to be there, often with great difficulty as they were all on the run.[47]

It is probable that much of the dislike Hayes inspired in Goertz and McCaughey stemmed from his dismissal of their ideas. Though plainly an intelligent man, a large part of Hayes's downfall must have stemmed from his own naïvety in not appreciating that this attitude would make enemies.[48] For these two *were* his enemies and they began to meet regularly, thus discovering that their aims were much the same, and that both blamed Hayes for all perceived failures, including the arrests by G2 of those contacted by Goertz.

McCaughey and Goertz shared a minor obsession with radio transmitters, or rather, with Dublin's lack of them. Yet it seems very likely that here, again, there existed no mutual definition of the objective. For McCaughey the transmitter was (as used in Belfast) for local propaganda broadcasting; for Goertz a far more powerful piece of equipment was necessary to maintain his contact with Germany. After the first transmitter, sent by Clan na Gael, was tracked down and seized in a matter of weeks, the authorities began to take the IRA seriously and Hayes was understandably lacking in enthusiasm for transmitters as a result of the new pressures. The intelligence services kept a check on people with technical knowledge and there were constant raids in which equipment was seized. Possession of a single radio valve was cause for arrest.[49]

Nevertheless, when Goertz arrived, he made the provision of a transmitter a condition for providing the arms and money needed by the IRA. Various initiatives, including the risky commissioning of a technician to assemble one, were tried and failed, and Goertz's eventual move to Held's house was solely because the latter had a transmitter. This proved not to be working. A garbled account of the transmitter saga, presumably heard from Goertz, who was by this stage panic-stricken and determined to leave Ireland, formed one of the planks in McCaughey's later accusations against Hayes.

Hayes was, therefore, on the run, and beset by two malcontents. McCaughey, now his Adjutant General, had been constantly aggressive and confrontational since their first meeting, while Hayes had been forced by the continuing arrests and internment of IRA men, to appoint McGlade and others from the Northern Command to take up the vacancies. Hayes could see the IRA deteriorating under his leadership while he had no assets to combat this: "Of late I had been deeply troubled with the state of the organisation. I had seen the organisation weaken around me and had asked myself if I was not making a bad job of it."[50] Nevertheless, in his dealings with McCaughey and Goertz, he had little idea of how to cope with those who disagreed with him, and also to have been too easily inclined to dismiss them when they refused to accept the facts: that the IRA was too few in numbers, too weakened by internment, and too poor to involve itself in their grandiose schemes. What McCaughey and Goertz wanted was an IRA invasion of Northern Ireland. Hayes, on the other hand, ignored McCaughey and Goertz as much as possible, avoided the police, and met his men in secret places, undisclosed to the attendees until the last possible minute, unaware that events were spiraling out of his control.

There are a number of accounts of the abduction of Stephen Hayes in June 1941: in newspapers, both local (Wexford) and national; in Quirke's work[51]; and in Hayes's own articles, principally "My Strange Story" in *The Bell* in 1951. This last was written a decade after the event, and Hayes, conscious that the passage of time could make a difference to memories, writes "Another difficulty in telling a story of things that happened ten years ago is that one can't keep from putting more wisdom into the telling than there was in him at the time."[52] These two articles are particularly significant in that they show Hayes's writing ability and clarity of thought about his own capabilities and, while humility is not evidence of complete honesty, it predisposes the reader to think well of him. In the main there are few differences in the details used in these narratives, probably because the newspapers got their information from each other or from the evidence given subsequently at Sean McCaughey's trial.

On 30 June 1941 three armed IRA men irrupted into Hayes's house in Coolock, Co. Dublin.[53] They bound his arms with copper wire and bundled him into a car. So sudden was this attack that Hayes was taken away in carpet slippers, and said ten years later "I find it difficult to believe even now that this thing could happen, above all to me."[54] There followed more than two months of accusations, interrogation, threats, beating and semi-starvation, punctuated by transfers to other houses, the writing of the confession,[55] and the court-martial,[56] which Hayes described as "a mixture between a schoolboy rag and an American gangster film."[57] There were two charges, with McCaughey acting as prosecutor:

> 1. That you, Stephen Hayes, conspired with the "Irish Free State Government" to obstruct the policy and impede the progress of the Irish Republican Army.
> 2. That you, Stephen Hayes, are guilty of treachery by having deliberately forwarded information of a secret and confidential nature concerning the activities of the Irish Republican Army, to a hostile body, to wit, the "Irish Free State Government."[58]

Liam Burke describes the two antagonists: "Failing to be specific on any point, Stephen Hayes continued only with monosyllabic rebuttals, frequently going off at tangents. Seán McCaughey went methodically from point to point."[59] This fails to take into account either the complete shock of one man, or the obsessional nature of the other.

At no time does Hayes admit to fear, although several times he was convinced that he was about to be shot, apart from on their arrival on the first night at the uninhabited farm house belonging to Roger Mac Hugh[60] in the Cooley hills: "It looked bad that my captors ... should smuggle me out of reach of the long-established I.R.A. units and their experienced fair-minded officers. It looked as if they themselves were frightened at what they had done. Men in such a mood are dangerous."[61] He came to the conclusion on that night "that I was not in I.R.A. custody at all. The men who had arrested me had merely ganged up on me."[62] This, he felt, left him "free to fox my way out, if at all possible."[63] His descriptions of his ill treatment at their hands contain no hint of self-pity, while a sense of shock is reserved for two occasions. The first was the discovery, in the first days of his captivity, that a two-way mirror in the room where he was held showed another prisoner tied to a chair in the next room: this was Bridie Hess, the mother of his small son, born only three weeks previously.[64] Bridie was held there for about two days, presumably to add to the pressure on the prisoner, but the implied threat must have lasted a great deal longer, because, though a few members of his family knew of her, and there are some letters from Mountjoy to "B," Hayes never mentioned her existence in writing, possibly because of the realization that he had brought such danger to mother and child.

The second occurred later, and seems to have been included in only two manuscripts: the article by Tarlach Ó hUid ("Stephen Hayes ag cosaint a chlu") of 1962, and in Quirke's typescript.[65] Hayes, as noted above, had never mentioned his knowledge of Irish in IRA circles, so none of his captors knew of it. Moreover his piety is well-attested throughout his letters from Mountjoy and the diary he kept while there, as well as by the words of those who knew him: "He was very religious. No matter how drunk he'd be, he'd kneel down by the bed to say his prayers and sometimes fall asleep where he knelt."[66] Condemned to be shot by his captors, and believing that the sentence would be carried out, he asked for a priest. Among themselves his captors frequently spoke in Irish, and this conversation was no exception. So Hayes was not surprised to hear his request reported in Irish to Sean McCaughey, but the answer horrified him: McCaughey snarled: "No priest for that rat!"

Many people would fail to understand a man who did not dwell on his fear of death but on fear for his immortal soul, nevertheless that is what happened. McCaughey, however, *did* understand. The memory of that moment never left Stephen Hayes. His ideals, his training, his whole life changed in one second when the Adjutant General of the IRA, most of whose members would cross themselves outside every church they passed on the way to a raid, coldly told the men who were to shoot him: NO PRIEST FOR HIM. Hayes spoke of this comment many years later: "*That ... was the moment when I abandoned the I.R.A. and its methods for ever* [emphasis added], the moment when I realized that the movement was now in the hands of men so vicious—these fighters for 'Holy Ireland'—that they could deny a man the consolation of religion at his last moment, something no Christian country does to the worst of enemies."[67] Even as an old man he recalled that moment with shock. The young man he had set so high in the IRA, and who had already let him down so badly, had denied him an elementary right open to all dying Catholics, no matter who they were or what they had done. This was the point when Hayes definitively severed himself from the IRA. He had given his life to the organization only to see it turn against him, in the person of a man who owed him a great deal.

While Hayes can certainly be accused of naïveté in his dealings with others, the venom displayed by McCaughey in refusing a priest goes far beyond dislike of his prisoner. It was an enormity nobody could have foreseen from another Catholic. McCaughey had tried, judged, and condemned Stephen Hayes on the basis of suspicion alone, and was now prepared to pursue him even beyond the grave. Hayes was profoundly shocked, as only a genuinely pious man can be. It is hardly surprising that he later said to Coogan "I don't think that McCaughey was the full shilling anyway,"[68] or that in Mountjoy he was to write "It is sad to think of the disaster—havoc a few Belfast curs have wrought in the organisation whose building up caused so much toil + tears to us all in years and years."[69] Nor can there be much doubt that, from that moment on, Stephen Hayes, IRA Chief of Staff, was a completely disillusioned man who regarded himself as divorced from the movement to which he had devoted so much of his life.

Subsequently he was brought, late at night, on foot, and still in the carpet slippers from the cottage to Mrs. Mac Eoin's house in Rathmines.[70] There, under duress, Hayes began to write the document later called the *Special Communiqué* (but more commonly "The Confession of Stephen Hayes"), possibly the longest IRA confession ever produced: the final version was about 10,500 words. Hayes always claimed that this confession was completely false, a mixture of lies and half-truths written and rewritten over many weeks according to McCaughey's dictation and demands. When ordered to write the names of all his contacts he simply listed all the names he could remember of the people who worked for Wexford County Council. McCaughey made him say that he and Dr. James Ryan, the Minister for Agriculture, had plotted to inform on the IRA in England, and that the failure of the English campaign was deliberately organized so that the IRA would be discredited. In this context it is worthy of note that the English bombing campaign began on 16 January 1939. As evidenced by secret papers recently released by the National Archives in London and used in the BBC Radio 4 program "Document," by 28 January of that year the Dublin government had already been in touch with the UK government, and by 6 February had agreed to supply information through the Gardaí "to prevent the organisation in Dublin of further criminal activities in the United Kingdom."[71] Negotiations in this matter were carried out through John W. Dulanty, High Commissioner for Ireland, and the culmination is a brief letter to the UK Attorney General bearing the significant final sentence "De Valera, I understand, has no objection to our saying that the facts in our possession have been communicated to Dulanty, but it would be better not to say anything about having asked Dublin to co-operate."[72]

Donnacha Ó Beacháin comments[73]: "It certainly would have undermined De Valera's image of being the pristine Republican leader who had heroically and unstintingly challenged the British. I think it would have been difficult for him to present that image, and it's something that he treasured."[74] The *quid pro quo* of this arrangement is revealed by the following:

> As regards Russell, it is believed that some ten or twelve years ago he was in Soviet pay as an agitator; if there is any information which could be made available to show that this was the case, or that at the present time he is in receipt of pay from foreign sources, it would be of the greatest possible assistance to the Dublin authorities in dealing with him, since it would practically eliminate the risk of his being treated as a patriotic martyr if they were able to show that he was merely a paid foreign agent.[75]

It would seem, then, that far from being de Valera's informer, Hayes was to become his scapegoat.

Hayes confirms that he wrote the confession very deliberately so that his readers would see how false it was, and that he was writing under duress. He thought that nobody would be credulous enough to believe a word of it but he was totally wrong, and unprepared for the reception the confession received: people not only believed it, they *wanted* to believe it, and this included many of his close friends as well as colleagues he had trusted.[76]

An interesting sequel to the confession bears out Hayes's constant claim that it was entirely composed of a mixture of lies and half truths, invented to save his life. On 15 October 1941, Patrick Murphy pleaded guilty "to membership of an unlawful organisation, possession of an incriminating document [the *Special Communiqué*], and the distribution of an incriminating document."[77] Two members of the Government and a Senator appeared at his trial before the Special Criminal Court at Collins Barracks: Dr. James Ryan, Minister for Agriculture; Thomas Derrig, Minister for Education; and Senator Christopher Byrne. Before they gave evidence the prosecuting lawyer, in his opening speech, spoke about the accusations against prominent figures in the document, and included his own view of its contents:

> in view of what is contained in these excerpts from the alleged Confession, it is impossible to imagine on what evidence the purported court-martial could ever have arrived at a verdict of guilty. If the evidence which I propose to tender to the Court is accepted as truthful and accurate, it will be apparent on going through the document that whoever was responsible for its production ... compiled what can only be described as a highly seditious, defamatory and imaginary document—in fact a complete fabrication and a tissue of lies.[78]

The three men, all of whom had been mentioned in the document, seem to have been questioned fairly briskly about their connections with Stephen Hayes and Larry de Lacy, and denied any recent knowledge of the two. Dr. Ryan went so far as to deny he had ever known Hayes.[79] The trial ended when Murphy was sentenced to twelve months' imprisonment, "not to be enforced on his entering into a bail bond to keep the peace for two years."[80]

For those who believed the confession, this would make very little difference: If Stephen Hayes was a Government informer, then of course the authorities would deny that the confession was true. Hayes had thought that he was writing such a ridiculous document that nobody of intelligence could possibly accept it. It was unfortunate, then, that one of the first people to deny its accuracy was working for the Government. Unfortunate also that the trial seems to have had an ulterior motive—the washing of Government hands. In the following year Stephen Hayes, on just one of the charges (membership of an illegal organization) leveled at Patrick Murphy, was sentenced to five years in Mountjoy. Murphy was given a suspended sentence for the same offence, so perhaps the trial was intended to provide a public forum for the Government to deny all the allegations. The reasoning behind this possibility becomes clearer if we look at Dr. Ryan's speech to a Fianna Fáil meeting in Wexford about two weeks later. Though he begins by reiterating his denials of any involvement with Hayes, he goes on to stress the value of Irish neutrality and the difficulties inherent in maintaining it.[81] Given the

2. The Emergency and After (1939–1974)

notoriety of both the Stephen Hayes Affair (as it came to be known in the press), and the *Special Communiqué* (possession of a copy was incriminating), it is not too great a leap to think that de Valera and his party had been very disturbed by the confession itself, and by the tendency of so many to believe in it once it was published in September 1941.

O'Halpin, Bowyer Bell, and others have scrutinized the Hayes confession, and disposed of those accusations which have not already been exposed as falsehood by time itself, for example: Hayes confesses to having conspired in the murder of Sean Russell in Gibraltar, whereas he died on the U-boat bearing him back to Ireland. According to O'Halpin "the only forensic analysis of it [the confession] traced dates from 1943, when it had become possible to test some of its claims through Pandora.... Hempel [the German ambassador] thought the confession an elaborate fabrication which might even be the work of British Intelligence."[82] Bowyer Bell claimed that "All the individuals named as agents swore the 'Confession' was a lie, as did all the members of the government in a position to know of any such plot, as did most of the individuals in the IRA listed as dupes or victims ... the 'Confession' ... is a maze of little errors and large assertions and assumptions, where every betrayal is denied by agent and victim."[83] While Coogan, referring to the later statement asserting his innocence made by Hayes to his solicitor, writes "Checking Hayes's statement against that of the I.R.A., any informed Irish person can see at a glance that, if one must make a choice, Hayes's document is much more likely to be accurate."[84] However, none of this informed analysis makes a difference to those who still believe in his guilt.

It does not seem to have occurred to any of Hayes's accusers to make comparisons. For instance, one of Hayes's miraculous escapes was during the 1939 raid on GHQ in Dublin when all the leaders except Hayes and Tuite were arrested. They arrived late and saw what was happening. Yet others had many lucky escapes: Goertz is a case in point. Hayes often advised the German to be cautious, and there were several occasions when he escaped while other men were arrested: Jim Crofton, for instance, ex–Special Branch, friend of Hayes and part of his intelligence network who, with his wife, Peg (sister of Bridie Hess), brought up Stephen Hayes's son in his early years. Liam Rice said of him "Jim Crofton may have been a distant relative of Stephen Hayes ... he believed Hayes was innocent and that Sean McCaughey was a troublemaker ... whenever the occasion arose, he would commence to rant about the Hayes affair."[85] This version was not altogether true; many years later Hayes's son recalls the arrival of Jim Crofton at his mother's house in the 1960s.[86] The purpose of his visit was to apologize because for many years he had actually been convinced of Stephen's guilt, but he now knew that he was innocent. He was crying and in despair: "If I was so close to him and couldn't believe him..."[87]

On 8 September 1941, one of Hayes's two guards was elsewhere in the Rathmines house talking to the landlady's daughter. The landlady herself came to the door of the room where Hayes was held.[88] When the second guard went to speak to her he left his gun on the mantlepiece. Hayes snatched the gun, threw himself out of the window and staggered down the road wrapped in chains. At that point he had no idea where to go, realized that he would be caught again if he attempted to go too far, saw the police station and went in. A garda who had seen his arrival at the Rathmines Garda station later commented that he was "looking like a lunatic, carrying a revolver in his hand, and he surrendered himself, an old man, as he looked.... He bore on his wrists and arms, shoulders, legs, thighs, and on the soles of his feet, and on his ankles the marks of his detention and the cruelty that had been inflicted on him."[89]

Hayes's escape from the house was seen by several local people and, as a consequence, caused a sensation in the press. McCaughey had been arrested earlier, on 2 September, when he got off a tram at the corner of Castlewood Avenue. He had in his possession a notebook and two keys which fitted the padlocks on Hayes's chains, and two latch keys which belonged to Hayes.[90] Stephen Hayes already thought his captors no longer knew what to do with him, and later there were rumors among the people of Wexford that he had been allowed to escape but his guards had not thought he would go to the barracks.[91] It is, however, plain that Hayes did not think so, at least at the time[92]: "If I could have thought that any of the powerful republican households would take me in, and defend me while I rallied some forces round me to convene a Republican Commission to find the facts in the whole sorry business, I would have got to that house somehow. But since I did not know of any such household, and my need was desperate, I made to the nearest Garda Barrack."[93]

Yet this was part of the evidence which was to damn him forever:

> To many the damning evidence was Hayes' willingness to seek refuge in a police station and, far worse, his testimony against McCaughey.[94] That by September Hayes was a dazed and broken man, who had lived in fear of death for ten weeks, was discounted. That Hayes might have sought revenge against McCaughey, the man who beat his body and tainted his honor, was discounted. That Hayes, who had spent his life in the IRA, might have been so repulsed by his ordeal that he no longer felt any loyalty for men who had almost been his executioners was discounted. For the stern and the pure, Hayes had sold out in court and in public, and that was enough.[95]

Ten days after his escape Hayes gave evidence against McCaughey when the latter was tried for abduction and assault by the Special Military Court at Collins Barracks. Hayes wanted to make a statement in court to explain his reason for testifying, but the President of the Military Court told him "Your explanation is quite unnecessary. It would be irrelevant to the case as far as the Court is concerned. There is a man charged here with a very serious offence, and anything that does not concern the evidence in relation to the charge, the Court would have to leave out."[96]

Arguably Hayes knew republicans would view his testimony in a bad light and hoped to defuse any accusations. The initial death sentence passed on McCaughey, the only sentence available to the three judges, was commuted to penal servitude for life. McCaughey was sent to Maryborough (Portlaoise) Prison, where he died in 1946 while on hunger and thirst strike for political status. This claim for political status rested on the fact that he was sentenced in a military rather than a civil court, "[and] it is alleged by his comrades that it was well understood by the prison authorities and by the government that he would have come off the strike if he had been removed to the Curragh."[97] His inquest revealed the appalling conditions in Maryborough to a shocked nation, and this, together with the manner of his death, led to protest meetings in Dublin and Wexford, as well as motions of sympathy in local councils in Wexford.[98] It also added to the general opprobrium surrounding the name of Stephen Hayes.

It could be argued that, once he was in police custody, Hayes's testimony against McCaughey was inevitable, but this was not so. As an IRA member he should not have recognized the court.[99] In fact, at his own trial in the Special Criminal Court he refused to plead, give evidence on oath or call witnesses, so the court entered a plea of not guilty. This raises the question of whether or not Hayes still saw himself as an IRA man at this juncture, and this is the crux of the matter. If he *was* a member, the accusation by republican posterity that he was an informer is technically correct. If he was not, which his reaction to the refusal of a priest indicates, then he was free to testify. Muddying these waters is that his testimony is also seen as revenge, the worst reason in republican eyes for informing. This is not impossible as a motive. Stephen Hayes was very much sinned against, but he was no saint, and there is evidence that he was inclined to be vengeful: "In 1938, when I heard of the appointment of Stephen Hayes to the staff, I told Russell that he drank too much and that, as a consequence, he might well turn out to be an informer. I did that from first hand knowledge, having spent five weeks in Co. Wexford ... when Hayes came to occupy the office of Adjutant-General, he uncovered my report, as a result of which I was expelled from the Army."[100] Two entries in his Mountjoy diary add weight: "Visit from Lizzie + Alice (née Byrne) before dinner. Lizzie told me she had left in some foodstuffs. Could not get cigs. Told in the evg. that parcel was handed back to her going out. Gateman, whoever he was, is evidently a 'friend' of mine. Will look him up and see what's about."[101] "Got another bad egg this evg. It is a shame to be allowing contractors to rob the OK sayers. I wd. love to get one of them in here for a month or two."[102]

There are parallels to the circumstantial evidence against Hayes. For instance questions could be asked about Charlie McGlade's career, given that he had precisely the sort of "luck" used by McCaughey to determine Stephen Hayes's guilt: why did McGlade step down as CO in Belfast to allow the youthful McCaughey, eight years his junior, to take his place? There was definitely an informer involved in the Crown Entry raid, yet there is still doubt about the executed men, but "It was McGlade's intelligence and sound deductions which brought the informer in the Crown Entry raid to justice."[103] Those arrested in that raid all faced the same charge, that of treason felony; the sentences varied from two to seven years; McGlade got only two years; after his release in 1938 he was on tour through Britain for a few months, and following his return the whole of the Belfast Battalion staff and many others were arrested, but McGlade was not.[104] Moreover, Bowyer Bell notes that in 1940, "McCaughey slipped down to Dublin and met with Assistant Superintendent Carroll of the Special Branch and Seán O'Grady, a Clare TD close to de Valera."[105] The same inferences could be drawn from all these facts as were drawn by Hayes's accusers from events during his tenure as Chief of Staff.

How easy it is to manipulate circumstantial evidence, and how difficult it can sometimes be to refute it. Moss Twomey recounts the same doubts about Larry de Lacy while he was in America, but concludes "While raising a question mark, these allusions add up to nothing conclusive." Twomey, a fair witness for the defense, considered McCaughey to be "devoted but not particularly clever," but "admitted that for Hayes to testify, in a life or death trial against McCaughey, *was a black mark*." Twomey arranged an interview in Dublin between Máire Comerford, who wanted Hayes's release from captivity, and McCaughey in 1941, and sat silently as an impartial observer. MacEoin writes "it is possible ... [that] as an old time seasoned campaigner, Twomey had his own doubts strengthened sufficiently to cause him to pronounce afterwards that the prosecution case ... was 'not proven.'"[106] Maire Comerford, however, had no doubts: "She was firmly of the belief that Stephen Hayes was NOT the informer."[107]

While the IRA was still in confusion following McCaughey's arrest on 2 September and Hayes's escape six days later, they decided to publish the *Special Communiqué*. According to Coogan "Dr Lombard Murphy, chairman of the board of directors of the Irish Independent Newspapers Ltd, was contacted and asked if he would publish the Hayes confessions [*sic*]."[108] Wartime censorship as well as editorial policy meant that he refused, so the IRA had the document printed, then circulated to Dáil deputies, the clergy, and certain of their own members. Printing and publishing an informer's confession was not standard treatment and their reason for doing so in this instance is unclear, though it may have been revenge on their Chief of Staff. The immediate result of their action was the second sequel to the confession and the final strand in this complicated series of events. It coincided with Hayes's sojourn in Rathmines Garda Barracks and tragedy ensued, because, in describing the fate of Michael Devereux, Quartermaster of the Wexford IRA, publication of the confession led directly to the death of IRA Volunteer George Plant.

The Devereux Affair

Michael Devereux, aged twenty four, was a lorry driver, used also as a courier to GHQ in Dublin where Stephen Hayes was Chief of Staff. He was arrested in August 1940, held for three days, then released without charge, and a short time later the Gardaí discovered an arms dump in Co. Wexford. This, together with reports from two other members, led to the belief that Devereux had informed, and Joseph O'Connor, Divisional Officer for the area including Co. Wexford, received the order to execute him. He selected George Plant and Michael Walsh to carry out the execution.[109]

The two men convinced Devereux that they all had to leave Wexford and they drove to Grangemockler, where they met up with some local men, including Patrick Davern.[110] Late on the night of 27 September 1940, Plant, Davern and Devereux left Grangemockler and walked up Slievenamon, there Plant accused Devereux of informing, Devereux denied this, and Plant shot him. He and Davern hid the body and separated.

In early September 1941 Patrick Davern was questioned by the gardaí and released. A short time later a detective convinced Davern that he was from the IRA, and got him to admit that he knew about Devereux. Eventually Davern gave the gardaí a detailed account of the shooting of Michael Devereux, led them to the spot where he was buried, and on 9 December 1941 George Plant and Joseph O'Connor were tried in connection with the murder. Davern, Walsh, and Simon Murphy, the three principal State witnesses, refused to give evidence and were also arrested. The government ordered the men, with the exception of Murphy, to be tried before a military court and, despite strenuous efforts from Seán MacBride, their defending counsel, they were brought to trial on 12 February 1942. MacBride was not alone in his attempts to save these men; a motion to annul the Emergency Powers Order was debated in the Dáil two weeks before the trial opened and offers a full description of the type of evidence to be used against the four men:

> Under the Emergency Powers Order ... it is not necessary to tender to the military court evidence on oath. A statement by a witness or by an accused person, even if not made voluntarily, will be admitted.... It will be possible for a police officer to threaten a person with imprisonment or internment and in these circumstances to extract a statement from that person ... and to tender that statement in evidence.... The prisoner will have no opportunity of cross-examining the person who made the

statement and the court will have no discretion whatever to refuse to admit evidence tendered in that way, no matter under what circumstances that statement may have been obtained either from a witness or from the accused.[111]

During the trial statements allegedly made by Murphy, Davern, and Walsh were accepted in evidence, though the men said they had been intimidated. O'Connor was found not guilty, the other three were sentenced to death. It was wartime and international interest was focused elsewhere, but a flood of petitions, letters and telegrams from the public, trades unions. and Bishop Collier of Ossory urging clemency resulted in commutation of the sentences on Davern and Walsh on 2 March 1942. Under the Emergency Powers Act, George Plant was executed by firing squad three days later. The reason for this is unclear, though there seems to have been some Government involvement, but the unfairness was perceived by the IRA. At the Devereux trial of February 1942 Seán MacBride, appearing for Plant, had said that it "was the first time that any court had been asked to forfeit the lives of men upon unsworn statements, not backed by evidence on oath.... The only evidence was that contained in the Hayes document namely the allegation that a man in custody, in conjunction with certain police officers, framed the victim in order to secure his murder."[112]

On the face of it this episode would seem to have little connection with Stephen Hayes, but the convoluted thinking of the time following Hayes's escape into the hands of the gardaí should not be underestimated. It is questionable whether Michael Devereux, as a messenger, came into contact with Hayes as Chief of Staff, who was, after all, on the run during these years. Nevertheless a case was made by those republicans who already believed that Hayes was a traitor, that he had ordered Devereux's execution to divert suspicion from himself. In this they were aided by one particular section of Hayes's confession:

> Dr. Ryan had told me ... that he would get concocted police reports in order to throw suspicions on to some victim or other as there were bound to be awkward questions on account of the number of raids and arrests for which there was no explanation.... Michael Devereux was detained by the police ... released and allowed to return home ... he [Ryan] looked on it [Devereux's arrest] as a good opportunity to cover up the leakage.... In spite of the fact that Devereux was innocent the result of all this was that the dump of gelignite was collected ... and the guilt for it fell on Devereux's shoulders.[113]

Hayes was held responsible by many people for the shooting of Devereux and, since George Plant was arrested after Hayes had taken refuge with the gardaí, the assumption was that he was also responsible for Plant's death. Yet the detectives and police who questioned and searched around Grangemockler, Co. Wexford, had been drawn there by the publication of the confession—in other words, by the conspirators themselves, not by Hayes.

2. The Emergency and After (1939–1974)

The Hayes Trial (19 June 1942)

The complete charge was that Stephen Hayes, in the years 1939–40–41, in the city of Dublin, usurped or unlawfully exercised the function of Government by maintaining and being a member and officer (Chief of Staff) of an armed force, to wit, an armed force styling itself the Irish Republican Army … not authorized on that behalf by or under the Constitution, contrary to Section 6 (1) of the Offences Against the State Act, 1939.[114]

While in Mountjoy awaiting trial, Hayes had written a letter, dated 21 December 1941, to Máire Comerford, a trusted friend with an impeccable republican reputation, a journalist with the *Irish Press* who thus had both cachet and access to publicity, "to answer all the things being said about him and to refute some of the things which had already been published in the *Special Communiqué*."[115] This letter, signed, stamped but unsealed, was read by the prison governor and passed on to the authorities. A Garda Superintendent went to Mountjoy and cautioned Hayes, who admitted that he had written it and that he had been acting Chief of Staff of the IRA until he was abducted.

There are some odd things about the letter to Máire Comerford, the most obvious being that it was ever written at all. She had been to see him, so could have been given this information verbally and far more safely; alternatively the letter could have been smuggled out, as sometimes happened. Stephen Hayes, as is evident from his own writings, though occasionally naïve, was clever, and must have realized that letters into and out of prison were always censored. He must also have worked out that, following his cautious low-profile stance while on the run, there was little or no evidence to substantiate the only charge against him, that of membership of the IRA. So his real purpose in writing might have been accomplished by the arrival of the Superintendent.

He begins by writing: "I know that time will vindicate me." Some eighty years after he wrote those words they have a poignant resonance, because, though his confession has long been accepted as false by historians, he has not been vindicated.[116] His accusers have simply pointed the finger at his evidence given at trial against McCaughey instead. There is also a sadness about this letter. It is a bitter defense against accusations which Hayes plainly feels should never have arisen. The sadness is occasionally lightened by flashes of an almost savage irony: "Now that the 'arch-traitor' [Hayes] had been run to earth, the Government would collapse.... People would have a decent standard of living, the Civil Service would be cleaned up, jobbery, bribery, and pensions would vanish for ever, and a thousand and one other reforms would be introduced to provide a dream world for the Irish people."[117]

On the surface the letter is what Hayes claimed it to be: a point-by-point refutation of the *Special Communiqué* and information for the journalist, but there could be a deeper, two-fold reason for it. In the first place, Stephen Hayes was a frightened man with nowhere to go if released, other than the Crofton household. Peg and Jim Crofton were staunch friends who were looking after his small son, but Stephen's presence in their house could be dangerous. In prison he was safe and so were they. So did he knowingly provide the police with the necessary evidence for his own conviction? This was, after all, the man who had saved his own life by writing such a long confession. He could have been engineering a prison sentence for his own safety. Moreover, the drama of his kidnapping and escape ensured that the press would be out in force at his trial and that the proceedings would be reported in full. What more sensible then than to provide them with a refutation of the *Special Communiqué* which would be disseminated in the principal newspapers and those in Wexford, thus reaching a far wider audience than Máire Comerford could command? It was read out at his trial by Mr. McCarthy, Counsel for the State, and taken down almost verbatim by journalists, with the version which appeared in *The Enniscorthy Guardian* being the most complete.[118] Accounts of the trial also appeared in the same newspapers, but these are mostly brief. Plainly it was decided that the letter was more interesting, though whether it influenced anybody not already convinced of Hayes's innocence is problematic.

Secondly, this is a very long letter (more than 3,800 words). Hayes's other letters still extant written from Mountjoy are between about 500 and 800 words in length, mainly written on small notebook-sized pages or on four sides of what seems to be the official prisoners' letter-sized paper.[119] His prison diary is written in very small handwriting on various differently sized pieces of paper. This would seem to indicate that writing paper of any kind was scarce among the prisoners in Mountjoy. So where did Stephen obtain enough paper to write at such length? Arguably, and adding to the theory that he was conniving at his own conviction, it could have been provided for this purpose by either the police or the prison governor.

Whether this theory is correct or not, it is ironic that the letter provides concrete evidence that Hayes informed, but against himself. Though many others are named in the letter, all of them were dead, in prison already, out of the country or no longer members of the IRA, thus none would be harmed by his words, while the contents of the letter, as well as his admission to the Garda Superintendent, provided ample evidence that he was indeed an IRA member and Chief of Staff. He accepted responsibility for the letter and was returned to Mountjoy to serve a five-year sentence. When found guilty he stated in court: "For over twenty-five years I have been associated with the national movement, and in all that time I have done what I considered my duty, conscientiously and according to my lights, fighting as a soldier always.

I can swear before God that I have never been guilty of a treacherous or traitorous act against the Irish Republic. Neither have I committed any crime against the Irish people."[120]

Conclusion

It is not easy to reach conclusions about Stephen Hayes, though the verdict, as far as the confession is concerned, is plainly in his favor. Even a cursory reading of the document reveals that it is not so much a confession as a diatribe directed at discrediting de Valera and his Fianna Fáil government, and that the sheer number of accusations, quite apart from their details, leads only to incredulity that anyone could possibly have taken it seriously. Nevertheless the Free State government *did* take it seriously, far more so than did historians and other analysts who agree that Hayes was innocent of the court-martial charge.[121] The government concerns were underlined by the appearance of two government ministers, Dr. Ryan and Mr. Derrig, and Senator C.M. Byrne, all three of whom were named in the confession, as witnesses at a very minor trial. It was admitted by Mr. D. Murnaghan, prosecuting, that these "were not considered very serious charges."[122] He first summarized excerpts from the confession at some length, then questioned the ministers and senator about the allegations relating to each of them, incidentally revealing that he found it "impossible to imagine on what evidence, the purported Court Martial could ever have arrived at a verdict of guilty," and described the confession as "a highly seditious, defamatory, and imaginary document."[123] As late as 1968 Gerry Boland discussed the matter with an *Irish Times* journalist and assured him that Ryan and Derrig were "incapable of such conduct or of the terrible crimes mentioned in the 'confession.'"[124]

The Stephen Hayes affair, however, is complicated by charges subsequent to his kidnapping: that he testified against Sean McCaughey in court, therefore is to blame for McCaughey's incarceration in Maryborough and for his death; and that he was responsible for the death of George Plant in the Devereux Affair. The first is particularly cogent, because "In Ireland the myth of hunger striking is more powerful than the history of hunger striking itself. Hunger striking fuses elements of the legal code of ancient Ireland, of the self-denial that is the central characteristic of Irish Catholicism, and of the propensity for endurance and sacrifice that is the hallmark of militant Irish nationalism."[125] But cogent also are the conditions in Maryborough, unknown to the public until McCaughey's hurried inquest when it was revealed that the prison was a Dickensian dungeon:

> spoken of by the few who knew it in horrified whispers. It was the decision of some ... policy maker in the Department of Justice who persuaded Gerald Boland that

anyone who offered armed resistance, *or who had his sentence commuted from death* [emphasis added], should be sent here. No visits, no clothes, no letters, no reading, no talk to anyone, never leaving the cell, that was the regime almost up to the death of McCaughey, in May 1946.[126]

Even after McCaughey's death, if conditions can be judged from the letters of protest in the *Irish Times* from such luminaries as Roger McHugh (1 June 1946), there was little or no change and, in one of the letters, Tim Healy advanced the theory that this was because "so many of our T.D.s were themselves prisoners in jails during the Sinn Fein war. They now admit that they had often exaggerated their prison grievances. This makes them sceptical of any complaints from present-day prisoners."[127]

The decision to go on hunger strike, as well as the constant will power needed to maintain it, is undoubtedly heroic, nevertheless it is personal, a matter of free will. McCaughey's actions towards Stephen Hayes cannot be seen as anything other than criminal: the charge at his trial was that he had unlawfully assaulted and imprisoned Stephen Hayes, and detained him against his will; and Dr. Sean Lavin, who testified at McCaughey's trial, described the condition of Hayes's body:

> As if he had been tied for a considerable time. Similar marks and scars on the wrists, three scars on the left arm, all the fleshy parts of which had hardened with evidence of considerable violence, while the thumb and first two fingers of the left hand had lost their power, and half of the hand itself was partly paralyzed, due probably to injury of a nerve. There were scars on the outside of the groin and all the muscles of the legs were tender. Both feet were blistered, the skin being missing on portion of one foot, and one of the blisters was two and a half inches in diameter.[128]

The claim for political status could be seen as casuistry, nevertheless, as a republican, McCaughey was in duty bound not to recognize the court and to seek political status. It was *not*, however, his duty to go on hunger and thirst strike. That was his personal choice.

Furthermore, certain questions remain unanswered: *Was* there an informer involved? Hayes certainly thought so, and over the years came to the conclusion that he knew who it was, and, though he told Quirke of his suspicions, the informer remains anonymous.[129] Was McCaughey influenced by the ambition to become Chief of Staff?[130] Hayes is charitable, he told Coogan that he "blamed the whole episode on the atmosphere of suspicion at the time"; and how far was Goertz involved in the conspiracy? Tempting though it is to elect the German spy to a pre-eminent position, he was too incompetent to be much more than a very minor *éminence grise* to McCaughey, though he shared the other man's opinions, as well as his ability to ignore uncomfortable facts *vis à vis* the IRA's future plans. In this context part of a November 1940 telegram sent to Germany by Dr. Eduard Hempel, the German ambassador, is interesting: "It was being persistently asserted in

I.R.A. circles that Germany wished to attack Northern Ireland in March or April. Regardless of the German Foreign Office's view to the contrary, the Army then proposed to attack Eire and thereby help the I.R.A. to overthrow de Valera. The I.R.A. knew all this through their regular link with the German High Command."[131]

The only link the IRA had to the German High Command was Goertz. It is impossible to think that this could stem from Stephen Hayes. This leaves the men from Northern Command to spread the allegation, which was consonant with their ideas: Hayes was to write a year later of several rumors set in motion by Charlie McGlade who had "responsibility for a fantastic article that appeared in ... [Belfast War News] after the Campile bombing ... [and that] Germany had guaranteed the I.R.A. that they would not bomb Belfast. This too, he told his compatriots, came from Dublin [GHQ]."[132] It is also consonant with Hayes's claim that it was to control the IRA that he was arrested by McCaughey and his men, of whom he wrote later: "I have been twenty-six years working in the movement in one capacity or another and I never did meet men who knew less about what they wanted and less about revolution."[133] Thus guilt or innocence remain a matter of interpretation and definition, and we are left to choose between Moss Twomey's "not proven" and the verdict of Máire Comerford who knew Hayes so well, while the legacy of the Stephen Hayes affair, both politically and otherwise, was wide-ranging in its effects.

The consequences for Hermann Goertz were on a par with all his other spying efforts: even after he was imprisoned (for six years) G2 continued to use him, because he communicated in code with his supporters, unaware that his system had been broken. Among those thus arrested was Jim Crofton, while he was assisting Goertz's abortive escape from Ireland.[134]

> G2 ... intercepted almost all of the Goertz messages, learning more by this means than was ever revealed in formal interrogations. Pretending to be the German high command, G2 asked for—and received—an eighty-page report from Goertz which outlined his activities and contacts since arriving in Ireland. The Irish felt so confident in ... their deception system that they unofficially promoted Hermann Goertz to the rank of major.... Goertz's gravestone lists this false rank.[135] Data collected from Goertz and other prisoners was passed on to MI5 under a secret security arrangement that dated from 1938.[136]

The 1946 inquest into the death of Sean McCaughey brought the plight of the other prisoners in Maryborough to the attention of the Irish people, and this contributed to the defeat of de Valera and the Fianna Fáil party in 1948, after sixteen years in power. The IRA was badly damaged in the short term, because many members shared the opinion of Tarlach Ó hUid that, irrespective of Hayes's guilt or innocence, the whole organization was discredited by the episode. Ó hUid wrote of it:

As far as I was concerned the Confession meant the end of the I.R.A. for me. There I was in Derry jail, already fed up to the back teeth with my comrades, and with the circumstances which had led me there, and this thing came. To me it meant that either Hayes was a traitor, in which case the I.R.A. was a lousy organization for having such a man at the top, or else he was innocent, in which case the I.R.A. was a doubly lousy organization to extract such a document from him. Either way I was finished.[137]

The disintegration of the IRA in the aftermath enabled Boland to boast that the IRA was dead, and that he had killed it, though this was proven premature when Anthony Magan suggested a reorganization of the Army in 1946 and the new policy of action directed solely against the Northern administration.[138]

The consequences for Stephen Hayes and for Bridie Hess, on the other hand, were lifelong. Bridie, as "Mrs. Browne" (the maiden name of Hayes' mother), moved to London in search of work, but possibly also as a result of the fear which remained with her until she died. Her son relates an anecdote illustrating her frightened reaction to Northern Ireland and even to the Northern Irish accent. In the late 1970s they both went to visit her dying uncle. The Irish male nurse looking after him, who was much liked by the whole family, suddenly revealed that he had formerly been a medical student in Belfast. Bridie froze in terror, she and Larry left the house and never went back. Even in the last eighteen months of her life, when she was vague about everything else, Bridie constantly talked about Stephen Hayes.[139] This attitude also had a great influence on her son, who has spent most of his life being warned by Bridie and other relations not to get involved.[140]

For Stephen Hayes, the clever man with the good job who had risen to the top of the IRA, the outcome was a lifelong obsession with proving his innocence. He had no further open contact with Bridie Hess or the Croftons.[141] He made no effort to hide after his release from Mountjoy in February 1946, nor to assume another name, but, apart from the continuing attempts to prove his innocence, did nothing to draw attention to himself. He lived with Mary (his sister) and her husband, Larry de Lacy, in Dublin and Blackwater, Co. Wexford, then, in the early 1950s, in Taghmon, Co. Wexford, as a lodger with the mother of Eileen Hayes while working as an electrician.[142] Most of his later working life was spent as a clerk, albeit for friends and relations who were doctors or solicitors; later still he worked for their sons in the same capacity.[143] Larry Browne referred to his father as "a disappointed man," and this echoes Eileen Hayes's summation. "He had a chip on his shoulder because he knew he could have done some good in the world which he didn't do."[144] During this time he wrote constantly: articles, letters, and statements about his ordeal. He did not return to Enniscorthy until 1972 when he went to live in the old people's home at St. John's Hospital, where he remained, still trying to establish his innocence, until his death in December 1974. Just three weeks earlier he had written to Máire Comerford about "a mysterious Clergyman or Christian Brother the confidant of McCaughey, during the period I was in their custody. Would this be the person I so long sought?"[145] As he had written to Bridie many years previously: "Often the tortures of the mind are far worse and leave more enduring wounds than those inflicted on the body."[146]

It is impossible to discover if the Hayes affair was instrumental in discouraging later informers. Given the extraordinary level of expertise in policing and intelligence work in the South during World War II, which undoubtedly used a network of low level informers, but was by no means dependent on them, it seems safe to assume that this situation continued until long after the war. This, together with the IRA lack of manpower until at least the launch of the Border Campaign in 1956, would have meant that informers at any level higher than purveyors of gossip were difficult to find. Moreover, this was not one of the periods when, as happened in Northern Ireland from the 1970s onwards, deliberate efforts were made to recruit them.

The Crime of Castlereagh

They came and came their job the same
In relays Ne'er they stopped.
'Just sign the line!' They shrieked each time
And beat me 'till I dropped.
They tortured me quite viciously
They threw me through the air.
It got so bad it seemed I had
Been beat beyond repair.
The days expired and no one tired,
Except of course the prey,
And knew they well that time would tell
Each dirty trick they laid on thick
For no one heard or saw,
Who dares to say in Castlereagh
The 'police' would break the law!

Source: Bobby Sands, "The Crime of Castlereagh," 1980, www.bobbysandstrust.com. Used with permission.

3

Persuasion in Castlereagh

"just sign the line"[1]

Tensions and weakness in the IRA continued sporadically from the 1940s until 1969 when, following a great deal of unrest on both sides of the border over Cathal Goulding's leadership of the movement, a split occurred at the General Army Convention in December.[2] Marcus Fogarty notes that this led to bitterness between the two sides throughout the country, especially in Dublin and Belfast, then, on 22 December, a twenty-six man group of those who opposed Goulding met in Athlone to elect an Executive and an Army Council.[3] Meanwhile, the unrest had been exacerbated by the Civil Rights march of August 1969 in Derry and the beginning of the Troubles in Northern Ireland.

It is impossible to state with any accuracy the number of paid informers in late twentieth-century Northern Ireland, if only because of the essential secrecy surrounding their activities, though Denis Bradley, author (with Lord Eames) of the Consultative Group on the Past's report of 2009, estimated that at any one time during the Troubles there were about 800 active informers in Northern Ireland at various levels.[4] The recruitment and motivation of the individual informer, however, differs markedly from previous eras, principally because the state forces, and in particular the RUC, began an intensive campaign which resulted in a wide network of informers. This was centered mainly, but by no means exclusively, on republicans: one of the earliest warnings to informers appeared in the *Loyalist News* in 1972, reminding "so called Loyalists ... prepared to betray their people and country ... that the Loyalist people will eventually emerge victorious.... The records and files of the ... police will then be in the hands of Loyal Ulstermen. What then, INFORMER?"[5]

It is, however, possible to be far more accurate about the growth of propaganda and censorship in the province since both followed the allegations of ill treatment of prisoners. Liz Curtis writes that, since partition, there had been a conspiracy of silence in Britain over Northern Ireland's affairs which lasted until 1968 when the civil rights movement shocked the nation into paying attention.[6] Then 1971 saw a media campaign in which "the British army could do no wrong and virtually every act of violence and ... rioting was blamed on the IRA."[7] Thus the introduction of internment without trial in that year, and subsequent claims of torture and brutality were largely ignored by the outside world,[8] despite the Amnesty International report of 1971, until so much was exposed at Strasbourg in 1974 and, in 1978, by another Amnesty International report.

In Northern Ireland in 1972, following the introduction of internment in August 1971, Castlereagh RUC Barracks, East Belfast, became a police holding center with responsibility for interrogating suspects, and reports of systematic abuse began to emerge. It should be emphasized at this point that interrogation was a function of RUC Special Branch, not the uniformed police, and that most of this questioning was done by four regional crime squads made up of 89 of the 464 Special Branch officers in the province. Nevertheless, certain of the uniformed men, particularly the sergeants at the interrogation centers, must have known a great deal. Vernon Laverty, who was taken to Castlereagh in March 1977, complained "to a Sergeant who made the remark that the plainclothes men were doing the beating and the uniformed men were being blamed" and Sean Macken met a uniformed sergeant who said to his interrogators "what are you trying to do, kill that young lad? have you seen his face? He needs a doctor."[9] There was no formal training in the techniques of interviewing, and "an officer new to interviewing duties accompanies a more experienced officer ... [who] may still be only a constable."[10] Former Northern Ireland police officer Michael Asher said "It had a grim reputation. Suspects were held there in windowless cubes for up to one week. They might be denied sleep, stripped, beaten or humiliated. No one wanted to be taken to Castlereagh."[11] Such words make the process sound unpleasant but finite. The case histories of some of those detained, though, such as Pearse Kerr and Brian Maguire, paint a much darker picture, one which had already been condemned by Amnesty International in 1971:

> The use of methods of interrogation which will be characterized as torture by those who have been subjected to them will tend ... to imperil the political objectives for which the Government is striving ... the credibility of the Government's claim that it is endeavoring to maintain civilized values is irretrievably weakened when the Government itself stoops to methods which many—including its own supporters at home and abroad—find abhorrent.[12]

This abhorrence had already been aired in the House of Commons during the 1971 debate on the Compton Report[13]:"The whole House will regret that there have been occasions when some members of the security forces have descended to methods of barbarism ... in obtaining information from people against whom no charge has been levied ... and against whom no evidence has been produced.... Is this not a disgrace to the whole purpose and procedures of the rule of law?"[14]

Arguably the RUC could never have succeeded in being anything other than a divisive force in Ulster. At its inception the RIC provided the basis for the new force, but at the time of partition many unionists did not trust them because about half of its members were Catholic. However, when northern landowners began to organize their own vigilante groups, it became clear that something must be done and the new Ulster Special Constabulary (A, B, C, and C1 Specials, all armed, with only the A Specials being a paid, full-time force) came into being in 1920 to act under the overall command of Colonel Wickham, the new RIC Divisional Commissioner. Reports about this innovation in the *Belfast Newsletter* stressed that once the new northern government was in place the RIC would probably be abolished, a new police force set up (the Royal Ulster Constabulary), and those who had served in the Special Constabulary should get preference for posts.[15] This was prescient as many who joined the RUC were from the illegal vigilante groups, now legally armed. Later the A and C Specials were disbanded, leaving the B Specials in existence for about forty years.

Once the RUC was in being Catholics initially accepted the new force, probably because many of the officers had been in the RIC and Catholics were fairly well represented among them.[16] The older men, however, had retired by the 1940s, and thereafter there was little attempt to encourage Catholic recruitment. By 1969 the Catholic proportion was down to 11 percent, and the RUC association with the surviving Special Constabulary, the loathed B Specials, was inevitably seen as keeping it in touch with militant loyalism. In 1980 the proportion of Catholics had further declined to about 6 percent and the B Specials had been replaced by the Ulster Defence Regiment, a number of whose members had been convicted of armed violence connected with loyalist paramilitary groups—notably the Miami Showband murders in 1975. The result was that, by 1983, the local security forces in Northern Ireland were seen as solidly Protestant, associated with loyalist paramilitary groups, and so distrusted by many Catholics.

The reverse was also true. The attitudes of both sides were a product of the situation, and frequently either misconstrued or overcompensated for on the mainland, while another of the factors which bedeviled Northern Ireland in its relationship with the rest of the UK related to misconceptions about the RUC—it never had the cozy "British bobby" image, but was always an armed quasi-military force. Their offices were barracks, thus reflecting the uneasiness of the state. Interpol figures for 1983 showed that "Northern Ireland was the most dangerous place in the world to be a policeman," twice as dangerous as in El Salvador, which had second ranking on the list.[17]

For the most part, the nationalist community did not differentiate between the uniformed branch of the RUC and the Special Branch. The latter was independent of the main force, under the control of a Special Branch Inspector, who interviewed those detained under the draconian 1922 Special Powers Act in the Interrogation Centers.[18] Palace Barracks, in Holywood, Co. Down, run jointly by the army and the RUC, was the first of these, and eventually became the blueprint for Castlereagh Interrogation Center. Army Intelligence supervised and Special Branch interrogated using the techniques developed by the British Army in the post-war years in Kenya, Malaya, Cyprus, and Aden. Thus detainees were hooded, subjected to a high-pitched noise, made to stand against the wall supported only by a single finger from each hand, and deprived of sleep and a proper diet.[19] Allegations of physical brutality gave rise to the Compton Report in November 1971 and to the closing of Palace Barracks Interrogation Center in 1972.

Castlereagh Interrogation Center

Following the closure suspects were questioned by police and army in police barracks, or in holding centers behind the police stations. The former army huts in the courtyard behind Castlereagh police station in East Belfast became Castlereagh Holding Center, and consisted of thirty-eight cells and twenty-one interview rooms. Suspects were the result of sweeps following either a particular incident or an investigation, and the interrogators tended to be young Detective Constables from one of the Crime Squads. The whole process was strictly planned, with an intelligence collator monitoring the progress of the interviews. The strategy was to break down one suspect, obtain a signed confession from him, and use his admissions on the others. However in, for instance, the first two months of 1977 306 complaints were lodged, of which 70 alleged ill-treatment. Deputy Chief Constable Harry Baillie referred to these as "a propaganda war in which every conceivable dishonesty, hypocrisy and threat is employed to support and sustain the physical campaign."[20] However "Some members of the RUC ... acknowledged the fact that many suspects had had statements beaten out of them, [they] admitted that one day there would have to be some kind of amnesty. One detective ... [said] he kept all his interview notes in case there were ever to be, at some distant date, a war crimes tribunal."[21]

Meanwhile Lord Diplock was appointed to review the existing judicial system because both witnesses and juries were liable to intimidation. These two factors, together with the ensuing reforms which, in 1973, led to the Diplock courts where the judge was the sole arbiter, paved the way for the later show trials and the emergence of the supergrass. Then Kenneth Newman became Northern Ireland's Chief Constable on 1 May 1976, and instituted various changes to develop a sophisticated intelligence network, to reorganize the CID, and to make Castlereagh a specialized interrogation center. In his Annual Report at the end of 1976 the Chief Constable announced rapid success: various terrorist units eliminated; a 121 percent increase in charges against the Provisional IRA; 708 suspects charged (over 100 percent more than in the previous year); an increase in charges for murder, use of explosives, hijacking, arson, and membership of an illegal organization. However, there had been 180 complaints of assault during interrogation in 1975, 384 in 1976, and that September had seen the publication of the European Commission Report which found the British government guilty of torture in Northern Ireland. The focus of the Commission's enquiry was mainly on events which took place in the autumn of 1971, nevertheless the findings were damning: "the systematic application of the [five] techniques for the purpose of inducing a person to give information shows a clear resemblance to those methods of systematic torture which have been known over the ages ... the Commission sees in them a modern system of torture."[22]

The Medical Evidence

The new regulations resulting from this critical report involved police doctors. Medical examinations were available before, during, and after interrogation to ensure that a suspect was healthy enough for interrogation and to discover whether or not he was already injured when he arrived in custody. Those who declined this initial examination were unable to prove afterwards that any injuries they received had occurred while under interrogation. Many did decline because they could see no point in it and little more than half consented to the final examination, either because they were afraid to do so (sometimes the "doctor" was a Special Branch man), or because they wanted to get away from the place as quickly as possible.[23] Even after release some would still not complain. Gerard Carson, arrested five times between November 1976 and June 1977, taken to Castlereagh on three of those occasions, and subsequently hospitalized twice, refused even to tell his mother what had happened there or to see a doctor.[24]

Before Castlereagh became an Interrogation Center, doctors from the Royal Army Medical Corps had responsibility for medical examinations. Later this was taken over by the Police Surgeons, under Dr. Robert Irwin, Protestant GP and Secretary of the Forensic Medical Officers Association. Finally it was undertaken by the Medical Referees Service, who decided if sick leave was genuine, during normal office hours, and by an on call rota covered by GPs and hospital doctors the rest of the time.

As a Police Surgeon Dr. Irwin routinely examined prisoners brought into police stations, one of which was Belfast's Townhall Street. All suspects were taken there after interrogation in Castlereagh, handed over, signed for, and asked if they had any complaints or if they wanted to see a doctor. In 1977 he began to see more and more prisoners coming from Castlereagh with injuries which were unexplained and, in the doctors' view, not self-inflicted. It was not in the doctors' brief to seek reasons for this state of affairs, nor to look at the priorities of the security forces, but many more suspects arrived at Castlereagh than were ever charged by the RUC. To take a representative period: between July 1976 and 7 November 1979, 5,067 suspects were questioned at Castlereagh; of these 1,964 were charged and 3,103 released.[25] At least 3,103 innocent people were held in Castlereagh between those two dates. This was the pool from which many informers were recruited during that period alone, though the resultant network was only a by-product of the real purpose: to remove as many prominent nationalists as possible from the community via the Diplock Courts. Neither innocence nor guilt really mattered.

Dr. Denis Elliott was the senior medical officer at Gough Barracks, Armagh. His medical room was not situated in the cell block, but at the end of the corridor containing the interrogation rooms, none of which were soundproofed. Dr. Elliot requested a transfer in March 1979 because of his concerns about the conduct of interrogation, and said "I do not wish to work at another holding centre."[26] The Police Surgeons, in a memorandum from their Association, also stated:

> Early in 1977 there was a large increase in persons having significant bruising, contusions, and abrasions of recent origin especially of the epigastrium and rib-cage areas. There was evidence of hyper-extension and hyper-flexion of joints, especially of the wrist; of tenderness associated with hair-pulling and persistent jabbing. There was evidence of rupture of eardrums and other injuries. At the same time, there was evidence of increased mental agitation and excessive anxiety states.[27]

Then, for the first time, Protestants also began to allege ill treatment at Castlereagh.

Dr. James O'Rawe had a group practice on the Crumlin Road which included patients from both communities. Previously injuries had been visible almost entirely on Catholic suspects, but now O'Rawe began to notice injuries on Protestants who had been interrogated at Castlereagh. It emerged very much later that this was the period when specialized interrogation teams of young detectives, formed in 1975 and expanded the following year, were beginning to see results. 1976 was the year that 307 deaths resulted from the Troubles, the second worst year of the Northern Ireland conflict, but 1977 brought the RUC a genuine belief "that they were turning the tide, that their strong-arm tactics were starting to win the war against the IRA, and … the loyalist gunmen."[28] The SDLP had publicly stated that it believed abuse was approved at a high level and not just caused by individual policemen. The

Police Authority attempted to communicate their growing concern to Kenneth Newman, who issued a statement in which he said that the allegations were a terrorist propaganda campaign and that the injuries were self-inflicted. Dr. Irwin gave no credence to this, like the other doctors he felt that most self-inflicted injuries were obvious, but by autumn 1978 he was still seeing evidence of injuries on patients arriving at Townhall Street from Castlereagh, though not on the same scale as before. Moreover, on three occasions that year he noticed that the spyholes in the doors of the interrogation rooms had been blocked or impaired.[29] Finally, in March 1979, Dr. Irwin spoke out in a television interview: "[He] claimed that up to 150 people he had seen at Castlereagh interrogation center had shown evidence of ill-treatment by RUC detectives."[30] This was followed by a House of Commons debate on the Bennett Report (which had not yet, as Gerry Fitt pointed out, been available for MPs to read), in which Dr. Irwin figured largely.[31] Mr. Fitt also made the point that:

> Since Dr. Irwin made his original comments on television, he has been subjected to a particularly vicious smear campaign on the grounds of his qualifications, the state of his mental health and other matters. On the front page of *The Daily Telegraph* today a story carries the headline: "Rape case bitterness denied by RUC critic." The opening sentence begins: "Suggestions, apparently by Government officials in Whitehall, that the police surgeon making brutality allegations ... is 'bitter and angry' because his wife was raped by two former members of the RUC."[32]

Amnesty International Report, 1978

"During 1976, Amnesty International received a number of allegations of maltreatment by security forces in Northern Ireland, and requested an official investigation into two such allegations.... The authorities informed Amnesty International that they were satisfied with the results of internal investigations into the allegations in both cases."[33] The allegations continued from both communities, and Amnesty International decided to send a research team to Northern Ireland. The 1978 report resulted from their mission there for the week between 28 November and 6 December 1977 when they examined the evidence in 78 cases where maltreatment by the RUC had been alleged, and its conclusion provides testimony from those who had been involved in interrogation of German prisoners during World War II, culminating in two quotations whose tenor damaged the British case irrevocably. The first says devastatingly "It is the simple truth to say that if one of our interrogators had suggested submitting any prisoner to any form of physical duress ... he would have been a laughing-stock among his colleagues."[34] The second, from a senior psychologist engaged in prisoner of war intelligence on behalf of the British Government, states equally baldly "If the Royal Ulster

Constabulary ... is using the methods reported, they are being singularly stupid.... Interrogation by overt verbal examination backed by fear is a blunt, mediaeval and extremely inefficient technique."[35]

Yet RUC Special Branch had been trained according to methods used by the army *after* World War II. Then "Inhuman and Degrading Treatment?" a Thames Television documentary was broadcast on 27 October 1977 despite RUC protests. The program included an interview with Newman, who said he did not rule out the possibility that a police officer might be tempted to overstep the mark, but insisted that the majority of injuries were self-inflicted, and continued "there is no policy for toleration of ill-treatment in this force, quite the contrary"[36]; and the Compton Report concluded: "Our investigations have not led us to conclude that any of the grouped or individual complainants suffered physical brutality as we understand the term."[37] In 1972, however, the Parker Report concluded more pointedly "The blame ... must lie with those who ... decided that ... we should abandon our legal ... wartime interrogation methods and replace them by procedures which were secret, illegal, [and] not morally justifiable."[38] Two years later the Irish government brought Britain to the European Court of Human Rights, and the commission's report of January 1976 included not only condemnation of the five techniques, but also disapproval. Legal opinion in the report notes that "the United Kingdom Government ... hampered, to a significant extent, the effective conduct of the investigation by the Commission and its delegates."[39]

The Bennett Report (March 1979)[40]

The Bennett Inquiry resulted from the Amnesty International Report, and certain of the seemingly mild observations in the report are barbed. Many of the RUC's interrogators, for example, were of junior rank and had no formal training. They appeared uncertain about treatment which would render suspects' statements inadmissible, and about the Judges' Rules.[41] In addition, though there had been successful claims against the RUC for brutality, and even out-of-court settlements, no police officer had ever been convicted of ill-treatment.[42]

Roy Mason (Secretary of State for Northern Ireland), insisted that the Bennett Report did *not* say that ill-treatment had taken place, though it summarized what doctors had been saying for nearly three years: the need for an urgent and drastic review of the RUC's interrogation procedures.[43] The report had a much greater impact in America, and a protest statement was issued by Senators Edward Kennedy and Daniel Moynihan, Tip O'Neill, Leader of the House of Representatives, and Hugh Carey, Governor of New York. In consequence Congress shocked the British by placing an embargo on delivery to the RUC of six thousand Ruger magnum pistols. It was uncomfortable for

Britain to be equated with the repressive régimes of the world. Mason attempted to ignore questions about Dr. Irwin while defending the RUC, culminating in the claim that: "Amnesty International and the Bennett report leave the reputation of the RUC uniformed branch completely untarnished." His opponents, including MPs Kevin McNamara, Clement Freud and Tom Litterick, were undeterred:

> Allegations of mistreatment and torture, particularly at Castlereagh, were already accepted by the nationalist community ... as established fact. Mason would brook no criticism of the security forces. Allegations of torture and mistreatment were all rejected by him and the Chief Constable as Republican propaganda. The importance of Irwin's and Elliott's work was that it came from the Forensic Medical Officers Association, "one of us," part of the establishment. The hysterical overreaction of the Northern Ireland office and the personal denigration of the Protestant Irwin and his colleagues showed how deeply the Northern Ireland establishment felt affronted and betrayed. Years of denial were shown to be just lies. Mason was again on the back foot, more munition for Strasbourg.[44]

Other repercussions followed: James Callaghan's Labor government fell, following their loss of a vote of confidence by just one vote[45]; Dr. Elliott resigned the week after publication of the report; and Kenneth Newman returned to England with a knighthood. Taylor points out that in the months following the report complaints of assault in police custody dropped sharply: 267 in 1978, 159 in 1979, and fifteen in the first two months of 1980; then, on 1 January 1980, Jack Hermon was appointed Chief Constable and announced his intention of relying on evidence rather than confessions. The judiciary had also become concerned, and in August 1977 the Police Authority decided to investigate the case of Pearse Kerr, possibly chosen because of the international ramifications.

Pearse Patrick Kerr

Pearse Kerr was born in Philadelphia of Irish parents. The family returned to Northern Ireland in 1972, when Pearse was twelve, because a relative was ill. He was a seventeen-year-old electrical engineering student at the local technical college until 18 August 1977, when he was arrested at 5 a.m. under Section 10 of the Emergency Powers Act and taken to Castlereagh. After two hours in a cell he was taken to an interview room and his first interview lasted from 10 a.m. until 12:30 p.m. He refused to sign a statement and asked to see a solicitor. Pearse appears to have been as rebellious as the typical teenager, though this provoked violence in custody:

> One Special Branch man propped himself up against the wall behind me, with his arms clamped around my chest.... Another one stood directly in front of me and

placed his fingers and thumbs up under each side of my jaws. He would push his fingers up until my breath would stop completely[46] ... I could feel myself losing consciousness and my vision got so blurred I thought it was because the pressure was making my eyes pop out. Then I'd come around a bit after they'd stopped. So they would go at it again.

During one of these strangling attacks, a Special Branch man, a different one, came in and said, "You may as well give up on this one. We're going to have to hang him." ... I was losing contact with what was going on.... I thought I was going to die...

While I was in that state they shoved the statement in front of me again. So I just signed it, because I thought if I didn't, I would have been a dead man.[47]

Three detectives were present and Pearse describes them in some detail, though he did not know their names and refers to them as nos. 1, 2 and 3. He also differentiates between the actions of each of them and between those present at subsequent interviews: it was, for instance, nos. 1 and 2 who were responsible for the hyperflexion[48] of both wrists (Pearse says, "I heard something crack in my left wrist and I knew it was broken"), and the strangling episodes which occurred both before and after the hyper-flexion.[49] At this point the U.S. vice consul, Wayne Roy, arrived and Pearse was taken into a separate room to see him. His broken wrist was handcuffed behind his back and a Special Branch man was with him, so Pearse was afraid to complain. Roy "reported that the youth was in good health and was not being abused or ill-treated in any way."[50]

At the second interview (from 2:00 until 3:00 p.m.) he was shown statements which said he was a member of the IRA and named some of his friends. An inspector came in and asked if he wanted a doctor to examine his wrist, Pearse refused, then wrote out a statement confessing that he had joined the Junior IRA[51] a month previously and gave details of his plans to bomb five business premises. This time there was no abusive treatment.

The third interview (4:00–6:00 p.m.) brought accusations of being a link man between the Provisional IRA and the Junior IRA. Again there was no ill treatment. Nor was there at the fourth interview (9:00–10:30 p.m.), conducted by an inspector. No. 3 came in and asked about a gun. Pearse initially denied this. Then, when the detective suggested that it might have been a plastic gun, he made a statement that this was so. That same evening the medical officer, who examined him at his request, sent him to the Ulster Hospital, Dundonald, to have his wrist X-rayed. There was a suspected fracture, so a cast was applied and Kerr was referred to the fracture clinic.

When Pearse appeared in court he was obviously in pain, his complaint of torture was supported by a doctor's statement, but he was remanded in custody to Crumlin Road Jail, Belfast. There the Medical Officer tried to find out how the injury had happened, but a Police Authority report said he "failed to establish how the injuries had been received and there was no medical report as to the man's physical condition on leaving Castlereagh Police Office."[52] Dissatisfied, they asked the RUC on 2 September to investigate the allegations in detail as soon as possible. The Police Authority met on 14 February 1978. Newman refused access to Kerr's file and to the doctors' reports, and claimed that the RUC's investigation into the case was complete, and that the papers had gone to the Director of Public Prosecutions.

Meanwhile Pearse Kerr remained in Crumlin Road Jail for three months until his unconditional release in November 1977. The UK government was undoubtedly sensitive to international (and especially American) criticism at this juncture, though Kenneth Newman continued to stonewall all requests for information. The Crown withdrew the charges when the U.S. State Department intervened, following the efforts of Joshua Eilberg, Congressman for Jenkintown, Pennsylvania, Jack McKinney, and other reporters, to secure his release. Though the case was covered in detail by *An Phoblacht* on 30 November 1977, no other newspapers took it up, with the exception of the *Philadelphia Daily News* once the U.S. State Department became involved. Pearse Kerr initiated a civil action for damages against the Northern Ireland Chief Constable, but it has not been possible to find out if it succeeded because, even thirty years later, Pearse Kerr is still unwilling to talk about this episode.

Brian Maguire

> The devil's sons and evil ones
> Gathered round like fire,
> And, Jesus Christ, their sacrifice!
> Was murdered Brian Maguire.
>
> The devils fled for life was dead.
> The law hid in its shame.
> The butchered air gasped in prayer
> And tears fell down like rain.
> The very walls were appalled,
> My eyes were red as fire,
> For I had cried a tearful tide
> In mourning of Maguire.[53]

On 22 April 1978 Constable Laird Millar McAllister was at home in Lisburn when a man called, drew a revolver and shot the policeman dead. In early May three people, including a woman, had already been charged in connection with his murder, and another was being interrogated. The latter was Brian Maguire.

Maguire lived with his mother in Lisburn. He was twenty-seven, an electronics engineer working at the Strathearn Audio plant in Andersonstown, and had just been told he was to be promoted. He was also a trades union official for the AUEW and due to be married the following January. He had one black mark against his character because he had robbed a pub, been remanded in custody for ten months but given a suspended sentence. Also, in November 1977 he had helped organize a march in West Belfast against repression. It has to be assumed, therefore, that he was known to the RUC.

Brian was arrested under the Prevention of Terrorism Act at 6 a.m. on 9 May and taken to Castlereagh. According to Chief Superintendent Peter Rawlinson, a divisional commander in the Merseyside force who later investigated the case, he was not held on a charge of murder. At most he was an accessory and his defense was duress.[54] He was interrogated on the morning of his arrest, then began to write his statement between 2:45 p.m. and 5:40 p.m. We do not know what happened to Brian Maguire in Castlereagh, but we can look at the experiences of others in the same situation: such as Felim Hamill, arrested a few days earlier in connection with the same murder, and Bobby Sands, who was arrested for vandalism in October 1976, spent six days being interrogated in Castlereagh and wrote an account of his ill-treatment there which has frequently been reproduced.[55] So Maguire confessed that he had been kidnapped by the IRA and threatened, that a girl came to his door on Saturday at lunchtime, took a gun from her bag, threw it on the floor, and he buried it in the garden. The next day the girl came back to remove the gun. He neither named nor described his kidnappers or the girl.

The next morning the light in his cell was turned on at 7:15 a.m. from outside, thus Maguire's every movement could be observed through the spyhole in the cell door. At 7:30 the constable brought his breakfast and found him hanged by a strip of sheeting from the ventilator grille over the bed and opposite the door.[56] He was the first to die in custody in Castlereagh. There followed allegations in the press that the grille would not have borne the weight of a man, and "previous victims of the seven-day detention orders in Castlereagh observed that the grilles in question were inaccessible—being some 12 ft. from the floor—and anyhow the grilles were of a size which did not permit anything being tied to them."[57] Nevertheless, Maguire *was* found hanging.

On 11 May, the day following Brian's death, there was a protest on the Falls Road, organized by Sinn Féin; his co-workers at Strathearn Audio walked out when they heard of his death; and a crowd gathered outside the British Embassy in Dublin. The publicity was widespread. *The Straits Times*, of Singapore, had a brief account of his death[58]; Joan Maynard, Labor MP, asked the Secretary of State for Northern Ireland, Roy Mason, to order a public inquiry "into the situation in Castlereagh ... [because] the Amnesty report ... calls for a public inquiry.... Britain has previously been condemned for brutal and harsh treatment of prisoners ... [and] doctors and lawyers are all critical of what is going on in Castlereagh"[59]; and the Chief Constable made

3. Persuasion in Castlereagh 99

a statement: "At our invitation a senior officer of the Merseyside Constabulary will arrive in Belfast today to take charge of the investigations into the circumstances of the death of Brian Maguire."[60]

Peter Rawlinson, the senior officer from Merseyside, wrote of the unexpected publicity surrounding his arrival in Belfast to investigate the death:

> I was horrified to find that my photograph was on the front page of the *Belfast Echo* as I stepped off the plane at Aldergrove. I was equally horrified later by a telephone call taken by my elder boy—"Your father has twenty four hours to live" and by the knowledge that Ken Oxford [Chief Constable of Merseyside] and I had a price on our heads (probably untrue!!). We carried guns throughout our visit and our drivers displayed genuine fears when taking us to "no-go" areas. Nevertheless we stayed quite openly at the Stormont Hotel. We were instructed to expedite our enquiry but to leave no stone unturned to discover the truth.[61]

The strict time limit meant that the Merseyside team confined themselves to the actual death of Maguire, including scientific evidence, and Maguire's home and business circumstances. Rawlinson and his team examined the scene (there was no sign of a struggle), the RUC investigations, the post-mortem report, and interviewed almost a hundred witnesses. They felt convinced of the integrity of Inspector (later Chief Constable) Flanagan, and the Reserve PC, an older family man, clearly distressed by the death, whose account fitted exactly with the evidence. The only dissenting voice recalled by Rawlinson was that of a fellow-prisoner, Earle, who claimed that the RUC gloated to him that they had hanged Maguire and showed him a photograph. An editorial in *An Phoblacht* possibly confirms this: "Later, a UDA[62] man who was held in the cell opposite Brian Maguire reported that RUC detectives asked him what he thought of their handiwork, referring to Maguire's death."[63] Was this Earle? If so, perhaps Peter Rawlinson and his colleagues did not give due weight to the significance of a UDA man giving evidence on behalf of a Catholic, nor to the possibility that RUC men might have thought a UDA man would approve of Maguire's death. But Rawlinson said, "There were no cells opposite Brian Maguire's."[64]

The team looked at how Brian Maguire died, not why, and presented their report after six weeks. Rawlinson summarized their findings: "There was not a scrap of evidence of RUC involvement—in fact the evidence all pointed to our conclusion that no other person was involved."[65] He went on to clarify this conclusion:

> You can never be sure that there is or is not more to uncover but we had more than enough evidence to convince us that Maguire's death was self-inflicted ... clearly both the bed sheet and the vent could bear the weight of a man rather heavier than Maguire. There were no marks on the body to indicate that Maguire had been assaulted. All the marks were attributable to the manner of Maguire's death.[66]

Peter Rawlinson noted that, following Maguire's death, supervision had been tightened; this bears out Bobby Sands's frequent references to "the Watcher" in *The Crime of Castlereagh*, while Maguire's post-mortem also showed no signs of injury or assault.

Brian's mother refused to believe his confession because she had been at home with him, and nobody came to the door. She also refused to believe in his suicide and Jim Sullivan, one of the Workers' Party councillors in Belfast, came to much the same conclusion: "The RUC stage mock stranglings of people under interrogation. This time the inevitable happened, and someone was murdered."[67] Others who supported Sullivan's assertion included Thomas McKearney from Moy in Co. Tyrone who said that "his head and trunk were covered with a black plastic sack, the type used for laundry and refuse collection. He said that he was beaten around the head while the bag was pulled tight around his throat. He managed to tear a hole in the bag so he could breathe."[68] While Edward Brophy, giving evidence in court, reported that "his head and neck were squeezed in such a manner that he fell to the floor, losing consciousness,"[69] and in October 1976, Bobby Sands wrote "The detective ... put his arms round my neck and pressed his two fingers in under my jaw.... I don't even remember falling, but I must have because I was being hauled off the floor and put on a chair when I regained my senses. I was given another cigarette ... and told. .. I could make it shorter and easier for myself if I just put my name to a piece of paper."[70] A few days before Brian Maguire's death, Felim Hamill, a zoology student from Queen's University, Belfast, had been charged and interrogated in connection with the murder of Constable McAllister. He was subsequently released. On 29 April he was examined by his GP who found extensive injuries consistent with Hamill's allegations and that "he had been choked to the point of unconsciousness and that he had a towel tightly wrapped around his face and neck."[71]

Suicide in police custody is not unknown, but there must be a reason. Peter Rawlinson offers fear "of the RUC or the IRA or his appearance in Court."[72] But even given that a seemingly stable young man might have killed himself, it still begs the question of the timing: How did he manage to do it in a busy police station while breakfast was given out, and in such a short space of time? Alternatively, *did* the RUC go too far with him? The interrogation tactics used at that time by Special Branch men were very questionable—it is impossible to disbelieve so many different accounts of torture—and it is significant that Special Branch formed no part of the inquiry.[73] Jim Sullivan said of the inquiry "At the end of the day ... the public will know just as much as the RUC wish them to know."[74] Significantly also, there is the case of Peter Hands who, in 1978, was held for a week, severely beaten, hooded, and half-hanged.[75]

Why was the Brian Maguire case so high profile, especially when Pearse

3. Persuasion in Castlereagh

Kerr, a seventeen-year-old American citizen, received almost no publicity? Some of the answers were revealed by the *Andersonstown News*, in January 2009. British documents from 1978, released under the 30-year rule

> revealed that up to 10 RUC men known as the "Goon Squad" were beating prisoners at interrogation centres throughout the North.... Official confirmation of the activities of the "Goon Squad" has led former Castlereagh torture victims to raise fresh questions about Brian Maguire's death. Mickey Culvert, whose torture by the RUC was investigated by Amnesty International, was one of the last people to see Brian Maguire alive. They passed each other in a Castlereagh corridor shortly before his death.... The British government documents contain lengthy statements from Dr Maurice Hayes, who insisted the maltreatment of prisoners had been approved by then RUC Chief Constable Kenneth Newman.

According to the same article, "Brian Maguire was the only paramilitary suspect to die in police custody during four decades of the Troubles."[76] This is the most obvious reason for the publicity at the time, because it was and still is the perception of most nationalists that he was killed by the RUC, nor have they forgotten him: more recent references to this case were made in Antony McIntyre's article "Death in Custody" for *The Pensive Quill*,[77] and in Allen Feldman's book, *Formations of Violence*, where he notes, "After that [Maguire's death] they installed cameras in Castlereagh. But the cameras are manned by Special Branch men, and there are Special Branch men interrogating you. So it's a joke. When they come into the interrogation room and just lift their coats off and hang them over the lens of the camera, that's the sign of the beating session."[78]

Whatever happened to Brian Maguire, he lives on in republican memory as well as in the poetry of Bobby Sands, who also died aged twenty-seven, and wrote a fitting epitaph for both of them:

> Oh! lonely winds that walk the night
> To haunt the sinner's soul.
> Pray pity me a wretched lad
> Who never will grow old.
> Pray pity those who lie in pain
> The bondsman and the slave,
> And whisper sweet the breath of God
> Upon my humble grave.[79]

Few adults could have been unaware of the advice to remain silent if interrogated, because it had been circulated throughout the nationalist community over many years since internment began. In 1976, for example, Ruairí Ó Brádaigh, formerly IRA Chief of Staff, was detained for nine days in Castlereagh. His treatment was benign in comparison with that of others detailed in these pages. He described it as the usual hot and cold business. I was asked general questions … about my family. I said nothing. I was put back in the cell then brought down to a different group…. There were about twelve of them, all in plain clothes. One stood in front of me and asked questions. The other eleven stood behind me where I couldn't see them.[80]. .. From me they particularly wanted to know about "Your people's talks with the British government." I said "You should ask your superiors in the British government." After I got out there was a message from the British government. They'd read the script of interrogation and were pleased to see that I hadn't revealed anything about the talks. That I was a person of my word. All I could do was laugh.[81]

Ó Brádaigh remained silent and refused to react to his interrogators. Eventually his solicitor arrived: "They came back after Kevin Agnew [the solicitor] had been there an hour and said we'd had enough time. Kevin laid into them."[82] There were no further interrogations, Ó Brádaigh was allowed exercise and released 96 hours later.

The case of Eamon Morris, aged eighteen, of Ballymurphy, West Belfast, had a completely different outcome. He was held in Castlereagh for three days in June 1984. Two men from Special Branch threatened that he would be detained unless he agreed to do a deal with them. He was told to meet them several days later, but did not turn up. This led to a year of threatening phone calls, and the RUC would often stop him on the street and hold him for an hour. A year later he was again taken to Castlereagh and endured further interrogation by the same two Special Branch men: "During his 3 day detention Morris was subjected to repeated threats and verbal intimidation. At one point an RUC man said that if Morris refused to co-operate his name and address would be passed on to the UDA."[83]

Such stories became increasingly commonplace, especially during the 1980s, in both *An Phoblacht* and the *Andersonstown News*, each article ending with the same advice: "[This] situation illustrates the depths to which the RUC Special Branch will sink in order to get nationalist youth into their clutches. I would plead again to anyone who finds themselves being pressurized by the RUC or Brits to get in touch with Sinn Féin."[84]

At this time the advice from Sinn Féin about how to behave under interrogation, which had been a constant feature in the nationalist newspapers, began to appear in loyalist newspapers, coinciding mainly with the first of the show trials to involve the Protestant community,[85] and Ruairi Ó Brádaigh happened to witness a loyalist prisoner under interrogation in Castlereagh:

> There were prefabs in the exercise yard … the windows came out in a piece and you could look in through a V shape and see what was going on. The man doing the interrogation was stripped to his vest. The prisoner sat opposite him. The man made a lunge across the table and made a motion to strangle him with his two hands. The prisoner was choking…. Two RUC men and a British soldier ran down the yard towards me and said "Enough of this. You mind your own business." They brought me back [to my cell] immediately.[86]

Ó Brádaigh adds, "I was barred from the yard after that, except in the early morning and late evening—when no interrogations were taking place."[87] The net was widening, yet most recruitment was still done within nationalist areas, or among the prison population, and most informers were men, as they always have been. However, there were a few women among their number, such as Angela Whoriskey and Catherine Mahon,[88] and attempts were made on a regular basis to recruit children.[89]

The majority of the women held in Castlereagh were very young and many of them came from the small Catholic Short Strand area of East Belfast. Eight young women from here (one was a girl of thirteen) were arrested between 6:30 and 7 a.m. on Monday 7 November 1977, and *The Castlereagh File* reproduces a number of their statements in full. Mrs. Geraldine Crane, aged twenty-one, for instance, was taken to the interrogation center for three days together with her two-year-old son. She weighed about eight stone when arrested and was seven stone 4lbs at a medical examination while she was there. She was threatened at successive interviews with a long period of imprisonment, with losing custody of her son, and finally told she would be released in return for the name of any man in the IRA or if she watched their movements: "They said to let them know and they would pay me well ... they would put the money in my son's name and nobody would know."[90] Mary McCann, aged 19, fared worse throughout thirteen interviews, including hyperflexion of her wrists, blows from the interrogators, some of whom were women, and threats of rape. She finally signed a confession and was sent to Armagh prison.[91]

There is also evidence that children were targeted during the 1970s, and that efforts were stepped up in the following decade. This was possibly for the reasons given by Sinn Féin: Margaret Thatcher's determination to overcome the IRA, and the aftermath of the hunger strike. A further reason could be seen in the activities of the Forces Research Unit (FRU) set up to handle informers in Northern Ireland in about 1980.[92] Their clients included the commanding officers of the British Army, MI5, and the RUC. The rivalry between the RUC and the British Army is well-documented by, for example, Martin Ingram, who worked within the FRU for seven years. He notes that the systems used by the FRU became more aggressive in the mid to late 1980s, so the RUC may have stepped up their own efforts in a reluctance to be outdone.[93]

It became a regular refrain in local Northern Irish newspapers, particularly the *Andersonstown News*, that in this recruitment campaign youth was no protection, just as it was no protection against imprisonment, victimization, torture, and death at the hands of the RUC, the British Army, and the various paramilitary organizations. The Sutton Death List, an index of deaths from the conflict in Northern Ireland, shows that Bernard Teggart, aged fifteen, an alleged informer, was shot by the IRA in November 1973. In February 1978 two fifteen-year-old boys from the Twinbrook estate in West Belfast were arrested and taken to Castlereagh for interrogation. In an interview one of the boys described his second interrogation which lasted about two and a half hours:

> Throughout the whole time I was either spread-eagled facing the wall on my fingertips, legs apart, or else standing with my hands on my head. Shouting continued. I was slapped about the head, back of neck, mouth, eyes. My wrists were bent back and my arms twisted. My ears were both simultaneously hit with open hands. I was punched in the stomach and kicked. My back was punched continuously particularly in the kidney area.
> I fell to the ground about a dozen times and was usually kicked while on the ground.... I was threatened that they would give my name to the UVF and UDA who would be only too willing to "bump" me off.[94]

The other boy was allegedly sexually assaulted and asked to tout on his friends and relatives. Both boys spent three days in Castlereagh and were released without charge. Nor did this abate as time went on. In May 1984 Jimmy Allsopp, aged only twelve, was seized by the RUC while with his friends, taken to North Queen Street Barracks, Belfast, and questioned about throwing stones at armored cars. The boy said "one of them threw a stone behind me and said that I dropped it.... When I was sitting down, the RUC man just went for me. He pulled my ear and grabbed me by the throat and lifted me up. The others had to pull him off.... They said they would let me go if I told them the biggest boy's name." When rescued by his father there were "numerous bruises and torn skin around the boy's neck and shoulders."[95]

Concrete evidence in support of the idea that the young and the vulnerable were deliberately targeted was provided in 1977 when a statement and a letter were sent to *Republican News*. The letter had been received by IRA Intelligence allegedly from within RUC barracks at North Queen Street, Belfast, and it read as follows: "Ginger, Please send your choice of 4 names of people in Unity for cat. III screening in the near future. I would suggest you choose the younger, weaker characters, who might crack, rather than the old hands.... If you wish to talk over with me about your choice of names come up P.M. Monday."[96]

Presumably the four weaker characters chosen from among the inhabitants of the Unity flats were like William Knight, from the Creggan estate in Derry, who, aged sixteen, appeared at a Sinn Féin press conference on 26 August 1987 to confess to receiving £175 from the RUC in return for information leading to the capture of IRA weapons and explosives. He was given twenty-four hours to leave the North and departed that same night. Willie Knight had received psychiatric treatment, spent several years in care, and according to his mother was unable to fend for himself. He had been an informer for over a year following RUC threats to reveal on the Creggan that his father was a soldier. Paul Kelly, who was given the same ultimatum, lived two doors away from Willie Knight. He had been a tout for the previous eighteen months. The Sinn Féin press conferences in Northern Ireland have always been intended to discourage informers by bringing home to them the dangers of the practice, and also to make the population aware that confessing such misdeeds of one's own accord obviates the almost mandatory death sentence. It is, of course, akin to the "Spies and informers beware" labels used by previous generations and, like them, guarantees newspaper publicity.

The editor of *Republican News* commented: "Trawling for informers is not a disorganized, haphazard RUC operation. It is a highly professional, officially sanctioned, and frighteningly systematic strategy. It exploits anti-social and criminal activity, personal weakness and instability. It is dependent on, and cynically abuses, psychiatric evaluation, a factor that, in itself should cause great concern among the medical profession."[97]

Much of this is confirmed in loyalist publications. Residents complained that the battle against crime had ground to a standstill because of the emphasis by certain Special Branch officers on recruiting touts in the early 1980s. *Ulster* quotes an ex–RUC man: "Young recruits nowadays are only in the force for the money.... Budding detectives, anxious to climb the ladder of success and promotion, have thrown their scruples out of the window in order to achieve their ambitions.... Many young men have placed their lives in peril, some have even taken the first plane out of the country because of the blackmailing tactics employed by unscrupulous officers."[98] *Mid-Ulster UDA News* tells of a member of the Royal Military Police (RMP), invited for supper to the home of a UDR man, who tried to get information about loyalist organizations from the teenage son of the house; and of other RMP men who frequent the Junior Ranks Mess of the UDR "to sniff about for information."[99] While *Ulster*, again, quotes the story of a RUC man in Ballymena "who was gleaning intelligence from kids at the local youth club."[100]

Perhaps the most alarming discovery in the 1970s was the so-called "Schoolboy Spy-Ring" in Belfast. This was a network of informers, their ages ranging from ten to sixteen, working for Special Branch and, in some cases, the SAS. Paul, Tony, and Danny were members of this organization. Paul, aged ten, was arrested by the RUC when he stole a Mars bar. He was taken to the Henry Taggart camp and told by a policeman "You could go on the beak if you give me names." His payment was £1 per name of anyone in the Fianna or the IRA. Tony, aged fourteen, was paid £4 a time for useful information, while Danny, also fourteen, was enticed by two other boys who gave names, told where rifles were hidden, and were paid £20 for each rifle. So many boys were involved that in 1975 the IRA declared a general amnesty for schoolboys involved with the RUC. In a nice piece of understated writing, the amnesty offer included the sentence: "Approaches have been made to their parents and the long-term danger of the boys' situation explained."[101] So effective was the explanation that the schoolboy network has never been resurrected. However not only older children were targeted: in 1974 the army descended to a new low when David Gill made headlines. He was approached in the school playground by soldiers and given 50p for identifying photographs. David was just six years old. Perhaps this or other similar occurrences were the inspiration behind the cartoon in the Andersonstown News, of 14 February 1979. It shows two bewildered soldiers talking while a delighted small boy is running away tossing a coin in the air. One soldier is saying "He said he would write down the names of three gunmen if I gave him 50p!!" The three names written by the boy are: John Wayne, Roy Rogers and Kojak. The attempts to use small children continued. Ten years later seven-year-old Gerard Rice was detained as he walked from school to his grandmother's house. His schoolbooks were thrown onto the road and the frightened child was interrogated until local women intervened.[102]

Jack Hermon succeeded Newman as Chief Constable at the beginning of 1980. This issued in a new era, when the RUC were to rely on evidence rather than confessions, but far from signaling the end of the informer tactics they became even more important. The problems this created quickly became evident to Sinn Féin, which emerged in the early 1980s as a significant political party after their electoral successes in the Assembly elections of October 1982. This was also the year when the RUC began to use paid perjurers, and recruitment tactics began to change in accordance with the lessons learned from the Stockholm Syndrome.

Stockholm Syndrome[103]

In August 1973 two robbers tied dynamite to four bank employees and held them hostage for five days in a bank in Stockholm. After the hostages were rescued they had developed a strong bond with the robbers and feared their police rescuers. This bonding became known to psychologists as the Stockholm Syndrome.[104] Four situations provide the foundation for this development: The presence of a threat to one's survival and the belief that the abuser would carry out the threat; the presence of a perceived small kindness from the abuser to the victim; isolation from perspectives other than those of the abuser; and the perceived inability to escape the situation.

All four situations outlined above were present in the supergrass system, and Eamon Collins, in his book *Killing Rage*, provides a textbook account of the process which fits so well with the Syndrome that it could be a deliberate attempt to get sympathy, were it not for similarities with other such accounts detailed in this study.[105] Each of the four situations can be seen in Collins's own experience:

(1) *The presence of a perceived threat*—this can be a direct threat to his life or to that of his family and friends, and the known history of violence by RUC interrogators would lead to the belief that the threat will be carried out: "I'm going to arrest your wife and she's coming here for seven days."[106]

(2) *A perceived small kindness*—a detective spoke of a lecture Collins had given about the republican movement: "He said he would have liked to have made his feelings known about his own people's role and place in Irish history.... He sounded genuinely hurt.... He also told me about the serious illness he had suffered recently. I felt sorry for him."[107]

(3) *Isolation*—the only people Collins saw were his RUC interrogators, and his cell was in the women's section of the jail.

(4) *Perceived inability to escape*—"The controller often uses extreme threats ('whether I talked or not I was going to be charged with murder ... before the week was out I would wish I had never been born.'[108]). He unveiled his strategy so gradually and skilfully that I did not grasp for a long time that he was working to a clear plan ... to close down gradually all possible avenues of retreat."[109]

The behavior associated with Stockholm Syndrome, seen by psychologists as a survival mechanism, can include the following:

(1) *Positive feelings by the victim toward the controller*—"After a while I would have believed anything he said for the simple reason that I wanted to believe it."[110] "I felt us becoming friends."[111]

(2) *Negative feelings by the victim toward family, friends, or authorities*—"I told myself that I had been exploited by the IRA and that I owed the army nothing. What had I got to lose by turning against it?"[112] "I no longer wanted to play a part in carrying the burden of centuries of struggle."[113]

(3) *Supportive behaviors by the victim*—"To me this cop seemed to be a decent and fair man."[114] "He had become my protector.... I had become totally dependent on him ... guided only by the controlling hand of my policeman savior."[115]

(4) *Detachment*—"I found myself adopting a pose of almost professional detachment as I looked at the photos."[116]

Gifford notes, in a perfect summary of the outcome of Stockholm Syndrome, that "his [the victim's] relationship with the investigating police officers becomes one of total dependence. He has cut himself off from his friends in the movement of which he was part. He needs the goodwill of the police officers in order to secure his immunity, or his light sentence, or his recommendation for an early release. He is in no position to resist any suggestions which they may make to him."[117]

In his semi-robotic state Collins imagined that his wife would understand. Instead he was confronted by a sudden burst of reality as she shouted at him: "You fucking bastard.... If I had a gun I'd shoot you myself. Now I know why all our friends have been arrested. All our friends. You've ruined our lives. My life and the children's lives have been ruined.... Only scum do this."[118] These phrases echoed and re-echoed in his thoughts until the spell finally broke when he saw her and his friends in the courtroom. Collins retracted his statements but was later killed by the IRA.

At much the same time the ever-increasing attempts by the RUC to recruit informers became so prevalent that details appeared regularly in the *Andersonstown News, An Phoblacht/Republican News,* and *The Irish People.* In each case the methods used were the same: arrest, often under the Emergency Provisions Act,[119] for some minor indiscretion[120] or for a spurious charge[121]; transport to the nearest interrogation center; then questioning by Special Branch, intimidation, brutality, blackmail, and bribes. Most were released without charge between three and seven days later.[122] Some agreed to co-operate initially because they were young and afraid, like John Duffy, aged eighteen, of the Short Strand area of Belfast. He reasoned that he would be released sooner if he agreed, then, on his release after only 36 hours, he contacted *Republican News,* and gave them a signed statement. This was published, together with a warning by the newspaper: "He has publicly exposed their futile efforts. We can recommend this course of action to further RUC victims as their wisest path."[123] Others, like Charlie Dunlop of Dungannon, contacted Sinn Féin. Francie Molloy, a Sinn Féin councillor, reiterated the constant warning: "Anyone approached by the RUC or already assisting them should come forward now and help expose this sordid tactic."[124] This, however, was not necessarily the end of their ordeal because frequently years of harassment from the police followed the initial arrest.

In an effort to provide their followers and sympathizers not only with information about the new show trials, and their tacit endeavor to strike fear into the entire community, but also emphasizing what could be done to help them, Sinn Féin produced a booklet in 1983 entitled *The Informers.* This booklet covers such topics as the financial and other inducements on offer to those prepared to turn informer, together with case studies of some of those approached in this fashion. Sinn Féin's motives in producing the booklet could not have been entirely altruistic, because as a political party they also wanted to be the primary recourse for the nationalist community.

The Informers is a more detailed exposition of the modern informer than had ever appeared previously and included the warning:

The RUC's use of paid informers must not be viewed in isolation, or simplistically as a terrifying new phenomenon. It is only the latest weapon in the arsenal of repression that the British and their Loyalist allies have relied on since the foundation of the six-county state in their efforts to quell the desire for national freedom.

Exactly why the informer tactic should have become such an important element of that repression over the last year or so can be attributed to a variety of factors. Foremost among these however was the belief in British establishment circles that Margaret Thatcher's intransigence during the hunger-strikes, and the resulting deeply-felt deaths of ten H-Block men, had inflicted a psychological defeat on the nationalist people which could be exploited by an increase in counter-insurgency activities, including black propaganda and the public use of informers.[125]

The description of the use of paid informers as "the latest weapon in the arsenal of repression" is incorrect. It is equally wrong to see it as something affecting only the nationalists, though there have been fewer informers among the loyalists. Nevertheless, during the 1970s and 1980s there does seem to have been an explosion in attempts to recruit ever more informers in Northern Ireland at every level.

As Sinn Féin observes in the booklet, the early 1980s, particularly following the deaths of the hunger-strikers, saw a marked resurgence in the recruitment of touts. Some of the children recruited then, such as Martin McGartland, became particularly notable later. In 1987 he was sixteen, had already been involved in petty crime with a gang of older boys, and was flattered on being approached by a friendly RUC man. At his first meeting with two men from Special Branch he was given £40 and readily agreed to keep an eye on certain people for them. In his memoir he says, "They had made me feel important. A real man."[126] He progressed in importance, at least in his own estimation, until he was twenty-one, and had to jump through a plate-glass window to escape interrogation by the IRA. He lost his country, his home, his wife, and children, and has lived in fear of discovery under various assumed identities ever since. Gerard Mahon is also typical of the many low-grade informers whose paymaster (1984–85) was the RUC.

Gerard and Catherine Mahon

The predominantly nationalist Twinbrook area of West Belfast, whose most famous son is Bobby Sands, was newly built in the seventies, and by the 1980s had many of the problems with poverty, vandalism, and petty crime associated with such estates throughout the UK. In 1984 Gerry Adams was shot in Belfast, allegedly by a UFF squad; the appearance of Martin Galvin, the Noraid leader, at a rally in Belfast ended in a riot which was shown on American television; and the IRA bombed the Grand Hotel in Brighton during the Conservative party conference. Tensions were high. Early in that year

Gerard Mahon, a mechanic from Twinbrook, was arrested for unpaid fines and taken to Tennent Street Barracks. Like others who went to the police station for a trivial reason, the experience led him to become an informer. From the many accounts of such arrests in both nationalist and loyalist publications it is not difficult to piece together events between Gerard Mahon's arrest, and his subsequent transfer to Woodbourne Barracks[127]: at least three days confinement in a low-ceilinged white painted cell, the horsebox; interrogations over lengthy periods by a number of different interrogators, accompanied by threats of physical punishment, and imprisonment in Long Kesh, together with acts of brutality and accusations of belonging to an illegal organization; then two easygoing police constables who pulled out cigarettes and spoke in a friendly manner, inquiring how the wife and family were taking this; then another two who would force the detainee to stand for a long time, or throw him wildly from one to the other until he was dizzy, when he would be told to sit down and tell them the truth.

At Woodbourne Barracks Mahon was approached by two Special Branch officers. Again, according to the published accounts, these men would have used the soft method: offering to get him released if he would work for them and pointing out the advantages of extra cash.[128] So Mahon agreed to work for Special Branch for £10 a week and bonuses, was given the code name "Spare Parts" and a telephone number 28511 Ext. 220.[129] He arranged to meet his two handlers at Upper Galwally Lane in South Belfast and was finally released.

Mahon's wife assisted him in his activities, which mainly consisted in reporting local gossip. Later, on instructions from his handlers, he contacted the IRA and offered to hold an arms dump in their flat which was then bugged by Special Branch. One bug was light sensitive and gave off a signal each time the dump was opened. Another was a special bleeper to contact Woodbourne Barracks. If Mahon were held by the IRA, his wife was to send a continuous bleep. For almost eighteen months Mahon received £10 per week and regular bonuses ranging from £100 to £150.[130] Their phone bill was paid by Special Branch and "On three occasions, when the RUC thought there was a possibility of 'hitting' IRA volunteers in the flat, they were both sent to Newcastle for the weekend. All expenses were paid by the special branch [sic]."[131]

The warnings to informers from the IRA are clear and constantly reiterated, in talk, on walls, in newspapers such as the *Andersonstown News*: "Anyone caught touting will be executed." Why would anyone risk death, especially for such paltry amounts? In the case of Gerard and Catherine Mahon the reasons are obvious. Firstly, the thought of a period in Long Kesh was enough to strike fear into any nationalist, because they knew about conditions there. Then, those from the nationalist community brought to the attention of the RUC were in danger of constant harassment. This meant the police arriving at all hours of the day or night, and this could go on and on without remission. Finally, anyone tempted by a regular weekly sum of £10 in 1983 must have been mired in the impotence of poverty. So for a small amount of work, the Mahons were relieved of the consequences of unpaid fines and given the wherewithal to pay their way for the future. As for the threat from the IRA, was this not nullified by the bleeper to warn the barracks? It would not have occurred to them that this signal was to allow the RUC to remove their expensive electronics from the flat, for, as became very clear, the couple were expendable.

Perhaps the greatest evil attendant on the whole system of informers was that their paymasters and handlers came to believe that anything at all (deceit, crime, murder) was legitimate as long as important sources were not compromised. So when, in 1985, the IRA suspected (accurately, he had been in the pay of RUC Special Branch since 1982) that Joseph Fenton, an estate agent, was a police informer, the RUC saved him by betraying Catherine and Gerard Mahon. Fenton, a far more valuable asset than the Mahons because he also provided the IRA with safe houses for their meetings, told the security branch of the IRA (the Nutting Squad) that the Mahons were informers to deflect suspicion from himself. Ironically, two years later, Fenton himself was shot and his body was dumped in an alleyway in Bunbeg Park in Lenadoon.[132] This was, apparently, to save Fred Scappaticci, a member of the Nutting Squad and himself said to be the highest ranking informer in the IRA, code named Stakeknife, whose paymaster was Army intelligence.[133]

The Mahons were taken together, with no time to activate the bleeper, and interrogated by Scappaticci. Interrogation by the Nutting Squad was almost ritualistic. It included elements of vengeance and humiliation, relied heavily on the guilt of the betrayer, and on the promise of forgiveness after confession. Once the confession had been extorted, it was then repeated and recorded, either in writing or electronically, for dissemination. The confession, an essential component of the IRA ritual for much of its existence, was not simply a warning to others, it also told the IRA exactly what information had been given to the Crown Forces, but few were forgiven, and the Mahons were not among those few.

On Sunday 8 September 1985, Gerard, aged twenty-eight, and Catherine, aged twenty-seven, their wrists tied, were shot dead, the first married couple to be killed for informing. From the position of the bodies it was assumed that Catherine was killed when she tried to escape after Gerard was shot.[134] Thus Catherine's claim to a place in history lies in the fact that she was the first woman to be executed as an informer by the IRA in Northern Ireland. Their families denied the allegations, but, given the details and the sparse rewards on offer, the accusation is credible.[135]

Seeing all informers as despicable and disreputable is overly simplistic.

Many, like Gerard Mahon, afraid of the immediate future, lacked the imagination and foresight to see the inevitable outcome of their actions. Even for those who survived, such as Martin McGartland, a new identity meant that they must leave everything and everybody they knew. One breach in the protective arrangements: a lower level of police vigilance or a corrupt policeman, a vengeful wife or mistress, even the informer's own loose tongue, and they are doomed. Yet those informers who wrote books (and even Brian Nelson who starred in a television documentary) do not seem to have been found as a result. It is doubtful that this is due to any special precautions taken by their publishers because this would have been costly, and so ruled out. Moreover, a brief web search for Martin McGartland gives 28,600 results and for Raymond Gilmour, 354,000. Obviously betrayal tends to come from someone much closer to home.

Denis Martyn Donaldson

The 2006 very public admission of guilt by Denis Donaldson places him firmly within the time bracket when informers increased so greatly: "I was a British agent.... I was recruited in the 1980s after compromising myself during a vulnerable time in my life."[136] On Tuesday 4 April 2006 the news magazine *Magill* was hosting its annual Politician of the Year awards in Dublin and intended to give an award to Denis Donaldson. That evening the news broke that Donaldson had been shot dead in Donegal.

Denis Donaldson embodied much of the republican history of Northern Ireland. He was brought up in the Short Strand area of East Belfast, the son of an IRA man, and sentenced to ten years in Long Kesh for explosives offences. There he met Bobby Sands and Gerry Adams, and bolstered his reputation as a committed republican and a serious thinker. Released in 1976, he stood as Sinn Féin's East Belfast candidate in 1983, and was part of the republican delegation which flew to Lebanon in 1987 to secure the release of Irish hostage Brian Keenan. When the Assembly was established in 1998, Donaldson, who had previously organized U.S. trips for Gerry Adams and Martin McGuinness, became head of Sinn Féin administration at Stormont. This meant that he was also one of the three men who faced charges of running an IRA spy ring, the so-called "Stormontgate" which brought down the Assembly in October 2002. The cases against the three men were dropped at the beginning of December 2005, with no explanation from the British government. The authorities in Northern Ireland had attempted to obtain a court gagging order in 2005, thus allowing the prosecution to conceal crucial evidence, and, presumably, Donaldson's status. The request was rejected.

Whether this had any relevance to the events of 16 December 2005 can only be conjectured. The previous week Denis Donaldson's Special Branch handlers told him that he was to be "outed" as an informer in a Sunday newspaper. He chose instead to confess to his Sinn Féin colleagues, and then to everyone else on 16 December at a press conference. Though assured by Sinn Féin that he would be safe, he was expelled from the party, and it was suggested by the press that he was told he would no longer be welcome in Belfast. *The Sunday Life* summed up his situation: "Donaldson sought, and was given, an assurance that he wouldn't be harmed.... Maybe when he spoke to a newspaper after being tracked down in the Glenties he sealed his own fate."[137] Those who couldn't stomach a tout in their midst may have felt he didn't keep his head down enough and decided it was an opportue moment to take him out."[138]

So Donaldson left his terraced house in West Belfast and went to a cottage owned by his son-in-law near the village of Glenties on the west coast of Donegal. Journalists made much of the supposed squalor (i.e., no electricity or running water) in which he was living, but he did not seem to be in hiding for on the night before he was killed he spent half an hour talking to Tim Cranley, a census official, who called at the cottage: "Mr. Donaldson wasn't in any way nervous or distressed ... he ... had quite good, bright lighting from a Tilley lamp.... It was very warm. The heating came from a sturdy old Stanley range.... No way was he living in abject squalor.... It was quite a cosy little place—neat and tidy."[139] The last person to see Donaldson was probably Pat Bonar, a sheep farmer who saw him driving his estate car at about 11 a.m. on Tuesday. Later that day a neighbor passed the cottage on her way to the shops and noticed that the window was broken and the door was open, when she returned the door was still open and she contacted the gardaí. Donaldson had been shot four times with a shotgun.[140]

There has been much written in the media about the identities of his killers. Donaldson is the twenty-third informer to be murdered since the 1994 ceasefire, and loyalists are believed to be responsible for thirteen of them, republicans for nine.[141] Donaldson's family did not believe he was killed by the IRA; they claimed his death was a direct result of the activities of Special Branch and the British Intelligence agencies. Amid much speculation and denial, it has to be said that compromising himself during a vulnerable time in his life has a familiar echo. It has already been established that in the 1970s and 1980s the RUC searched out the vulnerable, and, though nothing has been revealed about Denis Donaldson's recruitment as a Special Branch informer, the timing is right for him to have been a graduate of Castlereagh.[142]

Moreover, in the aftermath of his outing, five more republicans in West Belfast were told by the media that they would be outed: in one instance journalists camped outside the home of a republican whose name had been circulating as a possible informer. A senior republican said, "This is complete fantasy stuff on the part of British Intelligence, they are putting people's names into the public arena in the hope that Republicans will react.... They want to spread paranoia and fear amongst the Republican community as a follow-up to the Donaldson affair."[143]

While this may be true, the words of the senior security sources quoted in *Sunday Life* are more difficult to believe. They said that Donaldson was recruited following a standard Special Branch approach to republican activists: "[he] wasn't blackmailed or threatened, he was discretely [sic] approached and invited to discuss the political situation."[144] We have already considered the standard Special Branch approach, and there seems to be no evidence to suggest that any other was employed in the 1980s. Those same sources said that Donaldson was jointly run with MI5 "then the money came to Denis because they had a big budget." If there was this sudden influx of wealth why did nobody notice ?

One might imagine that this was the traditional killing of an informer. Against that, however, is the method employed. The traditional method is a lonely border road, a hood, a shot to the head, and sometimes a message left on the body. Donaldson's murder was not a textbook killing.[145] Perhaps his murderer, like so many others, will never be known. Meanwhile his inquest was adjourned five times at the request of the Gardaí, and this further fueled media speculation (not just in Ireland) that "he may have been ordered killed to prevent him revealing any more secrets."[146]

Conclusion

The conclusions of the Amnesty Report of 1978 placed Britain firmly among the nations who practiced torture:

(1) On the basis of the information available to it, Amnesty International believes that maltreatment of suspected terrorists by the RUC has taken place with sufficient frequency to warrant the establishment of a public inquiry to investigate it.
(2) The evidence ... does not suggest that uniformed members of the RUC are involved in the alleged maltreatment.
(3) The evidence ... suggests that legal provisions, which have eroded the rights of suspects held in connection with terrorist offences, have helped create the circumstances in which maltreatment of suspects has taken place.
(4) The evidence ... suggests that the machinery for investigating complaints against the police of assault during interview is not adequate.[147]

Such cogent questions as: "Did the authorities know of and condone the ill-treatment of prisoners?" "Was there an 'administrative practice' as defined by the European Court of Human Rights?"[148] and "Was official tolerance shown?"[149] needed once again to be answered. The court at Strasbourg had

3. Persuasion in Castlereagh 115

decided in 1974 that the answer was "yes" to all these questions. The British government insisted, in the teeth of both evidence and widespread condemnation, that Strasbourg had exonerated them. The argument they offered in defense ran as follows:

> The authorities are, in effect, engaged in a war against terrorism; terrorism must be defeated ... a continuous supply of tactical information relating to the identity of the enemy and the location of his weapons is vital ... and cannot be obtained without the use of physical ill-treatment; this may be illegal, it may ... be immoral, it may ... alienate many ... but its military value is established and that alone serves to justify its use.[150]

The Amnesty Report produced the words of former members of Army Intelligence who had plied their trade during World War II, to refute the government's argument. Moreover, in deciding if there had been a pattern of official toleration of ill-treatment, it should be remembered that the Amnesty team spent the week of 28 November to 6 December 1977 investigating the allegations of brutality in Northern Ireland. In December the doctors saw scarcely a case to worry them, and there were only eight complaints of assault, while the previous monthly average had been nearly forty complaints.

The Police Surgeons were very conscious of their position as servants of the state and had little sympathy with the paramilitary outrages. Nevertheless they made repeated attempts to bring the abuses to the notice of the authorities and the Chief Constable, only to find their efforts ignored. The Hermon Committee was established in October 1977 to deal with these problems but Dr. Irwin said that it had never been acknowledged that anything was wrong, and that "even the minutes weren't accurate."[151] In the end the General Practitioners began to refuse to attend at the interrogation centers in what amounted almost to a strike when, on 6 March 1978, they warned the Committee that the matter would be referred to the British Medical Association, and the Police Surgeons might refuse to examine any more terrorist suspects.

Few of those whose allegations about torture in Castlereagh are in print were subjected to violence in order to make them inform, Special Branch endeavors were directed towards obtaining confessions. Among the exceptions to this was George Watson Anthony, a loyalist who spent three days in Castlereagh in October 1975. He was interviewed nine times, once for thirteen hours without a break, in an attempt to force him to admit membership of the UVF, to inform for the RUC, and to agree to give evidence at a murder trial. After the third interview a uniformed constable whom he knew came into his cell, looked at his bruises and said, "The bastards wouldn't even do that to the Provies."[152] Nor should it be assumed that only Castlereagh was involved in the ill-treatment of prisoners, a plethora of accounts similar to those already related show that this was not so, the other centers: Gough,

Holywood, and Girdwood were also named, and RUC Barracks such as Springfield Road, Belfast, and Strand Road, Derry.

Meanwhile the RUC insisted that the allegations were all false, that the injuries were self-inflicted. It is true that some, like Sean Macken, arrested on 9 May 1977, and sent to Castlereagh, decided he could take no more of the beatings and cut his wrist with a plastic knife. It was not very sharp and it took about 20 minutes, but the doctors were perfectly capable of differentiating between self-inflicted injuries and the others.[153] Castlereagh closed at the end of 1999, and Alex Maskey of Sinn Féin said "that the history of the center stood as an indictment of the RUC and successive British governments, who ... had consistently turned a blind eye to ... the appalling brutality ... served out daily in Castlereagh."[154] Although Maskey's is not a neutral voice, the allegations were widespread and consistent, and the list of tortures in the Appendix provides further evidence which shows that the claims about Castlereagh differ only in severity. Even more telling is the reaction of the prison doctors to the injuries they were seeing and diagnosing as not self-inflicted. In addition, as recently as 2010, *Irish Republican News* reported that Amnesty International and British Irish Rights Watch had called for an inquiry into the torture allegations, while the Criminal Cases Review Commission has received more than 200 applications, and "a number of men who served as detectives with the Royal Ulster Constabulary (RUC) have told ... how senior members encouraged the systematic mistreatment of suspects at Castlereagh interrogation center in east Belfast, and elsewhere, after the establishment of the Diplock courts in 1973."[155]

It has been, then, accepted by all authorities, except the British government, that torture was rife in the interrogation centers of Northern Ireland. The recruitment of informers, particularly from within tightly knit communities such as exist in Ulster, demands the age-old spurs of the carrot and the stick. In earlier times, exemplified by the huge upsurge of informers of 1798, it is undoubtedly the case that the recruits' primary motivation was money. But their modern counterparts, more numerous (at least as a percentage of the population, but perhaps in actual numbers as well), were mostly driven by the stick that was Castlereagh. It stood out among the interrogation centers, not just because it was the first, but also because its reputation was such that detectives admitted many of the suspects arrived there consumed by such fear that some were ready to admit anything. Although the money mattered to the mostly unemployed suspects, fear was the mainspring, while for the interrogators and their masters the need was to control by any and every means. Beyond that must surely lie the regrettable suspicion, revealed to the world by the war crime trials at Nuremberg in 1945, that those who torture can leave their humanity so far behind as to regard it simply as a job or obeying orders.

Neither Pearse Kerr nor Brian Maguire was an informer, though both were from nationalist families, and thus could have provided information which might have resulted in the removal of other nationalists from the streets. Both, like many others before and after them, were innocent of the charges made against them, both were young men getting on with their lives. Yet Castlereagh broke both of them: Kerr, even in middle age, so long after the event and living in the U.S., still cannot bring himself to discuss it, and Maguire has been in his grave for thirty years. Moreover, the Maguire case gives rise to far too many unanswered and unanswerable questions. For Peter Rawlinson, used to policing on the mainland, there were no doubts over Maguire's death, because he applied mainland police standards to his investigation. Perhaps others, more conversant than he with the prevailing circumstances in Castlereagh, might wonder if the insistence on a strict time limit for his investigations had more to do with handicapping the investigating team, as with Amnesty, than in providing quick answers. Equally they might wonder if the distress of the elderly constable in charge of the cells was because a young man had died, or because he suspected the manner of his death, and feared he might incur blame. There had been, after all, so many other instances where men were brought to unconsciousness by smothering or strangling.

The touts are mostly not courageous, nor capable of either self-denial or self-sacrifice. Gerard Mahon was not a brave man. The implication behind the IRA statement after his death is that he agreed immediately to work for Special Branch. Whether or not this is true, given the threat of interrogation it is undoubtedly possible. Moreover, Fr. Denis Faul told the *Irish Times* in August 1983 that he believed the police searched the prisons for likely informers, and that they always picked on men who were weak and vulnerable. Again, there is written evidence to back up this claim. Also, the threat to those in custody, implicit in the very name of Castlereagh, was far more to be feared than any future danger, which was, after all, dependent on being found out—and that might never happen. The RUC promised many touts a happy and prosperous new life abroad, but it was a deceit.

The postscript to this period when Northern Ireland was ruled by the Diplock Courts is just beginning. Recent articles in *The Guardian* recount some of the cases reviewed by the Criminal Cases Review Commission (CCRC), which investigates alleged miscarriages of justice, and has received over 200 applications of which 47 are from people who were juveniles at the time of their conviction. By October 2010 the court of appeal in Belfast had already overturned convictions in twenty four out of twenty six cases heard, and admissions of brutality have been made by former RUC detectives[156]: "both IRA suspects and loyalists were beaten, burned with cigarettes or lighters, forced to assume stressful positions for long periods, stripped and humiliated, and sometimes threatened with murder. Some suffered such severe injuries that they were taken to hospital."[157]

The motivation behind all this violence was not specifically to recruit informers, though, as has been seen, if the occasion offered, and the prisoner showed the necessary weakness of character, this could be the end result. Instead "The driving force behind the brutality was a determination to secure more convictions in the judge-only Diplock courts that had been established in 1973 once it became clear that internment without trial was counterproductive."[158]

"The Informer"

People of Ireland, keep your eyes wide,
And be very wary in those you confide,
There are Informers and traitors who wouldn't half pause,
For the sake of a drink they would sell out the cause.

You'll find them in Dance Halls, you'll find them at work,
Wherever there's people, the Informer will lurk.

While drinking in pubs or shopping for food,
You'll meet the Informer, he's up to no good,
So when out in company, choose your friends well,
For you're the next fool the Informer could sell.

Source: The Volunteer, no. 23, n.d. no page numbers. NIPC, Linen Hall Library. The author has endeavored to find the original copyright owner of "The Informer," but has been unable to do so. If anyone can assist in establishing the copyright holder, the author will be pleased to acknowledge the owner.

4

British Intelligence and the Army

"choose your friends well"[1]

The first British troops arriving in Derry, on 15 August 1969, were greeted as saviors by the beleaguered community of the Bogside, facing the RUC and the B-Specials. Nevertheless, there was little hope that armed troops, trained for war, could ever be accepted as an impartial force on the streets of Northern Ireland. Such hope was further eroded by a nervous London government's refusal to contemplate direct rule, opting instead for piecemeal legislation: thus, among other things, security was transferred from the RUC to the army and the B Specials were to be disbanded. The results were alienation and disillusionment on all sides, and the Belfast riots of August 1969 when 83 percent of the damaged or destroyed buildings were Catholic-occupied. The troops had been ordered not to fire, the RUC refused to leave their barracks, and the attacking group came from the loyalist Cupar Street area. The inferences of sectarianism drawn by the Belfast Catholics may have been incorrect, but the logic is obvious.

Soldiers need an identifiable enemy, but in the heightened tensions of Northern Ireland in the early 1970s anyone could be the enemy. They came to identify Catholics with the IRA, but later this also applied to Protestants, when, on 11 October 1969, the Hunt report recommended the abolition of the B Specials. The Shankill burst out in fury, a constable was shot by a Protestant sniper, and Protestant mobs attacked the troops. So these young recruits were continually surrounded by an incomprehensible and possibly fatal hostility, and the uncertainty eventually led to the Falls Curfew of July 1970, when much of West Belfast was under virtual martial law for more than thirty-six hours. This not only had an adverse effect on nationalist attitudes towards the British army, it also proved very positive for the IRA.

The state's response to the unrest was personified in the arrival in Northern Ireland of Brigadier General Frank Kitson, who had served in Britain's colonial campaigns in such places as Malaya, Kenya, and Cyprus and was to use the same tactics in the province. Kitson's name would become an object of loathing for the nationalists: *Low Intensity Operations* was the book in which he outlined his ideas for dealing with resistance and undermining the popular movement in 1972.[2] The manual set out a series of recommendations for dealing with the situation wherever it was found: intelligence gathering; regular spot checks and searches; the development of surveillance techniques; infiltration of the various groups; the use of informants; psychological operations; and the spread of disinformation. This last was particularly important for causing confusion among the general population as well as the paramilitary groups, and, as will be seen especially in the Stakeknife case, it worked.

During the 1970s the RUC use of informers was predominant, largely because early army intelligence techniques in Northern Ireland were based on the undercover methods Kitson had found effective in Kenya in the early 1950s. Nevertheless, since so little intelligence was being passed on by RUC Special Branch (there was a good deal of territorial resentment between the two at this time), the army had to find a solution. They found that the IRA was structured in the British military fashion into brigades, battalions, and companies, meaning that very few informers were needed if they were well placed. These were recruited and began their work about November 1971. Their information was passed on to the newly set up Mobile Reconnaissance Force (MRF).

The weakness of army intelligence was counterbalanced by ever-increasing aggression on the part of the soldiers, culminating in internment, and then Bloody Sunday on 30 January 1972, and the result was "a tidal wave of support for the physical-force men, which increased the ranks of both the Officials and the Provisionals."[3] Nor was this support confined to Northern Ireland. In the wake of Bloody Sunday Jack Lynch announced a national day of mourning, and a protest mob in Dublin burned down the British Embassy while the gardaí stood by and watched.

Then long-term strategies began to be put in place, many of them following Kitson's advice: the legal system introduced the Emergency Provisions Act (EPA) in late 1973, which gave the soldiers a virtually free hand and helped to create the non-accountability which later extended to state killings. December in that same year saw the introduction of the Diplock courts and the new sweeping powers of stop, search, arrest, and detention; but increased surveillance was the most important change, because it made for insecurity, fear, and confusion in the community, and in 1973 Robert Daly, Professor of Psychiatry at UCC interviewed about twenty men who had been subjected to "extreme coercive pressure," including in some cases the hooding process, while in the hands of the security forces in the North. [Daly noted that] "Almost all of the patients I saw had overt psychiatric illness.... The commonest symptoms I found were of marked anxiety, fear and dread, as well as nightmares and startle responses.... These [are] ... characteristic of people who had been subjected to traumatic experiences like shell shock in wartime. Depression has been almost universal amongst these individuals. Weeping attacks are common."

He felt that it was particularly worrying that the problems of psychosomatic illness, such as peptic ulcers, headaches and buzzing in the ears had emerged in the men so quickly.... The shortage of the period in these cases might point to the severity of the experience.[4]

Other intelligence operations did not necessarily involve the MRF, and among the best known of these were the Gemini massage parlor on Belfast's Antrim Road, frequented by indiscreet IRA men and their friends from Ardoyne while soldiers listened and watched upstairs, and the highly successful Four Square laundry, whose van became a familiar sight in republican areas. The washing and ironing was done by a genuine laundry service, but the clothes were tested for traces of guns and explosives, while the van itself served as a mobile observation post.

The discovery and demise of the Four Square laundry came about when, in the autumn of 1972, a young Volunteer, Seamus Wright, failed to attend one of the IRA's routine daily meetings. Brendan Hughes, IRA commandant in Belfast, became concerned. Wright phoned his wife from England, she consulted Hughes and was told to tell Wright to come back. She returned without him, told Hughes that Seamus had broken under interrogation in the previous February after his arrest and interrogation at Palace Barracks, Holywood, Co. Down, and that he was afraid to come home. She was reassured that he would be safe, so he returned to Northern Ireland. The next day he was questioned by the IRA and mentioned a laundry van with an armed soldier hidden in a compartment above the driver. Hughes was horrified: "We had no idea that British Intelligence was running a laundry service and massage parlor ... until this information came in, no one suspected the Four Square laundry team were military personnel."[5] The IRA launched a combined operation on 2 October 1972 against the massage parlor and the laundry van. The outcome boosted IRA morale and was very useful in propaganda terms, but Seamus Wright was executed in January 1973.

Intelligence gathering in these years was still fairly chaotic, not least because of the rivalry between the RUC, MI5, and the army. The MRF was shut down in 1972, but Kitson's ideas remained influential and in 1974 a more sophisticated and highly trained organization eventually known as 14 Int became operative. It was not a SAS unit, though a number of SAS personnel was drafted into it, and so was Grenadier Guards officer Robert Nairac in the role of liaison officer in 1974.

Captain Robert Laurence Nairac

Robert Nairac was not an informer, but his service in Northern Ireland illustrates both the army's attitude to the general population and the ineptitude of its early attempts at intelligence-gathering. Worse, however, than arrogance, at least in terms of risk, was Nairac's delusion that a change of clothes and accent would hide his real identity, and make him one of this comparatively small community when the 1970s had brought Bloody Sunday and the Widgery Report; the bombing of Aldershot; violence between the Official IRA and the Provisionals; the sudden growth of the UDA; and what has become known as the dirty tricks campaign, the secret war which was to involve Robert Nairac.

Nairac had succumbed to the Ireland effect, like so many Englishmen for hundreds of years before him, while he was still at Ampleforth. He spent several school holidays at a friend's home in Spiddal, and the romantic side of his nature, later commented on by friends and senior officers alike, became so heavily imbued with the idea of Ireland that he became something of an authority on its history and its people. As with Erskine Childers, with whose career he had much in common, this was to be the fatal flaw which led to his death, because he forgot that, though he was a Catholic with a great love for Ireland, he was also just another hated British soldier with a gun.

By the end of his first tour in 1973, patrolling the streets of Belfast with the Grenadier Guards, he had decided that intelligence was the key to defeating the enemy and volunteered for specialist training. It seems to have been at this time that he took to frequenting the pubs in places like Kilburn, chatting to Irish laborers while trying to perfect an Irish accent, and making his first contact with Republicans. After he got to know Martin Squires the two men often went to Kilburn together, where Nairac, a former boxing blue, would sometimes get involved in fights. Squires said of him later: "there was no denying that he had this thuggish side of him"[6] While his friend, Major A, said that Nairac had no idea what he was coming to when he volunteered for special duties.

> We, the security forces, which included the RUC, were also effectively torturing people in the cause of gathering intelligence.... There was so much going on that was either being ignored, overlooked, covered up.... People were going haywire; some were going slightly mad. There were mean and petty jealousies within the intelligence business and especially between the Army and the RUC where communications all but broke down at one stage ... there were rumours of unauthorized shootings, secret graves, crime gangs mixing and matching with terrorists and the UDR alike so that you never knew who ... was your true enemy[7]

In 1974 Nairac was posted to the 3 Brigade area covering South Armagh as intelligence liaison officer between 4 Field Survey Troop, Royal Engineers,[8] the RUC and Special Branch (with both of whom, by all reports, he got along exceedingly well), and to the army units in the area, as well as liaising with army headquarters in Lisburn. As liaison officer he was second in command, his section commander was Captain Julian "Tony" Ball[9] and the two men became a formidable partnership, though Nairac was ultimately answerable to the SAS squadron commander.

To the outsider this conglomeration of different facets to his job points inexorably to the possibility that few people could ever have known exactly where he was at any given time. Added to this, he operated from the base at Castledillon and had a bedroom at Bessbrook. A recipe for disaster in the wrong hands, and Robert Nairac's were the wrong hands. A Special Branch man said of this period: "Even then, he was pushing out into the most violent place in the province. He was supposed to be liaison but it appeared to us that he was also going out in the field, on covert operations, and he was certainly in contact with informers, some of whom he snitched from us. Agent handling itself is a skilled and dangerous business. I could never be certain, but Robert appeared to be involved in that, too."[10]

Informer handling was not his job, but there are many other claims that Nairac was involved with informers. Important among these is the case of Columba McVeigh, a seventeen-year-old from Donaghmore, murdered in 1975. The IRA statement about his murder alleged that he was giving information to Captain Robert Nairac. The significance of this statement lies not in whether or not it is true, but in that it indicates that Nairac's name and job were already known to the IRA.

The Dublin and Monaghan bombings were widely believed to have been the work of UVF and UDA paramilitaries, but it was later claimed that Nairac and Ball had been involved in the planning, and that Nairac had been present at the murder of John Francis Green, an IRA commander hiding out over the border in Co. Monaghan. In addition, Nairac's name was linked to two informers known as "The Jackal" (Loyalist paramilitary Robin Jackson, a Special Branch informer and leader of the UVF unit known as the Glenanne Gang[11]) and "The Badger"(a senior Garda officer). John Weir, a former RUC Sergeant, gave evidence in his Affidavit that Jackson and Robert McConnell had murdered Green and had transported the bombs for the Dublin attack, so this may be the link between Nairac and the two events, though it still leaves the question of Holroyd's claims that he produced a Polaroid photo of the murdered man[12] and said he was a party to the killing. In the same vein John Weir said:

> I learned from a Republican informant that Robert McConnell ... had been set up by Army Intelligence and assassinated by the IRA. My informant told me that Army Intelligence Captain Robert Nairac had told him about McConnell.... I had discovered that Army Intelligence, through Nairac, was playing one side off against the other ...

that Army Intelligence had organised the murder of Robert McConnell after it had used him to carry out attacks on the Catholic population: it then arranged his murder by the IRA to ensure that he would never be able to reveal the truth about his role.[13]

Perhaps the best proof that this account is true is that the authorities immediately told the press that Weir was mentally and emotionally unhinged, a strategy which had already been used with Holroyd.

Nairac began to go out to local pubs, where he tried to engage Republicans in conversation, and stood up to sing rebel songs, a very risky and high-profile stance for an undercover soldier to adopt. "He seemed intent on setting himself up as a man who could be trusted and who would be accepted in Catholic areas and by the Provisionals themselves."[14] Many army sources have insisted that he pulled off some creditable achievements, but Adams, in *Ambush*, his book about the SAS, has a more realistic view of the situation: "It is a measure of the naivety of the army at this time that they thought that an army officer could simply walk out into the streets and be absorbed in the community, particularly an officer as classically British as Nairac. Some sources in the IRA claim that his Irish accent was so bad that he had become well known as a British officer, but was tolerated because he was so obvious that he was thought to be a plant."[15]

Much is made of Nairac's ability to reproduce Irish accents. Lilias Armstrong, the phoneticist on whom Shaw based the character of Professor Higgins, could listen to a speaker and know to within a few streets where he or she came from. To a much lesser extent the rest of us can do the same thing where our own locality is concerned. Major Clive Fairweather, despite his inability to make decisions in an emergency, seems to have been able to sum up Nairac better than most people. At their first meeting he saw that the young man was trying to impress him with his knowledge of the area and said "He talked in colloquialisms and he quite clearly wanted to be one of the boys. Despite the scruffy clothes, he still looked like a Guards officer."[16] Later on he warned Nairac " that no matter how much he learned about the Irish language he was never going to convince anyone that he was an Irishman because as a Scot.... I can spot anyone pretending to be a Scot within a couple of minutes."[17] The younger man was plainly convinced that he knew better, but the men at the Three Steps Inn certainly had little hesitation in identifying him as a British soldier.

His friends were also very skeptical of his claims: Julian Malins said: "He said he was working undercover, in intelligence. I simply could not believe this. A child could tell from fifty paces that Robert was Ampleforth, Oxford and Guards,"[18] while Martin Squires, to whom he boasted about his contacts with the IRA, said: "He talked about how far he'd got inside that whole community and the only thing I can say is that if half he told me was true, I'm just amazed he wasn't bumped off before."[19]

A good deal of arrogance is evident in his behavior, particularly in his consistent flouting of SAS rules, above all those concerned with back-up units and not going out alone. Worse, however, than arrogance, at least in terms of risk, was his delusion that a change of clothes and accent would hide his real identity, would make him belong to this comparatively small community. Fairweather commented: "It is kind of unhealthy to walk through somewhere like Crossmaglen and places like that in uniform one day and be talking to local people, and then be in the pubs wearing the donkey jacket or whatever else come nighttime, talking in an Irish accent and pretending to be Danny McAlevey, a Sticky from Ardoyne ... local people and the local IRA were beginning to spot what he was doing."[20]

Many aspects of Nairac's character are borne out by his teachers, his friends and army personnel. Mary Price, a former girlfriend said that he "lived very much in a world of fantasy," that he was "extraordinarily cold ... and ruthless" but with "a certain charm,"[21] before going on to describe him in 1976 at a ball in Chelsea, the last time she saw him: "I found him very altered and furtive. He kept looking over his shoulder, thinking someone was spying on him.... He was like a man obsessed; he told me that evening that because he was a Catholic and because he was in the Army, he felt that he could personally bring the two sides together. In that sense, I think he was living out a fantasy and in his personal life quite definitely did."[22]

Teachers at Ampleforth and fellow officers commented on his similarities to T.E. Lawrence, his "need to come first" and that he was "personally desperate for success."[23] After his death his mother said: "all he ever wanted was to help bring peace to that troubled land."[24] All of this adds up to a man obsessed by the idea of himself as the self-elected *Boys' Own* hero who charges into the conflict and saves the day. Moreover it helps explain his conviction that he could patrol the streets of Crossmaglen in uniform by day and visit the pubs as "Danny McAlevey" at night; or that shaggy hair and a false moustache could hide his identity at the Three Steps. After all, when Superman swoops into town, who recognizes Clark Kent?

On Saturday 14 May 1977, the night of his death, Robert Nairac left Bessbrook Army Camp at 9:25 p.m. in a red Triumph Toledo.[25] He told the operations officer, Captain David Allan Collett,[26] that he was going to the Three Steps Inn at Drumintee, gave no reason for the visit, but said he would return to base at 11:30 p.m. At 9:50 p.m. he reported that he was travelling towards Drumintee, and at 9:58 p.m. that he had reached the Three Steps and was closing down radio contact. This was his second visit to the Three Steps in two days, and rumor later had it that he had been there several times in previous weeks. The landlord saw a red Triumph Toledo come from the Jonesboro Road and park at the top of the car park facing the main road. The man who got out of the car wore dark clothes, had bushy hair and a moustache.

4. British Intelligence and the Army

The John Murphy Band, from Creggan, Crossmaglen, was playing to a crowded bar that Saturday night. People later told police that they had seen Nairac, and that a number of men showed an interest in him and checked up on his conversations. The barman remembered serving him twice, each time with a pint of Guinness and twenty cigarettes, and Edmund Murphy, a member of the band, noticed him:

> He was in the company of some people. There might have been four or six involved. He went to the toilet about three times. At 11.15 when he was coming out of the toilet, he asked me if a Belfast man could sing a song. I told him to write it down on a piece of paper. He said "no" and I was just to call it out.[27] He gave his name as Danny McElean.[28] After singing he rejoined the same people at the bar. The band finished playing at 11.35pm and began to pack up, and one of the band, perhaps noticing, as others did, that he seemed to be agitated, offered him a lift, but he declined.

In the car park of the Three Steps Inn, Nairac was going towards his car when a man behind him (Terry McCormick) called on him to halt. As he got to the car Nairac stopped and reached for his pistol, but McCormick, who was well-known for his boxing ability, punched him on the jaw, at the same time throwing his arm wide and knocking the pistol out of Nairac's hand. Three men ran up and joined in the struggle, Nairac was overpowered and bundled into a car. The gun was picked up and brought with the party.[29]

Two cars drove with Nairac over the border towards Ravensdale Forest; they turned left on the Newry-Dundalk Road and crossed the River Flurry. In the field on the left beside the little hump-backed bridge the men took from him his holster, the spare magazine for his gun and a driving license with a Belfast address, then he was beaten and interrogated. Nairac claimed that he was a Stickie[30] from Belfast. He even gave an authentic name of an Official IRA man, Seamus Murphy, from Dundalk, but he did not admit that he was a soldier.

Two of the men were sent to get "Townson or some of the boys."[31] While they were waiting Nairac made a futile escape attempt, and in the ensuing struggle McCormick was accidentally shot.[32] After the arrival of Liam Townson Nairac made another escape attempt, endured another beating and was shot dead. Townson went home across the fields immediately. The rest of the group scattered. Fr. Murray wrote, in *The SAS in Ireland*: "Someone, however, must have moved the body that night. It was seen as late as 10.30 am the next day in a sitting position, legs stretched out, propped against the wall of the bridge. The body must have been moved on Sunday 15 May."[33]

At midnight Nairac was thirty minutes overdue back at Bessbrook Mill and Captain Collett phoned his commanding officer. It was decided that they would give him a few more minutes. At 12:15 a.m. the commanding officer rang Major Clive Fairweather, SAS officer and the intelligence co-ordinator for Northern Ireland[34] and told him that Robert Nairac was missing. They discussed the situation. Nairac had been late before, and, though he had no back-up team, this had also happened previously. They agreed to wait. Two hours later it was decided not to alert very senior officers in case he turned up because, Fairweather said: "we were going to end up getting an awful lot of people out of bed for nothing," but they would send a helicopter to look for him at first light.[35] Fairweather then spent most of the night making and receiving phone calls. Why? To whom?[36] Some may have been to inform the RUC, who were furious that Nairac had gone out alone, especially in that area, and that they had not been informed of his disappearance until 5:45 a.m.[37]

After quite an extraordinary delay, Nairac's car was found at 9 a.m. on Sunday. An RUC man who went to the car park saw bloodstains and a damaged wing mirror. The matter passed out of Fairweather's hands and became a joint RUC-Army operation. Then the search for Nairac began in earnest as troops, helicopters and extra police were drafted into the area, and roadblocks were set up. Conferences and meetings went on all day at Army HQ in Lisburn and at Bessbrook. Nairac's room was searched fruitlessly, nor was there any sign of the Filofax-type notebook full of information that he usually carried. The next day the Provisional IRA issued a statement, summarized later that week in *An Phoblacht*:

> Captain Robert Nairac, an SAS man operating in the South Armagh area, had been arrested and executed, after interrogation, in which he had admitted that he was a member of a SAS unit.
> The statement went on to say that the intelligence department of the First Battalion had had a number of photographs of SAS members and that Captain Nairac had been recognised from one of these and arrested ... the execution was in retaliation for a series of incidents in the south Armagh area by the SAS, including the murder of Peter Cleary.... The usual fate of spies captured in wartime is execution.[38]

Media interest began only when Cardinal Hume, who had known Nairac when he was at school at Ampleforth, made an appeal for his safe return before anyone realized that he must be dead. When the appeal appeared in the newspapers, Fr. Murray wrote: "British Intelligence was in hot water. His disappearance hit the headlines. It had questions to answer. It directed attention from itself by making him a hero. He was given the George Cross in record time. Medals usually come slowly and proceed from citations down the line. This one came from the top. The move diverted the press from investigating."[39]

For a time *Republican News* carried a comic strip called "Captain Nervewreck," about an incompetent ex-public schoolboy with a taste for adventure,[40] but otherwise the diversion worked until Fred Holroyd's allegations were first made public by Channel Four in 1984. Since then, over the years, of all the soldiers killed in Northern Ireland, Nairac's name is the one which has resurfaced continually, in books and newspapers, even including an article, "Shadow Man," in *Esquire*.[41] Then Liam Patrick Townson, a twenty-four-year-old unemployed joiner from Dromintee, living in Dundalk,[42] was arrested by Gardaí on 28 May and charged with the murder. Dublin's Special Criminal Court found him guilty of murder on 8 November 1977 and he was given a life sentence.

Just over a year later five men from South Armagh[43] were convicted in connection with the murder by Lord Justice Gibson at a Diplock Court in Northern Ireland[44] and given sentences ranging from 3 years to 22 years. "The impression of observers at the trial was that the British Army was embarrassed by the whole affair and did not push the case to extremes; all the men sentenced in the North were released in minimum periods."[45] Two of the other men, Crilly and Maguire, went on the run in the Republic after the murder, and McCormick went to the United States. No attempt was made to extradite them. Nairac's body has never been found, nor has his Filofax notebook.

In the furor of speculation and comment about the disappearance of the body, the IRA were the first to capitalize on the possibilities offered by propaganda. Having classified Nairac as a member of the SAS in the original statement about his murder, they followed this up in the same edition of *An Phoblacht*, and on the same page, with the headline: "Brits admit Nairac was a spy" and quoted the MOD as saying that "Captain Robert Nairac, 'on occasions would have been' actively working with the SAS."[46] Nor would it have escaped the attention of the people of South Armagh that only a few weeks earlier *An Phoblacht* had run an article stating that: "[A] Brit SAS unit has been using the roof of St. Joseph's Intermediate School at Crossmaglen as a secret spy post over the past two months and had deliberately contaminated the school's water supply system ... by using the school's water supply as a toilet they had threatened the health of pupils and teachers.... The school management confirmed that the water contains deleterious matter and that sanitary authority officials have been called in."[47]

So successful was the assertion that he belonged to the SAS that all those writing about Nairac in the years following his death have gone to inordinate pains to clarify the position occupied by a Grenadier Guards officer working for and with the SAS. Clive Fairweather, though, advanced the theory that Nairac himself had been telling people that he was in the SAS, because he was just a captain, so low in the pecking order, and tended to overstate his own importance. Fairweather had received quite a lot of intelligence reports that "they were going to get the curly-headed SAS man"[48]; he had warned Nairac about this and been ignored.

There is much evidence in *Secret Hero*, John Parker's biography of Robert Nairac, that all the characteristics leading almost inexorably to his death were already present in Nairac from his schooldays. He *had* to be a hero, but a hero needs a cause, he found it in Ireland and convinced himself that he alone had the necessary qualifications to solve the problems. From this point on obsession and fantasy were intertwined. Even the fact of his being a loner fits in with this hypothesis—the *Boys' Own* hero is always alone, and this adds to his heroism. Moreover, the falsity of this superimposed character is possibly one reason why so many of his fellow soldiers were very uneasy about him.

It is undoubtedly true that Nairac spent far too long in Northern Ireland, and that he gradually became ever more a loner as time went on, until he reached the point where he imagined that donning a false moustache and wearing scruffy clothes, together with his accent and his knowledge of the Ardoyne made him invulnerable. It is probable that there was also an element of "thick Micks" in his thinking. It may or may not be true, as Fred Holroyd claimed, that he and Tony Ball were linked to the killing of John Francis Green, the Miami Showband massacre and other Loyalist activities. Nairac's records have still not ben released, so we cannot know for certain. But it is also true that his senior officers should have called a halt to his questionable activities, thus perhaps preventing the sadness of this young man's clumsy death in the ultimate isolation of a field in Ireland at the hands of a makeshift gang of very amateur Republicans.

A member of the IRA told Martin Dillon:

> Nairac was out in the open. IRA intelligence reckoned that he was possibly a decoy and was there to entice would-be informers to approach him or to draw attention away from somebody more important than himself who was operating in the same area. There was also a recognised possibility that he genuinely believed he was in deep cover and that his cover was good enough to fool people. IRA intelligence was content to wait and watch. By the time of the Three Steps Inn episode he was someone who knew the neighbourhood and many of its occupants but he had changed his image from the guy who was seen around Crossmaglen. That would not have fooled the IRA, but he might well have thought that it would.[49]

Finally, a question that never seems to have been asked: according to Dillon, McCormick was not a member of the IRA, how then did he know that "Townson or one of the boys" would come out in the early hours of the morning to shoot Nairac? Had the IRA been watching Nairac's visits to the Three Steps? Had they used McCormick to set him up? Perhaps the answer lies in John Weir's statement:

> Captain Robert Nairac ... had infiltrated both sides, Loyalist and Republican, in an attempt to intensify the conflict so that each side would wipe each other out. A Republican informant, the late Packy Reel, from Dorsey, South Armagh told me ... that Nairac had supplied explosives to the IRA and I knew from my Loyalist contacts in Portadown that Nairac was involved with Robin Jackson. Reel told me that Nairac had informed him, and therefore the IRA, that police and security forces were

responsible for the attacks on Donnelly's Bar and that he (Nairac) had given Reel the names of those responsible.... Reel explained that the IRA had, for a time, believed Nairac to be sympathetic to their cause, which was the reason he had been allowed to participate in IRA meetings; but that Nairac's cover had been blown when he was recognised at the Army shooting of IRA activist Peter Cleary[50] in South Armagh. Nairac paid the price for his attempt to play off both sides.[51]

It is entirely possible that, if Robert Nairac had not died, today he would be a 59-year-old nonentity. It was his death which made him a *cause célèbre*, the darling of the media and a hero posthumously (and very hastily) awarded the George Cross for his exploits. Moreover, the multitude of unanswered (and, so far, unanswerable) questions surrounding both his activities and the manner of his death have ensured that, even after the passage of many years, interest in him remains high.

Notwithstanding the Nairac debacle the army was undeterred, informers were still needed, though there was plainly a tacit decision to use soldiers native to Northern Ireland and the days of 14 Int were numbered. By the 1980s it was decided to set up the Force Research Unit (FRU), to recruit and handle informers from all parts of Northern Ireland, especially those who were members of paramilitary organizations. "Rob Lewis," a soldier in the FRU, tells of their approach to the task: "Potential targets for recruitment would normally be ... close friends and associates of known terrorists, any of the known players rumored to be disenchanted with the situation in the Province, and neighbors who could report sightings and other low-level information."[52] He adds the following information about the search for suitable recruits: "Numerous weeks, often months, were spent searching for the character who was able to move freely within this community without suspicion, was accepted without question, and was brave enough to provide the intelligence we needed."[53]

So the army intensified its efforts to find locally born soldiers to provide the necessary information, and later recruits came from a totally different background to that of Nairac, as can be seen in the following accounts of Peter Keeley and Willie Carlin. Both men were natives of Northern Ireland who became British soldiers, thus they had a fund of local knowledge and would obey orders. It means, also, that some credence must be given to their insistence that they are agents, not touts. Nevertheless, a look at the initial training of both men, when they began to betray friends and acquaintances, casts a great deal of doubt on their denials. Neither of them, certainly in the eyes of the British army, was a soldier for long, so, for the purposes of this work, the difference in title is arguably only semantic. This period, and, in particular, the career of Brian Nelson discussed below, is full of complications, accusations, and counter-accusations. Therefore, to simplify some of these, it is necessary to look briefly at the Stevens Enquiry of 2003 and the Cory Inquiry of 2004.

The Stevens Enquiry, which began in September 1989 as a direct result of the murder of Loughlin Maginn by the UDA a month earlier, lasted for a period of some fourteen years. This was an official British Government inquiry into collusion in Northern Ireland between loyalist paramilitaries and the state security forces. It was led by Sir John Stevens and ultimately became three inquiries with Stevens 3 finally published on 17 April 2003, despite the obstruction the investigators identified as "cultural in its nature and widespread within parts of the army and the RUC."[54] A notable incident in this obstruction was the burning of the Enquiry's offices, together with all the documentation held there in January 1990, previous to the first interview with Brian Nelson. However, the investigative team had taken the precaution of keeping copies of all documents elsewhere. Stevens 3 also includes a brief but damning summary of the findings of the Enquiry: "My Enquiries have highlighted collusion, the wilful failure to keep records, the absence of accountability, the withholding of intelligence and evidence, and the extreme of agents being involved in murder. These serious acts and omissions have meant that people have been killed or seriously injured."[55]

The reports of both the Stevens Enquiry of 2003 and the Cory Inquiry of 2004 were a response to allegations of collusion between the security forces and the loyalist paramilitaries, and both covered the murder of Pat Finucane, while Cory alone covered the later murders of Robert Hamill (a Catholic from Portadown), Rosemary Nelson (a human rights lawyer), and Billy Wright (the LVF leader, killed in 1997).

Mr. Justice Cory produced separate reports covering the allegations of collusion in each of the above-mentioned deaths and sets out his task in a foreword: "I had the preliminary role of assessing whether there is a case to be answered as to possible collusion ... by members of the security forces in these deaths such as to warrant further and more detailed inquiry."[56] Cory makes it clear that, unlike Stevens who interviewed all those involved, he looked only at the documentary evidence and found that in each case "there are matters of concern which would warrant further and more detailed inquiry."[57] Common to both reports is the inexorable pointing towards Douglas Hogg's statement to the House of Commons on 17 January 1989: "some solicitors were unduly sympathetic to the cause of the IRA."[58]

"Kevin Fulton"

Peter Keeley (later known almost universally as Kevin Fulton) was born c. 1960 in Newry, Co. Down. His grandfather had fought during World War II, and his stories imbued the boy with a strong desire to be a British soldier. In 1973, when Fulton was thirteen, Kevin Heatley, a Newry boy of his own age,

4. British Intelligence and the Army

was killed by a British soldier. This resulted in a parental curfew. For the next three years Fulton had to be home every evening by seven o'clock, and consoled himself by reading *Boy's Own* and military adventure books, waiting for the day when he could be a soldier. He also began to realize that his ambitions would come up against resistance from his family, so, at sixteen, he joined the merchant navy. Six months later he returned home and began to look for a job. His search culminated in his joining the army without telling his family, who thought he had gone to sea again. His deception was later aided by his FRU handlers who arranged for postcards from him to be sent from all over the world. His horrified mother finally discovered the truth by accident.

In 1979 Fulton was interviewed by "Andy" and "Gerry" from their army HQ at Bessbrook. He claims that he was eager to impress them, agreeing not only to identify photographs of Newry people, but also to lie to his fellow soldiers, if necessary, about his association with the two intelligence men. All these things: easy money, secrecy, and lies leading to betrayal, set a pattern from which Kevin Fulton was seldom to deviate in the years to come, and, presaging the future, the first photograph he identified for Andy and Gerry was that of an old school friend. Later he was to write of himself: "I'm not a grass. I'm not someone who crossed over to the other side to save my own skin. I was a British soldier, actively recruited by British military intelligence for the specific task of infiltrating the IRA, and working my way up within the organisation. Which is exactly what I did."[59]

From Fulton's account, which, like the majority of books written by informers and the security forces, is intended to paint the author as hero, and thus is, in the main, both unreliable and exaggerated, it appears that the FRU men were skilled at their job. He depicts them as beguiling him with exciting stories about espionage and intrigue, thus making his months of looking at photographs and his gossip about IRA sympathizers seem innocuous. At the men's request he introduced them to two other friends, and watched as Andy and Gerry rapidly made themselves indispensable companions to the two, open-handed when they all went out together, joking about simple ways of earning money, until "they had two willing and watching sets of eyes in the heart of two housing estates in Newry."[60]

At the same time Fulton's grooming continued at their weekly meetings until they finally told him he was the perfect recruit for military intelligence, if he was interested. If Fulton is to be believed the prospect frightened him and he asked himself "How could a squaddie with few qualifications be of such worth to British military intelligence?"[61] But he had already delivered up three of his friends (the first was the old school friend), and this could not have gone unnoticed by the FRU.

There followed a prolonged period of fears and reassurances. The FRU men had all the answers: he would be given a dishonorable discharge from the Army on fictitious but convincing grounds for the benefit of IRA inquiries; he would still receive his Army pay each week, in cash; he would be a hero, saving lives; his security would be their main priority. "The fact that I wouldn't have to do anything I didn't want to was probably the single most persuasive factor of all."[62] A hated transfer to Berlin made up Fulton's mind, so, on 26 May 1981 Kevin Fulton was discharged from the British Army and began his new career.

However, Fulton's motivation was not confined to his idea of a newfound personal freedom. He does not admit a fact obvious to those who read *Unsung Hero*: that a soldier's life had become the last thing he wanted. In addition, the flattery implicit in his situation may have drowned out his misgivings:

> Chosen by military intelligence ... that was the second major spur for me. Here I was, a lowly teenage squaddie with no formal qualifications, being groomed for a role as a special agent, to become their man in Newry, and getting paid my Army wage to live out this Boy's Own adventure! That I had been singled out by Andy and Gerry—two men of unquestioned calibre and standing—made me feel ten feet tall. I was bowled over.[63]

Few lives can be so empty of people important enough to warrant more than a walk-on role as Fulton's memoir would indicate. Andy and Gerry, the men from military intelligence who flatter him are omnipresent, the wife he married in March 1984 is not. He admits that he lied to her from the start because he was protecting her,[64] and this may indeed be true, just as her anonymity and infrequent presence in the book may have been for the same reason. His readers, however, would be forgiven for gathering that Fulton's sympathies have always and only been for himself, the "Special Agent," never "the informer," and for his solution to his financial problems: £130 per week from military intelligence; a job in the local meat factory; bed and breakfast guests in their house, and a plan to hijack a lorry. Both the lies and the decision to steal the lorry's contents are the first definite evidence of a dishonesty patent throughout the rest of his career.

The hijack plan went badly wrong and the FRU men, disinclined to dealings with either the RUC or the law courts, told him to admit his crime to the RUC. He was sentenced to two years in Crumlin Road Prison and, given a week's parole in July 1986, he rang his handlers, was given an offhand reception, and found that he was now a liability: "I suddenly realized a terrifying truth.... My life was literally in their hands."[65] There was nobody else he could rely on for money and an escape route.

Fulton had previously made overtures to the IRA in Dundalk, in accordance with instructions from his handlers, only to be frightened off by a nasty joke masquerading as an initiation ritual. Fulton and a friend, invited to meet the top IRA man in Dundalk, were greeted by hooded men with guns, thrown to the floor, stripped, blindfolded, and interrogated, before being hauled off for execution as touts. Then, abruptly, they were taken back upstairs, the blindfolds were removed, and the hooded men laughed at them.[66] Nevertheless on his release from prison in November 1986 he contacted them again, hoping at the same time to repair his reputation with his handlers. This time he had some credibility: he had done his time and named no names; the police were convinced he was an IRA man; and he was accepted by Dundalk IRA men "Conor"[67] and "Niall."[68] This friendship led to many introductions among the Provisional IRA in Dundalk, as well as to the discovery that "all these men suspected each other of being a tout. Paranoia ruled supreme."[69] This was, of course, the point of Kitson's strategy.

Once again Andy and Gerry took charge. On their instructions he bought an ice-cream van with a secret compartment in the back, and they installed a hidden video camera above the windscreen. There followed a period as cross-border IRA messenger and chauffeur for Conor. Fulton began running guns, helping to build bombs, and getting to know many Provisionals. Yet, after nearly seven years, he was not a member of the IRA, and now Conor told him he had to join them. His handlers were delighted, but Fulton was reluctant. The reasons he gives for this reluctance are unconvincing, and include the amazing statement that "I feared I would find their historical justifications for the mindless slaughter of innocent people hard to swallow. I dreaded it."[70] Yet he had swallowed much the same from Andy and Gerry without difficulty and would later swallow even more, as, for instance, when his new MI5 handlers "Bob" and "Pete" said to him: "Another IRA person gets shot, ... so what? Another dead Provie is hardly bad news for anyone, is it? And it's the ultimate cover for you. Who'd ever suspect that someone executing informants is an agent?"[71] However, a warning from Niall, his IRA tutor, jolted Fulton into reality about the dangers he would face from every quarter if he continued along this path: "You know, ... all the IRA can offer you is heartache. It's a shit life, being a volunteer. You go to prison. Your loved ones go through hell. You lose friends. You lose loved ones. All the time you're half-expecting to be arrested, or blown up, or shot. If the Army or the police or the Orangemen don't get you, the stress will.... I've had two heart attacks ... and I'm not yet thirty."[72]

From time to time, throughout Fulton's account of his life as an IRA man, he protests his horror at his own actions: one of his bombs narrowly missed killing a sleeping child, and he had to kneecap Eoin Morley.[73] However, it is noticeable that his qualms seemed to apply only to what happened in front of him (and they lessened a great deal as time went on), while his plan (in September 1988) that the IRA should attack forty British soldiers in Germany is only detailed because he was pursued around Paris by a mysterious man in black.[74] The overall impression is that he was far more efficient and useful to the IRA than to the British Army, and scattered throughout this narrative of nefarious activities is the constant defense: "I wanted to use my position in the Provisional IRA actively to prevent someone from being murdered. If I could save more lives than I helped to take, then my role as a special agent would be worthwhile and justifiable."[75] At the same time he pleads frequently for sympathy and understanding: "I lived every minute of every day with the terror of being shot by a Loyalist death squad or by the SAS ... being harassed, threatened and abused by the RUC ... I began to receive death threats on the phone at all hours of the day and night."[76] While, in what seem likely to be the ghostwriters' words rather than Fulton's, he excuses his actions by telling us: "In my full-time role as a double agent, I was losing any sense of myself. When I was with my comrades in the Provisional IRA, I morphed into a character I no longer felt any emotional attachment to.... I stopped feeling the pain and the doubts and the anguish—all those emotions which would hinder my efficiency as a double agent. I was becoming de-sensitized, de-humanized, robotic."[77]

The year 1991 brought several changes. His handlers were now Pete, from the FRU, and Bob, of MI5; Fulton made an effort to get away, took a painting job at Euro Disney in Paris, in August 1991, and enjoyed a feeling of freedom for just two weeks until, he claims, the security services leaked information about his being an IRA man to the *Sunday Express*.[78] A week later Fulton returned to Northern Ireland where he was promoted to the IRA's security unit.[79]

Many of Fulton's claims about his own suffering and sacrifices must be viewed askance. Nevertheless, his attempted escape to Paris after twelve years as an informer attests to a degree of stress arising from this life, and perhaps this, together with his brief weeks of freedom there, was responsible for another bout of rational thinking on his return, when he discovered that his handlers, far from seeing added danger in his promotion, were overjoyed by it. He began to wonder about the real priorities of Pete and Bob, and came to an uncomfortable conclusion, which may be retrospective thinking. "I began to wonder if, to them and their colleagues in MI5 and the Force Research Unit, Northern Ireland was one big elaborate playground where they had carte blanche to do exactly as they pleased ... if it was in anyone's interest for the war to cease ... [because] If the war ended, so would their power, status and influence."[80]

Despite these alleged reservations, the betrayals went on. "Johnny" had been Fulton's fellow bomb-making graduate[81] who had escaped to New York with a fake passport provided by Fulton in the name of his own completely innocent brother-in-law. The FBI now wanted Johnny, and Fulton obliged: "Even though I liked Johnny as a person, he was an IRA bomb-maker. He deserved what was coming to him."[82] Fulton had begun his career by betraying a friend, now his betrayal of his friend Johnny was almost his last act as an informer for the FRU.

February 1994 saw him arrested by the RUC, sent to Castlereagh, and interrogated about the attempted murder of Derek Martindale, a senior RUC man. He was not ill-treated, but he was terrified of discovery, and found that his wife had also been arrested. Following this came the disputed interrogation by the Nutting Squad[83]; then his agitated demand that his handlers should keep the promises made to him and pull him out of Northern Ireland. His request was refused, on the grounds that he had not been discovered, so he went to London independently and, several increasingly panicky phone calls later, realized he was on his own, an expendable liability to his former employers.

Kevin Fulton takes every opportunity in *Unsung Hero* to emphasize his fear, his risks, his sacrifices, and the constant stress he suffered during the years of providing intelligence to his FRU handlers. Yet he did not take this opportunity to turn his life around, nor did he stay away from Northern Ireland. Indeed, in a self-serving statement about not knowing what to put on his CV if he applied for a job, despite his every previous claim of having been a soldier, he writes instead about an inevitable drifting "back into the one field I knew about."[84] Thus he became an informer to HM Customs about IRA smuggling operations, then to the RUC anti-racketeering squad. He gives no dates for these activities and HM Customs refused to confirm or deny employing him.[85] This state of affairs makes his own self-pitying epitaph pure nonsense: "I had spent the past twenty years in a near-constant state of anxiety, but with my cover blown—and without the safety net of relocation—I would be looking over my shoulder until the day I died.... But they'll get me in the end."[86] It was this very situation which was to lead to his subsequent notoriety, aided as much by his sudden addiction to self-promotion as by the investigation report of the Police Ombudsman for Northern Ireland into the aftermath of the Omagh bombing.

The Omagh Bomb: 15 August 1998

Fulton's allegations that he had warned the RUC about the Omagh bomb beforehand were published on 29 July 2001, in the *Sunday People*. Shorn of newspaper rhetoric, his claims were that he had passed information to his CID handler five times between June and August 1998[87]; and that information passed on 13 August 1998, was specifically about an imminent bomb attack.[88] He did not mention Omagh, but this did not prevent the newspaper using it as the headline ("I told cops about Omagh") and suggesting in the body of the article that the attack could have been prevented if the RUC had acted on Fulton's information. This article gave rise to the Ombudsman's investigation,[89] and the furor among the people of Northern Ireland which followed publication of the article must have been the spur for Fulton's next career change: interviewee for journalists writing about informers or the IRA generally which, in turn, gave rise to his spate of accusations naming senior IRA men as informers. As well as offering (for a price) to name Stakeknife, he pointed the finger at such people as Sean Mag Uidhir, editor of the *North Belfast News*, but, as Mick Hall asks in *The Blanket*, how would Fulton know? "We can take it for granted that all agents and informers working within the Republican Movement are not given a Christmas party once a year organized by their employers, the British State, at which they swap notes and stories about each other."[90] Gerard Bradley, who had known Fulton in Newry in 1993, said with equal disbelief: "Who was fighting the war when Keeley was running around? Because it seems to me that he was only consorting with a convention of Brit agents. Everyone he ... met now seems to have been an agent."[91]

This whole whistleblowing exercise culminated in Fulton's forming a team of sixteen informers to make a video revealing the identities of senior British intelligence officers, disclosing the handlers' techniques, and publicizing some of the worst operations of the British security forces in Northern Ireland in 2002. Supposedly aimed at exposing the truth behind the so-called "Dirty War," given Fulton's past record it comes as no surprise that the video, "Agents: No More Lies." was intended as an instrument of blackmail. They wanted their criminal records cleared, relocation packages, and full military pensions. He is quoted as saying "We want to get this information out so the MoD will honor its debt to us. If the MoD settled our disputes, this video would never see the light of day."[92]

As with so much in Northern Ireland's Troubles, there are unanswered questions about Kevin Fulton's activities, as well as conflicting answers, and a great deal of confusion, but it becomes abundantly clear in the whole Fulton/Keeley story that his motivation was financial. During his initial interview with the RUC, for instance, Fulton said he had been working as an informant with the Irish Customs in Dublin, but no longer wished to do so because they paid badly (he had been paid £750 for information about a large shipment of drugs). In 1997 information about a bank robbery, and IRA money laundering brought him "Participating Informant" status, a reward of £5,000 from the bank, and £12,000 paid in three stages from the RUC.[93]

Far from maintaining early protestations about his moral dilemma, he had long thought of his activities as simply a job. This is clearly evidenced by his return to informing after his escape to London, though perhaps it would be more correct at this juncture to use the word "spying." The Cryptome website is American, and, in its own words, "welcomes documents for publication that are prohibited by governments worldwide, in particular material on ... national security, intelligence, and secret governance"; much of its content is anonymous, unproven, even perhaps unprovable, and so possibly unreliable as a source, nevertheless it contains much that is of interest to this study.[94] In particular the file "SECRET," allegedly the statement of Detective Sergeant "Z" who became Fulton's Drugs Squad handler at Belfast's Antrim Road Police Station in June 1996.[95] "Z" supplies two other useful pieces of information: "Money appeared to be the motivation for Fulton. Most of the information that he supplied was accurate and yielded results"; and "As his handler I had never encouraged or tasked him to seek information from any terrorist organisation."[96] Nevertheless he notes that on 5 January 1998, Fulton began to give information about IRA members in Dundalk, and that he had since been told by Special Branch that "Fulton had told lies and had made tape recordings of conversations with officers."[97]

Kevin Fulton survives and, presumably, continues to pursue his trade in the secrets of others. His career has developed from the informer betraying his own to the informant who will betray anyone at all provided that the money is right. Did that career shape his character, or vice versa? Do we consider such factors as personal responsibility and the conscienceless actions of the eighteen-year-old boy from Newry? Or can we point the finger inexorably (and simplistically), as Martin Ingram does, and say "Kevin Fulton was a British agent actively encouraged to take part in operations that were immoral, and illegal."[98] As a teenager Kevin Fulton inveigled his young friends into following his example, in order to enhance his own standing with his first handlers; and over the years he used all those with whom he came in contact to further his own ends. Greed and self-interest have always been his watchword, and his more recent actions have done nothing to disprove this.

William Carlin[99]

Willie Carlin was born into a Catholic family in Derry and served for nine years as a soldier in the Queen's Royal Irish Hussars until, in 1974, he was recruited by MI5 to infiltrate the IRA. "The recruiting routine was the same for all of them. At first they were asked if they recognized photographs of potential republican sympathizers. Secret meetings with senior officers over tea and biscuits continued for several months until the soldiers were finally asked if they would be prepared to go back home to take part in what was called 'The Programme,' i.e. infiltrating the IRA."[100]

Following his return to Derry it took him a number of years to become sufficiently acceptable in republican circles, but eventually in 1982 he joined Sinn Féin as a party worker in Derry, and began to come into contact with such senior republicans as Martin McGuinness and Mitchell McLaughlin. At the same time Carlin was meeting his MI5 handlers, who were based at

Ebrington Barracks, HQ of the British Army's 8 Infantry Brigade, and passing on information about republican political strategy. His main role was allegedly "to report on McGuinness's political development and encourage him and others to abandon their military campaigns for a political solution."[101] It is, however, difficult to attach too much credence to this because it is conceivable that in 1974 Martin McGuinness would not have held this sort of importance for British intelligence; and less than a year after this claim Carlin told another journalist that "the purpose of the FRU ... was to redirect 'loyalist killing gangs' away from sectarian murder towards 'legitimate' republican targets."[102]

Carlin, code named "The Fox," claims that in 1981, after the murder of Joanne Mathers, a Protestant census worker, he began to question his role within Sinn Féin. This did not prevent his helping to organize the Sinn Féin election campaign in 1982 in which McGuinness was elected to the Northern Ireland Assembly, nor does it accord with his activities as an informer, which were, after all, directed towards the subversion of republicanism, not its continuance. Moreover, though he also claims to have distanced himself from both Sinn Féin and MI5 for a time, he again became involved with the FRU and worked for them until 1985. Had this distancing from Sinn Féin been definitive, Carlin would have been of very little use to the FRU. In this context three possibilities are apparent: firstly, that he may have begun to exaggerate the importance of his information to MI5, felt that his financial rewards from them were insufficient to reflect his value and yielded to a higher offer from the FRU; secondly, the distancing may have stemmed from a sudden realization of his dangerous position, until greed forced him to cast around, as did Fulton, for another employer; thirdly, his use to MI5 may have diminished, perhaps he began (as Fulton did later) to rehash old information, and thus became unreliable. Given the tendency to self-importance evident throughout his book, the first explanation seems the most likely.

It is also possible that his elevation to press officer, Sinn Féin treasurer in Derry, and controller of the IRA's fraud and embezzlement scams there, as well as his previous Army background, drew the FRU's attention to him. His informing for the FRU continued until March 1985, when Michael Bettany, while on remand in late 1984 in Wandsworth Prison, became friendly with Pat Magee, a fellow prisoner, and told him of a British informer close to Martin McGuinness in Derry.[103] The description was undoubtedly that of Willie Carlin. This information was relayed back to McGuinness by Magee's republican visitors, an investigation began but Carlin's handlers were told that his cover had been blown. He, his wife, and three children were removed from Northern Ireland on 3 March 1985 and relocated with new identities and a new home.[104] The marriage failed and in 1998 he was living in Dunblane, Scotland, with "Toni," and they decided to write a book about his experiences.

This relationship came to an end in November 2000 and the book was never written. The following year he claimed to be in more danger from British intelligence than from the IRA and moved from Dunblane.

Dealing with the material available on Willie Carlin is not easy. This is, in part, because so many newspaper articles are simply rewritten copies of others, and British newspapers (including the *Sunday Herald*) do their best to put a heroic slant on Carlin's actions, mainly because of the need to defend the British image in Northern Ireland. The factor which causes most of the confusion, though, is the difference between what Carlin is alleged to have said in one interview, and what he has said to a different journalist some time later. His initial claim to have known Martin McGuinness well is at the very least doubtful. McGuinness said of him that "although Mr. Carlin was associated with the Sinn Fein in the Waterside he hardly knew him and Mr. Carlin had manufactured the alleged conversations."[105] Of these two opposing claims made to the Saville Inquiry (1998), it seems obvious that McGuinness's would be the easiest to disprove, given his high profile in Derry, yet there appears to be no evidence of refutation. This, of course, casts further doubt on every other claim made by Carlin. Perhaps this is another instance of the phenomenon so prevalent among the Northern Ireland informers: a tendency to overestimate their own importance. Compare Carlin's alleged escape in the Prime Ministerial jet, and Fulton's words to Neil Mackay: "I was told there'll be no medals for this, and no recognition, but this goes the whole way to the Prime Minister. The Prime Minister knows what you are doing."[106] What *is* known, however, is that "Thatcher did grant the FRU extra funding to recruit agents in the wake of the IRA's Remembrance Day bombing in Enniskillen" in November 1987.[107] Thus it is necessary to bear in mind that the fact that a man was an informer, and that he lived a lie for many years, does not automatically mean that he is a liar now. Nevertheless, once judgment of Carlin's post-informing activities is based on his habit of exaggeration, and an addiction to self-aggrandizement in the press, much of the confusion disappears, especially in view of the Kitson influence.

During the spate of publicity over Carlin's "heroic" decision to give evidence to the Saville Inquiry he told the press an increasingly extravagant series of facts, most of which he could not have been in a position to know: that Martin McGuinness had, through Michael Oatley, been working with MI6 since 1974, and that this had been sanctioned by the IRA Army Council; that the British purpose was to facilitate the IRA's way into politics, and so Carlin had been encouraged to rig the 1982 Northern Ireland Assembly elections; that John Francis Green was assassinated by loyalists acting on information received by the British Army; that "loyalist attackers were 'encouraged,' and given bomb-making training to plant car-bombs in Dublin and Monaghan which killed 33 people in 1974."[108] At the same time Carlin was one of

Fulton's team of informers who, still in pursuit of their perceived rights, requested a meeting with the Taoiseach, which made for headlines, but looks less impressive when seen from the Dublin viewpoint: A spokesman for the Department of Foreign Affairs said "A group of people claiming to be former British agents wrote to the Taoiseach requesting a meeting. They were given a standard reply as you or I would if we made such a request."[109]

It also makes for different thinking about Carlin's contact with MPs Michael Martin, Tam Dalyell, and Andrew Hunter in the hope that they would bring the matter of the informers' army pensions to the attention of Parliament. This was, presumably, following his co-ordination of earlier attempts by the group to gain political support for their aims. Their constant publicity-seeking efforts showed that they had a poor grasp of reality, like most of the other informers of their era, nevertheless only two (Carlin and Fulton, together with Martin Ingram) are named in the newspaper reports.

Speaking for this moles's union, Carlin claimed that all contact with handlers ceased in 1998 with the Good Friday Agreement, that their regimental records showed only that they were discharged from the Army, and that the MoD was dismissive, advising them to contact the police if they felt threatened. He described himself and his fellow informers as "victims of the ceasefire" because "We were officially discharged from the Army so as not to raise suspicion, but we were told by the Army we would be taken care of financially."[110] There can be little doubt that Willie Carlin, the man who could write as recently as 2007 about many of his friends, including Martin McGuinness, now being in high places, is still lying.[111] Moreover, given that, even in recent newspaper accounts, the activity of informers in Northern Ireland is still widely acknowledged, only a man steeped in the fantasy of his own importance could possibly imagine that his country owes him anything.[112]

Taking into consideration all the ingredients contributing to the "Dirty War," not least of which was the use made of the media in both Britain and Ireland, the addition of all these efforts to gain publicity must bring us close to wondering if Italian journalist Silvio Cerulli is right when he says in his article about Fred Scappaticci: "One thing seems certain: nobody can discount that Carlin, Fulton, Martin Ingram and the other 'rebels' may not still be in the pay of the Crown."[113]

Stakeknife

On the surface the saga of the unmasking of Fred Scappaticci is just one more instance of treachery in high places within the hierarchy of the IRA, if rather more sensational than most given Scappaticci's former place in that organization as one of the triumvirate known as the Nutting Squad.[114] However, analysis of the evidence, and of both Scappaticci and Martin Ingram, ultimately his principal accuser, provides a different picture.

"It was 8:10 p.m. on Saturday, 10 May 2003, and Scappaticci had just been named on an American spy website[115] as Stakeknife, the jewel in the crown of the British Army's network of agents inside the republican movement."[116] Liam Clarke, Northern Ireland editor of the *Sunday Times*, had revealed the existence of an Army agent called Steak Knife in 1999.[117] It was later said that the agent had been trained in interrogation techniques in Libya in the 1980s, and was paid £80,000 per year for his information, but the money remained largely untouched in a secret bank account in Gibraltar. The Stakeknife name appears to have emerged in 2000 in connection with the Stevens Enquiry,[118] with the balance of opinion (including that of Sir John Stevens, who referred to "the legend of Stakeknife")[119] inclining towards thinking it merely rumor. The *Telegraph* wrote: "There may be no Stakeknife—or if such an agent exists, he may not be the man whose name was bandied about over the weekend. He may be somebody even higher up in the IRA, whose identity the security services are trying to protect. In the world of espionage and counter-espionage, countless lies are told."[120] Martin Ingram later stated: "There are still some within republicanism who believe Stakeknife was not a person but the codeword for all intelligence-gathering operations inside the IRA."[121] Given that the FRU is alleged to have had a separate team for dealing with Stakeknife, such thinking cannot be easily dismissed. Could any informer in Northern Ireland possibly be so prolific as to occupy the attention of a team of people, while at the same time safeguarding his own anonymity? And safeguard it he did, for the above scanty facts were all that was known for certain about Stakeknife in May 2003.

Of Scappaticci, however, a good deal is known. He was born into a republican family in the Markets area of West Belfast in the late 1940s, became a bricklayer, was a low-level IRA member in the 1970s, and was interned in Long Kesh in 1971. He came to prominence only in 1991 when Danny Morrison was tried on charges of falsely imprisoning Sandy Lynch.[122] By May 2003, however, Scappaticci was living in Andersonstown and had been inactive in the IRA for about thirteen years. What information, then, could he have been passing on to the dedicated FRU team?

Sandy Lynch's story of his imprisonment is unpleasant,[123] but far more repulsive, if true, is the now often quoted occasion when Eamon Collins nervously asked Scappaticci if they always told people they were going to be shot.[124] Whether or not the following story is true, there can be little doubt that during his time in the internal security unit he was a deeply frightening man, but at the same time the story is not evidence that he was the man known as Stakeknife:

He [Scappaticci] turned to [Magee] and started joking about one informer who had confessed after being offered an amnesty. Scap told the man that he would take him home ... [but] to keep the blindfold on for security reasons as they walked away from the car.

"It was funny," he said, "watching the bastard stumbling and falling, asking me as he felt his way along the railings and walls, 'Is this my house now?' and I'd say, 'No, not yet, walk on some more.'"

"...and then you shot the fucker in the back of the head," said John Joe, and both of them burst out laughing.[125]

Though more and more information about the touts of Northern Ireland is now being revealed, largely by the province's journalists, few in the years under discussion would have known which of their fellows was also an informer, and it would have made little difference if they *had* known. Loyalty was not their watchword and many were ready to kill in order to protect themselves. The *Irish News* claims that in 1996 Mark Haddock, UVF informer to RUC Special Branch, killed Thomas Sheppard, UVF and a suspected informer[126]; while South Belfast UDA commander Stephen "Inch" McFerran, a Special Branch informer, was tried in February 2007 for the killing of Roy Green four years earlier when Green was suspected of informing.[127]

The stories of Stakeknife and Fred Scappaticci as well as that of Kevin Fulton converged on the Cryptome website.[128] The allegations were anonymous, but unleashed hysteria across the media. While it is notable that journalists with some expertise in the doings of Northern Ireland and of the caliber of Ed Moloney[129] neither accepted nor denied that Scappaticci was Stakeknife, much of the subsequent writing veers wildly from acceptance to dismissal. *The Guardian*, for instance, had no less than seven articles about Scappaticci in its edition of 12 May 2003, many of them repetitious and some highly inaccurate. They use the tabloid trademark word "murky," constantly use the names "Stakeknife" and "Scappaticci" as synonyms of each other, and bear few signs of balanced reporting.[130]

There followed a great deal of guesswork about the identity of the anonymous contributor to Cryptome. The *Daily Telegraph* had no doubts: "Stakeknife's identity was exposed by another double agent, a loyalist terrorist with a false identity. He was angry that the IRA man was receiving a better financial and relocation package from the intelligence services than he was."[131] The others who pointed the finger decided it had to be Fulton, because of his previous threats to the MoD to reveal Stakeknife's real name. They might have changed their minds had they read Hansard for the previous January, where Lord Fitt cites an article in the previous Monday's *Irish News*:

> It is understood that one of Fulton's police handlers ... advised the former agent he would receive "compensation" if he dropped threats to reveal the identity of the IRA mole known as "Steak Knife" ... Kevin Fulton, is on record ... [as] having gone to a

British Sunday newspaper and signed a deal for £50,000 that he would identify this mole.... [A] reporter said ... that he was "a notorious double dealer behind a string of dubious hoaxes."[132]

There is, however, a better candidate for the Cryptome revelation than Fulton. Apart from the financial aspect, which Fulton would have been very unlikely to jeopardize, he could not have known Stakeknife, despite his claims, except through his association with Martin Ingram. Ingram was an ex-soldier, he had worked with the FRU, and was co-author of the book *Stakeknife* with Greg Harkin, the journalist. Their book, naming Scappaticci as Stakeknife, was due for publication in 2004 and sales would benefit immensely from the ensuing publicity, while Harkin, of the *Sunday People*, had "been itching to publish Scappaticci's name as Stakeknife for months, but been ... restrained by ferocious injunctions from the Ministry of Defence."[133] The revelation on Cryptome could have cost Harkin his job. Ingram would have had no such inhibitions. Given his constant efforts up until then to propagate the name of Stakeknife, he is the candidate of preference. Moreover, though it could be said that he would not have known Scappaticci, there is the obvious link between Harkin and Ingram—the co-authored book *Stakeknife*, published only one year later. It is possible that the revelation on Cryptome was publicity-seeking. If so, it was a huge success. Certainly Anthony McIntyre wrote later: "It is generally accepted that Ingram was the primary source behind a process which ultimately led to Freddie Scappaticci being identified as Stakeknife."[134] Moreover, despite the injunctions: "The *Sunday People* was evidently not taken by surprise by publication on the internet: it had prepared eight pages on the story."[135]

Scappaticci's response to this sudden shock was not to go on the run. As so often urged in republican newspapers, he consulted Sinn Féin and then a solicitor, Michael Flanigan, who issued a comprehensive denial of all the allegations on behalf of his client: "He is not 'Stakeknife.' He has never been an informer, has never contacted the intelligence services, has never been taken into protective custody and has never received any money from the security services."[136]

The following day, Wednesday 14 May, while it was being reported that Scappaticci had fled to a safe house in Britain, he appeared in an interview on BBC (Northern Ireland) television news. Then his solicitor told the media "Mr. Fred Scappaticci was present at our office today, 14 May 2003.... He has not been in England and during the course of the past few days has not left Northern Ireland.... I have been instructed to examine all the material recently published with a view to defamation proceedings."[137]

Since that time Fred Scappaticci has repeatedly denied that he is Stakeknife. Martin McGuinness said at the time that he believed Scappaticci's denial; Danny Morrison wrote: "the story of Stakeknife is full of holes. Claims about Stakeknife have been used in recent years by British Intelligence in an attempt to sow confusion and fuel Republican dissent"[138]; Gerry Adams said that he should be considered innocent until proven guilty. A comparison can be made here with the death of Paddy Flood in 1990. The FRU wanted him dead, but the shoot-to-kill policy was politically unwise. A former agent said of them "If you wanted a player out of the way and you could get him whacked by his own people you were onto a winner. FRU tricked the Provos into killing Paddy Flood."[139] Moreover, as already noted, one of the British intelligence goals was the spread of disinformation, primarily to alienate the nationalist population from the IRA. This was in keeping with Kitson's ideas, but may also have been the application of common sense to the situation. That the policy never met with much success can only be laid at the feet of all those members of the Crown Forces who failed to differentiate between nationalist and republican, as, for example, in the cases of Pearse Kerr and Brian Maguire. Thus the RUC and the soldiers continued to demonstrate to wide swathes of the population that the enemy was not the Provisionals.

As for Fred Scappaticci, no matter what he did throughout this time he could not shake off either media attention or media theories about his every action, past and present, complete with copious and devious use of the conditional perfect tense. Otherwise there were neither incidents nor attempts on his life, which being a complete departure from the norm seems to indicate that the Provisionals did not believe the media furor and that Scappaticci was, in fact, innocent.

It is necessary to assess Martin Ingram's credibility because he figures so constantly as a provider of information throughout this whole episode. His own words aid in this endeavor: "I spent seven years working for the FRU in Northern Ireland.... Inevitably we talked about our work though each case was meant to be kept secret. My many conversations with my colleagues led me to know the details of most of the cases being handled by the unit."[140] This is not the type of evidence historians would automatically find acceptable, nor would it be good enough for a law court. Though he did spend seven years working for the FRU, he was just twenty years old when he began, with an undistinguished academic record, two years of nameless jobs, and ten weeks in the Parachute Regiment behind him. At this point he was interviewed at Templar Barracks in Ashford, home of the Intelligence Corps, and joined 85 Squadron. His social life took precedence over coursework, so he failed three consecutive weekly tests and, with his friend Kev, was demoted. Given a second chance the two men took precautions. "Each week, usually on the Wednesday night before a Friday exam, we broke into the offices ... and stole the carbon copy which had been used to print the exam papers."[141]

An article by Ingram, reproduced on Cryptome, emphasizes his own credentials and denigrates those of most other people, especially Adams and McGuinness, whom he accuses, albeit obliquely, of being touts.[142] Though he throws doubt on the entire IRA leadership, his main target is McGuinness, whom he dislikes intensely. This article generated much correspondence, most of it saying openly or implying: "Why should we believe Martin Ingram? He could very well still be a British agent." Of these, probably the most interesting noted:

> The person who calls himself Martin Ingram but is in fact ex Int Corps SSgt Ian Hurst (known as rocky) [sic] is a liar of the highest order. His book STEAKNIFE is almost complete fiction, as are his assertions that Martin McGuinness was an agent of the state. He is dementedly lying completely about his past service in FRU. He only ever served in sleepy backwaters of the Province and never came face to face with anyone except low level eyes and ears agents. He never ran STEAKNIFE or even met him. In short, his book is a complete fabrication.[143]

Ingram tells us himself: "It was very much in the interests of British intelligence agencies to sow alarm, despondency and paranoia in IRA ranks by having a regular supply of informers allegedly 'unmasked.'"[144] And "By this stage confusion reigned in republican ranks.... The FRU strategy—to create tension and confusion amongst republicans ... seemed to be working."[145] Moreover, it should be remembered that Ingram was the man who accused Martin McGuinness of working for the British security forces in 2006 thus, once again, unleashing excitement and logorrhoea among the journalists.[146]

Was the alleged outing of Scappaticci ultimately an exercise in manipulation of the press, orchestrated by Martin Ingram in order to spread panic among republicans and destabilize the political climate? The bitter rivalry between the various branches of British intelligence operating in Northern Ireland is well-documented, while divide and conquer is a very old British strategy, and, as Johnston writes, "The apparent unmasking of an informer has the potential to inflict significant damage on current and future operations in the province."[147] So a good many people, not least Ingram himself, benefited from the furor, as did MI5, which had tried for years to wrest control of intelligence in the province from the police. They were to succeed in this in 1993.

Ingram could not possibly have achieved sufficient seniority in the time he worked for the FRU to be given any kind of jurisdiction over Stakeknife, when the informer was llegedly important enough to have his own dedicated team of handlers.[148] From Scappaticci, the denials continued: "Listen, I've been building blocks all day. Does it look as if I've been getting £80,000 a year? ... It's ten years since I was involved with politics. Do you think I'd be here if it was me?"[149] And later spoke again in despair: "I'm a lifelong republican and my reputation's destroyed. I'm just taking one day at a time. I couldn't tell you what I'll be doing in six months.... I'm only fifty-seven, I've another eight years before retirement. I'm just a working class man and now I can't go out to work. My life's been turned upside down."[150]

This is circumstantial evidence; nonetheless it is evidence, and so a better basis for judgement than allegations and trial by media. The Stakeknife story attracted an enormous amount of attention in the media, partly because of its beginnings on a website dedicated to secrets, and partly on Martin Ingram's own efforts to seek publicity for his theorizing and his book. So let us recall Kitson's ideas and permit Jim Gibney to make what is, perhaps, the most important point in this particular saga: "The point is not whether Stakeknife really exists or if he is the product of a fertile mind in Military Intelligence. The point is that Downing Street used death squads and authorized the killing of those it considered to be its own citizens."[151]

If we accept, as we must, that the ultimate responsibility rests with the Prime Minister, Gibney is undoubtedly correct and, furthermore, it is quite possibly an unacknowledged reason for the amount of press attention the story unleashed. An American website that uncovers secrets, a top informer who has been unsuspected for many years, the likelihood of Government and MI5 involvement at high levels, and all of this in the UK—how could Stakeknife *not* have become a household name, and how could the media *not* have jumped with alacrity onto the bandwagon? Even today, some eight years after the resultant ill-informed hysteria, there are still articles about and references to Stakeknife in the media, the most recent being first a statement to the Smithwick tribunal,[152] particularly noteworthy because once again the allegations come from Martin Ingram, under his real name: Ian Hurst[153]; then, more recently, we learn of the projected Operation Kenova via a BBC *Panorama* program which revealed nothing new in the way of evidence.[154]

Brian Nelson[155]

Brian Nelson, born in 1947 into a loyalist family in the Shankill area, was one of six children. His father worked at the Harland and Wolff shipyard, where the sons of workers often gained apprenticeships, as did Nelson. Perhaps the expectation of a guaranteed job may have been the reason for his lack of success in school,[156] but he gave up his joinery apprenticeship at the shipyard after only sixteen months. He spent the next four-and-a-half years as a soldier in the Royal Highland Regiment (the Black Watch), and soldiers who served with him said: "Nelson was ... the most disobedient, rebellious recruit in the barracks. He was constantly going AWOL ... When he did have authorized leave, he would return late. He often fell asleep on duty."[157] When he left the Black Watch in early 1969 he was twenty-two years old, became a follower of Ian Paisley, and set up a paramilitary group of Paisley's Ulster Protestant Volunteer Force (UPVF). His army experience meant that his methods of drilling new recruits gained him a great deal of respect and from 1972 he was working for the Ulster Defence Association (UDA), the umbrella group for loyalist vigilante groups and Northern Ireland's largest paramilitary group, proscribed in August 1992. A former UDA comrade said of him: "Brian was up for anything that was going.... He was a small, almost weedy man. It clearly helped his ego when he was given a job to do, and he was given many jobs to do."[158] Thus he had finally found a niche where he was respected and where his burgeoning sectarianism was an asset. The most glaring early example of this was the abduction and torture of Gerry Higgins, registered blind, and a Catholic peace campaigner, on 25 March 1973. At the subsequent trial in 1974 police officers said, "there was no doubt that [Nelson] ... was the ringleader."[159] There is no doubt either that Higgins's life was only saved by a chance encounter with an army patrol.

Nelson was sentenced to seven years and released in 1977, after which he rejoined the UDA before, in 1983, beginning his career as an informer by offering or being encouraged to give his services to the FRU. The details of his recruitment remain unclear and there are conflicting accounts. It seems most likely, given that the RUC often trawled the prisons for possible informers, that the FRU would do the same among imprisoned serving or former soldiers with a Northern Ireland background. This would mean that Nelson was recruited during his sentence or immediately after his release. It is also noteworthy that, at this time, the Force Research Unit was "a highly classified grouping known only to Special Branch, MI5, the RUC hierarchy and the British Cabinet."[160] During this first period as an informer, when he became the UDA's Senior Intelligence Officer for West Belfast, Nelson's most notable exploit was his key role in the loyalist arms transaction with South Africa in June 1985. Then he took his wife and children to Regensburg, in Germany.[161] According to McDonald and Cusack the reason for his emigration was that "he came under suspicion by other UDA men of tipping police about an operation on the Shankill Road,"[162] and Ingram says that while he was in Germany he spied on the Irish community there for both the Army and MI6.[163]

Had Colonel Gordon Kerr not been appointed commander of the FRU in 1986 at a time when loyalist killings had increased,[164] Brian Nelson might have remained in Germany, where he worked as a roof tiler and was making a good living. As it was, Kerr said, "In January 1987 we were reviewing our current agent coverage and we identified a gap in our coverage of the loyalist paramilitaries.... We examined the case of Brian Nelson and decided that we should try and re-recruit him."[165] There was opposition from MI5[166] but, despite this, at the beginning of 1987, Nelson was first sent to Repton Manor,

Ashford, Kent, for computer training, code-named 6137, then brought back to Belfast shortly after the Anglo-Irish Agreement. "Geoff," his handler, gave some of the practical details: "We brought his family back into this dangerous job, paid the deposit on a house and car and set him up in a taxi firm. Initially we paid him a salary of £200 a week, rising as time went on, to do this job specifically for us. He was also paid generous bonuses on a regular basis."[167]

Nelson's sudden prosperity was explained by a fictitious German lottery win of £20,000. In April 1987 on his return to Belfast he took up his previous life where he had left off, met Andy Tyrie, commander of the UDA, and John McMichael, his second-in-command and the UFF leader. In December of that year Nelson became UDA Senior Intelligence Officer for the whole province after McMichael was killed by the IRA. He inherited McMichael's files and FRU commander Kerr had them checked and updated by FRU analysts before returning them to him. Then Nelson created his own meticulous filing system, and began to use it with increasing success. "[He] relied upon various items of information, including radio transmissions, electoral registers, and republican newspapers. However, his primary source material consisted of photo-montages and hand-written information acquired from either the military or the RUC."[168]

He turned out to be a hugely successful (in UDA terms) Intelligence Officer, mainly because FRU helped him to organize and collate material on a computer provided by the UDA. Intelligence documents, gathered by loyalists from sources such as the RUC and UDR, which at first were passed from Nelson to the FRU, photocopied and returned, later became data on a disk and so easier to pass on secretly. Ultimately this became a two-way traffic when the FRU began to provide him with intelligence details and documents. Apart from this, Nelson was encouraged to inform his handlers about the UFF's targets. They would pass this information on to their superiors who, in their turn, would inform Kerr. Subsequently either the target would be warned or steps would be taken to prevent the attack. It seems certain that Gerry Adams' life, for instance, was saved twice by this system, once in April 1984 when he was attacked by UFF gunmen as he left Belfast Magistrates' Court, the second time in early 1987 when the plan was to attach a limpet mine to the roof of his car. There were, however, times when Nelson did not tell his handlers everything or when the information was not acted upon. In September 1988 Gerard Slane, claimed by the UFF to have been involved in the shooting of a prominent UDA man, was killed. Nelson had provided the killers with Slane's address and photograph, then warned his handlers twice that the man was being targeted, but neither warning nor protection was given to the victim.

The UFF targeting and murder in February 1989 of Pat Finucane, organized by Nelson, was Nelson's greatest error in that it brought him to the attention of the Stevens Enquiry. He had compiled the dossier on Finucane, given a photograph of the lawyer to gunman Ken Barrett, and driven Barrett to show him Finucane's house.[169] Then and now the killing of the Catholic solicitor has been the cause of much furor. Finucane's successful defense of Patrick McGeown, a former hunger-striker charged with involvement in the killing of two FRU men, was followed by RUC Chief Constable Sir John Hermon's report to the MoD. This culminated in Junior Home Office Minister's (Douglas Hogg) statement in the House of Commons.[170]

Nelson was not the only informer connected with Finucane's death, nor is this surprising since the RUC alone had twenty-six loyalist informers inside the UDA during the 1980s.[171] Loyalist informers Billy Stobie, who provided the gun, and Ken Barrett, eventually convicted of the murder, were also directly involved.[172] It is not clear why the Northern Ireland situation caused so many loyalist informers, nor (as with the republicans) how many there were. It may have been simply the prevailing climate, when the government agencies were so eager, it seemed, to pay anyone at all for information, and so many men, particularly in the upper echelons of the loyalist paramilitary organizations, saw themselves as untouchable despite the harsh lessons of the past. In support of this, there is one incredible story which, if true, implies a great deal about the whole situation. This first surfaced in an allegation by Martin Dillon and has since been repeated several times in the media, with the most recent repetition appearing in *The Sunday Times* in 2008. Joe "The Hawk" Haughey was almost legendary in the IRA, not least because of his catchphrase: "I'm the Hawk from the Walk and I don't talk." He "ran agents for the IRA within the loyalist paramilitaries, the most famous of which was Jimmy Craig who directed the UDA's building site rackets."[173]

However, though the Finucane case drew an uncomfortable amount of international attention to the situation in Northern Ireland, it was the murder of Loughlin Maginn in August 1989 which caused the most damage. Nelson, in order to add to the information in his files, had asked soldiers to film their intelligence bulletins. These were lists of suspects posted routinely on the walls of their barracks, and on one of these Loughlin Maginn was named as a suspected IRA intelligence officer and subsequently shot by loyalists. The Maginn family denied that Loughlin was an IRA man so, to prove that they only shot IRA men, the loyalists posted some of Nelson's files in public places throughout Belfast. Nelson became worried about his own cover, especially when this action brought demands from the Irish government for an inquiry and the British government agreed to their demands. Though Nelson's eventual downfall was caused inevitably by his own character flaws (principally his arrogance), the murder of Loughlin Maginn precipitated the event. Tommy "Tucker" Lyttle, close friend of UDA commander Andy Tyrie, and a Special Branch informer for nearly twenty years, reacted to the renewed demands for an inquiry into allegations of collusion by giving a journalist documents exposing the links between the security forces and the UDA/UFF. This led to the arrival in September 1989 of John Stevens, Deputy Chief Constable of Cambridge, and a team of detectives. The affair culminated in MI5's victory, three years later, in their hidden battle to achieve primary control in the intelligence field.

Nelson was convinced that the Stevens Enquiry had nothing to do with him because the army had told the enquiry that they had no agents in Northern Ireland. In addition, "Brian believed, not that he was bullet-proof, but that he had protection from us and that what he was doing, he was doing at our request and therefore he had immunity. And he didn't."[174] He was to be disillusioned when information about Stevens' plans to arrest him was leaked to the loyalist paramilitaries and the press by Special Branch.[175] "He had started to become a major embarrassment to the SB ... who were concerned at his access to information which was regularly highlighting RUC collusion by officers, many of whom had no official sanction."[176] Warned by his handlers, Nelson left home the night before his arrest was due, while they removed all his documents to Holywood's Palace Barracks. He was ordered by his bosses to give himself up a week later, after being debriefed in Ashford and prepared for his interview. Though the Stevens incident room had been destroyed by fire the night before the new date set for his arrest, Nelson's career ended on 12 January 1990, when he was finally arrested by the Stevens team. During that month he made an 800-page statement[177] implicating himself in murder and asking for immunity but this was turned down by the DPP. Too much adverse publicity had focused on immunity during the 1980s and Nelson had already made a full statement so there was no benefit in attempting to bribe him. Brian Nelson's trial, two years after his arrest, was brief and marked by two factors: the first of these was that the original thirty-four charges, including two counts of murder, were reduced to twenty; the second was the appearance of the FRU's Colonel Gordon Kerr as the sole witness, identified in court only as soldier "J," whose evidence was an encomium to Nelson's heroism, and to the numbers of lives he had saved. Kerr depicted him as a very courageous man, a hero, and a victim of the system. This had the desired effect on the trial judge. Though Nelson was sentenced to a total of 101 years, the sentences were to run concurrently, so, on 22 January 1992, "Nelson was sentenced to 10 years' imprisonment. His decision to plead guilty meant that the security services did not have to justify their actions in court."[178]

Sentence was passed on 3 February 1992, and Nelson was released, and received protection in late 1996. "On his release he was given a new home, £100,000 and a new identity in England."[179] However, by the time Mr. Justice Cory's report (2004) had demolished soldier "J's" evidence by revealing that its relationship with the truth was at best approximate, Gordon Kerr (pro-

4. British Intelligence and the Army 153

moted to Brigadier and awarded the military OBE) had been suspended from his new appointment as British Military Attaché in Beijing, following the Stevens report.[180] The Cory Report said of Kerr's evidence:

> it appears that, by the time of the trial in 1992, senior officials were well aware that the statistics referred to in Soldier "J's" testimony were inaccurate and could not realistically be sustained. In a letter sent to the Secretary of State for Defence on 25 April 1991, the Attorney General pointed out that the evidence in the possession of the DPP[181] and others indicated that Nelson's intelligence had actually resulted in only two lives being saved and that "The Chief Constable of the RUC agrees with this conclusion."[182]

Brian Nelson at twenty-two had been a sectarian bully and murderer, yet at 40 he was not only prosperous but industrious, efficient, and organized, "always keen to impress the bosses."[183] On the surface this would seem to be a complete *volte-face*, but the driving motives behind both sections of his life were the same: his hatred of Catholics, his enjoyment of violence against them, and a growing feeling of power and influence over all those with whom he came in contact. The importation of arms "improved the standing and prestige that Brian Nelson enjoyed within the UDA, which in turn meant more influence,"[184] just as, later, his increasing mastery of the computer files led to improvements in targeting victims and further impressed the gunmen of the UFF.[185] At the same time, viewed simply from the perspective of Nelson's importance to the FRU, it seemed that he could do no wrong. In London Margaret Thatcher, in her determination to overcome the IRA, was asking for more and more intelligence; Nelson, ordered to recruit helpers, enlisted forty more informers and provided that intelligence.

Nelson began to feel invulnerable. He told his FRU bosses less and less about his actions, began to drink heavily, and made indiscreet and abusive phone calls to his handlers late at night from bars. The FRU discussed this problem, with some officers wanting to get rid of him, while others felt he could be brought back into line. Nelson hit back. He responded to threats to disown him with threats of his own to spill the beans, and subsequently did so.[186] Other informers have written books about their heroic deeds, Nelson went one better: in 2002 he made a television documentary, of which the main focus was the murder of Pat Finucane, with BBC's *Panorama*.[187] The program established collusion, both generally and in the case of Finucane's murder, between the security forces and the UDA and, as John Ware says in the documentary: "Within a year military intelligence were reporting that thanks to their agent [Nelson] the targeting by loyalist murder gangs was more professional."[188] Even at this stage Nelson must have thought his position was unassailable, for few informers wish to see their photographs in the papers, yet Nelson was on film, revealing himself to be the archetypal informer, at least in appearance. Though his activities are revealed more *in absentia*, through the words of Ken Barrett and of Carole Creighton, Nelson's sister (who said of him that he was like a secret squirrel), he told the programme: "I would like to state that all information concerning the Finucane affair I passed on to military intelligence through my handlers. At no point did I ever conceal or withhold any information that I was party to from them."[189]

The most fruitful period of Nelson's activities was between April 1987 and 12 January 1990. A conservative estimate, based loosely on the figures given by Geoff, reveals a cost of at least £200,000. The results of Nelson's work during those three years were: the exposure of a number of his fellow loyalist informers (Lyttle, Craig, Barrett, Stobie); the (temporary) downfall of the FRU[190]; the saving of two lives, not the hundreds attributed to him[191]; many deaths among the Catholic population, most of whom were not republicans; and also deaths among the loyalists, as, for instance, John McMichael. Yet Geoff could still say of Nelson, "He seemed quite a nice person. A family man.... He told me he hated violence and he didn't agree with the way in which loyalists were carrying out their attacks. He saw himself as the spearpoint in the attack against terrorism."[192] Geoff's stance is unusual. Other handlers in this study may use flattery to keep the informers in line, but never show them sympathy, and their prevailing attitude is a veiled contempt for their charges. The informers themselves accept the mantra that they are saving lives, and go on using it *ad nauseam* to disguise their actions from themselves and others. Perhaps Nelson was preying on a perceived naïvety in Geoff, because the former wrote more truthfully in his personal journal: "I was bitten by a bug.... Hooked is probably a more appropriate word. One becomes enmeshed in a web of intrigue, conspiracies, confidences, dangers and the power of being aware of things that others around you aren't. The power of this phenomenon acts like a drug."[193]

The man who wrote these words is obviously more of a thinker than his violent career would suggest, and this helps to explain his sudden transformation from rebellious soldier to efficient organizer. If this is correct, it places Nelson firmly in the ranks of those informers whose weakness was identified and exploited by the security forces, and who subsequently discovered that power was a heady drug. There is also the possibility that at some point, perhaps while he was in prison, Brian Nelson changed. Is it really feasible that the man who had spent so much of his life murdering and aiding others to murder, who had even attended a celebration party after the murder of Finucane, should suddenly see the error of his ways? Others have done it, and Nelson had already undergone one complete turnaround in his life. In this case we have only the evidence of his personal journal and the fact that in 1998 he was offered a seven-figure sum by a group of New York lawyers and businessmen if he would provide evidence about the Finucane murder.[194]

They seem to have had no response to their offer, so perhaps money was no longer an inducement. The apportioning of blame is best left to the realistic Mr. Justice Cory: "FRU considered the normal rules—including the rule of law—to be suspended and the gathering of intelligence to be an end that was capable of justifying questionable means. Indeed, this attitude was essentially confirmed by the CO FRU [Gordon Kerr], when he gave his testimony at Brian Nelson's trial."[195]

Nelson died in Cardiff in April 2003.[196] As this was just a few days before publication of the Stevens 3 collusion report, it led to much press speculation that his death was no coincidence. Lack of any confirmation from the MoD caused a series of widely conflicting claims in the press about where and how he died, and even a further contribution from Martin Ingram, claiming that he may still be alive.[197] Yet the effects of his actions are still felt today, particularly by the Finucane family, who are still fighting for an independent enquiry into Pat Finucane's death. British Irish Rights Watch put Nelson's life into perspective when they wrote:

> Through its secret Force Research Unit (FRU) ... the state sought out loyalist Brian Nelson and infiltrated him into the Ulster Defence Association, which carried out its campaign of murder under the flag of convenience of the Ulster Freedom Fighters (UFF). FRU used Nelson to enhance the loyalists' intelligence on people it was targeting for murder, and that intelligence rapidly spread throughout other loyalist paramilitary groups.[198]

Conclusion

Kitson's disinformation theories worked well, and would possibly have been even more effective had the soldiers on the ground not covered their fear of Northern Ireland with so much aggression. The IRA had discovered long ago with Michael Collins that intelligence was the key to defeating the enemy, and now the British army had finally caught up with them, even to the point of realising that the republicans expected to find informers in their ranks. Just as, for the soldiers, anyone could be an enemy, for the IRA, anyone could be an informer. In fact, the majority of the army informers seem to have been both ex-soldiers and of Catholic nationalist or republican families. Nelson was one notable exception, though McDonald and Cusack note the possibility that one or more of the UDA's Inner Council were also informers and, in 1992–3, loyalist informers identified as the result of an amnesty were all killed by the UDA or fled.[199] Therefore the military went to great lengths to conceal their moles by such methods as dishonorable discharge from the army: a tactic later to prove so inconvenient to the moles' union.

Recruitment followed a well-trodden path, as can be seen from the experiences of Carlin and Fulton, and provided a contrast both with the RUC's methods and the attitudes of the soldiers on the streets of Northern Ireland. This was the tea-and-biscuits approach, relying on seemingly innocent beginnings and flattery: be a hero; save lives. Many lies later, on both republican and loyalist sides, the money became all-important until the danger was finally realized, but it was too late.[200] The other major route to recruitment was to seek out the disenchanted. Rob Lewis details the turning of "Brenda," a republican horrified by the killing of the two British soldiers at the funeral of Kevin Brady in 1988.[201] Brenda, who lived in an unidentified border town, had the motivation and worked for Sinn Féin. It is, however, questionable that the imputed motivation was strong enough to make her agree to be used in a honey-trap operation and become the mistress of Liam Donnelly, a man in whom the FRU was interested.[202]

The disinformation tactic could be called an unqualified success, given that so many still doubt its operations nearly forty years later. The Stakeknife/Scappaticci furor and the *succès de scandale* of Ingram and Harkin's eponymous book happened comparatively recently[203] and opinions are still divided on the subject, though possibly the most convincing argument in favor of Fred Scappaticci's innocence of the charge is that he is still alive. Before that time and after it there have been many other accusations of touting, each one sowing doubts and nibbling away at IRA support among nationalists, many of whom no longer knew who could be trusted. When the local laundry van or the ice cream van turn out to be surveillance vehicles, when informers are believed to be at every turn in the road, what is left but suspicion? The subsequent paranoia spread throughout the population, including the paramilitaries. This situation had already caused the death of Ardoyne resident Jimmy Hanlon. He was seventeen, shot as an informer by the IRA on 16 March 1972 because doubts were aroused by his arrest and imprisonment for some days in Girdwood Barracks a few days before his death. Those who arrested him surely knew that this would engender suspicion. The IRA later apologized and exonerated him.[204] He was just one of the innocents who were accused of informing and thereby lost their lives. Michael Kearney was killed in July 1979 for the same reason. He cracked in Castlereagh, reported this immediately to the IRA on his release but was shot three weeks later.[205] The most horrific of such incidents concerned Paddy Flood, "the best bomb-maker in the Provisional IRA," who went out in early June 1990 and was found dead on a border road seven weeks later. Greg Harkin claims that the FRU wanted him dead, so they used their agents inside the IRA to point the finger at him.[206]

The unmasking of an informer had serious consequences for the IRA, because it threw doubts on the leadership as well as creating tension and confusion in the ranks. Thus the revelations about Stakeknife sent shock waves throughout the organization, in much the same way as the allegations against Stephen Hayes had done in the 1940s. The advice appended to any story about informers in republican newspapers: to contact Sinn Féin if approached by the Crown Forces seeking information was the best weapon against these tactics, and many took advantage of it, including some who had already been informing. Its efficacy was tacitly admitted when the loyalist newspapers followed suit soon after the Joe Bennett trial of 1983 which had sown so much consternation among the loyalist community. The sub-text, which did not need to be spelt out because it was widely known, was an excellent reason for taking that advice: if the IRA find you out before you confess punishment will be swift. This was why so many felt that the shooting of Seamus Wright and Franko Hegarty, both of whom had confessed, albeit not in person, after they had been encouraged by the leadership to return to Northern Ireland, was a betrayal which created more mistrust.

The IRA approach to the punishment of informers tended to be almost ritualistic: confession, always recorded for later dissemination in order to spell out the message, and because it was important to know exactly what the enemy had been told; then the penalty which, in some cases (for instance the very young) was usually banishment, but in others was a corpse left on a border road. Loyalists, on the other hand, perhaps less inclined towards ritual than their Catholic counterparts, simply shot informers at the first opportunity once their guilt had been accepted, as with the UDA amnesty. Given that all these things were common knowledge, the greatest mystery is why these (mostly) men should put their lives in such constant danger. The only possible answer is a lack of imagination, they thought they would never be caught. To this tendency, so common among the informers themselves, can be added such characteristics as Nelson's sectarian bias, his addiction to power, and his arrogance, as also the greed, allied to a sort of helplessness, displayed by Fulton and Carlin, all over-familiar in the context of the touts of the province. However, a factor perhaps greater in its influence than all of these things, is the role of the handler. The army had learnt quickly that the subtleties of flattery, added to the payments, were far more effective than brutality.

"Daddy, who was Judas?"

"Daddy, who was Judas, was he really bad?"
My little girl looked up at me, her face so very sad.
Before I made my answer, my mind drifted far away
And from within my heart a quiet voice did say
"Yes my love he really was a very evil man,
He sold his soul for money, he betrayed the Son of man."

Things have changed so little since those days so long ago
You only have to study what the Diplock records show.
In place of evil Judas we have the modern "Supergrass"
Perhaps he is a murderer, all his crimes are vast.
He really has no principle, just a wretched no good tout
Whose evidence to Judges is a pack of lies throughout.

My heart was greatly saddened as I thought of recent days
How I'd become a victim of the Supergrass Malaise.
Judge Murray he condemned me on the word of one such tout.
A lying woman killer whose name we all should shout.
A traitor called Joe Bennet whose only claim to fame
Is that he is a thief, a liar, a heap of human shame.

A little voice rang out again so very loud and clear
"Please daddy give an answer, don't pretend you didn't hear."
What could I tell my little girl, she wouldn't understand
About the sins of Judas deep within the heart of man.
"Daddy who was Judas, was he as bad as people say?"
"My little love be patient, we'll know on Judgement day."

Source: Combat, vol.4, issue no.65. In Northern Ireland Political Collection on microfiches, Linen Hall Library, Belfast. The author has endeavored to find the original copyright owner of these untitled verses, but has been unable to do so. If anyone can assist in establishing the copyright holder, the author will be pleased to acknowledge the owner.

5

The Supergrasses

"Just a wretched no good tout"[1]

In 1980 the IRA became increasingly focused and efficient as a result of restructuring from battalions into closed cells. This, which helped to preserve anonymity, and their use of anti-interrogation training, together with the effects of the Amnesty International and Bennett reports on the RUC's conduct of interrogation, led to a decline in convictions and intelligence gathering. In turn, this meant that the RUC had to rethink their intelligence strategy. Gifford noted of this period that many lawyers "had been told by clients of invitations and inducements being made by the police to give evidence against other people."[2]

In January 1982 a two-week IRA amnesty was offered to all informers who would reveal within two weeks what arrangements they had with the RUC, which further stemmed the flow of information from nationalist areas to the police, and caused them to change their tactics. Instead of sending informers back into their communities to provide information, the RUC began to offer them protective custody, huge sums of money, and immunity from prosecution if they gave evidence in court. The following November Stephen McWilliams, a petty thief and informer in the pay of the British Army, wrote to the *Sunday World* confessing that he had been bribed to tell lies under oath, and warning "people like [Christopher] Black that life will be so hard for him after the Brits are finished with him. I say to anyone thinking of doing this terrible thing: DON'T."[3]

The emphasis of interrogation thus shifted from physical force to other techniques in the early 1980s. Hugh Brady, of Derry, described his interrogation in Castlereagh, where he was held on the word of Raymond Gilmour:

> I have been arrested on countless occasions; the first being in September, 1973 ... On any previous occasion ... the RUC have tried to fool me into making a self-incriminating statement, or to beat one out of me ... now [in the early 1980s] ... there is no force used except mental / psychological force. Their whole attitude has

changed.... They threw down the perjurer's statement and said: "We have you by the short and curlies. We've no need to question you."[4]

The deaths of the ten hunger strikers occurred in the summer of 1981. This, as well as the apparent failure to achieve their demands, had a huge impact on the nationalist community because they were exhausted, and the feeling of defeat was demoralizing. In May 1983 Sinn Féin claimed that this was an important factor in the rise of the supergrass strategy because of "the belief in British establishment circles that Margaret Thatcher's intransigence during the hunger-strikes, and the resulting deeply-felt deaths of ten H-Block men, had inflicted a psychological defeat on the nationalist people which could be exploited by an increase in counter-insurgency activities, including black propaganda and the public use of informers."[5]

The use of accomplice evidence has a pedigree as long as that of the legal system itself. To remove one villain from society and use him as a lever to remove others at the same time is practical and efficient. In modern times its best known use has been in Italy, where a great number of *mafiosi* have appeared in court to denounce former comrades or bosses. The policy was tried in Britain in the 1970s to convict ordinary criminals, but it was found that juries were so unwilling to convict on uncorroborated evidence that the Director of Public Prosecutions "issued a directive that no prosecution should even be started on uncorroborated evidence," and the tactic was abandoned.[6] Despite this, Tom Hadden points out:

> There are established legal rules for dealing with the evidence of accomplices. In all such cases the judge is required to warn the jury of the dangers of relying on the uncorroborated evidence of an accomplice.... But there is no legal requirement that the evidence of an accomplice must be corroborated.... [This] means that the conviction can be based entirely on the often dubious evidence of a supergrass.[7]

The influential Gifford Report resulted from an investigation undertaken by Lord Gifford QC at the request of the Cobden Trust, a charity dedicated to research and education, and is limited to a consideration of just four of the supergrasses (Bennett, Black, McGrady and, briefly, Grimley), but also considers the law on accomplice evidence, and the arguments for and against the supergrass system.

Lord Gifford defined a supergrass as "a person who has repeatedly taken part in serious criminal enterprises, and who agrees to give evidence against alleged participants in those same crimes."[8] In Northern Ireland the first real supergrass was Christopher Black, an IRA activist at the time of his arrest in 1981.[9] His promised immunity from prosecution was the beginning of the supergrass strategy, which eventually had less to do with the trial of those accused than with allowing the RUC to rid the streets of Northern Ireland of those they mistrusted. Thus, when Black gave evidence against 38 people from Ardoyne, most of the offenses were minor; for instance (and for the first time) some people were charged simply because republican activists had visited their homes. The whole purpose, as Sinn Féin later averred, was to sow seeds of suspicion and fear in the minds of nationalists, to attack the idea that every nationalist door in the province was open to republicans, and to make them distrust their neighbors. Presumably elated by the success of this new tactic (though denying that it was a deliberate policy[10]) the RUC pitted Joe Bennett against the loyalist paramilitaries in May 1981, and the system was launched.

The whole thrust of police activity under interrogation was now to create supergrasses and gradually a pattern emerged: "It is a simple tactic—you implicate someone in a serious offense (whether they were involved or not), and implicate their wives and families if you can; then if they show weakness, offer them a way out by turning supergrass. Then, after two years of tuition at the hands of the police, produce them in court with a plausible tale, and you put away whoever you want."[11] Later came other refinements: when faced with their horrified families the supergrasses tended to weaken and retract their evidence, so the RUC began to isolate their informers in the Annex in Crumlin Road; but when facing large numbers of defendants in court at the preliminary hearings, again they retracted. Indeed the Clifford McKeown and Sean Mallon cases ended in chaos because both informers retracted earlier statements during the preliminary enquiries (in July and September 1982 respectively) when confronted by defendants and family members. Therefore a legal weapon, the voluntary Bill of Indictment, was invoked and its powers reinterpreted in such a way that the DPP could dispense with the usual preliminary enquiry. The *American Gael* sums up its effects succinctly: "The so-called <u>Bill of Indictment</u> has removed the necessity for a preliminary hearing thus:

(1) eliminating a confrontation with the defendant as well as distressed family members.
(2) preventing the defense counsel from evaluating and probing the evidence against the defendant."

Essentially this meant that the informer did not need to face those he was accusing until the trial began, but it also allowed the RUC to prolong the informer's isolation, and keep the defendants on remand without bail from their arrest until the trial. Numerous people, then, could be detained without trial for up to two years (sometimes longer, as in the case of Cathal Crumley, remanded between August 1982 and November 1986). Sinn Féin made the important point that "[this] tactic is directed primarily at ... community support for the national liberation struggle, rather than at the IRA itself."[12] Yet the parallels with internment were immediately apparent to both communities. The women of the Shankill-based Families for Legal Rights put the whole issue in perspective when they recounted: "[A] man incriminated at the end of 1983 was charged with 'conspiracy to murder a person or persons unknown between the months of 1 January 1975 and 31st December 1975.' His case will not be heard until 1987 and if he cannot prove his innocence he faces a twenty year sentence."[13]

The supergrasses chosen as case studies here are included for a variety of reasons: Joseph Bennett was not only the first of the loyalist supergrasses, but his trial was undoubtedly accelerated to demonstrate that this new security strategy was being employed impartially[14]; Raymond Gilmour is a prime example of those nationalists who were deliberately targeted when very young and cajoled into imagining themselves to be a superhero saving lives, when in fact they were, or became, totally venal and self-centered. He was responsible for the highest number of victims, as well as being the root cause of the turning of Robert Quigley and Eamon Doyle; Kevin McGrady was an obvious choice, given that he was the only one who lived up to Sir John Hermon's description of the converted terrorist; while Angela Whoriskey, though in essence no different from others who were frightened into becoming paid perjurers, was the only woman among the supergrasses.[15]

Joseph Charles Bennett

Joe Bennett, born 19 July 1946 in East Belfast, trained as a welder after he left school, but his criminal tendencies had already shown themselves when convicted of larceny at the age of eleven. At fifteen he added convictions for firearms offenses and within a few years became a heavy gambler. He joined the UVF, then an illegal organization, in 1972, when he lived with his wife and two children in Dundonald, on the outskirts of Belfast. In August of that year he was charged with possession of firearms, ammunition, and explosives, but released on bail. Bennett was rearrested on 30 March 1974. His Shankill house was found to hold an arms dump; he pleaded guilty to possession charges and was given a twelve-year prison sentence. He was released in 1980, became a UVF company commander, and worked first as a barman, then as a bar manager (in a UVF pub) but left in March 1981 after stealing £1350 from the till. A UVF court martial sentenced him to death in his absence for this.[16] In May of the following year, with two other men, he took part in the robbery of a Post Office at Killinchy, County Down. There was a struggle, one of the sisters of the elderly postmaster was stabbed and died soon afterwards. Bennett was arrested on 20 May. He made a series of statements over the following months, some taking as long as two days to complete, which implicated eighteen suspects in the robbery and other offenses ranging from murder to membership of the UVF. Bennett agreed to testify against all of them in return for immunity, a new job, and a new life in another place.[17]

> I did not want to go to prison again.... I volunteered to give evidence to the Detective Sergeant ... and I asked if I did this would I be given immunity.... I knew I was in real danger of going down on a murder charge. I would be away for life and I was shocked. I was inside for life or sentence of death outside. The future was bleak. The police offered a third alternative.... My safety depended on my ability to name as many as possible.[18]

The Trial: *R. v. Graham* (16 February–11 April 1983)

Mr. Justice Murray described Bennett in court as "a ruthless, resourceful and experienced criminal ... [who committed] the daring armed robberies from which considerable sums of money were stolen and divided amongst himself and his accomplices." Justice Murray, nevertheless, justified his belief in Bennett's evidence in the following words:

> It is my firm view that Bennett chose the perilous task of turning Queen's Evidence because he simply could not face another long spell in a prison cell. I ask myself, is it conceivable that he would add to his peril by going to Court and naming someone who might have a complete alibi that would show him to be a liar? This would forfeit any protection the police were prepared to give him, and would be signing his own death warrant.[19]

The evidence at the trial relied almost completely on the statements Bennett had given to the RUC, so a great deal of weight was placed on his character, credibility, and the immunity deal which could affect his reliability as a witness, yet Bennett's own testimony was the only evidence that he had been granted immunity.[20] Justice Murray was highly critical of the Crown's failure to provide details of this but still allowed the trial to proceed, deciding that the lie Bennett told in court about receipt of a UVF welfare cheque for £600 was "extraneous," and said that Bennett's evidence "had a clear ring of truth in my ears."[21]

The Bennett trial was significant because it was not only the first involving a loyalist supergrass but also the first to come to court, thus allowing the authorities to claim that the new policy was being applied in a non-sectarian way. There was evidence that the DPP's office deliberately speeded up the timing of the Bennett trial to achieve this claim: two other cases pre-dated it, but were held up by remand periods; Bennett was arrested in May 1982, the preliminary inquiry held in December, and the trial began in February 1983; normally there was a delay of six months or more between the preliminary inquiry and the trial (the Bennett trial ran concurrently with the Black trial for part of the time, but fourteen months elapsed between the preliminary inquiry and the trial in Black's case).[22] Secondly the standard of evidence accepted was very low, because "the vast majority of Bennett's evidence was not corroborated in any way."[23] In fact, in accepting Bennett's evidence, Murray gave approval to the tactic itself and a firm indication that the judiciary would accept the flimsiest of evidence to put people in jail.[24]

One week after the trial the *Sunday World*'s northern edition reported a claim from the UVF that Joseph Bennett had been executed by his British controllers. However, in May 1986, *Combat* announced that Bennett was in custody in Lincoln Prison, charged with robbing a bookmaker and intent to rob a bank. He was being held in a special category annex with access to anything he required, and his guards were present only to prevent anyone getting near him, not to prevent his escape. The news emerged when three other prisoners realized who he was and told their families. As his immunity related only to crimes committed before the trial, he was awaiting a decision from the Home Office about his recent crimes. If the story in *Combat* is correct, and given Bennett's previous record, it might be safe to assume that he continued to spend a great deal of time in jail.

Though most of those convicted at the Bennett trial were freed on appeal in 1984, loyalists had been alienated, including "many who are far removed from support for terrorism."[25] Their outrage was completely understandable: Bennett, a convicted criminal, escaped punishment and innocent people were imprisoned. Peter King wrote that a number of loyalists "stated they can now begin to appreciate the plight of the nationalist community."[26] Indignation began in the loyalist community as soon as the news of Bennett's accusations reached them, and this rapidly became criticism. The legal system was called into disrepute and the integrity of the judiciary questioned. The loyalists also commented on the parallels with internment, and, adversely, on Sir Michael Havers, especially given his attitude to supergrasses in the English courts:

> When a prosecution witness is given immunity from prosecution, this fact is disclosed to the defence and to the court and there is no bargain or arrangement between the witnesses and the prosecution. The Director has given instructions that ... the Chief Constable will furnish him with a statement of all financial arrangements made for the support of the witness and his family ... and that these particulars will be disclosed to the defence and will be available to the court of trial.[27]

The loyalist emphasis on immunity, in objecting to the supergrasses, frequently caused comment among nationalists. However, given the evidence supplied by Joe Bennett's life, it is hardly surprising that they insisted, "there is no guarantee that they will not revert to their old ways when released into society ... by being given a form of immunity [they] can see that this process could be used again to their benefit if a similar situation arose."[28] More sympathy-provoking, though, are the words written in *Combat* which encapsulate all the confusion of the loyalists at being treated in the same way as the nationalists: "The outstanding question of all remains unanswered.... If all or even part of Bennett's evidence was true, why would the British Government go out of their way ... to attempt to crush the only militant resistance to British withdrawal from N. Ireland?"[29] It might be surmised, however, that by 1986 when Roisin McDonough wrote her protest to *Fortnight* in which she stated: "Only nationalists and republicans remain convicted on such evidence,"[30] loyalist confusion, if not loyalist fears, could have abated.

Raymond Gilmour

Raymond Gilmour was born in Derry in 1961, the youngest of eleven children. He grew up in a terraced house on the nationalist Creggan council estate in the city. He describes it as "filthy ... [with] rusting iron beds and burned-out cars in the alleys at the back of the houses.... The gardens ... and the public spaces ... were minefields of broken bottles and bits of scrap metal."[31] There follows a graphic picture of dereliction, of unemployment, burned out shops, boarded up flats, and smashed street lights, alleviated by the proximity of the surrounding countryside. He claims to have been an unhappy child and to have disliked the feel of the crowded house, yet his brother says "I think we had a good house."[32]

Gilmour makes an interesting case study because, unique among the supergrasses, there is so much material available about him from differing viewpoints: apart from his own book, Pete, his handler, has also written about him[33]; his high profile even among the supergrasses ensured attention from those who have written about the supergrass system[34]; he figured largely in the newspapers of the time, local and otherwise (even in the U.S.)[35]; during the Donaldson furor of 2005, journalists quoted his views on life after informing[36]; and his brother has been interviewed. In *Dead Ground* Gilmour tries to illustrate the inevitability of his becoming an informer, while always pointing the finger of blame at others: he liked the RUC because of his mother's views; he stole because of the example of his brothers and almost everybody from the Creggan did it; he alone was sensitive to the suffering around him. All this is necessary in order to portray himself as the hero. Nowhere in the book, however, is there any admission of guilt, nor does he have enough self-knowledge to see that he is living a fantasy life with little connection to reality. His brother says of him that he dressed in a tweed coat and slacks like a Special Branch man; before the trial he told Pete: "If you can't protect me, then I won't do this. I don't want to be looked at as an informer or grass, I want to be looked at as a policeman." His trusted friend Pete's reply was: "There's no way that you'll be thought of as an informer or a grass. I don't think of you that way."[37]

The attitude, then, of his minders in August 1982 when he was first in hiding came as a shock: "I expected a bit of respect for what I'd done, but they seemed to look down on me.... I got the feeling that they weren't classifying me as one of their own, but as just another criminal who'd turned Queen's Evidence to save his hide or make a few quid."[38] This brings to mind the scornful words of the IRA security unit quoted in Eamon Collins's book *Killing Rage*: "You're not an IRA volunteer. You're a tout, and I want you to get on your bike, get back home, and write down everything and everybody you touted about on paper and get it up here. Now off you go."[39]

Perhaps Pete was also touched by fantastic ideas: in the epilogue to his book *Shadows* he writes "I merely wanted to tell a simple but true story of sacrifice, courage, patience and betrayal,"[40] and was amazed and embittered when arrested and charged under the Official Secrets Act. However, while it is temptingly easy to point out the fallacies in Gilmour's thinking and the numerous points in the book where he betrays himself far more damningly than he betrayed others, it is necessary, in the interests of balance, to look at other aspects of the affair.

Raymond Gilmour was thirteen years old when he was arrested by the Scots Guards, hurt, beaten, terrified, and ordered to inform on the IRA men around the Creggan.[41] His father, Patrick Gilmour, knew exactly what to do. A visit to Martin McGuinness, then the elected Sinn Féin Assemblyman for Derry, followed by a press conference and an article in the *Derry Journal*, gave Raymond his first taste of fame with none of the repercussions he had feared. At sixteen he was involved in a break-in, slapped around by two RUC men, and left crying in a cold cell. It was a relief to meet the Special Branch man who "didn't seem like a policeman at all, and didn't talk to me like one. It was as if we were just a couple of mates, passing the time of day. He said his name was Pete, and I took to him right away."[42] Pete was then twenty-three, an adult to a boy of sixteen, and at that time it was flattering for a teenager to be invited to use an adult's Christian name and be treated as an equal.[43] Ray escaped with a warning, but the seeds were sown and the end result was perhaps inevitable.

In August 1978 Ray and a friend robbed a post office and were seen running away: this was the period when the heavy handed methods of recruitment were coming under increasing and international criticism, and when a certain amount of psychology was being used, particularly against the younger, weaker members of the nationalist community. Ray was young, his school record was abysmal, he was scared, and open to flattery. The idea of working as an undercover police agent saving lives was tailor-made for him. Nevertheless his understanding that Special Branch would be appreciative of his services was immediate: "How appreciative, exactly?"

[Pete] smiled. "If you did well for us, it would be more money than your Da's ever seen in his life, or you're ever likely to in yours."

... The thought of the money was ... a very powerful attraction to a sixteen-year-old kid with no qualifications and no prospects whatsoever. I was still too young and naïve to know or care about the short life-expectancy of agents and informers, and the thrill of working undercover was almost as compelling as the cash.[44]

But Pete was not too young or naïve to know this, and money is mentioned very frequently in Gilmour's book, with the occasional hasty addition of "saving lives."[45]

Even a superficial reading of Gilmour's and Pete's books reveals that, if the incidents described are the most significant of the operations in which Gilmour was involved, neither Gilmour nor Pete can have been important. The fantasy went on, however, with Gilmour constantly referring to himself as the top agent and both men reiterating the mantra "saving lives" throughout their books. There was even greater emphasis on this when persuading the "secret police agent" to testify in court, once it became obvious that he was about to be exposed.[46] This is one of the points where the two accounts differ: "Pete's boss ... asked how many people Gilmour could testify against ... [and] there were in the region of 108 people that he could implicate in connection with terrorist crimes.... It was a phenomenal number."[47]

Gilmour did not stand a chance of refusing. He was twenty-one and had been an informer for five years. If Pete had not persuaded him to testify, there can be no doubt that he would have been threatened with exposure to the IRA to force the issue. In the event, Gilmour was panicking but still susceptible to the idea that he was doing an undercover job, so, given two options by his handler (disappear with his family, or finish the job by putting these guys away for a long time)[48] the decision was never in doubt, but Pete writes that he "volunteered."[49]

On 16 August 1982 Raymond Gilmour drove out of Derry with his wife, Lorraine, and their two children. At that point Lorraine was told what he had been doing. One week later, when the RUC were seen breaking into the Gilmours' flat and removing the contents, the people of the Creggan knew that Raymond was an informer. The news reached his family via the sister of Johnny Gilmour's girlfriend. "Da went to bed."[50] His mother "Suffered heavily with her nerves, ... and then ... after Raymond ... disappeared ... she started smoking, she started drinking, neither of which she had done in her life before."[51] Life was never to be the same again for any member of the family. Some people thought the whole family had informed; some spat in Johnny's baby son's pram; that night there were 300 people, including some of their best friends, rioting outside their door and threatening to hang Raymond's father, Patrick[52]; most assumed that the family must have known about Raymond's activities.[53] Finally IRA men told the mob to leave. Johnny

Gilmour says scathingly that the rioters were: "The fireside republicans who never threw a fucking stone in their lives."[54]

Protective Custody

For Gilmour the isolation, despite the presence of his wife and children, was complete, and cruelly emphasized by the presence everywhere he went (Lisburn, Ipswich, Cyprus, London, Pontefract, Newcastle) of his minders. He and his family were all forbidden to speak to outsiders and all four of them were monitored, observed, followed every day, and instructed on a daily basis by the RUC. In Ipswich, Lorraine said "He told one ... that he was thinking about retracting and the next thing they took him out to all these discos and started filling his head with shit again. They were always at that—always pressurizing and threatening with their hints of what would happen if we didn't go ahead."

The isolation had its effect on Lorraine and the children, she desperately wanted to go home, "but every time I brought the subject up they told me if I did I'd know what would happen to me and the children. That the IRA had 'done it before and they'd do it again.' I know I shouldn't have believed them but it's different when they've got you."[55] Fear of the IRA was a constant presence and the pressure was, initially, to produce reams of statements; then, during the months following his disappearance, 71 people were arrested on his word alone; later he was schooled and rehearsed by the police for his court appearances.

The Kidnapping

Patrick Gilmour, Ray's father, was taken from his home in Derry to a place over the border by an armed and masked IRA unit on the night of 17 November 1982, and his family were told that his safety depended on his son. The RUC immediately sent Raymond and his family to Cyprus, probably in case the threat to his father might break him. Raymond's response was a suicide attempt.

There was some gossip in Derry that Raymond's father might have colluded in his own kidnapping. He was fairly close to Sinn Féin and to Martin McGuinness, who had already proved his worth in the earlier attempt to make Raymond inform, and Patrick would have seen the value, in terms of pressure on his son to retract, of his own disappearance and threats to his life. It is also certain that he knew that an informer who gave himself up was far more likely to survive than one who did not.[56] Johnny Gilmour, however, denies that his father would have done this to his family. He said: "The family suffered terribly when he was kidnapped and were not told of his whereabouts—there is no way my father would have put my mother and us through that."[57] Raymond decided it was a bluff "and one in which he might even have been a willing participant."[58] This reasoning left him stress- and guilt-free as far as his father was concerned.

Patrick's family in Derry were crushed by this fresh blow and there were protests from many quarters, answered by a public statement from the IRA: "Following a number of public and private calls to us to release, or clarify the situation regarding Patrick Gilmour, we can confirm that we intend to continue holding this man to show his son, Raymond, that the cost of collaborating will be personally dear to him. Mr. Gilmour is being treated well ... his release is conditional upon the activities of Raymond Gilmour."[59]

After ten months in custody Patrick Gilmour was unexpectedly released by the IRA, late on Monday, 26 September 1983. He made it clear that he had not been ill-treated, but had never been left alone, and his homecoming was marked by a violent mob which attacked his house and the houses of his family. The following day Patrick and Bridget Gilmour left Derry to stay in Ellesmere Port, Merseyside, with Dessie, another son. Raymond wrote that he was unmoved.[60]

Martin McGuinness appealed to the relatives of the victims of the show trials not to take out their understandable anger over Raymond Gilmour on Patrick and his family. "It is obvious that his son, Raymond, has been brainwashed beyond compassion for the heart-break and broken homes he is causing in Derry.... It is also obvious that while we could use the arrest of Mr. Gilmour as pressure on his son, there was no way we could ultimately hold him responsible for the actions of Raymond."[61]

While in Cyprus Lorraine managed to make unsupervised phone calls to her mother. She continued this contact despite the constant moves to new locations. At much the same time, and while Patrick was still being held, Martin McGuinness began to have contact with her family in Derry. Then, on 13 March 1983, Raymond phoned his sisters from a coin box, making his regrets clear and claiming that the RUC were "treating his wife and children like dirt" but that he did not know how to go about severing his connection with them.[62] Whether or not his father's abduction was relevant to this call is unclear, but common sense suggests that Lorraine's phone calls home had much to do with it. At the suggestion of his sisters Gilmour agreed to speak to McGuinness. On 20 March he made several more calls, but it seemed to the family that he was not alone, and when asked if the RUC were with him he did not answer. He spoke to McGuinness in March, but very guardedly and promised to ring again. That call did not happen. Martin McGuinness said:

> Raymond Gilmour has been in total isolation for eight months. He is totally dependent on his Special Branch guards. They control his every word, his every action. In

his excitement at making what he thought was a free and confidential contact with his family, he has overlooked the possibility of his relatives' phones being tapped.

Such evidence of the RUC's apparently limitless power only serves to reinforce Gilmour's fears and his dependence on his guards.[63]

The following week McGuinness made another statement, interesting enough to be quoted in its entirety:

> Last Thursday I issued a statement in connection with Raymond Gilmour, the informer. This statement shed new light on the situation. Subsequently the statement was heavily censored by the editor of the *Derry Journal* after the RUC had threatened the paper with contempt of court citing the sub-judice nature of the Gilmour case.
>
> The RUC are well aware of the legal and moral implications involved in the widespread use of informers.
>
> It is not in the RUC's interest that the issue should receive thorough public critical comment and analysis. They claim Raymond Gilmour to be a "free agent," but after speaking with his family and indicating his fear, worry and desire to retract, and having spoken with him myself, I totally refute that contention.
>
> It is my opinion that the media in general has plainly allowed itself to be muzzled by the RUC. On previous occasions the media has often flaunted its investigative ability and integrity, and I would ask why it refuses to examine in any depth the use of informers. Has it been so intimidated by the RUC?[64]

Lorraine went home to Derry with the children on 18 April 1983, knowing that her father-in-law was still a captive.[65] She said of her decision to return: "I know it was the only thing I could have done. I would only have driven myself mad.... My hopes for the future are that he will realize soon that if he retracts they'll have no hold on him."[66]

The Trial: *R. v. Robson and others* (8 May 1984)

The trial itself (preceded by preliminary enquiries when most of those originally accused were remanded in custody) was notable for various reasons, though few of these were connected with the legal procedure. It was a typical show-trial, as the supergrass trials began to be called, held in a Diplock court, presided over by one judge, and without a jury. It differed, however, from preceding show-trials, in that it was already notorious as the largest trial ever mounted by Britain in the UK, and when it ended it had cost the British taxpayer an estimated £0.75 million. Thirty-six men and three women faced a total of 186 charges, and it took nearly two and a half hours to put these charges to the defendants: "The scene in the Belfast Crown Court as the trial opened clearly showed the abnormal nature of this trial. As the courtroom was not large enough ... most of the defendants had to sit in the public galleries. They were surrounded and outnumbered three to one by police and prison warders, leaving little room for the public. Either side of the judge stood an armed RUC guard."[67]

Denis Dillon, district attorney of Nassau County, New York, an observer at the trial, commented: "I think the legal system is being used to deal with a political problem."[68] Raymond's appearance was carefully thought out. He wore, for the first time in his life, a grey suit, white shirt, and striped tie, in contrast to the defendants (most of whom had already been detained on remand for up to two years) in jeans. Nell McCafferty described him thus: "He exhibited no signs of human emotion and responded as if he had been programmed. A general feeling among journalists, lawyers, the public and the prisoners was that the police controlled every word."[69]

Probably the most telling proof of this, certainly in that Belfast court, was his reference to "Londonderry." This, from a young man who had spent his whole life in Catholic nationalist "Derry," was unbelievable. Then there was much laughter, even among the defendants, when he got his own birthdate wrong, was unsure of the ages of his children, and showed confusion over other dates. His evidence was further marred by claims that, while on active service with the IRA, he went to great lengths not to shoot anyone. *An Phoblacht* categorized Gilmour's testimony as "vague and insubstantial ... much of which concerned alleged planned operations against crown forces which, by Gilmour's own admission, were never carried out."[70] Such claims were a constant feature of evidence presented by previous supergrasses since the Christopher Black trial.[71]

Raymond's family was represented by his mother, sitting with Martin McGuinness, and surrounded by RUC men; two of his sisters, Dymphna and Geraldine, sat with his brother Johnny at the back of the courtroom. This situation came to an abrupt end when Gilmour began to testify. Bridget Gilmour left the court, pausing to speak to him as she did so, thus causing the RUC to eject her forcibly. Her two daughters leapt to her defense and were manhandled from the room over the heads of the crowd; at this point Johnny jumped to their aid and was dragged away by six RUC men. While this was happening Gilmour and his minders turned and left the court.

Raymond Gilmour concluded his direct evidence on 22 October and the trial was adjourned by Lord Chief Justice Lowry until 5 November, when Gilmour would face cross-examination. Then defense lawyer, Desmond Boal, in his cross-examination, made much use of Lorraine's words in exposing her husband's lies, especially his denials that, prior to his court appearances, the RUC had given him a book of evidence, which contained all the statements he had signed to incriminate the prisoners; Boal also pointed out substantial discrepancies between Gilmour's claims of his financial arrangements with the RUC and the figures supplied by the prosecution.

Part of the cross-examination was observed by two delegates from

Birmingham Trades Council, Dave Brooks and Allan Thomas, because one of the defendants, had asked for this to be arranged. On the subject of their presence at the trial, Brooks said: "trade unionists like myself should visit a part of the UK where you can be arrested without charge, detained without trial, tried without a jury and condemned on the evidence of a 'supergrass' whose testimony is tainted."[72]

Finally, on 19 December 1984, Lowry called an abrupt halt to the trial. The problem, he said, was not Gilmour's "scandalous character, oblivious to every natural obligation of marital and fatherly affection and friendship," but that he considered him to be "entirely unworthy of belief."[73] Nevertheless, and despite his having said much the same thing about the evidence of another supergrass, Kevin McGrady, in May 1983, Lowry made it clear that uncorroborated evidence by alleged accomplices had no bearing on his decision.[74] This was emphasized in 1984 by Douglas Hurd, then the Secretary of State for Northern Ireland, when he refused in Parliament to stop the supergrass system, saying "There is no reason to reject, in principle, evidence simply because it comes from an accomplice who has given information to the police."[75] Most of the people who were acquitted had been remanded without trial since August 1982, while Cathal Crumley, later the first Sinn Féin Lord Mayor of Derry, and eight others remained in custody as they were also accused on the word of supergrass Robert Quigley. They were finally freed on appeal in November 1986 after spending over four years in prison. In addition, a few days after the collapse of the Gilmour trial, the first appeal against conviction by a supergrass (Joe Bennett) took place, and the fourteen men previously jailed on his word were acquitted. Their acquittal did not, however, signal the end of the strategy.

Certain questions remain, especially those concerning Martin McGuinness' sympathy with Raymond Gilmour. Plainly it was to the advantage of Sinn Féin to have Gilmour retract, on the other hand, it would have been unlikely to score very highly with the people of Derry whose view of Gilmour was at one and the same time the traditional view of the informer, and fear in case they would be the next named. If McGuinness' overtures were not genuine, and geared solely towards making Gilmour return to Derry in order to be killed, that too could have had a very negative effect.[76]

Johnny Gilmour said of the people of Derry, "It was unbelievable how some people treated my family," and of Raymond, "I would've shot him when my temper was big because my parents were hurt."[77] Nevertheless, despite all that his family suffered, and although Lorraine changed her name, he cannot hate him. He says, "Well of course I love him, he's my brother, and I sit here and I think about him and I hope he's OK,"[78] and Claire, Johnny's wife, was defensive, insisting that Raymond was very selective about people and was careful not to mention those who were friends.[79]

Was Raymond Gilmour's selective betrayal deliberate? Was it in some way better than betraying his family's friends? Or did he just, like so many others, echo the names dictated to him by Special Branch, so that the lack of friends' names on the list was mere coincidence? Or, indeed, given that Hugh Brady, who lived on the Creggan, had been friendly with Gilmour ("they used to run about together"[80]) and was later named by him, is it more simply an attempt to defend the indefensible? Whatever the answers the inescapable fact remains that, as Bobby Sands observed in *The H-Block Trilogy*, there were those who informed and there were those who refused.[81] Perhaps Johnny Gilmour summed it up accurately. When asked why he refused to tout, both as a child and when he was older, he said, "Because I'm never helping them bastards."[82]

Kevin McGrady

Kevin Joseph McGrady (born in 1956) lived with his parents, sister, and five brothers in the predominantly nationalist Markets area of inner-city Belfast. When he left school he began an apprenticeship with a butcher not far from his home, joined the local IRA battalion in 1975, and had never been in trouble with the police up to that point. "He claimed he enlisted in the IRA because he identified with the nationalist cause, distrusted the Protestant community, and because his brother Sean had been interned in the early 1970s."[83] He was an active member for less than six months, from his first operation in July 1975 until the following October, when he went on the run (unsuccessfully, because he was in police custody by December, and remained there until June 1976). Six months in any organization is something less than significant, nor can it be assumed that Kevin could have progressed much in the IRA in so short a time, yet the prosecution, in May 1983, gave much weight to his membership, and Judge Lowry referred to his "thorough familiarity with his fellow terrorists. His knowledge of them was by no means casual or transient. This is a very important side to this man."[84]

By the time he was arrested in December 1975 he had been involved in some serious crimes, though he was only charged with one of these: the murder of Ernest Dowds. The charge was dropped when the owner of the car said to have been used in the shooting withdrew his evidence.[85] His brother, Sean McGrady, however, had made a statement, confessing to have been a look-out, after a previously broken arm was broken again when his RUC interrogator beat it against a wall. Subsequently Sean was given a life sentence for the murder, and Kevin was given three months imprisonment for assaulting an RUC man during interrogation. Since he had already been remanded in custody for seven months, he was released immediately and six weeks later he went to work as a butcher in London. There he spent eighteen months before going to Amsterdam where he worked in a hotel, and lived in a youth hostel controlled by an American evangelical group, Youth with a Mission (commonly known as YWAM). In March 1978, apparently after a religious conversion, he became a member of YWAM and then worked as a registered member of the staff of the hostel between January and September 1981. When he applied for the job of assistant manager he was told he must clear his conscience first.[86]

In January 1982 Kevin McGrady returned to Belfast and gave himself up to the RUC, then, in Castlereagh, confessed all his crimes. Yet, despite his voluntary surrender, Special Branch wanted more, and especially they wanted James Gibney, formerly a National Organizer of Sinn Féin and election agent for Owen Carron in the Fermanagh-South Tyrone by-election in 1981. A Detective Constable admitted in court that Gibney was "high on the list of people the RUC wished to convict."[87] Given the brevity of McGrady's membership of the IRA, and his long absence from Northern Ireland, it is unlikely that he could have known Gibney. It should also be noted that all of the evidence presented at the trial related to 1975, some seven years previously. The Belfast Bulletin printed a graphic and bitter summary of the trial:

> the subsequent conduct of his case closely mirrors that of the other supergrass trials … the careful schooling of McGrady in the art of giving evidence (there were 47 pre-trial visits by police and religious minders), the psychological manipulation of McGrady to ensure that he endured throughout the long pre-trial period and trial, police minders in Court providing support and reassurance when the cross examination got rough, and a deal of sorts with the referral of Kevin's brother, Sean McGrady's, case back to the Court of Appeal given the new evidence of his innocence provided by Kevin's confession.[88]

Kevin McGrady had exonerated his brother and confessed that only he and John McConkey (later also a supergrass) had been involved. McConkey had admitted that this was correct. On 26 June 1982, therefore, Kevin McGrady pleaded guilty to "twenty-seven charges, including the murders of William Stephenson, Andrew Craig, and Ernest Dowds, and four attempted murders, in all of which he claimed to have played a secondary but willing role as a look-out or as a driver of the getaway vehicle."[89] He had not asked for immunity or money, nor had they been offered, he had just wanted to free his brother.

The Trial: *R. v. Gibney and others* (5 May 1983)

The trial was the third of the show trials (it was preceded by the Bennett and Black trials) and lasted almost six months. The ten defendants faced a total of 45 charges between them, including: three murders (Andrew Craig, 8 September 1975, William Stevenson, between 1 October and 4 October 1975, Ernest Dowds, 10 October 1975); attempted murder; conspiracy to murder (Sir James Flanagan, then Chief Constable of the RUC); attempted murder, and attacks on public houses. All the defendants were also charged with membership of the Provisional IRA.

The main significance of the trial was that it gave Lord Chief Justice Robert Lowry the "opportunity to lay down guidelines for the other seven High Court Judges regarding the admissability [sic] of informer evidence."[90] This had wide implications for the conduct of the show trials and was interpreted by the media as the definitive statement. It was accepted that written or verbal statements made by the defendants constituted corroboration of the statements made by informers, but Lowry took this one step further in the McGrady trial. James Gibney had made no statements, but the police claimed that, when confronted by McGrady, he looked uneasy, and became flustered. Gifford's comment on this is: "at the most it gave rise to suspicion, but then so did McGrady's evidence about him. Adding suspicion to suspicion does not amount to proof."[91] The judge accepted this as corroboration and Gibney was sentenced to twelve years. Yet of McGrady's evidence in the case of two of the murder charges (Craig and Stevenson), totally disproved by forensic evidence, Lord Lowry commented: "to have convicted ... in these groups of charges would have been a perversion of justice ... so contradictory, bizarre and in some respects incredible was McGrady's evidence and so devious and deliberately evasive was his manner of giving it."[92]

Whenever Kevin's evidence could be tested against forensic evidence it was shown that he was lying: "On the killings of Craig and Stephenson, which McGrady claimed to have witnessed, his version was proved impossible by the evidence of the forensic pathologist."[93] Eugene Pinkey was in prison at the time he was alleged to have been involved in IRA activities, so his brother, Thomas, was substituted for him. In like manner, Gerard McMahon was accused originally, then his brother Patrick was substituted because Gerard had been in prison between 1974 and 1976. As this included the whole time of Kevin McGrady's involvement with the IRA he could not possibly have known him as an active IRA member. Again Lord Lowry commented: "Were the glaring absurdities merely due to a foolish desire to 'improve' a good case? Did McGrady believe those whom he accused were guilty and then pretend to have been present? Or did he make the whole thing up? I find it hard to say, but perhaps the choice is between the second and third hypothesis."[94]

Yet Lord Chief Justice Lowry managed to find a unique solution which enabled him to convict seven of the defendants, including Gibney. "He decided that, at times, McGrady was telling the truth, but at other times he was telling lies."[95]

Much was made in newspapers and books of Kevin McGrady's religious conversion, his return to Northern Ireland, and his evidence in court. The charitable have described him as a young man in need of psychiatric treatment.[96] Perhaps, though, they all approached the problem from the wrong direction and assumed that he must have been lying about everything. The *Belfast Bulletin* was clearly ambivalent about this, referring to it as "the most problematic aspect of the Kevin McGrady case.":

> There is no doubt that he did return and confess to a number of crimes. His motivations for so doing are clearly important. Was he really troubled by his conscience and the knowledge that an innocent man was in prison? Was he truly converted to a new religious philosophy which rejected his earlier activities? Or was he gambling on cleaning the slate, doing a short term in an English prison and getting his brother Sean off the hook at the same time?[97]

Why did this young man become a supergrass? He had plainly been reasonably successful at school (this is borne out by his apprenticeship and the later attempt to become assistant manager in the hostel); he had never been in trouble with the police during his school years; and he was strongly enough attached to his family to follow in the footsteps of Sean and Anthony, his brothers, and to return from Amsterdam to rescue Sean. Moreover, when he arrived in Amsterdam he chose to live in a Christian youth hostel. It seems possible that his brief experience of the IRA and the world outside his home had not been life-enhancing, and that he was looking for the security of his childhood, centered around home, school and parish church.[98] YWAM offered this, and more:

> YWAM provides a positive alternative for energetic young people. For some, the choice can be as clear and dramatic as rebellion versus submission. The danger and thrill of drugs, gangs and the street seduces them into rebellion from their parents' world. However, YWAM offers similar excitement through an alternative means—submission to Jesus Christ. YWAMers love God and follow him with the same reckless abandon that characterized the first century disciples.[99]

Kevin McGrady was certainly naïve, and perhaps easily impressed by authority of any kind and unquestioning of its edicts. This would explain his sudden conversion when in contact with YWAM, an organization with wide experience of young people all over the world, whose claims to be interdenominational might also impress a young man from Belfast. It also seems that he became very dependent on this new community and was assiduously courted by them (McGrady made two trips to the U.S., courtesy of YWAM, in as many years). He found security and a purpose with YWAM.[100] This is obvious, not least because he had no wish to return to Belfast. He returned there originally in 1981, then went back to Amsterdam, too afraid, perhaps, to carry out his intention (moreover, his mother had died and his father became seriously ill before he went to Holland). Nevertheless, he *did* go back a second time, voluntarily surrendered himself to the RUC, and confessed his involvement in three murders and other crimes. While in Amsterdam, according to the *Belfast Bulletin*, his record shows "dependence, manipulation and having others make his decisions for him." It is possible that he then transferred this dependence to the police. The *Belfast Bulletin* also decided that Kevin was "weak-minded and impressionable" and referred to the ease with which he changed his mind and his story. Yet it also said of him that "Every major decision in his life was either taken casually or under the strong influence of others," and that "In the experienced hands of the RUC he must have been like putty."[101] So there is another explanation for these apparent vagaries: The usual schooling by the RUC would have been very confusing for a young man determined to be truthful.

Kevin McGrady was Sir John Hermon's ideal converted terrorist. In fact he was the only supergrass who deserved that description, and, if one accepts his religious conversion as genuine, it explains a great deal. He did not ask for anything, not even immunity. He wanted Sean to be released on the grounds that he, himself, was guilty of the crime for which his brother was serving life. This is both laudable and understandable, as is the fear he must have had to conquer in order to pursue it. He not only failed (indeed at one point both brothers were serving life imprisonment for the same crime—the murder of Ernest Dowds) but ended up as yet another informer, exiled, and looking over his shoulder for the rest of his life. This happened partly because of his own naïvety in assuming that the police would accept his confession, but largely because the RUC viewed him opportunistically and manipulated him: "He testified in Court that he had not intended to name names, and that *it was the police who persuaded him to do that*. In fact, according to his own statements, he wasn't aware that he could give evidence against the others."[102]

Those lies told in court, which attracted such scorn on every side, were they Kevin's lies? If Kevin McGrady was a liar why did he tell the court that "Sean had been a lookout at the Craig murder in 1975, an offense for which Sean had not been prosecuted," and offer to give evidence for the prosecution against Sean?[103] After all, his main motive, apart from clearing his conscience, was to free Sean and this was no way to do it. Did he perhaps suffer from the scourge of all the newly converted: the assumption that others want to or should do as they themselves are doing? Or did it have something to do with his claim in court that he had been assaulted while in Castlereagh? The RUC Inspector questioned about this claim said (on oath) that McGrady was a liar. The same Inspector in answer to the value of McGrady's evidence against other men said McGrady was an honest and truthful man.[104] Or was he just doing as he was told, keeping his bargain with the RUC to attain Sean's freedom? The RUC reneged on this, perhaps by default, when Sean McGrady's conviction was upheld by the Court of Appeal in 1984 on the grounds that Kevin's evidence was unreliable because it was contrary to the evidence of some soldiers and others.

In fact, since Kevin McGrady was not motivated by personal gain, as the *Belfast Bulletin* states: "there is some reason for assuming that he may be a credible witness," and that this case "by all common sense criteria, should be sympathetic to those who support the supergrass strategy." Nevertheless, they also went on to deliver a condemnation of the Northern Ireland system of justice, claiming that:

> The extent to which the system of "justice" in N.I. has become a farce, a show, is illustrated not only by the conduct of the trial ... but also by the fact that within weeks of delivering judgement in the McGrady case (the essence of which was the acceptability of uncorroborated evidence) the same Lord Chief Justice allowed an appeal by a Special Branch detective who had been convicted, on informer evidence, of armed robbery and possession of firearms.[105] Lowry's reason for releasing McCormick, the Special Branch detective, was that: "the prosecution case lacked the cogent and compelling corroboration required in cases of this kind."[106]

Kevin McGrady was sentenced to life imprisonment in June 1982 for his involvement in the murder of Dowds. Earlier that year Sean McGrady had tried in vain to visit his brother in prison. He came to the conclusion that his efforts were being frustrated by the RUC, who feared his influence, and finally accepted that he could only get a message to him via the media:

> Eight months ago my brother Kevin gave himself up and cleared me of my involvement in the killing for which I am now doing life.
> I believe my brother is now being used by the RUC and that my release is conditional on him now giving evidence against other men who are innocent.... I therefore appeal to my brother ... not to allow himself to be pressed into giving false evidence against innocent people.[107]

Kevin was released from Maghaberry Prison in April 1988. Thirty of the forty-five charges based on his evidence were thrown out of court and three of the ten defendants were freed. Of the remaining seven, two, including James Gibney, were given twelve years.[108] Kevin McGrady did not manage to free his brother. Sean McGrady's appeal was heard on 4 May 1984 when he had already served eight years of his life sentence, and was refused on the grounds that Kevin's evidence was "quite unpersuasive and incredible."[109]

Angela Whoriskey

Although women played a more active role in republican activities during the 1970s, much of the ideal concerning them remained: that they should be respected and treated with gentleness. So, despite the persistent rumors in January and February 1972, that a wing in Armagh Jail had been designated for women internees, none were interned until Elizabeth McKee, aged nineteen, became the first woman to be interned without charge or trial in January 1973. She was not alone for long: in 1974 Mary Kennedy was interned, leaving her children to fend for themselves.[110] From then on ill-treatment of women in nationalist areas and the prisons was noted with increasing frequency in republican newsletters and by relatives' action groups.

In 1980 Fr. Denis Faul produced a compilation of allegations about the treatment of republican women protesters in Armagh Jail and commented "For the past two years a policy of repression has been in vogue, control and punishment with no redress for grievances." He went on to describe the actions of the Special Prison Officer Riot Squad following what seems to have been deliberate manipulation of the women: "Men in riot gear were sent to the cells armed with batons and shields. They beat and dragged the girls to the guard room, twisting their hair.... The girls were starved of food and drink.... The toilets were locked and the girls were not allowed to the toilets."[111]

From January 1980 physical violence, petty harassment and filthy conditions became more common for republican women, and this extended to other women prisoners.[112] Far worse, however, than any of this was the strip-searching—generally agreed by all the women to be the most distressing aspect of prison life.[113] Strip-searching was introduced in November 1982. From then until December 1983, 1,621 strip-searches were carried out in Armagh Jail on a maximum prison population of 40, ten of whom were ordinary criminal prisoners. The Northern Ireland Office told the House of Commons that strip-searching in Armagh was "no more frequent than in Scottish prisons,"[114] and that all strip-searches are essential for security and are carried out by caring staff.[115] Nothing was ever found.

> One argument about strip searching is, if strip searching is done with "care and consideration" it is alright [sic] ... it is not alright.... You are naked and vulnerable.... You are being examined to take something away from you—using your body against you.... We know from my own and others' experience that it is a horrendous experience which has proven adverse emotional and psychological effects.[116]

Such were the conditions when Angela Whoriskey was convicted. She was twenty-five, the single parent of an eighteen-month-old daughter, who lived on Strand Road, Shantallow, a nationalist area of Derry described as "the most poverty-stricken of the 566 districts in the North of Ireland."[117] She had a history of psychiatric problems and, on 9 October 1985, she was arrested and accused of complicity in the murder of RUC Inspector Norman Ruddy. Like so many of the others she was vulnerable to pressure, and Angela Whoriskey became a supergrass.

Apart from the fact that she was the only woman among the supergrasses, the case of Angela Whoriskey is singular in that, for the first (and perhaps only) time, most public comments made about her actions were tinged with a good deal of sympathy and understanding. Whether this was because she was a woman, or because both journalists and Sinn Féin commentators were beginning to understand how often the weak in nationalist areas were pressurized to inform, is impossible to say.

On 15 October, a week after Whoriskey's arrest, the RUC and the British Army conducted a series of raids in Derry. The procedure began at 4 a.m. and lasted for over five hours. Nineteen people were arrested, taken to Interrogation Centers, subjected to the usual treatment, and twelve of them were later charged on the basis of statements made by Whoriskey. She applied for bail and asked for police custody, meaning she would be remanded at the local police barracks rather than Armagh Women's Prison, but Justice O'Donnell denied both requests, though police custody had been agreed with the RUC. O'Donnell's decision may have been intended to send a message to the women of Derry because the main significance of this setback was the fear, by this point endemic among nationalist women, of being sent to Armagh.

On 16 October the people of Strand Road knew what had happened when a large force of RUC, with British troops and several masked figures in tracksuits, arrived at Angela Whoriskey's home at 7:30 a.m. They loaded everything from the house into an unmarked furniture lorry. This was the unmistakable sign of the supergrass: it had been seen too often in preceding years. At much the same time her father, her sister, her brother, and her small daughter disappeared from the house, an indication that the RUC were using the family to pressurize Whoriskey, and isolate her from all outside contacts. "Derry Sinn Féin Councillor Mitchel McLaughlin said he believed that the father is now being used by the RUC as 'extra leverage' to ensure that Angela Whoriskey testifies, a tactic he described as 'a very blatant use of emotional blackmail.'"[118] Martin McGuinness noted of her case: "I am convinced that this is part of a deliberate RUC attempt to resurrect the use of paid-perjurers in Diplock courts. Angela Whoriskey, a single parent, separated from her family, friends and young child, is especially vulnerable to the sophisticated techniques of blackmail and suggestion used and perfected by the RUC."[119]

On 25 October a High Court Judge, Mr. Justice MacDermott, was told by a defense lawyer that there was a question mark over Whoriskey's informer status. He said: "they were reserving their position on her alleged admissions to police and that they did not necessarily accept them."[120] Then, on 7 March 1986, in an indication that Whoriskey had been offered an early release in exchange for her testimony, Mr. Justice Hutton did not stipulate any minimum recommended sentence when she was given a life sentence after confessing involvement as a look-out in the killing of Inspector Norman Ruddy.[121]

5. The Supergrasses

Much of what is known about Whoriskey's time in prison has been told to republican newspapers by Patricia Moore. She was twenty-two, worked as a quality control examiner in a Derry shirt factory, and was arrested on Whoriskey's evidence following the raids on 15 October. She said "I was never ever inside an RUC barracks in my life before that morning I was arrested. I was shocked and nervous but because I knew I'd nothing to hide and I was innocent, I kept thinking 'Do seven days and you'll get out.'" Moore was held for seven days in Castlereagh and it is conceivable that she was transported there from Derry because of Castlereagh's reputation. Moore endured threats during that week that she would be shot by the SAS, and pressured to become an informer for Special Branch. Finally Whoriskey was brought in to identify her. Patricia Moore said "She never once looked at my face."[122] She had no need to do so since, as an editorial in *The Irish People* makes plain, it was "A one-to-one confrontation which begins with the RUC announcing the accused's name. It is a farce intended to make certain that Whoriskey can point out the right individual in court."[123]

There followed five months in Armagh Jail, until it closed in 1986, then a transfer to Maghaberry Prison where Moore's cell adjoined the unit occupied by Whoriskey. "Virtually every day, Whoriskey was visited by RUC Special Branch men carrying thick files and maps who were there to rehearse Whoriskey.... It really added to the stress, to sit behind bars knowing that you're totally innocent and knowing that the Special Branch were going in to school her to lie not only about me but about everyone else. And there was absolutely nothing I could do about it."[124]

Whoriskey had been given a life sentence, but was allowed extra visits, given her own choice of food and clothes, and was taken out on shopping expeditions and for periods of twenty-four hours, while the remand prisoners were repeatedly strip-searched even when seriously ill. The case of Patricia Moore, who was returned from hospital to Armagh, is ample evidence that strip-searching had nothing to do with security. She fainted in the search area, but was not strip-searched until she was again conscious. She was later operated on for a burst ovarian cyst.[125] When, a year later, Patricia Moore was freed in Lisburn Courthouse, her bitterness is understandable: "All of a sudden I was arrested and kept in jail for a year for things which I didn't know anything about, never mind did.... Nobody's ever going to hand me back that year, nobody's going to be able to take away all the hurt and the worry that I've had to go through—not only me, but my family and all the other people arrested and their families."[126]

She and eighteen others from Derry had all charges against them dropped when, in October 1986, a year after their original arrest, "for reasons which have not been made clear, the DPP for Northern Ireland announced that they would not be prosecuted."[127] *Troops Out* commented: "It seems that months of RUC tuition could not produce a witness with even the meagre credibility required in a Diplock court."[128] Of Whoriskey's case, Martin McGuinness commented:

> After a year of collusion between the RUC and DPP they have finally accepted that Angela Whoriskey can no longer be presented as a willing, a truthful or indeed an effective witness ... [This] does not, however, signal the end to the paid perjurer strategy. On the day this case collapsed the trial of three men based on the word of another RUC blackmail victim, Owen Connolly, began in Belfast.... The collapse of the Whoriskey case is a victory for those who oppose injustice and oppression. But we must all redouble our efforts to end once and for all this squalid strategy.[129]

The supergrass strategy ended without fanfare. Greer lists the reasons for its demise: the Anglo-Irish Agreement in November 1985; the campaigns and the international pressure they engendered were influential on the courts; the danger of alienating the loyalist community; the Gifford report, though unofficial, was hard-hitting and widely read; and finally, despite claims to the contrary, the impact of the supergrass system on levels of violence was insignificant.[130] The main significance of the 1985 Anglo-Irish Agreement in this context lay in Article 7(c) which emphasized the need to "improve relations between the security forces and the community, with the object in particular of making the security forces more readily accepted by the nationalist community ... [and] to increase the proportion of members of the minority in the Royal Ulster Constabulary."[131]

However, the loyalists saw it as a betrayal of Ulster: they had been excluded from the negotiations; the Dublin government was to discuss Northern Ireland matters with British ministers and this was perceived as a threat to the position of Northern Ireland within the United Kingdom; and unionists had to accept the power-sharing *régime*. In addition. "for the first time, the British Government has officially committed to promoting legislation for a united Ireland if a majority is in favor."[132] The subsequent protests made it quite clear that the Agreement had no support within the loyalist community. Thus the Anglo-Irish Agreement may have temporarily distracted both loyalists and nationalists from their concerns about the supergrasses, but Greer overestimates its importance as a factor in bringing about the end of the supergrass strategy.

Conclusion

Some twenty-seven names come under the supergrass umbrella, varying in importance according to the numbers of those whom they accused, which ranged from three (Sean Mallon) to forty-five (Raymond Gilmour). The main success of the strategy lay in its duration, because for those five years between

1981 and 1986 the victims implicated by the supergrasses were held in prison without trial for considerable periods. This did not initially result in the public outrage and organized opposition which had characterized internment, because the impact fell mainly on nationalist working-class communities with the large numbers implicated by Christopher Black. Then the advent of Joseph Bennett and the consequences to the loyalist paramilitaries, intended to circumvent accusations of sectarianism, backfired when loyalists began to realize how the nationalists felt. Bennett was followed later by other loyalist supergrasses, such as James Crockard (UVF, eleven victims), William "Budgie" Allen (UVF, twenty-two victims), and Clifford McKeown (UVF, twenty-nine victims). The topic began to appear in print in the loyalist publications as frequently as in those of the republicans, and the loyalist women of the Shankill took up the struggle on behalf of their men. They formed Families for Legal Rights, protested at Stormont and Westminster, organized events to raise funds, and lobbied MPs (including Lord Longford)[133] and Assembly members. Alexa McCrossan of this group said: "all right thinking people should do what they can to bring down this unjust system."[134] While Joseph McCann, a victim of Budgie Allen, wrote: "One can only conclude that the Northern Ireland officer [sic] and the Judiciary are conveniently bending the law in the mistaken belief that this will help bring a solution to the problems which exist in Northern Ireland. History shows us that such a course will do nothing but exacerbate the situation."[135]

Roisin Loughlin's husband, Gerald, was one of 38 people charged and held on remand on the word of Christopher Black. Gerald was arrested on 21 November 1981 and given a life sentence. Determined to fight this new injustice, Roisin got together with other women to begin the Anti-Show Trials Campaign. So although the political impact of the supergrass system was limited it had an immense effect on the wives and families of the victims. The Crumlin Road Families Centre, originally set up to serve the relations of those in Belfast Prison, was in high demand during the supergrass trials from hundreds of relatives (of the informers as well as the accused). Often while mothers and wives were in court, the children were left there all day. Joan McNally, the Canteen Supervisor, was in a good position to see the effects of the trials on these families:

> the main one is stress ... this is partly the normal apprehension about a family member getting a prison sentence. But the supergrass system does have special effects. Many relatives feel frustrated and aggrieved that their men are being tried on the word of despised informers.... The day of the verdict is the worst ... this is a terrible trial for children ... by the time the day is over, Daddy may be serving 20 years.[136]

She noticed that there was no difference between the women of both communities when she saw them advising each other and discussing their problems together during the Black (December 1982–August 1983) and Bennett

(February–April 1983) trials. Particularly hard on the wives and children was the fact that when their husbands were in prison their unemployment benefit stopped, and all the wives, in order to support their families, had to reapply every week for supplementary benefit which involved queuing for hours.

In February 1984 the Anti-Perjurer Joint Delegation, led by Bernadette McAliskey,[137] went to London. It comprised the Concerned Community Organizations, Stop The Show Trials Committee, and Relatives For Justice. They met politicians, Amnesty International, the National Council for Civil Liberties, and lawyers. None of the Conservative MPs accepted the invitation to meet them.[138] Bernadette McAliskey's words at the time, spoken about nationalists, should have resounded uncomfortably throughout the UK: "We have a position where we are all guilty and that is the position we start off with. It has not yet been determined of what we are guilty, but we are guilty by birth, we are guilty because of the position we occupy in society."[139]

Public concern grew rapidly, generating protests from the relatives of the defendants, lawyers, politicians, trade unions, church leaders, and prominent figures in the Irish government and the British Labor Party. Ultimately various protest groups formed. Some were international, such as Action Europe: begun following a visit from a French lawyer to Derry and leading to accusations of British violations against the Human Rights Charter in the European Court of Human Rights[140]; others were initiated and run by the defendants' wives and lawyers.

Later, following the efforts of the women to publicize events, though there had not been a great deal of concern in the British newspapers, news spread throughout the English-speaking world, and caused the anger felt by the general population in Northern Ireland to be reflected across the U.S. and Australasia. There was wide condemnation of the British and the RUC, so the impact was very negative. Moreover, the Gifford Report asserted that "the conviction of defendants by single judges on the uncorroborated evidence of supergrasses is not an acceptable means of doing justice"; that it led to the telling of lies and the conviction of the innocent; and that the RUC regularly programmed supergrasses to concoct and rehearse statements.[141] Despite the collapse of the Whoriskey trial and the Gifford report of 1984, on 22 October 1986 the Attorney-General stated publicly that the supergrass system would continue. This confirmed Roisin McDonough's words a few months earlier when she refuted Greer and Jennings' article in *Fortnight*, which implied that the system had ended.[142] She named four appeals and four cases, including Whoriskey, as still outstanding; and also mentioned that there were no appeals or trials pending from the loyalist community.[143] Though Whoriskey's was the last trial, more potential supergrasses were still being held in Crumlin Road Jail, including Eamon Collins, who eventually retracted.

Yet legal writers had insisted earlier that the system had ended with the collapse of the Grimley trial in November 1983, though wisely appending a question mark to the title of their article.[144] Two years later they again made the same claim, this time in connection with the conviction of twenty-seven defendants in the Kirkpatrick trial in December 1985.[145] The reaction to this, in a letter from Roisin McDonough of Relatives for Justice, shows the different attitude of those caught up in the supergrass net when she refers to "an extremely dangerous assumption that the system has ended." She also challenges Whoriskey's position as either the first or the only woman supergrass, citing the little-known case of Catherine Yendall, of New Lodge Road, North Belfast, who, "Whilst her evidence was utterly discredited and the charges thrown out, three people whom the RUC had decided to imprison for 6 months were successfully detained without a public outcry."[146] However Yendall had little in common with the supergrasses: she was a notorious shoplifter and drunkard, used by the RUC to convict three Sinn Féin members who were freed when their trial collapsed in November 1985.[147]

Much information about the supergrasses is difficult to find, though there is always the possibility that the future release of archives pertaining to Northern Ireland may make this available, but a large amount of material has reportedly been destroyed. *Saoirse* claimed that on December 31 2006: "Prison authorities in the Occupied Six Counties destroyed 52,382 files in the months before the Freedom of Information Act was introduced."[148] In addition the material on the supergrasses whose arrests did not result in a trial is sparse. Of the twenty-seven, seventeen supergrasses retracted their statements: four were loyalists, and two (Whoriskey and Barry Llewellyn) were probably unaffiliated.

Among those who retracted the most notable has to be Robert Lean, of Ballymurphy. Lean was married with five children, an active member of Sinn Féin, and a campaign worker on Gerry Adams' election committee. This last, like any other political activism, plainly made him an ideal candidate for Kitson's "unwanted members of the public." He had been arrested and charged on the word of James O'Rawe (March 1982), then of William Skelly (September 1983).[149] Lean's wife, Geraldine, was also under suspicion, and so there was a risk that their children would be taken into care. Lean's importance lay in the widespread boasting of the RUC, who alleged that he was second in command of the Belfast IRA and that his evidence would devastate both the IRA and Sinn Féin in the city. This ensured wide media coverage first of his arrest in 1983, then of a series of leaks by the RUC about the numbers of people arrested on Lean's information, and the newspapers produced graphic descriptions of republicans fleeing Belfast in panic. *An Phoblacht/Republican News* reported:

While all of Sinn Fein's offices were fully staffed and working as usual, the press was reporting wild allegations of "panic spreading through West Belfast" (*Irish Times*), of scores of republicans "on the run" or "having fled over the border" (*Evening Press*). The *Daily Mail* quoted RUC sources as saying they were "confident they could clean up" West Belfast of republicans, with Lean's help. The *Sunday News* of September 11th went further and printed a James Bond type story alleging that Lean had been an "RUC mole" for years.[150]

Instead, only weeks later, the republican press, in delighted detail, was reporting Lean's escape from protective custody in a stolen police car. The added fillip was that, as he drove through the gates, he was saluted by the RUC man on duty there. Maura McCrory, of the Stop the Show Trials Co-ordinating Committee, said: "The facts are that the 'converted terrorist' theory is a nonsense, merely a propaganda myth. If Robert Lean did anything, he pulled the bottom out of this silly assertion."[151]

Whether or not it was this incident which gave rise to the theory that Lean was a plant by the IRA to discredit the supergrass strategy, there is a certain amount of evidence to support this idea: Lean had ensured his wife's escape some days previously, his own escape was newsworthy, and he followed this by making a retraction statement in the form of an affidavit to his solicitor; then held a press conference at the Felons' Club in West Belfast. Immediately after this, the RUC arrested him for stealing the police car, thus ensuring widespread newspaper coverage of the entire incident. Though other retractions were reported in the press, none had the drama or formality of this one.

Apart from the high proportion of retractions, a pattern emerges from a study of the supergrass phenomenon. Many of them, such as Goodman and Allen, were already criminals, some, like McAllister and Kennedy, were already RUC informers. Among this group Clifford McKeown stands out for his previous and subsequent involvement in violent crime, and for his murder of Catholic taxi driver, Michael McGoldrick, during the 1996 Drumcree crisis.[152]

Though some trials took place in the 1970s, of particular interest was firstly the McWilliams trial of March 1980, then *R. v. McCormick* in March 1982.[153] The significance of the latter case was that Justice Murray refused to convict without corroborative evidence, and also criticized the police for coaching their witness (the informer Anthony O'Doherty) prior to the trial. This judicial attitude can be compared to the same judge's conduct of the Joseph Bennett trial in the following year when he advanced his argument for believing Bennett's evidence. Gifford demolishes this "curious argument" in a few sentences: most of the offenses had taken place up to two years before Bennett was arrested, some much further back (1973–4); many charges were based on a single conversation and were vague about dates and details, e.g., "conspiracy on a date unknown between 1 January 1980 and 1 May 1982 with persons unknown to possess explosive substances."[154]

Between 1982 and 1984 twelve supergrass trials took place. Of these, William "Budgie" Allen, Joseph Bennett, and John Wright were UVF men, and Christopher Black, Raymond Gilmour, Jackie Goodman, Jackie Grimley, Harry Kirkpatrick, James Kennedy, Kevin McGrady, John Morgan, and Robert Quigley belonged to the IRA or INLA. The Grimley trial stands out because it ended abruptly, with seven of the eighteen defendants acquitted, when Lord Justice Gibson found Grimley's evidence to be completely unreliable. In all cases the process of arrest, inducement, implication of others, statements, and trial were the same. Both the supergrasses and Lord Gifford agree (the latter reluctantly) that many of the statements were written by the RUC to implicate those involved in any kind of political activism, and scant attention was paid to whether or not the informer concerned had ever known those he was implicating.[155] Gifford comments of Grimley, a habitual criminal with no regard for the truth "his use as a star prosecution witness makes one wonder whether there is any effective control by the authorities over the supergrass process."[156] The inducements were enough to tempt even an honest man, and most of these men were not honest, though Sinn Féin stated that the RUC had consistently denied offering such bribes. In March 1982, nevertheless, Sean Seamus O'Hara, the brother of dead hunger striker Patsy O'Hara, told a press conference in West Belfast that he had been offered £50,000 and a new identity in South Africa by the RUC in return for giving evidence against INLA members, some of whom he had never met. John Carson from Ballymurphy, West Belfast, was offered the same amount, and the pamphlet goes on to claim that: "Others who have been interrogated in Castlereagh have been offered staggering sums of £250,000 ... in return for giving evidence against prominent republicans."[157] Bonner, considering the supergrass trials in *The Modern Law Review*, is careful about the claims of pressure from and inducements offered by the RUC. He writes of the allegations: "whether their claims represent the truth of the matter or are designed to explain or justify their aberrant conduct to their colleagues is impossible to say."[158] However, in February 1985 the Secretary of State for Northern Ireland said that "total direct expenditure on the protection of individuals who gave evidence against former accomplices in terrorist organisations in the last seven years amounted to just over £1.3 million."[159] Robert Lean told Lord Gifford what he had been promised: "How it works, we choose a place where you won't stand out, where you blend ... give us three countries where you would like to go, and we will pick one ... the kids could go to private boarding schools ... you won't get a lump sum because you would blow it ... we'll pension you off ... like Supplementary Benefit only far more ... a house fully furnished ... you negotiate your terms."[160]

Yet others, besides Bennett, were more influenced by the promise of immunity or a much reduced prison sentence. Those they accused were subjected to the same pressures and inducements: Quigley had been implicated by Gilmour; Lean and other retractors had also been accused by previous supergrasses; and victims freed by one retraction were frequently on the list of the next informer, as in the case of Lean. Given the nature of the pressure and the rewards on offer, it is surprising that so few were turned by the police. It is also interesting to realize how brief the supergrass era was, and to attempt to establish what brought it to an end. The Gifford Report is very readable and full of commonsense and humanity for all those involved, but in 1986 the Attorney General, urged by Gifford "to prevent prosecutions based on uncorroborated supergrass evidence,"[161] announced that the system would continue. Though it did, in fact, dwindle away, this probably had more to do with the numbers of acquittals of those convicted in earlier show trials, thus making it difficult to keep up the momentum. Moreover, neither its brevity nor the acquittals made it a failure. It has long been assumed by the Northern Ireland community that the whole purpose of the supergrass system was to act as a replacement for internment by removing certain individuals from circulation. In this respect it undoubtedly succeeded. In 1985 *Troops Out* stated this bluntly:

> The entire "supergrass" strategy is based on police coercion of informers ... with the aim of fostering fear and divisions within the Nationalist community. "Success" is not seen purely in terms of convictions but in terms of how long people are held in prison before trial. In this case, most defendants had been in custody more than two years.... Others, still awaiting trial ... have been in prison for over three years! This amounts to selective internment.[162]

Greer regards this claim of internment under another name as conspiracy theory.[163] Bonner, however, admits that it would be unwise to dismiss such claims out of hand and notes that these "expressions of concern transcend the sectarian divide in a way that few other issues have done in Northern Ireland."[164] He also notes the allegation, in the case of Patrick McGurk, who retracted just before the trial in October 1983, that the Crown was told over a year previously that he was not going to testify against anyone. The families of over 500 people, remanded without bail while awaiting trial on the word of the supergrasses, were in no doubt that the reason for this strategy was to remove certain people from the streets. Nor did it matter much whether they were innocent or guilty: originally 55 percent of those charged were convicted, on appeal the conviction rate dropped to 24 percent, but the innocent had still been in jail for a considerable amount of time.

While Raymond Gilmour, some twenty years after the event, can still deceive himself about his actions, not all the supergrasses were incapable of accepting the consequences of their treachery.[165] In Eamon Collins's *Killing*

Rage, James Crockard, the loyalist supergrass, incarcerated with Collins in the Crumlin Road Annex, said to him: "We are all in the same boat, Eamon. None of us is certain of anything. None of us knows exactly what will happen." Collins, thinking about these words, decided: "we all had one thing in common: we broke, we betrayed our comrades, our beliefs, and our communities ... the safety and security ... had gone."[166] Yet others neither broke nor betrayed. Danny Morrison compares the two strategies:

> Arrested second time in September 1978 and questioned for seven days—the worst part was the screams of men coming from other cells down the corridor and men crying like children.... Was in C/Reagh in Jan 1990 for the last time—the interrogation and attempts to break one down were all intellectual/cerebral/psychological and actually quite entertaining though at the end of it I was charged with conspiracy to murder, kidnapping and IRA membership.[167]

So the pressure exerted on the supergrasses cannot be disputed, but it should not be forgotten that there were those who refused, often at great cost to themselves, both in terms of mental and physical suffering and in the effect of their refusal on their families. Ray Gilmour's family say of him that he did not accuse any family friends, but Hugh Brady was one of Gilmour's own friends. This defense says more about his family than it does about him, because, young though he was, his brother Johnny was no older when the RUC tried and failed to turn him. Many families' lives were ruined because of the supergrasses, including those of their own families, and the effects could be renewed at any time. Following Raymond Gilmour's plea to return to Derry in 2007, and the publicity it engendered, his family was once again running scared. In a BBC interview in 2007 Gilmour said: "I am suffering for it now. I have a heart complaint, I'm an alcoholic. You name it—I have all the psychological problems that go along with the things that I have done in the past."[168] His regrets are all for himself.

Nevertheless, while we can accept that the supergrasses were (and are) victims of the conflict in Northern Ireland, when recalling those who said "No" and suffered the consequences, the revulsion felt in the local community, epitomized by their rejection of Gilmour, is understandable, and Frank Kermode's description of the informers' lives is apt: "Wretched dregs, soaked in fear and vice; yet they had gambled with death, staking their lives on the razor's edge of a lie.... The only human emotion they had was the tormenting agony of their own cowardice. From fear of death they faced death every day."[169]

Conclusion

An attempt to discover the full extent of informing during conflict in Ireland is doomed to failure. This is not a homogeneous group of people known to each other, but an assortment of individuals who would write no Witness Statements and whose families would not boast of such activities. Nor is there an abundance of material to document them: in some cases only a name survives. In fact, those informers whose careers we can track in detail were the failures of the system. We cannot know if others remain unknown to history because they were not documented, nor how many people in every era would have passed on local gossip, as happened at Dripsey, simply because it was interesting. Even so it does seem that they were most active in Dublin, the center of IRA activities, and Cork, with its large concentration of British forces.

The full impact of the informer is best seen in the context of Northern Ireland from the 1970s and, in the latter part of this work, a picture of the province emerges seen from one particular perspective—that of the informers, who were formed and informed by the society in which they lived. Throughout that time, particularly in the actions of the RUC and the army, there are constant ugly echoes of the Kitson influence as epitomized in his most infamous words: "The law should be used as just another weapon in the government's arsenal and in this case become little more than a propaganda cover for the disposal of unwanted members of the public.... The activities of the legal services have to be tied into the war effort in as discreet a way as possible."[1] This influence is seen chiefly in the Stakeknife account, the recruitment of the supergrasses and the uses made of them, but earlier efforts in the RUC Interrogation Centers relied on brutality.

"The Crime of Castlereagh," Bobby Sands's long poem written while he was imprisoned there, is about the terror felt by the prisoners, the fear of death, the fear of giving in, and his understanding of what that fear can do to people:

'Twas times like this in wretchedness
A man fell down and prayed.
'Twas times like this in cowardliness
That men would break their code,
And spill the beans in cowardly screams
To shed this murderous load.[2]

Brian Maguire, one of the two examples of attempted recruitment, is mentioned frequently in the poem, ensuring him a sort of immortality, and so his story has been included here: he stands for all those who suffered in Castlereagh. The other is Pearse Kerr, whose American citizenship did not protect him from torture, though it did eventually gain him his freedom, but not before he had signed his name to the confession beaten out of him.

Later army intelligence demonstrates a learning curve in recruitment terms: between Nairac's abortive attempts to infiltrate the nationalist/republican community and the effects on that community of Stakeknife, much knowledge had clearly been acquired. Here also we find betrayal, first in the attempts to suborn schoolchildren, then with the very young soldiers who saw themselves as heroes but had no real understanding of what they were being asked to do or of its effects on their lives. It is poetic justice that Carlin and Fulton, the examples of locally born soldiers, were later to blackmail the MOD into providing them with pensions.

Hermon's arrival signalled a change in RUC tactics which mirrored those adopted by the army as they began using subtlety: the informers, mainly little men recruited when young, slowly became addicted to an exciting mixture of money, power, and importance. The first step was photographs, some were of their friends, but they *were* just photographs and so innocuous. This, however, was the important step, the first betrayal. The origins of this strategy by both army and RUC may well have been inspired by army psychologists: the term Stockholm Syndrome was used from 1973 but the condition, a survival mechanism based on the human desire to belong and be safe, was already known to the experts. Yet the brutality had not entirely disappeared. Kevin McGrady gave himself up to the police, but he too complained of beatings by the RUC, suggesting that he was forced to give evidence against those convicted at his trial. Here the treachery is systematic: the supergrasses betrayed as many people as required and, in addition, spread fear throughout both nationalist and loyalist communities.

In earlier years, while there was no overarching system, then as now reputation could be destroyed by a whisper. Stephen Hayes is the main example of a man whose life is destroyed by the accusations of informing. This episode meant betrayal on all sides for Hayes: by the government, many of whose members were old IRA men; by McCaughey and his accomplices; by the IRA, many of whom believed in his guilt; and even by posterity, given that his name is anathema in Wexford, his own place, to this day.[3] Willie Joyce's link to the main theme is through his age: can there be any doubt that the adult paramilitaries, by permitting him to spend a great deal of time in their company and thus ensuring his bad local reputation and putting his life in danger, did not betray this young boy?

Yet there is no betrayal without the expectation of loyalty, love or protection. Thus Robert Nairac was not an informer, though he had "infiltrated both sides, Loyalist and Republican, in an attempt to intensify the conflict so that each side would wipe each other out,"[4] because his loyalty belonged to Britain and to the British Army; while Fulton and Carlin *are*, despite membership of that same British Army, by virtue of their background and upbringing as Irishmen. Probing reveals only how intangible this all is, and how dependent on the ideas illustrated by "Kate Maloney," which gives the traditional view of informing as an action so despicable that even death is preferable and no motive is acceptable.

Though money is important among the reasons for informing, clearly seen in the later actions of such men as Fulton and Carlin, as Danny Morrison says: "Often financial reward is not top of the list and most touts usually act chiefly out of self-preservation (after being compromised), become increasingly ensnared by each successive piece of information they give, and then become perversely addicted to the excitement of their secret life."[5] There were very few like Joe Bennett, the first loyalist supergrass and career criminal who claimed that he was never offered money, yet was a heavy gambler.[6] Willie Joyce, even when young, was a traitor by nature because he enjoyed treachery, and Nelson admits that power was the drug. Of the others the vast majority succumbed to blackmail or fear, later to psychological tactics, and relied on their captors empty promises. Denis Donaldson is not only the most recent informer used in this study but also one of the highest grade, yet his status did not save him from being outed in a Sunday newspaper following his involvement with "Stormontgate."

It is clear from the case studies that certain characteristics are common among informers: they are all greedy, though not necessarily for money; they have an exaggerated sense of their own importance; their own safety and desires are paramount, to the exclusion of all others including mothers, wives, and children; most of those who wrote books believed themselves heroes, but were gullible, living their own fantasies and falling again and again for the same arguments from their handlers: "If you don't do it, someone else will"; and finally waxing indignant over their own betrayal by their army or RUC bosses. So to conclude that the informers were important might seem to give them a status they did not and do not deserve. And yet, as so very often some action or treachery of theirs completely altered the course of history, no other word can be used.

Implicit in every case study and every chapter is a great deal of misery, both in the lives of the informers and in those connected to them. This is another factor which increases exponentially with the century, so that it is far more telling in Northern Ireland. Yet the people's spirit is indomitable and their sense of humor shines through most of the cartoons, as also through the Castlereagh anecdote recounted by Ruairi Ó Brádaigh. He had given advice to a loyalist prisoner, Lowry Quinn, in the next cell, and later read of his arrest in the newspaper: Quinn, accused of being a lieutenant in the UDA, had hidden his revolver wrapped in brown paper under the dog kennel in a neighbor's yard. The dog dug up the parcel and dragged it into the street where it was found: but the brown paper wrapping had Quinn's name and address on it. While Danny Morrison can say "I was roughed up a few times by the Brits when I was arrested for screening [4 hours in the barracks while they got every detail they could about your family and the color of your wallpaper]."[7] Perhaps most striking of all, in this context, are the words of Johnny Gilmour, speaking of his lost little brother who can never come home, when he laughs about the day Raymond left home: "He dobbed my best suitcases. They were American and cost $200. That was the last time I saw him. Wouldn't you think, with all the money he had, he could have bought his own?"[8] There can be a lot of pride in laughter: humor can be a way of feeling in control, even when the humorists know that the situation is painful, and that betrayal must always lead to tragedy.

Yet the system continues, and the PSNI[9] are still using the RUC recruitment methods, as in the case of Francis Carleton, of North Belfast, who was arrested in June 2011. Since then the PSNI have repeatedly tried to recruit his brother, John. The most recent attempt involved stopping him as he drove along the A1 Belfast to Dublin road, and asking him to lure a certain person across the border by offering him discounted toys in a Newry toy shop. Once in the shop the man would be arrested and all charges against Francis Carleton would be dropped. John Carleton says: "I have a young family and I'm afraid of what's going to happen next…. It's pure harassment and the stress it's putting my family under is unbearable. I have no connection to any organisation and I feel my life is being put at risk by all the attention around me and my home." The article claims that "A number of other attempts to recruit informers have been reported in recent weeks to capitalize on people's financial problems ahead of Christmas."[10]

Certain cases discussed in these pages might lead eventually to a more balanced attitude to accusations in the future; in particular, such examples as that of Stephen Hayes might serve as a reminder of the frailty of reputation and that nobody is truly safe from slander. While if responsibility for the informer scenario must be apportioned: the man for whom control is so important that he is willing to pay for knowledge of a neighbor, lies at its heart; he must find the person willing to betray a neighbor for gain; and the conditions must exist to make the neighbor's secrets sufficiently vital. Thus, in the Ireland of today it is certain that, while conflict persists, there will continue to be a market for the informer's services, and the loathing of his treachery will still be shared by his victims and those who use him. Moreover, to quote Danny Morrison once again:

> I do not know the detail of what damage Donaldson did or his selfish motivation. Often financial reward is not top of the list and most touts usually act chiefly out of self-preservation (after being compromised), become increasingly ensnared by each successive piece of information they give, and then become perversely addicted to the excitement of their secret life.
>
> An informer only admits being ashamed after being caught; then, in the words of Maxim Gorky, he begins living "the life of a useless man."[11]

Appendix: Principal Methods of Torture Used in Holywood and Girdwood Barracks

1. Placing a man in "search position," single finger of each hand to the wall, legs well apart and well back, on the toes, knees bent, for prolonged periods.
2. Heavy punching to the pit of the stomach to man in "search position."
3. Kicking the legs from under a man in the "search position" so that he falls to the ground, banging his head on the wall, or radiator, or ground.
4. Beating with batons on the kidneys and on the privates in "search position."
5. Kicking between the legs while in the "search position." This is very popular among the RUC officers and they often do it for periods of half an hour or an hour.
6. Putting a man in "search position" over a very powerful electric fire or radiator.
7. Stretching a man over benches with two electric fires underneath and kicking him on the stomach.
8. Rabbit punching to the back of the neck while in "search position."
9. Banging the head against the wall.
10. Beating the head with a baton in crescendo fashion.
11. Slapping the ears and face with open hand.
12. Twisting the arms behind the back and twisting fingers.
13. Prodding the stomach with straight fingers.
14. Chopping blows to the ribs from behind with simultaneous blows to the stomach.
15. Hand squeezing of the testicles.
16. Insertion of instruments in the anal passage.
17. Kicking on the knees and shins.
18. Tossing the prisoner from one officer to another and punching him while in the air.

19. Injections.
20. Electric cattle prod was used.
21. Electric shocks given by use of a machine.
22. Burning with matches and candles.
23. Deprivation of sleep.
24. Urinating on prisoners.
25. Psychological tortures:
    (a) Russian roulette
    (b) Firing blanks
    (c) Beating men in darkness.
    (d) Blindfolding.
    (e) Assailants using stocking masks.
    (f) Wearing surgical dress.
    (g) Staring at white perforated wall in small cubicle.
    (h) Use of amphetamine drugs.
    (i) Prisoners are threatened; threats to their families, bribes offered, false confessions are used.

Source: British Army and Special Branch RUC Brutalities, December 1971–February 1972, *compiled by Revv. D. Faul and R. Murray from accounts by parishioners.*

Chapter Notes

Introduction

1. Racine, *Britannicus*, acte IV, scène 4. [There are no secrets that time does not reveal]

2. *Andersonstown News*, 14 February 1979.

3. Hatfield House, part of which was the childhood home of Elizabeth Tudor (later Queen Elizabeth I), is in Hertfordshire, England, and the Rainbow portrait can be seen online.

4. William Cecil was Elizabeth's chief councillor; Francis Walsingham was her secretary of state; Robert Dudley was a royal favorite.

5. A. Haynes, *The Elizabethan Secret Services* (Stroud, 2000), p. 27.

6. *Ibid.*, p. 28.

7. W. Lecky, *A History of Ireland in the Eighteenth Century* (London, 1892), p. 252.

8. *Ibid.*, p. 148.

9. *Ibid.*, p. 153.

10. M. Byrne, *Memoirs* (Dublin, n.d.), p. 19.

11. W.J. Fitzpatrick, *Secret Service Under Pitt* (London, 1892), p. 58, note.

12. R.R. Madden, The United Irishmen; their lives and times (London, 1842–1846), p. 205.

13. Thanks largely to John Magee, owner of the *Dublin Evening Post* and *Magee's Weekly Packet* who lampooned Higgins as "Frank Paragraph" and "Signor Shamado" continually until Higgins sued him in a trial so skewed in its bias that it was subsequently discussed in Parliament (W.J. Fitzpatrick, *The Sham Squire, and the Informers of 1798* (London, 1866), pp. 1–3).

14. J. Connolly, "The Irish Masses in History," *The Harp* (September 1908).

15. A. Manning, Donegal *Poitín: A History* (Donegal, 2003), p. 15.

16. *Ibid.*, pp. 123–4.

17. *Ibid.*, p. 198.

18. Register of Informants, National Archives of Ireland (NAI), British in Ireland microfilm, CO 904/183. No page nos.

19. Nero was probably Cork journalist Patrick Cogan. See O. McGee, *The IRB* (Dublin, 2005), p. 192.

20. Nor has this come to an end. In an article about the Smithwick Tribunal of Inquiry into collusion by the gardaí in the murder of two senior RUC men, Henry McDonald writes: "One thing is certain. At this time of resurgent dissident republican terrorism, the state is recruiting a new generation of agents to ensure a low-intensity, sporadic Irish terror campaign does not spiral out of control." "Smithwick tribunal: Hurst evidence shines light on a covert war" (*Guardian*, 11 September 2011).

21. Royal Ulster Constabulary.

22. *The Irish Rebellion of 1798: A Bicentenary Perspective* (Dublin, 2003); *Revolutionary Dublin: The Letters of Francis Higgins to Dublin Castle, 1795–1801* (Dublin, 2003); "Leonard MacNally: Playwright, United Irishman, Barrister and informer" in Hiram Morgan (ed.) *Media and Information through the Ages* (Dublin, 2001).

23. *MI5 and Ireland, 1939–1945: The Official History* (Dublin, 2002); "Three failures and a success: Dublin Castle's intelligence war, 1795–1803" in *Intelligence and statecraft in History* (Dublin, 2006); *Spying on Ireland* (Oxford, 2008).

24. H. Bhabha, "Narrating the Nation," in J. Hutchinson and A. Smith (eds.), *Nationalism* (Oxford, 1994), p. 310.

25. B. Anderson, *Imagined Communities* (London, 1991), p. 19.

26. The Brehon Law (possibly) antedates the Iron Age and lasted until Cromwellian days in the seventeenth century. Its basis was the code of honor which could be compared to Stephen Hayes's attempts to clear his name. See Chapter 2.

27. "Supergrasses," Belfast Bulletin No. 11, Workers' Research Unit (n.d.).

28. F. Braudel, *Ecrits sur l'Histoire* (Paris,

1999), pp. 20–21. (All translations are the author's unless otherwise stated).
29. *Ibid.*, p. 299.
30. *Ibid.*, p. 34.
31. *La Divina Commedia*, Dante Alighieri, *Inferno*, Canto 33, 129–133. Dante lived from 1265–1321, the dates of his writings are inexact.
32. *Ibid.*, Canto 32, 13–15.
33. The Jerusalem Bible, Genesis 3:12–13, p. 7.
34. G. Murphy (ed.), *"I am Eve": Early Irish lyrics, Eighth to Twelfth Century* (Oxford, 1956), pp. 50–52 (translator, Kuno Meyer).
35. Shakespeare, *All's Well that Ends Well*, Act III, scene 6.
36. A.R. Elangovan and D.L. Shapiro, "Betrayal of trust in organizations," in *Academy of Management Review*, vol. 23, no. 3, 1998, p. 548.
37. S. Rachman, "Betrayal: A psychological analysis," in *Behaviour Research and Therapy*, vol. 48, 2010, Abstract.
38. Meow Lan E. Chan, "Why did you hurt me?," in *Review of General Psychology*, vol. 13, no. 3, 2009, pp. 263–265.
39. *Ibid.*
40. Marc Bloch, *Histoire et Historiens* (Paris, 1995), p. 12.
41. Táin Bó Cúailgne (The Cattle Raid of Cooley), once seen just as mythology, is nowadays seen by archaeologists as the repository of much information about Iron Age living.
42. I. Jackson, *The Provincial Press and the Community* (Manchester, 1971), p. 42.
43. *Ibid.*, p. 46.
44. *Ibid.*, pp. 219–20.
45. *Ibid.*, p. 42.
46. A D-Notice is an official request to news editors not to publish or broadcast items on certain subjects for reasons of national security.
47. Chief Secretary's Office, Minute Sheet, 11 May 1921, NAI CO 904/162.
48. Letter, Foreign Office to the Chief Clerk, Irish Office, 27 April 1921, NAI CO 904/162.
49. "Somewhere in the Land of Terror," *The Catholic Register*, n.d. vol. xxvix, no. 15, p. 1.
50. Copies of all the statements have been accessible in the National Archives of Ireland (NAI) since 11 March 2003 and are now online and searchable.
51. Joseph Togher, Galway, Witness Statements (hereafter W.S.) 674 and 1729.
52. Bloch, p. 13.
53. Irish Republican Army, sometimes known as the Volunteers. In the earlier years of the century I.R.A. was more usual, but IRA throughout avoids confusion.
54. Collins, p. 191.
55. *Ibid.*, p. 158.
56. *Ibid.*, p. 275.
57. He was a law student at Queen's University, Belfast, before becoming a customs officer.
58. By Mick McGovern.
59. Clár 2, "Coinsias," *Brathadóiri* [Programme 2, "Conscience," *Informers*]: Series made by Scun Scan Productions for TG4, 2008.
60. Johnny Gilmour said that in later years his mother blamed the police, because Raymond was only a child. (Email to author, 7 October 2006).
61. Gilmour, p. 22.
62. *Ibid.*, p. 29.
63. "The police never left our front door, we were naughty boys." Johnny Gilmour, interview, 21 March 2006.
64. *Ibid.*, p. 11.
65. Fulton, pp. 15–17.
66. *Ibid.*, pp. 196–201.
67. *Ibid.*, pp. 235–6.
68. S. Greer, *Supergrasses* (Oxford, 1995).
69. A. Boyd, *The Informers* (Dublin, 1984).
70. Greer, p. 12.
71. *Ibid.*, pp. 12–13.
72. Boyd, p. 14.
73. *Ibid.*, p. 97.
74. A. Seldon and J. Pappworth, *By Word of Mouth: Élite Oral History* (London, 1983).
75. Died 1754.
76. Daly, p. 2.
77. T. Kinsella, *The New Oxford Book of Irish Verse* (Oxford, 1986), pxxvii.
78. Corkery, p. 126.
79. Undated, but obviously very early because it preserves the pre–Christian viewpoint, is the poem "Ticfa Talcenn." "Ticfa Talcenn / tar muir mercenn, / a thi thollcenn, / a chrann crombcenn." [He is coming, Adzed-Head, / on the wild-headed sea / with cloak hollow-headed / and curve-headed staff. // He will chant false religion / at a bench facing East / and his people will answer / 'Amen, amen.'] 'Adzed-Head' is generally accepted as referring to the tonsure, which among Irish monks meant shaving the hair ear to ear. After the Synod of Whitby in the seventh century the Roman tonsure was universally accepted. Kinsella, *The Dual Tradition* (Manchester, 1995), p. 8.
80. The Cattle-Raid of Cooley (Táin Bó Cúailnge) is the central epic of the Ulster cycle.
81. Sands was elected Member of Parliament while in prison. His hunger strike lasted for sixty-six days.
82. Both *The Volunteer* and *Combat* have ceased publication, though *Combat* seems to have sired a new magazine: *The Purple Standard*.
83. Mac Réamoinn, p15.
84. Cited in L. Ó Broin, *Dublin Castle and the 1916 Rising* (Dublin, 1966), p. 151.

Chapter 1

1. M. Skinnider, *Doing My Bit for Ireland* (No publisher, n.d.), p. 100.

2. Royal Irish Constabulary, predecessors of the Garda Síochána.
3. Volunteers and IRA are used in this chapter as interchangeable terms, much as they were used at that time.
4. Colonel Eamon Broy, W.S. 1280, p. 10.
5. Nathan to Birrell, 10 April 1916. Cited in L. Ó Broin, *Dublin Castle and the 1916 Rising* (Dublin, 1966), p. 73.
6. David Daly, Commandant First Battalion, Athlone, W.S. 1337, p. 4. This is borne out by O'Halpin's research into the financial side. See below.
7. See below.
8. Máire Comerford, cited in K. Griffith and T. O'Grady, *Curious Journey* (Dublin, 1998), p. 83.
9. Joseph McGuinness, a convict in Lewes Prison, was returned for Sinn Féin by thirty-seven votes.
10. E. O'Halpin, "The secret service vote and Ireland, 1868–1922," *Irish Historical Studies*, xxiii, no. 92 (November 1983), pp. 350–353. The amounts available varied between £932 12s 0d (1916–17) and £63,602 4s 9d (1920–21).
11. *Ibid.*, p. 352.
12. Broy, W.S. 1280, pp. 38–39. G Division was the detective section of the Dublin Metropolitan Police (DMP) and the only section which was armed.
13. DMP did not regard themselves as members of the Crown forces. (Broy, W.S. 1280, pp. 77–79).
14. 21 January 1919.
15. October 1920. *The Irish Republican Army* (from captured documents only), printed booklet, p. 23. (EPS/2/2, Imperial War Museum Department of Documents).
16. Cited in M. Foy, *Michael Collins's Intelligence War* (Stroud, 2006), pp. 67–68.
17. William Stapleton, W.S. 822, pp. 36–37.
18. Joseph Dolan, W.S. 663, p. 4.
19. Vincent Byrne, W.S. 423, p. 61.
20. *Irish Times* (31 January 1921), p. 5. Irish newspapers at this time came under British censorship, so the anodyne phrase should be interpreted in this context.
21. Colonel Charles Dalton, W.S. 434, p. 10.
22. Christopher Harte, W.S. 2, p. 1.
23. Frank Thornton, W.S. 615, p. 21. Thornton's Statement is invaluable for details about Collins's Intelligence network and how it worked.
24. Foy, p. 40.
25. E. O'Halpin, "The secret service vote and Ireland, 1868–1922," p. 351.
26. Real name: John Charles Byrnes, but also referred to as Byrne or Burns. For a full account see P. Hart, *The IRA and its Enemies* (Oxford, 1999), pp. 224–236.
27. Joe Leonard, W.S. 547, p. 14.
28. Griffith and O'Grady, p. 163.
29. Frank Thornton, W.S. 615, p. 40. The death of "Jameson" at Glasnevin and the mystery surrounding his name meant wide press coverage which continued until his body was claimed by a woman who refused to answer questions.
30. Foy, p. 106.
31. Cited in J. Borgonovo, *Spies, Informers and the 'Anti-Sinn Féin Society'* (Dublin, 2007), p. 136.
32. Anyone seen on the streets of Dublin talking to uniformed men during curfew hours was automatically suspect.
33. Sergeant Mannix, cited in Frank Thornton, W.S. 615, p. 18.
34. Frank Thornton, W.S. 615, p. 23.
35. E.M. Forster, 'What I believe,' in *Two Cheers for Democracy*.
36. Hart, 2006, p. 292. Perhaps Collins, with all his experience in such matters, was warned subliminally by a change in Childers' attitude?
37. NAI, DE 2/304:2.
38. Coogan, Michael Collins, p. 242.
39. Lloyd George, cited in Ring, *Erskine Childers*, p. 264.
40. And see below for "Cruxy" Connors.
41. F. Gallagher, *The Four Glorious Years 1918–1921* (Dublin, 2005), p. 243.
42. Charles Pinkman, W.S. 1263, pp. 7–10.
43. Patrick Lennon, W.S. 1336, p. 11.
44. E. O'Malley, *On Another Man's Wound* (Dublin, 2002), p. 343.
45. See Borgonovo, 2007.
46. Though Borgonovo, 2007, Chapter 4, includes information and tables using numbers culled from RIC records, and Murphy (G. Murphy, *The Year of Disappearances* [Dublin, 2010]) used a variety of sources for his estimate, it is impossible to be certain of the numbers executed as informers in Cork.
47. So-called because he had won the French Croix de Guerre. Interesting as this man's story is, he was generously brought to the attention of the author by John Mulcahy of Blarney who has amassed a considerable body of research on Connors with the intention of publishing. The author would not wish to pre-empt that.
48. Pat Margetts, a soldier stationed at Victoria Barracks who gave information to the IRA. (Cited in Borgonovo, 2007, 91). Anyone who entered Victoria Barracks was automatically suspect.
49. On the first Sunday of their new life Mrs. Lindsay led her husband and James Clarke to the front pew in Magourney church. The Rector told her that there was a traditional order of seating and they were obliged to move further down the church. (T. Sheehan, *Lady Hostage* [Dripsey, privately printed, n.d.], p.

76). All biographical details are taken from Sheehan, pp. 73–80, unless otherwise stated.
	50. Figures courtesy of Dr. Nicola Morris, University of Chester.
	51. Following the death of her favorite nephew she put one of the famous "Your Country Needs You" posters on the wall of Magourney church, provoking an argument with the Rector, and attempted to set up a V.A.D. (Voluntary Aid Detachment) unit in Coachford.
	52. Borgonovo, 2007, pp. 91–92.
	53. *Ibid.*, pp. 94 and 96.
	54. Colonel Eamon Broy, W.S. 1285, p. 27.
	55. Feeney, p. 127.
	56. Sheehan, p. 91.
	57. For details see Sheehan, pp. 91–94.
	58. Feeney, p. 134.
	59. Sheehan, p. 102.
	60. Des Long, interview, 17 October 2010. Des Long has been a member of the republican movement since 1959, and is the author of "The Provisional IRA in Munster: 1969–1974" (unpublished MA thesis, University of Limerick, 2010).
	61. Feeney, pp. 134–135.
	62. A copy of a report from the Adjutant of the 1st Cork Brigade to the Adjutant General at GHQ states "about 400" British soldiers. ("An I.R.A. Ambush," Foulkes, Kings College London (KCL), 7/32, 2 February 1921). Charles Howard Foulkes was Director of Irish Propaganda in 1921.
	63. General Order, Deserters, and General Order, Death Penalty (both 2 April 1921), The Irish Republican Army (from captured documents only), p. 15. Though both of these were promulgated after the Dripsey ambush there can be little doubt that such punishment already existed.
	64. 4 February, adjourned until 8 February 1921.
	65. *Irish Times* (18 February 1921), p. 5.
	66. Feeney, p. 157.
	67. Jeremiah Murphy was a local farmer. There were so many Murphys in the area that most had nicknames.
	68. It was eventually revealed in Strickland's diaries that, on Sunday 27 February 1921, Mrs. Bowen-Colthurst and the Dean of Cork went to ask General Strickland to reprieve the men (Sheehan, p. 159). O'Callaghan gives 11 March as the date of her death, Sheehan has 21 February. An anecdote, told to Ruairí O Brádaigh by Miss O'Sullivan in 1959, makes the latter impossible, but does not confirm the former: The sister of Michael O'Sullivan went to Victoria barracks to identify her brother, who had been killed by Crown forces on 23 February, 1921. She did so, and on the way out was stopped by an officer who said General Strickland wanted to speak to her. She was brought into his office. He said he regretted her brother's death and that he was concerned about Mrs. Lindsay, who had been missing for some time.
		a. She said: "It's pretty clear that the Dripsey ambush prisoners are likely to be executed. It's been made clear that if they are reprieved Mrs. Lindsay won't be harmed." He said there was nothing he could do—the law must take its course.
		b. She was surprised by this conversation because she was involved in serving Mrs. Lindsay's meals and had given her breakfast that morning (but she didn't tell him that). (Ruairí O Brádaigh, telephone interview, 5 April, 2010).
	69. Sir Neville Macready, *Annals of an Active Life*, Vol. II (London, 1924), p. 543.
	70. Summary of Lindsay case, including text of her letters to Strickland, Foulkes, KCL 7/37, n.d.
	71. Letter, Jeremiah Murphy (4 February 1926) (NLI, MS 44,045/2).
	72. Cited in J. Borgonovo, *Florence and Josephine O'Donoghue's War of Independence* (Dublin, 2006), p. 84. According to Jeremiah Murphy there were 55 men at his farm (Jeremiah Murphy, 4 February 1926. NLI, MS 44,045/2).
	73. The sequence of events is related in a series of letters and statements from Grace Conway and Mrs. Lindsay's two sisters held in the files of Mrs. Benson's literary executor, Frau Rosamund Huebener of West Germany (reproduced in Sheehan, pp. 166–169).
	74. Cited in F. Costello (ed.), *Michael Collins: In His Own Words* (Dublin, 1997), pp. 25–26.
	75. Somebody was lying.
	76. Sheehan, p. 176.
	77. Cited in O'Callaghan, *Execution*, p. 179.
	78. Cited in Costello, pp. 25–26.
	79. The Earl of Selborne, *Hansard* (4 August 1921), vol. 43, cc. 320–2.
	80. "Mrs. Lindsay was warned not to remain in her house which could not be protected indefinitely, but she refused to leave and was eventually murdered after undergoing great hardship" (Macready, p. 543). This gives the impression that she was protected initially. There is no other mention anywhere that this was so.
	81. Author unknown, but the song was written shortly after his death in November 1920. Notable in the present context because Barry refused to inform on his comrades.
	82. Patrick Mannix, W.S. 502, p. 4.
	83. Colonel Frank Saurin, W.S. 715, p. 4.
	84. Mrs. Lindsay's car was found there in early April (*Freeman's Journal*, 5 April 1921, p. 6).
	85. 29 July 1921. Cathal Brugha was then Minister of Defence in the Provisional Government. "…one fact emerges from a close scrutiny

of the circumstances, namely that 'Cathal Bruga' [sic] was lying to Mrs. Benson in attributing Mrs. Lindsay's execution to General Strickland's failure to reprieve the Cork prisoners" (Foulkes, 7/37).
86. Cathal Brugha's letter to Mrs. Benson (*The Times*, 30 July 1921, p. 10).
87. Their leaving Ireland may have been a part of the general Protestant exodus in 1921–22, or perhaps Mrs. Benson's crusade drew I.R.A. attention to the sisters and they were ordered to leave.
88. Letter, Rev. Thos. J. O'Connor to Richard Mulcahy, Minister of Defence, 10 February 1922, NLI, MS 44,045/1.
89. NLI, MS 44,045/1.
90. Letter, Mrs. Benson to Jeremiah Murphy, 5 January 1924, NLI, MS 44,045/1. Her emphasis.
91. Letter, Jeremiah Murphy (4 February 1926), NLI, MS 44,045/2.
92. F. O'Donoghue, *No Other Law* (Dublin, 1954), p. 160.
93. Feeney, p. 125.
94. For example, in March 1921 Mrs. Fletcher was ordered out of Cork for being "on friendly terms with police and military" (Borgonovo, 2007, p. 102, n107).
95. General Orders (New Series), no. 13 (17 November 1920). The Irish Republican Army (from captured documents only), p. 23.
96. A. Matthews, *Renegades: Irish Republican Women, 1900–22* (Cork, 2010), p. 277.
97. 7 December 1920. *Ibid.*
98. General Order, no. 17 (2 April 1921). *Ibid.*, p. 15.
99. General Order, Spies (20 April 1921). *Ibid.*, p. 15.
100. General Orders (New Series), no. 13 (17 November 1920). The Irish Republican Army (from captured documents only), p. 23.
101. O'Callaghan, p. 133.
102. Feeney, p. 136.
103. *Irish Times* (7 July 1921).
104. Letter from E.L. Kineen to Connacht Sentinel, cited in "Irishman's Diary," *The Irish Times*, 8 March 1941, p. 4.
105. Gilbert Brooke, Derbyshire police statement. (18 March 1940). Reproduced in P. Martland, *Lord Haw Haw* (Kew, 2003), p. 168.
106. Michael Joyce was also renting property to the RIC in Mayo from July 1910. This was burned by the IRA in May 1920 (Kenny, pp. 69 and 264, n39).
107. "his father's profession is given on the rolls as architect" (Kenny, p. 45). William was later to claim this occupation for his father during the war years when Michael was a vacuum cleaner salesman (National Registration entry, 18 October 1939. Reproduced in Martland, p. 116).

108. Kenny, pp. 37–61; Martland, pp. 3–10; F. Selwyn, *Hitler's Englishman* (London, 1987), pp. 12–21.
109. Report from MI5 agent "M" (Charles Henry Maxwell Knight), 21 September 1934. Reproduced in Martland, pp. 120–123. But see below.
110. Selwyn, p. 35. As a result of his interview Joyce was not allowed to sit the examination.
111. William Joyce, 9 August 1922.
112. MI5 report, 13 June 1945. Reproduced in Martland, p. 131.
113. Kenny, pp. 84–86.
114. 1 Rutledge Terrace, Rockbarton, Salthill. The sale was completed on 29 October 1913 (Kenny, p. 265, n13). "Still standing, this is a two-storey comfortable-looking house, with a tiny walled garden, in a pleasantly-secluded position just off the promenade" (Cole, p. 20).
115. *Ibid.*, pp. 47–8.
116. Told that his mother, a Protestant, would not achieve salvation, he severed his connection with the Catholic Church when he was 14 (Selwyn, p. 16). In actual fact, though this was presumably what he understood, it could not have been what was said.
117. The boy had called him an Orangeman (Cole, p. 20). It should, perhaps, be noted that Cole has a slight tendency to make excuses for William Joyce often without giving either reasons or references for his statements. For example, Cole writes about his Jesuit education: "He had less reason to be grateful that his upbringing had implanted in him a feeling of guilt about sex" (Cole, p. 21); and "The memory of these two incidents [seeing a dead policeman, and seeing an IRA man hunted and shot dead by the police] haunted him all his life" (Cole, p. 23).
118. W. Joyce, *Twilight Over England* (Berlin, 1940), p. 7. Ad Majorem Dei Gloriam [To the greater glory of God] is the Jesuit motto. More often rendered as A.M.D.G.
119. Selwyn, p. 34.
120. A. W. Miles Webb, report to Wiltshire police (26 June 1945). Reproduced in Martland, p.124.
121. His passport application shows his adult height as five feet six and a half inches.
122. Douglas Duff, RIC sailor, cited in Kenny, p. 57.
123. Miles Webb, report. Reproduced in Martland, p.124.
124. Selwyn, p. 18.
125. Kenny, p. 265, n31.
126. Ronan Kelly, unbroadcast interview, 1996. Cited in Kenny, p. 56.
127. T.G. McMahon (ed.), *Pádraig Ó Fathaigh's War of Independence* (Cork, 2000), p. 24.

128. His body was not found until 1998 (Kenny, p. 58). There were a few other instances where the Crown forces made such efforts to find an abducted informer, as in the case of Tom Downing in Cork (Borgonovo, 2007, p. 28), but it did not normally happen. Even in the case of Mrs. Lindsay (see below) the search was not solely for her. This leads to the supposition that informers in Galway were in short supply, and thus, indirectly, to the assumption that the services of William Joyce, despite his age, would have been very much appreciated by the Auxiliaries.
129. *Southern Star* (2 July 1921), p. 5.
130. Fr. Griffin was a member of the Gaelic League and used Irish whenever possible. The housekeeper who heard the conversation said it appeared to be friendly (*Galway Observer*, 20 November 1920). Though there are no references to Joyce's competence or otherwise in speaking Irish, he was good at languages and he must have learned Irish in school because it was (from 1910) a mandatory requirement for entry to Ireland's National Universities.
131. Togher, W.S. 1729, p. 8.
132. *Galway Observer* (20 November 1920).
133. *Ibid.* (28 October 1922).
134. Togher, W.S. 674, p. 4.
135. Togher, W.S. 1729, pp. 2–3. Eglinton Street Barracks was the HQ of the Black and Tans in Galway.
136. *Ibid.* p. 5.
137. *Ibid.* pp. 8–9.
138. See Borgonovo, 2007, p. 28.
139. Togher, W.S. 1729, p. 5.
140. Cited in Selwyn, p. 18.
141. Miles Webb, report. Reproduced in Martland, p. 124.
142. Maxwell Knight, report, 21 September 1934. Reproduced in Martland, pp. 120 ff.
143. Togher,W.S. 1729, p. 6.
144. *Ibid.*, p. 9.
145. *Ibid.*, p. 8.
146. Murphy, p. 36.
147. Frank Martin Joyce, William's younger brother, evidence given before the Home Office Advisory Committee during his wartime detention for fascist activities. (5 July 1945, reproduced in Martland, p. 115).
148. J. A. Cole, *Lord Haw-Haw: The Full Story of William Joyce* (London, 1964), pp. 23–24.
149. William Joyce, writing in 1944, cited in Kenny, p. 38.
150. "in 1939, Knight ... tipped Joyce off that he was about to be arrested under the wartime Regulation 18B" (*New Statesman*, 5 May 2003, vol. 132, Issue 4636, p. 20). An undated memorandum recommended Joyce's detention in the event of war with Germany (reproduced in Martland, p. 167).

151. See, for example, Raymond Gilmour in the Supergrasses chapter.
152. "Scores of bodies were dumped in fields, lanes or ditches tagged with messages like 'Spies and informers beware' or 'Convicted spy.'" (Hart, p. 295).
153. L. Mac Gabhann, "Freedom-fighter on a bicycle," *The Irish Times* (3 August 1968), p. 6.
154. "Callous conduct," *Freeman's Journal* (12 March 1923), p. 3.
155. Matthews, p. 277.
156. "Agenda," *The Irish Times* (20 March 2006), p. 13.
157. "Irish hierarchy's warning," *Freeman's Journal* (11 October 1922), p. 5.
158. "Agenda," The Irish Times (20 March 2006), p. 13.
159. Letter to female "Operative No. 23," cited in "Agenda," *The Irish Times* (20 March 2006), p. 13.
160. *Southern Star* (30 June 1923), p. 8.
161. Seán Irwin, letter to Michael Hayes, 3 November 1970. Cited in A. Dolan, *Commemorating the Irish Civil War: History and Memory, 1923–2000* (Cambridge, 2003), p. 1.
162. *Ibid.*, p. 150.
163. *Ibid.*, p. 148.
164. F. S. L. Lyons, *Ireland Since the Famine* (London, 1971), p. 460.
165. P. McMahon, *British Intelligence and Ireland 1916–1945* (Woodbridge, 2008). Des Long says that the State and the police rarely released civil war documents. Telephone interview, 20 March 2011.
166. C. O'Malley and A. Dolan (eds.), *"No Surrender Here!" The Civil War Papers of Ernie O'Malley, 1922–1924* (Dublin, 2007).
167. *Ibid.*, p. 21.
168. *Ibid.*, pp. 62, 86, 96, and passim.
169. *Ibid.*, pp. 51, 96, 103, and passim.
170. *Ibid.*, p. 53.
171. *Ibid.*, p. 250.
172. *Ibid.* p. 35.
173. *Ibid.* p. 505.
174. *Nenagh Guardian* (21 October 1922), p. 6.
175. O'Malley and Dolan, p. 511.
176. *Ibid.*, p. 240.
177. *Ibid.*, p. 257.
178. *Freeman's Journal* (10 May 1922), p. 6.
179. *Nenagh Guardian* (25 November 1922).
180. *Irish Independent* (7 December 1922), p. 7.
181. *Freeman's Journal* (12 April 1923), p. 6.
182. *Freeman's Journal* (24 April 1923), p. 5.
183. *Leitrim Observer* (27 October 1923), p. 2.
184. Cited in Murphy, p. 293.
185. The anonymous verses, from a private collection, are entitled: "Take It Down From

the Mast." The sentiments are echoed by a memorandum, dated 3 August 1922, from Liam Lynch to Ernie O'Malley: "Owing to the abuse of the Tricolor by Free Staters during the present hostilities, it has been decided that the Republican Flag, when used by us, will bear the letters I.R." (O'Malley and Dolan, p. 85).
    186. Hart, 1999, p. 308.
    187. McMahon, pp. 73–96.

Chapter 2

    1. "Let Erin Remember," private collection.
    2. In 1924 Patrick McGilligan, Minister for Industry and Commerce, told the Dáil: "There are certain limited funds at our disposal. People may have to die in this country and may have to die through starvation." (Dáil Éireann debate, 30 October 1924, vol. 9, col. 6).
    3. After the Truce of July 1921 the Civic Guard (renamed the Garda Síochána na hÉireann on 8 August 1923) was formed by Michael Collins and the Irish Government to replace the RIC.
    4. Foley, pp. 49–50.
    5. IRA Chief of Staff from 1927–1936.
    6. U. MacEoin, *Harry* (Dublin, 1986), p. 46.
    7. J. Bardon, *A History of Ulster* (Belfast, 1992), p. 539.
    8. On 18 June 1936, Gerald Boland, the new Minister for Justice, declared the IRA to be unlawful and most senior IRA officers went into hiding.
    9. Harry White, cited in MacEoin (1986), p. 123.
    10. Bardon, p. 532.
    11. S. Hayes, "My Strange Story," part I, *The Bell*, vol. XVII, No. 4 (July 1951), pp. 13–14.
    12. Hayes's escape in this raid was to form part of the "evidence" that he must be an informer.
    13. Oglaigh na h-Eireann, *Special Communiqué*, dated 10 September 1941. Sean O'Mahony Papers (NLI, MSS 44,107/2), p. 1, c.2. This document is the printed version of the confession of Stephen Hayes written during his captivity.
    14. S. Hayes, Extracts from Mountjoy Diary, July 1945–March 1946, was acquired by Wexford County Archives (WXCA) in 2008 (P 246/1). The document was handwritten in Mountjoy on variously sized pieces of paper. It ends just before Hayes's release from prison. The only indication that it was not a part of a longer diary is the comment on 21 July 1945, that Hayes had been suffering "fits of depression so frequent since June 8th—date I hoped to get out." The diary, therefore, could have been a coping strategy during this time.
    15. "He had a passion for carpentry and woodwork. His tool collection was his pride and joy." (Larry Browne, telephone interview, 28 January 2009).
    16. Also, by 1920, he had become a sporting hero in the GAA and was, that year, an All-Ireland Champion athlete.
    17. The order was withdrawn about three years later. This is cogent in terms of motivation. I have asked people who knew or were related to Stephen Hayes whether he was ever motivated by money. Even those totally convinced of his culpability said he was not.
    18. Stephen Hayes, cited in T. Ó hUid, "Stephen Hayes ag cosaint a chlu," [Stephen Hayes defends his reputation], *Republican News* (23 November 1962).
    19. Eileen Hayes, telephone interview (2 October 2008). All the information from Eileen Hayes stems from the period, at some unknown point after Stephen Hayes's release from Mountjoy until circa 1950–51, when he was a lodger in her mother's house in Taghmon, Co. Wexford.
    20. Hayes, July 1951, p. 13.
    21. *Ibid.*, p. 14. Of his time as Chief of Staff he said "The main thing ... was to try and keep the organization intact, and we were sending fellows round the country to try and organize things." Cited in Coogan, *The I.R.A: A History* (Colorado, 1994), p. 116.
    22. 22 December. However, it was an axiom that men on the run did not return home, most particularly at times such as Christmas or Easter when the police were most active in their searches.
    23. R. Quinn, *A Rebel Voice* (Belfast, 1999), p. 65.
    24. Hayes, *The Bell* (August 1951), p. 42.
    25. "[The] lack of communication is not exaggerated. Pearse Kelly, one of the first people I interviewed for this book, compared my lack of knowledge on starting my research to his incomprehension about Dublin's affairs when the Hayes investigation first took him to the South" (Coogan, 1994, p. 131n).
    26. Foley, p. 182. Coogan notes: "There was at the time a strong Fascist influence in Belfast I.R.A. circles" (Coogan, 1994, p. 132).
    27. Foley, p. 194.
    28. Des Long, letter (13 April 2009).
    29. The Hayes's confession claims it was a government plot with the proviso "that the ammunition or the major part of it would be recovered" (Special Communiqué, p. 2, c.2). Also according to the confession, six lorries had been arranged but three or four extra had turned up (Special Communiqué, p. 3, c.1). That does not add up to thirteen. Was this an intentionally false piece of information which was disregarded?

30. Jim Crofton was one of these. It should be noted, however, that the Gardaí relied heavily on the knowledge of the former IRA men in their ranks. Also "Gardaí documents released in 2009 claim that the force had informants, ranging in rank from ordinary volunteer to O/C, in almost every area where the IRA organized in the Free State during the mid–1930s. These men were paid for their assistance and while some were motivated purely by financial reasons, others hoped their helping Gardaí would mean their locality saw little trouble" B. Hanley, *The IRA, a Documentary History 1916–2005* (Dublin, 2010) p. 114.
31. Mainau, a beautiful island on Lake Constance, became the code word for Ireland.
32. M. Hull, "The Irish Interlude: German Intelligence in Ireland, 1939–1943," *The Journal of Military History*, vol. 66, No.3 (July 2002), p. 696.
33. *Ibid.*, p. 695 (Abstract).
34. No relation to Stephen Hayes
35. "The so-called 'Dublin Link' with MI5 insured [*sic*] that information gathered in Ireland would ultimately go to the benefit of the Allied war against Nazi Germany." (*Ibid.*, p. 716).
36. Cited in *ibid.*, p. 700.
37. Other notables among the twelve German World War II agents must include: Walter Simon, who asked two plain-clothes detectives on the Tralee-Dublin train if they knew anyone in the IRA; Henry Obéd, an Indian who had never been in Ireland, but who was the guide for two other agents. The trio lasted about two hours before being arrested; and Ernst Weber-Drohl, the 67 year old circus strong man, who set off in a rubber dinghy from a submarine in Sligo Bay, but capsized, lost his transmitter almost immediately and had to be rescued from drowning by the U-boat.
38. Pro-German husband of Iseult Gonne. Francis Stuart was in Germany throughout WWII and wrote some of William Joyce's (Lord Haw Haw) broadcasts.
39. Hull, p. 703n.
40. J. Bowyer Bell, *The Secret Army* (Dublin, 1989), p. 184.
41. Held was a Dublin businessman with German heritage.
42. E. Stephan, *Spies in Ireland* (London, 1963), p. 124.
43. Hull, p. 704.
44. He published a series of articles in the *Irish Times* and wrote a great deal, in both English and German, after his arrest on 27 November 1941. This output included statements for the Irish Secret Service which Stephan examines in detail throughout his section on Goertz.
45. Stephan, p. 119.

46. *Ibid.*, p. 121.
47. W. Quirke, "Story of Stephen Hayes" (Wexford County Archives, P 246/2), pp. 75–76. This unpublished and incomplete typescript, written circa 1991–1992, was acquired by Wexford County Archives in 2008. Quirke's knowledge came from interviews with Stephen Hayes during the two years before his death, and the author has relied on it heavily in this chapter. Access to the formerly unknown typescript has been particularly invaluable in seeking an understanding of Hayes's character. The document consists of the first few chapters of the Stephen Hayes story, intended ultimately for publication as a book, and written by Billy Quirke, a Wexford journalist. The rest of the book exists and is in the possession of the copyright holder.
48. He shows the same attitude throughout the confession.
49. Quirke (WXCA/P 246/2), p. 77.
50. Hayes, *The Bell* (August 1951), p. 43.
51. Quirke (WXCA/P 246/2), p. 10.
52. Hayes, *The Bell* (August 1951), p. 43.
53. These men are not named in *The Bell*, but Hayes knew them. They were Sean McCaughey, Charlie McGlade, and Liam Rice.
54. *The Bell* (July 1951), p. 16.
55. It was written later in the house in Rathmines, and the writing took until 8 September.
56. 23 July 1941. The court martial lasted from 9 p. m. to 7 a.m.
57. Hayes, *The Bell* (August 1951), p. 46.
58. *Special Communiqué*, p. 1, c.1.
59. Quinn, p. 71.
60. Ruairi Ó Brádaigh, letter to author, 22 December 2011.
61. *The Bell* (August 1951), p. 44.
62. *Ibid.*
63. *Ibid.*, p. 46.
64. 7 June 1941. This incident was related to the author by Larry Browne, son of Stephen Hayes and Bridie Hess, and, until contacted by the author, he had never spoken about his father to anyone other than his mother. Browne, interview (24 November 2008).
65. Quirke (WXCA/P 246/2), p. 15.
66. Eileen Hayes telephone interview (17 September 2008). Hayes's drinking is frequently mentioned, but Eileen Hayes speaks only of the time after he was released from Mountjoy.
67. Stephen Hayes, cited in Tarlach Ó hUid, "Stephen Hayes ag cosaint a chlu" [Stephen Hayes defends his reputation], *Republican News* (23 November 1962).
68. Coogan, Sunday Independent (23 August 1970), p. 8.
69. Hayes, Mountjoy diary, 12 January 1946.
70. See below for the doctor's description of the condition of his feet.
71. E.J. Harding, Home Office memoran-

dum, 31 January 1939. (BBC Radio 4, "Document," 28 March 2011). National Archives (DO 35/893/6).
72. *Ibid.* H.G. Bushe, letter to the Attorney General, dated 3 February 1939.
73. Lecturer in Politics, Dublin City University and author of *The Destiny of the Soldiers: Fianna Fail, Irish Republicanism and the IRA 1926–1973* (Dublin, 2010).
74. M. Thompson, "How De Valera asked UK to smear IRA chief Sean Russell," BBC News World (28 March 2011).
75. (DO 35/893/6). Signed with initials—possibly JES and DO. n.d.
76. Quirke (WXCA/P 246/2), p. 48. Near the beginning of the confession Hayes wrote: "I did not take the Army seriously." (Special Communiqué, p. 1, c.1). This, from a man who had spent all his adult life in the IRA, was obviously intended to act as a signal to his readers that the whole confession was false. It failed. He states that people wanted to believe the confession (Quirke, p. 48).
77. *The Free Press* (18 October 1941), p. 2.
78. *Ibid.* G.D. Murnaghan, instructed by the Chief State Solicitor's Office.
79. According to Eileen Hayes, Dr. Ryan had originally worked for Wexford County Council and must have known him. Dr. Ryan's nephew said to Eileen much later: "Dr. Jim should not have said he didn't know Stephen Hayes" (Eileen Hayes telephone interview, 17 September 2008).
80. *The Free Press* (18 October 1941), p. 2.
81. De Valera's insistence on neutrality had as its foundation his single-minded determination to ensure the survival of the Irish state during the war years, and there was little he would not do in this connection.
82. Pandora was the British cover name for decoded German diplomatic traffic, which became readable from January 1943. O'Halpin, p. 173.
83. Bowyer Bell, p. 208.
84. Coogan, 1994, pp. 117–8.
85. U. MacEoin, *The IRA in the Twilight Years: 1923–1948* (Dublin, 1997), p. 536.
86. Browne was not at home, but says of the visit "I would guess, around 1963–67... It was as if Jim had had a conversation with another party and as a result felt guilty about his past assumptions.... What is interesting is that Jim never seemed to voice his doubts about Steve, in front of me" (Larry Browne, email to author, 3 March 2011).
87. Larry Browne, telephone interview (26 January 2009).
88. This was Mrs. MacEoin, mother of Uinseann MacEoin, interned in the Curragh (Ruairí Ó Brádaigh, letter to author, 22 December 2011).
89. *Enniscorthy Guardian* (20 September 1941), p. 3. "The IRA says that Hayes was continually interrogated but not tortured or harmed in any way" (Coogan, 1994, p. 114). Nevertheless, when first kidnapped his hair was brown; two months later when he escaped it was white (Browne, telephone interview, 26 January 2009).
90. *The Enniscorthy Echo* (20 September 1941).
91. Eileen Hayes, telephone interview (31 January 2009).
92. Nor did Liam Burke, one of his guards: "In these first few confused days of September 1941, the options of when to execute Hayes and where to place his discredited corpse were being trawled over" (MacEoin, 1997, p. 447).
93. *The Bell* (August 1951), pp. 50–51.
94. He later made a fuller statement to solicitor Eoin O'Mahony (dated 18 March 1949) refuting the confession point by point.
95. Bowyer Bell, p. 210.
96. Cork Examiner (19 September 1941).
97. Coogan, 1994, p. 149.
98. This was the occasion when Sean MacBride famously forced Dr. Duane, the prison doctor, to admit that if he had a dog he would not treat it in this fashion (Coogan, 1994, p. 149).
99. An extract from the IRA Oath of Allegiance reads as follows: "I do further swear that I do not and shall not yield a voluntary support to any pretended Government, Authority, or Power within Ireland hostile or inimical to that Republic" (Coogan, 1994, p. 33). This would include the courts of justice of the Free State. McCaughey did not recognize the court.
100. Bob Bradshaw, from Northern Ireland, in MacEoin, 1997, p. 431. The fact of Hayes's constant drinking is widely accepted, but very few people seem to have witnessed it. Perhaps, as Hayes himself claims in the Quirke typescript, this was put around by his enemies.
101. Hayes, Mountjoy diary, 8 December 1945.
102. *Ibid.* 6 October 1945.
103. Yet McGlade was not the intelligence officer, he was the quartermaster. *An Phoblacht* (7 September 2006).
104. *Ibid.*
105. Bowyer Bell, p. 194.
106. MacEoin, 1997, pp. 848–849.
107. Danny Morrison, friend of Comerford, email to author, 16 February 2011.
108. Coogan, *The I.R.A.*, p. 118.
109. George Plant was a Protestant who joined the Fianna when he was fourteen years old following ill-treatment by the RIC some two years earlier, he then graduated to the IRA, and took the republican side in the Civil War. Later he spent some years in the U.S. and

Canada but returned to Ireland when Sean Russell became Chief of Staff. Walsh was a local IRA training officer in Kilmacow, Co. Kilkenny.
110. An illiterate IRA man of over sixty who worked as an agricultural laborer.
111. Emergency Powers (No.139) Order, 1941—Motion to Annul, Dáil Éireann, Volume 85 (28 January 1942, pp. 1453–1454).
112. "Most amazing case ever heard," *The Irish Times* (26 February 1942), p. 1.
113. *Special Communiqué*, p. 3, c.2.
114. *Irish Times* (4 June 1942), p. 3.
115. S. Hayes, Letter to Máire Comerford, 21 December 1941, Sean O'Mahony Papers (NLI, MSS 44,107/5).
116. O'Halpin, Bowyer Bell. See above.
117. Hayes, Letter to Máire Comerford, §16.
118. 27 June 1942, p. 3.
119. A number of these letters, written to B, are in the possession of her son. The collection includes one written after Hayes's release from Mountjoy, signed with a fictitious name. They were all given to Browne by Jim Crofton's son.
120. *The Free Press* (Enniscorthy), 27 June 1942, p. 3.
121. O'Halpin (p. 173), Bowyer Bell (p. 208), and Coogan, 1994 (pp. 117–8).
122. *Cork Examiner* (16 October 1941).
123. *Ibid.*
124. M. McInerney, "The Stephen Hayes Affair," *Irish Times* (16 October 1968).
125. Padraig O'Malley, cited in C. Ní Bheachain, "The Lost Republicans: Sean McCaughey and the disruption of the Free State narrative" (unpublished MA thesis, University College Galway, 1997), p. 57.
126. MacEoin (1986), p. 167. Prisoners suffered from sleep deprivation because the lights were turned on in their cells every fifteen minutes during the night, the warder would knock and they had to answer.
127. T. Healy, letter (dated 30 August) to the *Irish Times* (7 September 1946).
128. *Cork Examiner* (19 September 1941).
129. The Quirke typescript (WXCA/P 246/2) ends at this point. The rest is unattainable.
130. Coogan, 1994, p. 116.
131. Sent in November 1940. (Stephan, p. 190).
132. Hayes, Letter to Máire Comerford, 21 December 1941, §9.
133. *Ibid.*, §17.
134. This led to years of poverty for Peg Crofton, her family, and Hayes's small son during the time he was in Mountjoy. He comments about birthday and Christmas (1945) presents received: "Have a lot of surplus foodstuffs which I will send to Peg. All preserved so they'll last, will help brighten the New Year for Kids." (Mountjoy diary, 26 December 1945).
135. He took cyanide on 23 May 1947, fearing deportation to Germany.
136. Hull, p. 704.
137. Coogan, 1994, p. 118.
138. Cited in Foley, p. 206.
139. Bridie died in 2007, aged 94. (Browne, telephone interview, 21 March 2009).
140. The first time Browne spoke about his father to anyone other than Bridie was when he began to speak to the author. He says that if his mother were still alive he would not have done so. (*Ibid.*)
141. Browne, telephone interview (24 November 2008).
142. Eileen Hayes, telephone interview (20 November 2008).
143. Browne, telephone interview (21 March 2009).
144. Eileen Hayes, telephone interview (2 October 2008).
145. Hayes, last letter to Máire Comerford (7 December 1974).
146. Hayes, letter to "B" (Mountjoy, 10 April 1945).

Chapter 3

1. Bobby Sands, "The Crime of Castlereagh" 1980 (www.bobbysandstrust.com).
2. One of the causes for dissatisfaction was Goulding's dismissal of Cumann na mBan from the movement. "Liam Lynch," cited in Long, p. 85.
3. *Ibid.*, p. 87.
4. D. Bradley, Public lecture "Who are worst at dealing with the past—the British or the Irish?" (Institute of Irish Studies, University of Liverpool, 31 March 2011).
5. *Loyalist News* (25 November 1972), no page nos.
6. L. Curtis, *Ireland: the Propaganda War* (London, 1984), p. 18.
7. *Ibid.*, pp. 25–26.
8. See "The Record of British Brutality in Ireland," a booklet published by Northern Aid and the Association for Legal Justice, n.d. but internal evidence suggests 1971–72.
9. Fr. D. Faul and Fr. R. Murray, *The Castlereagh File* (Dungannon, 1978), pp. 51 and 61.
10. H.G. Bennett, "Report of The Committee of Inquiry into Police Interrogation Procedures in Northern Ireland (March 1979)," paragraph 59. (The Bennett Report).
11. Cited in M. Urban, *Big Boys' Rules* (London, 1992), p. 93.
12. Amnesty International, "Report of an enquiry into allegations of ill-treatment in Northern Ireland (1971)," part 3, 7(viii), p. 44.
13. In 1971 the Heath government had set up the Compton Committee "To investigate

allegations ... of physical brutality while in the custody of the security forces."

14. Kevin McNamara MP, *Hansard* (16 November 1971), vol. 826, c.220.

15. M. Farrell, *Arming the Protestants* (London, 1983), p. 46.

16. In 1927 30.9 percent of officers and NCOs were Catholic (*ibid.*, p. 267).

17. C. Ryder, *The RUC: A Force Under Fire* (London, 1992), p. 2.

18. Civil Authorities (Special Powers) Act (NI) 1922.

19. This régime was known as the "Five Techniques."

20. Cited in D. McKittrick, "Northern Notebook," *The Irish Times* (19 March 1977).

21. P. Taylor, *Beating the Terrorists?* (Harmondsworth, 1980), p. 339.

22. Ireland against The United Kingdom of Great Britain and Northern Ireland, Report of the Commission of the European Court of Human Rights, 25 January 1976, pp. 402, 420, 473. None of the interviewees is identified by name. Case no. T6, identified only as a teacher with an ulcer from Pomeroy, Co. Tyrone, whose case is discussed on pp. 409–413 of the report, is Michael Harvey. Harvey's full story is told in S. Ó Tuathail *Torture: The Record of British Brutality in* Ireland (Dublin, 1971), pp. 25–29. Each of the stories in this publication is witnessed. In Harvey's case the witness was Fr. Denis Faul.

23. Sean Macken, for instance, stated "[the interrogator] came in with another man who said he was a doctor... He asked me where was sore. I said 'My stomach and jaw' ... he punched me in the stomach and jaw, he said that was the best medicine for a terrorist bastard like me" (Faul and Murray, 1978, p. 60). Leo Martin, between his arrest on Saturday 12 August 1977 was seen by doctors (one of whom sent him to hospital) eight times before his release on the following Monday. He filled in the Release Form saying he had not been mistreated. (*Ibid.*, pp. 74–77.)

24. *Ibid.*, p. 47.

25. At Gough, a total of 897 persons were interviewed between 28 October 1977 and 31 October 1979. Of this number, 197 were charged and 700 released. Chief Constable's Annual Report, 1977 (cited in Taylor, p. 194).

26. *Irish Independent* (23 March 1979).

27. Taylor, p. 178.

28. I. Cobain, "Hundreds of Northern Ireland 'terrorists' allege police torture," (*Guardian Unlimited*, 11 October 2010).

29. The Pat Finucane Center website includes a Fact File on Ronnie Flanagan, who became Chief Constable of the RUC in November 1996. It comments that in 1978 Flanagan became Duty Inspector in charge of Castlereagh Interrogation Center, and cites the Bennett Report (1979): "The key role of the Duty Inspector (DI) is underlined in the Report. The actual business of supervising interviews falls largely to the inspector on duty. (para. 112) Permission for interrogations to begin or be continued after midnight was the responsibility of the DI ... [there was a] requirement that the DI must return to the interrogation center before overnight interrogations could even be permitted. (para. 97) Any 'untoward incident,' including allegations of ill-treatment, were [sic]to be reported to the Duty Inspector. (para. 120) Officers in charge had the clear responsibility to ensure that 'breaches of the regulations are not committed.' (para. 121) The decision on whether or not a suspect may consult a solicitor rested also with the Duty Inspector (para. 122)" (Fact File, pp. 2–3).

30. BBC News (30 December 2009).

31. H. G. Bennett, "Report of The Committee of Inquiry into Police Interrogation Procedures in Northern Ireland (March 1979)." For all details of the debate see *Hansard* (16 March 1979), vol. 964, cc. 961–84.

32. Gerry Fitt, MP for Belfast West.

33. Report of an Amnesty International Mission to Northern Ireland (28 November 1977–6 December 1977), chapter 2.

34. Letter to *The Times* (27 November 1971) from L. St. Clare Grondona, Commandant during World War II of the Combined Services Detailed Interrogation Centre. Cited in Amnesty Report, p. 46, 7 (xi).

35. Letter to *The Times* (25 November 1971). Cited in Amnesty Report, p. 46, 7 (xiii).

36. *Irish Press* (28 October 1977).

37. Sir E. Compton, "Report of the enquiry into allegations against the Security Forces of physical brutality in Northern Ireland arising out of events on the 9th August, 1971" (The Compton Report) (London, 1971), no page numbers.

38. Lord Parker of Waddington, "Report of the Committee of Privy Counsellors appointed to consider authorised procedures for the interrogation of persons suspected of terrorism" (The Parker Report) (London, 1972).

39. Ireland against The United Kingdom of Great Britain and Northern Ireland, Report of the Commission of the European Court of Human Rights (25 January 1976), p. 494.

40. H.G. Bennett, "Report of The Committee of Inquiry into Police Interrogation Procedures in Northern Ireland" (The Bennett Report) (London, 1979).

41. The Judges' Rules were formulated in 1964 and introduced into Northern Ireland in 1976. "It has been a well established proposition of the laws of evidence for over 100 years that a confession is admissible at trial only if it was made voluntarily and without inducements,

threats, tricks, or force. It is to this primary rule of the Common Law that what we know as the Judges' Rules owe their origin." T. E. St. Johnston, "The Judges' Rules and Police Interrogation in England Today," The Journal of Criminal Law, Criminology, and Police Science, vol. 57, No. 1 (Chicago, 1966), p. 85. Among the provisions of the Judges' Rules was access to a solicitor.

42. D. McKittrick, "Northern Notebook," *The Irish Times* (19 March 1977).

43. The Bennett Report said "Our own examination of medical evidence reveals cases in which injuries, whatever their precise cause, were not self-inflicted and were sustained in police custody" (Bennett Report, p. 316). The debate is in *Hansard* (16 March 1979), vol. 964, cc. 961–84.

44. Dr. Kevin McNamara, email to author (18 November 2010).

45. 28 March 1979, after Dr. Irwin's television interview on Sunday 11 March, and publication of the report on Friday 16 March.

46. Bobby Sands recorded receiving the same treatment in Castlereagh in 1976. (*Behind the Wire*, no. 8, May 1989, p. 12).

47. Pearse Kerr, as told to Jack McKinney of the *Philadelphia Daily News*. Reproduced in *An Phoblacht* (8 February 1978), p. 4.

48. A systematic bending of the hand back while holding the elbow, sometimes called dorsiflexion.

49. Pearse Kerr, as told to Jack McKinney of the Philadelphia Daily News. Reproduced in *An Phoblacht* (8 February 1978), p. 4. This was a common occurrence and is borne out by, for example, Liam McColgan of Derry City, in February 1977, who claimed that his wrists were "bent to such an extent that the blood leaked through the pores of my skin." (Faul and Murray, 1978, p. 48); and Sean O'Neill of Co. Derry, in October 1976, who alleged that one of his interrogators "began to force my fingers backwards ... this made me go down on my knees in pain — he then changed to my left hand and repeated the action; he did this twice on each hand." (*Ibid.*, p. 46.)

50. Irish Prisoner of War, No.1 (n.d.), p. 2. "(c) consular officers shall have the right to visit a national of the sending State who is in prison, custody or detention, to converse and correspond with him and to arrange for his legal representation" (Article 36, Vienna Convention on Consular Relations, 1963, p. 15).

51. Presumably the Fianna.

52. Police Authority confidential report. Cited in Taylor, p. 203.

53. Sands, "The Crime of Castlereagh," (Part 1 of The H Block Trilogy), in R. Sands, Writings from Prison (Cork, 1998), pp. 124–5.

54. Letter, Peter Rawlinson, 4 December 2005.

55. See *Behind the Wire*, no. 8 (May 1989), pp. 11–13. For a graphic first hand description see also much of the text of "The Crime of Castlereagh."

56. Peter Rawlinson confirms this position.

57. *IRIS*, November 1981.

58. 11 May 1978, p. 24.

59. *Hansard* (15 June 1978), cc. 1161–4.

60. *Constabulary Gazette* (June 1978).

61. Letter to author, Peter Rawlinson (26 October 2005).

62. Ulster Defence Association, the largest Ulster loyalist paramilitary and vigilante group in Northern Ireland.

63. 6 December 1999.

64. Letter, Peter Rawlinson (26 October 2005).

65. *Ibid.*

66. *Ibid.* 21 November 2005.

67. *The Irish People*, 19 May 1978, p. 1. There were also allegations of attempts to put pressure on the vagus nerve near the ears: "the ... man had thumbs in pressure points on the backs of the ears." (Peter McCoy, cited in Faul and Murray, 1978, p. 66); "they stuck their fingers beneath my ears and kept pressing in" (Austin Devine, *ibid.*, p. 52). Vagal inhibition stops the heart by stimulation of the vagus nerve in the neck. This can be caused by pressure on the neck.

68. Cited in Taylor, p. 218.

69. *Ibid.*, p. 306.

70. Cited in *Behind the Wire*, no. 8 (May 1989), p 11–13.

71. *Republican News* (25 November 1978), p. 4.

72. Letter, Peter Rawlinson (26 October 2005).

73. *Ibid.*

74. *The Irish People* (19 May 1978).

75. *Ibid.*

76. Ciarán Barnes, *Andersonstown News* (2 January 2009).

77. 5 October 2009.

78. A. Feldman, *Formations of Violence: the narrative of the body and political terror in Northern Ireland* (Chicago, 1991), p. 129. Feldman had personal experience of interrogation in Castlereagh.

79. Bobby Sands, "Weeping Winds," in *Prison Poems* (Dublin, 1981).

80. Bennett, paragraph 181, was to insist three years later that not more than two officers should interview a prisoner at any one time.

81. Ruairí Ó Brádaigh, telephone interview (15 October 2010). He makes the point that this treatment is not typical. After his release he was served with papers ordering him to live across the border.

82. *Ibid.*

83. *An Phoblacht* (25 July 1985), p. 5.

84. *Ibid.*, 30 May 1985, p. 5.
85. See Joe Bennett, Chapter 5.
86. Ruairí Ó Brádaigh, telephone interview (15 October 2010).
87. Ruairí Ó Brádaigh, letter to author (22 December 2010).
88. See Gerard and Catherine Mahon, and Angela Whoriskey, Chapter 5.
89. For the purposes of this study children are defined as anyone up to the age of sixteen.
90. Faul and Murray, 1978, pp. 140–143.
91. *Ibid.*, pp. 143–146.
92. The date is uncertain because the FRU replaced a unit known as the Det, which had the same function.
93. M. Ingram and G. Harkin, *Stakeknife* (Dublin, 2004), p. 209.
94. *Republican News* (18 February 1978), p. 4.
95. *An Phoblacht/Republican News* (10 May 1984), p. 7.
96. The signature looks like Alan Int. Sgt. (*Republican News*, 17 September 1977, p. 6).
97. *Republican News* (3 September 1987), p. 2.
98. *Ulster* (December 1981), p. 5.
99. *Mid-Ulster UDA News* (11 May 1974), p. 6.
100. *Ulster* (June 1987), p. 15.
101. *Republican News* (6 December 1975), pp. 1, 4–5.
102. *An Phoblacht/Republican News* (10 May 1984), p. 7.
103. All details and quotations in this section are from Carver except where otherwise stated (J. Carver, *Love and Stockholm Syndrome: The Mystery of Loving an Abuser* [www.drjoecarver.com]).
104. For example: battered wives, cult members, incest victims, etc.
105. See, for instance, the description in Chapter 5 of Ray Gilmour's demeanor in court.
106. Carver, p. 267.
107. *Ibid.*, pp. 270–71.
108. *Ibid.*, p. 261.
109. *Ibid.*, p. 281.
110. *Ibid.*, p. 275.
111. *Ibid.*, p. 276.
112. *Ibid.*, p. 277.
113. *Ibid.*, p. 267.
114. *Ibid.*, p. 275.
115. *Ibid.*, p. 280.
116. *Ibid.*, p. 278.
117. Lord Anthony Gifford QC, "Supergrasses: the use of accomplice evidence in Northern Ireland" (London, 1983), p. 26.
118. *Ibid.*, p. 283.
119. Caroline Williams, single mother aged 34. *An Phoblacht/Republican News* (28 August 1986), p. 10.
120. Patsy McKea, charged with disorderly behavior. *Andersonstown News* (17 June 1987), p. 11.
121. Ivan Coyle, aged twenty. *An Phoblacht/Republican News* (25 September 1986), p. 7. All three were released without charge.
122. *Troops Out* (February 1984), p. 4.
123. *Republican News* (20 January 1979), p. 5.
124. *An Phoblacht/Republican News* (8 May 1986), p. 5.
125. Sinn Féin, *The Informers* (Dublin, May 1983).
126. M. McGartland, *Fifty Dead Men Walking* (London, 1998), p. 70.
127. See, for example, "RUC threats ignored," *An Phoblacht/Republican News* (19 November 1987), p. 4, and "RUC pressure tactics exposed," *An Phoblacht/Republican News* (19 March 1987), p. 7.
128. For bribes and the promise of rescue if necessary see, for example, "Frame-up threat," *An Phoblacht/Republican News* (18 September 1985), p. 7. Bribes in the South may have been more sizeable: Michael Clarke of County Tyrone, living in Dublin, was offered £10,000 by Dublin's Special Branch (*An Phoblacht/Republican News*, 4 December 1985, p. 6). In 1985 newly built houses in the Dublin area were selling for £30,000–£36,000 (*Irish Press*, 4 January 1985, p. 16).
129. "Enemy agents executed," IRA statement re: Mahon shootings, *An Phoblacht/Republican News* (12 September 1985), p. 2.
130. *Ibid.*
131. *Ibid.*
132. G. Harkin, "How husband and wife were 'nutted,'" *The People*, 18 May 2003.
133. Given the rivalry between the RUC and the army, this explanation seems unlikely.
134. "Revulsion over IRA 'execution,'" *Irish Press* (10 September 1985), p. 1.
135. *Andersonstown News* (14 September 1985), p. 3.
136. Donaldson, at a Dublin press conference (16 December 2005).
137. Donaldson was tracked down by Colin Breen, a retired RUC man said to have close ties with Special Branch, and Hugh Jordan, a reporter on the Sunday World, about two weeks before he was killed.
138. "Donaldson betrayed," *Sunday Life* (9 April 2006).
139. "Donaldson 'cheerful' in 'cosy cottage': census man," *Irish Independent* (9 April 2006).
140. Forensic experts find it difficult to trace shot, unlike bullets.
141. "Gardaí pledge to catch Donaldson murderers," irelandclick.com, n.d.
142. Guesses have been made by journalists about what made him vulnerable. Most refer to his propensity to chase women, but others say he might have been involved in a fraud.

143. *THE POST.ie* (1 January 2006). Claims by the media about other informers, subsequent to the unmasking of Stakeknife, were later shown to be untrue.

144. 1 January 2006.

145. Others argued that the IRA hired a Continuity IRA gunman from Co. Cavan to murder Donaldson ("Provos hired hitman to kill Donaldson," *Irish Independent*, 9 April 2006).

146. *Irish Republican News* (27 August 2010).

147. Amnesty Report 1978, Conclusions.

148. To prove this there had to be a pattern of ill-treatment at a particular place and at the hands of a particular agent.

149. Either the direct superiors knew and did nothing, or they were indifferent to the allegations by refusing to conduct an investigation.

150. Cited in Amnesty Report, p. 42, 7(i). Amnesty received little or no official cooperation and was denied access to the medical reports compiled by Police Surgeons at Castlereagh and Gough Barracks.

151. *Ibid.*, p. 289. Hermon was then Deputy Chief Constable.

152. Faul and Murray, 1978, p. 126.

153. *Ibid.*, p. 64. Sean Macken's case is fully covered in this publication, including his own detailed statement, medical reports and the involvement of a solicitor (pp. 57–66).

154. *RTÉ News*, 10 December 1999 (www.rte.ie).

155. *Irish Republican News* (12 October 2010).

156. I. Cobain, "Hundreds of Northern Ireland 'terrorists' allege police torture," *Guardian Unlimited* (11 October 2010).

157. I. Cobain, "Inside Castlereagh: We got confessions by torture," *Guardian Unlimited* (11 October 2010).

158. *Ibid.*

Chapter 4

1. "The Informer," *The Volunteer*, no. 23, n.d., no page numbers.

2. F. Kitson, *Low Intensity Operations* (Philadelphia, 1971).

3. T. P. Coogan, *The Troubles* (London, 1996), p. 556.

4. Eolas, *August 1973*, no page numbers. Startle is the word used for a very exaggerated response akin to jumping at a sudden noise but lasting far longer and without any external stimulus apparent to the onlooker. When the Compton Report was published (November, 1971) the British government denied that hooding could cause mental injury.

5. Cited in Taylor, *Brits: The War Against the IRA*, p. 135.

6. Martin Squires. Cited in Parker, p. 133.

7. SAS Major A. Cited in Parker, p. 38.

8. One of the detachments of what later became known as 14 Int.

9. There are two very conflicting opinions about Tony Ball: some colleagues said "Ball was a nasty bit of work, a psychotic, I would say. He bit his fingernails down to the white half-moons and was living on his nerves continually, possibly taking drugs." (O'Neill, p. 122); while Colonel G, one of his senior SAS officers, said, "He was sharp, aggressive and streetwise ... tough and hard ... completely admired by most of his contemporaries" (Cited in Parker, p. 69).

10. Cited in Parker, p. 66.

11. According to a number of former British army intelligence operatives, Robert Nairac was working with the Glenanne gang and was involved in the planning and carrying out of the John Francis Green assassination as well as the Miami Showband massacre (*Irish Republican News*, 3–5 August, 2010).

12. Nairac had a collection of photos of scene-of-crime events in Northern Ireland which verged on morbidity.

13. John Weir's *Affidavit*, 03.01.99, from www.seeingred.com, §30. This statement was given to *The Sunday Times*, February 1999.

14. Parker, p. 67.

15. Adams, p. 84.

16. Major Clive Fairweather. Cited in Parker, p. 181.

17. Fairweather. Cited in Parker, p. 186.

18. Julian Malins, friend. Cited in Parker, p. 165.

19. Martin Squires. Cited in Parker, p. 166.

20. Fairweather. Cited in Parker, pp. 203–4.

21. Cited in Parker, p. 222.

22. Cited in Parker, p. 223.

23. Parker, p. 223.

24. Parker, p. 224.

25. Registration CIB 4253. (Dillon, p. 169). The Press Association release at the time described the car as "an unmarked, British army issue Triumph Dolomite" (*An Phoblacht*, 18 May 1977).

26. Collett belonged to the Worcester and Forresters Regiment and was responsible that evening for logging personnel in and out.

27. He sang Republican songs: "The Broad Black Brimmer" and "The Boys of the Old Brigade."

28. Cited in Dillon, p. 170. Dillon says that the "spelling of McElean derives from police notes of interviews with several people who were in the Three Steps on 14 May. However, since there is no Catholic name spelt in this way, I believe that the name was probably McErlean and that Robert Nairac was unable to introduce an 'r' sound into his speech sufficiently to imitate a Belfast accent. The tendency of an English person would be almost to erase

the 'r' sound in McErlean" (Dillon, p. 171). It is also worth noting that previously in pubs Nairac had given his name as Danny McAlevey, and this is the name Parker uses.

29. Murray, p. 151.
30. Member of the Official IRA
31. "Of all those legally held to be connected with either the abduction or death of Nairac, only Fearon [a member for only six months] and Townson admitted to IRA membership" (Dillon, p. 177).
32. Dillon, pp. 179–80.
33. Murray, p. 152.
34. This included Special Branch (Fairweather, cited in Parker p. 180).
35. Fairweather, cited in Parker, p. 215.
36. "The length of time it took the army to respond to what was clearly an emergency showed a lack of appreciation of the situation" (Adams, p. 86).
37. "I do not understand the reason for such a delay in communicating the problem to the police, who were equally if not more familiar with the territory" (Dillon, pp. 171–2).
38. *An Phoblacht*, 18 May 1977, p. 8.
39. Murray, p. 154.
40. Curtis, p. 116.
41. Undated. www.esquire.co.uk
42. Dillon says from Meigh, outside Newry (p. 173).
43. Gerard Patrick Fearon (20), Thomas Patrick Morgan (18), Daniel Joseph O'Rourke (32), Owen Francis Rocks (33) and Michael Joseph McCoy (19). NB: There is a discrepancy in ages between sources, particularly in the case of Rocks.
44. "It was the first murder case to be conducted in Northern Ireland when the victim's body was still not found" (Murray, p. 153).
45. Murray, p. 154.
46. 18 May 1977, p. 8.
47. *An Phoblacht*, 26 April 1977, p. 6.
48. Parker, p. 204.
49. Member of the IRA, cited in Dillon, p. 185.
50. Shot by the army on 17 April 1977.
51. *John Weir's Affidavit*, 03.01.99, from www.seeingred.com, §35.
52. R. Lewis, *Fishers of Men* (London, 1999), p. 116.
53. *Ibid.*, p. 163.
54. Sir John Stevens, Stevens Enquiry 3, Overview and Recommendations, 17 April 2003, §3.1.
55. *Ibid.*
56. P. Cory, "Collusion Inquiry Report: Patrick Finucane" (London, 2004), p. 3.
57. *Ibid.*
58. Taken to be a reference to Finucane. Widely cited both at the time and later. For example: BBC News, 17 April 2003.

59. K. Fulton, *Unsung Hero* (London, 2006), p. xiii.
60. *Ibid.*, pp. 16–17.
61. *Ibid.*, p. 17.
62. *Ibid.*, pp. 20–21.
63. *Ibid.*, p. 25.
64. *Ibid.*, p. 46.
65. *Ibid.*, pp. 66–67.
66. *Ibid.*, pp. 39–44.
67. Pseudonyms are used for all the IRA men in Fulton's work. "Conor" was a top IRA figure (Fulton, p. 59).
68. Niall was "regarded as something of an IRA legend ... [and] had stiffed anything from four to ten people" (*ibid.*, pp. 70–71).
69. *Ibid.*, p. 71.
70. *Ibid.*, p. 81.
71. *Ibid.*, p. 164.
72. *Ibid.*, p. 82.
73. *Ibid.*, p. 114. Morley was an active member of the Provisional IRA who later joined the IPLO.
74. *Ibid.*, pp. 84–88.
75. *Ibid.*, p. 130.
76. *Ibid.*, p. 156.
77. *Ibid.*, p. 151. *Unsung Hero* was ghostwritten by Jim Nally and Ian Gallagher.
78. *Ibid.*, p. 158. Attempts to confirm this have failed.
79. Fulton, Conor and Niall were in charge of Dundalk, Armagh, and South Down.
80. *Ibid.*, p. 165.
81. *Ibid.*, p. 196.
82. *Ibid.*, p. 197.
83. He claimed to have been questioned by "Michael" (Fred Scappaticci).
84. Fulton, p. 235.
85. Barry McCaffrey, *Irish News* (31 January 2002).
86. *Ibid.*, p. 245.
87. This was accepted by the Ombudsman.
88. The details (Fulton, pp. 236–8) are convincing because of Fulton's previous experience in bomb making.
89. The Ombudsman's report was limited to the subsequent police investigation into the attack and, though there had been some lack of cooperation by the RUC into O'Loan's enquiry, her chief criticism was "the judgement and leadership of the Chief Constable and ACC Crime have been seriously flawed" (Ombudsman, Statement by the Police Ombudsman for Northern Ireland on her Investigation of matters relating to the Omagh Bomb on August 15, 1998, 12 December 200, §7.4).
90. Hall, "More Questions than Answers," *The Blanket* (August 2003). When Hall wrote the article it had been revealed on the Cryptome website (cryptome.org) that Fulton's real name was Peter Keeley.
91. Gerard "Whitey" Bradley, cited in *An-*

dersonstown News (3 June 2004). Bradley describes Fulton as "a Del Boy."

92. N. Mackay, "Rogue British agents name MI5 bosses in video expose," *Sunday Herald* (30 June 2002).

93. Participating Informant status is "R.U.C/P. S.N.I. speak for bent terrorist. They know he's a bomber, but the value of his information exceeds the threat of his terrorist activities" (Peter Rawlinson, email to author, 30 June 2007).

94. Statement taken from the website.

95. His statement was taken by Detective Inspector "BD," reportedly a PSNI Detective Inspector (Sergeant "Z," "SECRET," Cryptome, 27 December 2001).

96. *Ibid.*, p. 3.

97. *Ibid.*

98. Martin Ingram, Foreword, Fulton, p. x. Ingram (a pseudonym for Ian Hurst) is co-author of *Stakeknife*, and formerly a member of the FRU.

99. Though in chronological terms Carlin precedes Kevin Fulton, his career as an ex-informer includes much that refers to the latter's subsequent activities, so this order is more useful for the purposes of this study.

100. Carlin, cited in Hopkins and Cowan, "IRA moles plead for protection," *Guardian Unlimited* (28 April 2001).

101. McDonald, "Spy says McGuinness did not fire on Bloody Sunday," *Guardian Unlimited* (6 May 2001). Henry McDonald, Ireland editor, Guardian, in this same article, supposedly quotes Carlin as saying "the IRA want to lift me, take me away somewhere and torture me until I talk. Then I'll get one in the head in the middle of saying the Our Father." The author cannot believe that even a very lapsed Irish Catholic would confuse the Our Father with the Act of Contrition. Mistake or invention?

102. Sage, "Army Trained Loyalist Death Squads," *PA News* (27 March 2002).

103. Bettany was a former MI5 officer unmasked by a Russian defector and convicted of espionage.

104. The *Sunday Herald* reported that they were flown out of Northern Ireland in 1985 in Margaret Thatcher's Prime Ministerial jet. (N. Mackay, "The Army asked me to make bombs...," *Sunday Herald* (23 June 2002).

105. British Irish Rights Watch, Bloody Sunday Inquiry reports no. 107, p. 25.

106. Mackay, "The Army asked me to make bombs...," *Sunday Herald* (23 June 2002).

107. *Ibid.*

108. Sage, *PA News* (27 March 2002). This last allegation was already current.

109. *Ibid.*

110. Carlin, cited in Hopkins and Cowan, "IRA moles plead for protection," *Guardian Unlimited* (28 April 2001).

111. Willie Carlin, email to author (23 November 2007).

112. E.g. articles about Denis Donaldson, such as "Real IRA says it executed Denis Donaldson," *Republican News* (10–16 April 2009).

113. Cerulli, "Che cosa sta succedendo?" [What's going on?], *irlandanews* (22 May 2003), p. 6.

114. The centralized IRA internal security unit which replaced "The Unknowns" when the general reorganization took place in the late 1970s and early 1980s.

115. Cryptome.

116. Ingram and Harkin, p. 241.

117. This was after Martin Ingram had contacted him.

118. Martin Ingram brought the name to Sir John Stevens' attention.

119. Hopkins, "Questions Stevens wants answered by top Army spy," *Guardian* (12 May 2003).

120. Editorial, *Daily Telegraph* (13 May 2003).

121. Ingram and Harkin, p. 16.

122. Lynch, a self-admitted police informer for seven years, was interrogated by Scappaticci, and rescued by the RUC. There was no evidence to show that Morrison had been in the house where Lynch was held and he was not mentioned in Lynch's statement. D. Morrison, *Then the Walls Came Down: A Prison Journal* (Cork, 1999), pp. 81–2.

123. Ingram and Harkin, pp. 138–148.

124. Collins, with John Joe Magee and Scappaticci, made up the internal security unit.

125. Cited in Cowan, "He did the IRA's dirty work for 25 years," *Daily Telegraph* (12 May 2003).

126. Barry McCaffrey, "Former detective says Special Branch protected UVF informer," *Irish News* (28 October 2005).

127. McCaffrey, "Guilty plea meant loyalist's double life remained secret," *Irish News* (15 April 2007).

128. British Irish Rights Watch say that these stories did not appear on Cryptome, but this author has seen them on the website.

129. *Daily Telegraph* (15 May 2003).

130. Scappaticci "was outed on several websites," "was spirited away to a safe house in England by undercover agents" (Cowan and Hopkins, "British Army spy at heart of IRA death squad unmasked," *ibid.*, 12 May 2003).

131. Harding, "I'm no spy, says the man named as Stakeknife," *ibid.*

132. Lord Fitt, *Hansard* (8 January 2003), c. GC28.

133. Ware and Palmer, "This father of seven claims to be just an ordinary man," *Sunday Telegraph* (18 May 2003), p. 23.

134. McIntyre, "Spooks, Spies and Spoofers," *The Blanket* (5 August 2003).

135. *Ibid.*
136. Statement of 13 May 2003 (British Irish Rights Watch, "Stakeknife").
137. Statement read by solicitor Michael Flanigan to Brian Rowan (BBC) and Anne Cadwallader (Independent Radio News). Cited in Ingram and Harkin, pp. 248–249.
138. Cited in Ware and Palmer, *Sunday Telegraph* (18 May 2003), p. 23.
139. Greg Harkin, "How FRU got IRA to murder top sniper," *Sunday People* (23 June 2002).
140. Ingram and Harkin, p. 7.
141. *Ibid.*, p. 23.
142. www.indymedia.ie/article/76319
143. Jack Grantham, www.indymedia.ie/article/76319#comment 172043.
144. Ingram and Harkin, p. 83.
145. *Ibid.*, p. 247.
146. Suzanne Breen, "The tale of two Martins," *Sunday Tribune* (5 June 2006).
147. The key word here is "apparent." Johnston and Harding, "Stakeknife suspect in dramatic TV appearance," *Daily Telegraph* (15 May 2003).
148. Martin Ingram notes indignantly in Stakeknife that a former colleague, Rob Lewis (also a pseudonym, the author of *Fishers of Men*), circulated emails giving Ingram's real identity. (Ingram and Harkin, p. 261.)
149. Scappaticci, cited in *ibid.*, p. 243.
150. Scappaticci, *ibid.*, p. 253.
151. Jim Gibney, cited in Cerulli, p. 6.
152. The Smithwick tribunal opened in June 2011 to look at collusion between the Gardaí and the IRA.
153. "Statement of Ian Hurst," *Guardian* (11 September 2011), pp. 15–19 and 22–24.
154. The inquiry is to open in June 2017 and its subject is Stakeknife, which might lead to speculation about the timing of the BBC program (11 April 2017).
155. The early biographical details are taken from Ingram and Harkin, pp. 160–166, except where otherwise stated.
156. School reports described him as lazy (*ibid.*, p. 161).
157. *Ibid.*, p. 163.
158. *Ibid.*, p. 165.
159. *Ibid.*, p. 169.
160. M. Dillon, *The Trigger Men* (Edinburgh, 2004), p. 252.
161. McDonald and Cusack, UDA, *Inside the Heart of Loyalist Terror* (Dublin, 2004), p. 139.
162. *Ibid.*
163. Ingram and Harkin, p. 179.
164. There were four such killings in 1985, fifteen in 1986.
165. Kerr, cited in Taylor, p. 289.
166. Officers from MI5 had visited Nelson in Munich in an effort to recruit him (Davies, *Ten Thirty-Three*, Edinburgh, 1999, p. 62).
167. Geoff, Nelson's handler, cited in Taylor, p. 289. For purposes of comparison in 1986 a lecturer (Grade II) in Higher Education (university) would have earned £10,251 per annum.
168. J. O'Brien, *Killing Finucane* (Dublin, 2005), p. 115.
169. Ken Barrett, "A Licence to Murder," BBC *Panorama* (19 June 2002).
170. 17 January 1989
171. McDonald and Cusack, p. 152.
172. Stobie and Barrett were Special Branch informers (Moloney, 27 August 2000).
173. Liam Clarke, "McShane took a hardline on touts," *Sunday Times* (17 February 2008). Craig was killed by the UDA for passing information to the IRA resulting in McMichael's death in December 1987.
174. Geoff, Nelson's handler, cited in Taylor, p. 293.
175. Stevens Enquiry 3, Overview and Recommendations appeared in April 2003.
176. Security source cited in Moloney, "Security forces created Shankill UDA" *Sunday Tribune* (27 August 2000).
177. See Cory, pp. 43–58.
178. CAIN, "Collusion—Chronology of Events in the Stevens Enquiries."
179. Harkin, "Agent was simply a bigot—pal," *Sunday People* (23 June 2002).
180. Kerr's first response to Stevens in 1990 is noteworthy: "I find it incredible that I should be required to account for our handling of the case [Nelson]" (Ware, "It's a deadly business, saving lives," *Guardian*, 19 June 2002).
181. Director of Public Prosecutions, Head of the Crown Prosecution Service.
182. Cory, p. 114.
183. Ingram and Harkin, p. 165.
184. A senior FRU officer, cited in Ingram and Harkin, p. 191.
185. "Since 6137 [Nelson] took up his position as intelligence officer, the targeting has developed and become more professional." MISR (Military Intelligence Source Report) dated 3 May 1988 in Taylor, pp. 289–290.
186. Davies, p. 191.
187. BBC *Panorama*, "A Licence to Murder," (19 June 2002).
188. John Ware, *ibid.*
189. Nelson, *ibid.*
190. The FRU subsequently became the JSG (Joint Surveillance Group).
191. One (or even both, perhaps) of which was Gerry Adams.
192. Geoff, cited in Taylor, p. 288.
193. Cited in O'Brien, *Killing Finucane*, p. 11.
194. *Irish Echo* (8–14 April 1998).
195. Cory, p. 93.

196. The cause of death was a brain hemorrhage. This is as reported in the British media. CAIN says Nelson died in Canada.
197. McCaffrey, "Nelson may still be alive—ex-agent," *Irish News* (3 September 2003). But this can surely be dismissed as more publicity-seeking from Ingram.
198. British Irish Rights Watch, 1999, p. 1.
199. McDonald and Cusack, pp. 151–2 and 163. It is noteworthy that, though arguably there were lower levels of loyalist informers, more of them may have been executed by former comrades.
200. Brian Nelson was an exception to this. For him the attraction was power.
201. Brady was one of the three killed by Michael Stone, the Protestant extremist who ran amok at the Gibraltar funeral in March 1988.
202. Lewis, pp. 167–184.
203. 2003 and 2004 respectively.
204. "Executed," *Irelandclick.com* (23 September 2002).
205. "Volunteer cleared in IRA probe," *ibid.*
206. Greg Harkin, "How FRU got IRA to murder top sniper," *Sunday People* (25 June 2002).

Chapter 5

1. "Daddy, who was Judas?" *Combat*, vol. 4, issue no. 65, n.d.
2. Gifford, p. 11.
3. A. Boyd, *The Informers* (Dublin, 1984), p. 79.
4. "Supergrasses," Belfast Bulletin No. 11, Workers' Research Unit (summer, 1984), p. 4.
5. "The Informers," Sinn Féin (Dublin, 1983), p. 3.
6. *Fortnight* (November 1984), p. 13.
7. *Ibid.*, May 1983, p. 9.
8. T. Gifford, *Supergrasses: The Use of Accomplice Evidence in Northern Ireland* (London, 1984), p. 4.
9. The main differences between the informer and the supergrass are that the latter appears in court and is better paid.
10. The RUC preferred to use Hermon's phrase "converted terrorists," implying that the informers were coming forward of their own free will (but see Kevin McGrady, Chapter 5).
11. *Resource* (September 1983), p. 3.
12. "The Informers," Sinn Féin, n.p.
13. *Shankill Bulletin* (June 1984), p. 2.
14. Thus the UDA and the UVF were also badly hit by the supergrass system.
15. But see Catherine Yendall.
16. Alleged by Bennett at the trial. Among those against whom he gave evidence was James Irvine, a member of the UVF court martial.
17. *Combat*, August 1986 (no page numbers)

alleged that he was also given £1000 per month and a police 357 magnum pistol; and that Australia, New Zealand, Canada and South Africa all refused to allow him to live within their territory.
18. Joseph Bennett, *R. v. Graham* (1983). Cited in S. Greer, *Supergrasses* (Oxford, 1995), p. 62.
19. Murray cited in *Belfast Bulletin*, p. 5.
20. None of the accused had made written or verbal confessions, and all went to jail protesting their innocence. Corroboration, where available, came mainly from RUC statements.
21. Murray, cited in Gifford, p. 16.
22. *Belfast Bulletin*, p. 5.
23. Gifford, p. 15.
24. *Belfast Bulletin*, p. 5. In all, fourteen men were sentenced to prison for periods ranging from five years to life on the basis of the Bennett trial.
25. Gifford, p. 17.
26. "The Death of Justice in Ireland," *The American Gael* (May/June 1984), p. 4.
27. Sir Michael Havers, in a written submission to the House of Commons (24 October 1983), recorded in *Hansard*, cited in Combat, May 1984, p. 1.
28. *Combat*, vol. 4, issue 63, n.d., no page numbers.
29. *Ibid.*, vol. 4, issue 59, n.d., no page numbers.
30. R. McDonough, letter, *Fortnight* (24 February 1986), p. 14.
31. R. Gilmour, *Dead Ground* (London, 1998), p. 12. There is no mention of any other author, copyright belongs solely to Raymond Gilmour, but this does not necessarily mean that there was no ghostwriter involved.
32. Johnny Gilmour, interview (21 March 2006). Johnny has not read *Dead Ground*, but refutes many of Raymond's claims of ill-treatment at home when he emphasizes that Ray was never hit.
33. Alan Barker, *Shadows: Inside Northern Ireland's Special Branch* (Edinburgh, 2006).
34. Lawyers such as Boyd and Greer.
35. *An Phoblacht/Republican News* (26 August 1982), p. 3; The Irish People (a U.S. publication), 29 November 1988, p. 1; and many others between these dates. It is noteworthy that the RUC "threatened the Derry Journal with contempt of court if they published a statement issued by ... [Martin McGuinness] about the case" (*Troops Out*, May 1983, p. 4).
36. "Raymond Gilmour ... says that since Christmas [2005] he has been given only psychological counselling for post-traumatic stress disorder, and no physical protection. 'I have been told to ring 999 if I think I am in danger,' he said." (*Timesonline* 9 April 2006, no byline).

37. Gilmour, pp. 377–378.
38. *Ibid.*, p. 355.
39. Cited in E. Collins, *Killing Rage* (London, 1997), p. 348. But Collins was both more intelligent and more of a realist than Gilmour.
40. Barker, p. 239.
41. "This was common place [sic], they asked and threatened most of those lifted if they were young ones." (Johnny Gilmour, email to author, 8 October 2006).
42. Gilmour, p. 60.
43. Johnny Gilmour also suggests that Raymond was impressed by Pete's nickname: Scarface. (Johnny Gilmour, email to author, 7 October 2006.)
44. Gilmour, pp. 68–69.
45. See, for example, Gilmour, pp. 78, 80, 105, 108, passim. "One sister suspecting [sic] him of informing cos he would make calls from her house and because he had more money." (Johnny Gilmour, email to author, 7 October 2006).
46. He was one of only three people who had known the whereabouts of the powerful M60 gun which had just been captured by the RUC.
47. Barker, pp. 211–212.
48. Gilmour, p. 327.
49. Barker, p. 211.
50. Johnny Gilmour, interview (21 March 2006).
51. Claire Uí Suileabhain, Johnny Gilmour's wife, interview (14 February 2006).
52. Johnny Gilmour, email to author (7 October 2006).
53. "Raymond always had a car after prison ... suspicions were aroused in the family but some thought he got money from doing 'jobs' [for the IRA]... It was at a time when the IRA were giving people money for doing jobs, causing many of the original supporters to turn away." Johnny Gilmour, email to author, 8 October 2006.
54. Johnny Gilmour, interview (21 March 2006).
55. *The Irish People* (30 April 1983), p. 8.
56. Although this is the impression given by IRA statements and encouragement to informers to come forward, Johnny Gilmour saw it differently: "A few minor informers in the early days were encouraged to come forward, got off with it but mostly were told to get out of Derry, Raymond would almost certainly have been shot." (Email to author, 7 October 2006.)
57. *Ibid.*
58. Gilmour, p. 363.
59. *An Phoblacht/Republican News* (10 March 1983), p. 3.
60. Gilmour, p. 365.
61. *An Phoblacht/Republican News* (29 September 1983), p. 2.
62. *Ibid.*, 31 March 1983, no page number.
63. *Ibid.*
64. Martin McGuinness, 31 March 1983. Cited in *An Phoblacht/Republican News* (7 April 1983), p. 5.
65. At this point Lorraine was just twenty-one. Raymond was one year older and he had already been treated for the first of four gastric ulcers.
66. Lorraine Gilmour, *The Irish People* (30 April 1983), p. 8. Johnny Gilmour said: "She didn't always have an easy time of it, but McGuinness took care of her" (Email to author, 7 October 2006).
67. *Troops Out* (June 1984).
68. *The Irish People* (27 October 1984), p. 1.
69. Socialist Republic (September 1984), no page numbers. The supergrass trials had become notorious internationally and other observers came to Belfast to see them. See *Andersonstown News* (30 June 1984), p. 6, for Noel Saint-Pierre of the Quebec Jurists Association.
70. *An Phoblacht/Republican News* (25 October 1984), p. 7.
71. For example, he claimed that during an attack in Derry, when a British soldier was shot dead, he kept the safety catch on his rifle, and on another occasion he deflected the gunman's aim by making the car lurch. The RUC were adamant that they never offered immunity to killers.
72. Dave Brooks, observer from Birmingham Trades Council, cited in *An Phoblacht/Republican News* (8 November 1984), p. 4.
73. *Ibid.*, 20 December 1984, p. 5.
74. See Lowry's judgment in *R. v. Gibney*, 1983 (the McGrady trial) (*Belfast Bulletin*, p. 24).
75. Debate on the Baker Report on the Emergency Provisions Act in Northern Ireland, 21 December 1984. Cited in *Troops Out* (February 1985).
76. "Many of the family believe that it was a trap, apparent sympathy in order to trap him" (Johnny Gilmour, email to author, 7 October 2006).
77. Johnny Gilmour, interview (21 March 2006).
78. *Ibid.*
79. Claire Ui Suileabhain, interview (14 February 2006).
80. Claire Ui Suileabhain, email to author (1 February 2007).
81. Bobby Sands, "The H-Block Trilogy," *Prison Poems* (Dublin, 1981).
82. Johnny Gilmour, interview (21 March 2006).
83. Greer, p. 79.
84. From Lowry's judgement, cited in *Belfast Bulletin*, p. 24.
85. Greer, p. 80.
86. *An Phoblacht/Republican News* (29 March 1984), p. 12.

87. *Ibid.*, 27 October 1983, p. 5.
88. *Belfast Bulletin*, p. 23.
89. Greer, p. 81.
90. Concerned Communities Organisations, "The Supergrass" (Belfast, 1984), p. 23.
91. Gifford, p. 24.
92. *Ibid.*, p. 22.
93. Concerned Communities Organisations, "The Supergrass" (Belfast, 1984), p. 32.
94. Lowry, cited in the Gifford Report, p. 22.
95. Concerned Communities Organisations, "The Supergrass" (Belfast, 1984), p. 32.
96. He "suffered from acute religious delusions," *ibid.* p. 31.
97. *Belfast Bulletin*, p. 24.
98. "The Markets area is a small, very close-knit and long-established working-class community." *Ibid.*, p. 25.
99. Gregory Fritz, President, Caleb Project. This is one of the many eulogies cited on the YWAM website: www.ywam.org.
100. "[He] came under the strong influence of a number of key people in the YWM [sic] organisation, among them a U.S. pastor named Floyd McClung, who gave him advice on when to return to Belfast" (*Belfast Bulletin*, p. 25).
101. *Ibid.*
102. *Belfast Bulletin*, p. 25.
103. Greer, p. 81.
104. This contradiction raised no questions (*The Starry Plough*, September 1983, p. 8).
105. The informer was Anthony O'Doherty.
106. *Belfast Bulletin*, p. 23.
107. Sean McGrady, cited in *The Irish People* (18 September 1982), p. 7.
108. *Belfast Bulletin*, p. 26.
109. *An Phoblacht/Republican News* (10 May 1984).
110. Her husband was already interned in Long Kesh. (*IRIS*, 11 September 1974).
111. "Beating Women in Prison," *National Newsletter* (April 1980), pp. 4–5.
112. See, for example, *An Phoblacht/Republican News* (15 February 1980), p. 6.
113. See "Strip-Searches," in S. Calamati, *Women's Stories from the North of Ireland* (Belfast, 2002), pp. 86–88.
114. *Saoirse* (4 August 1987), p1.
115. *Andersonstown News* (5 January 1985), p. 23.
116. Stella Mann-Cairns, strip-searched at Greenham Common in December 1983, later awarded costs and damages against the MoD. Cited in *Troops Out*, August 1988, p. 11.
117. Local newsletter *Fingerpost*, cited in Calamati, p. 109.
118. *The Irish People* (9 November 1985), p. 10.
119. Martin McGuinness, cited in *Ireland's War* (January 1986), p. 10. At that time McGuinness was the elected Sinn Féin representative for Derry.
120. *800 Years*, October (n.d. but internal evidence indicates 1985).
121. This is a considerably lesser charge than the original, but it is probable that both confessions were signed under pressure during interrogation.
122. *The Irish People* (November 1986), p. 12.
123. *Ibid.*, May 1986, p. 4.
124. *Ibid.*, November 1986, p. 12.
125. When she went for a post-operative check-up it was discovered that her records had disappeared.
126. *The Irish People* (November 1986), p. 12.
127. Greer, p. 145.
128. *Troops Out* (November 1986), p. 5.
129. cunamh.org/content/derry_news/PATRICIA_MOORE.PDF
130. Greer, "The Supergrass: A Coda," *Fortnight* (March 1987), p. 8.
131. CAIN, text of Anglo-Irish Agreement.
132. http://news.bbc.co.uk/onthisday
133. *Hansard*, Northern Ireland: "Supergrass" System. HL Deb 03 April 1985, vol. 462, cc. 306–35.
134. *Shankill Bulletin* (June 1984), p. 2.
135. Letter, Joseph McCann No.164, H.M.P. Maze, *ibid.* (June 1984), p. 5.
136. Interview in *Niacro News* (January 1984), p. 10.
137. As Bernadette Devlin she was, at the time of her election, the youngest woman ever elected to serve as a Member of Parliament.
138. Though Lord Hailsham and the head of the Conservative party later met the Shankill-based Families for Legal Rights.
139. Bernadette McAliskey, speaking in London (2022 February 1984). Cited in *Troops Out* (April 1984), p. 2.
140. The EU case came under Sections 8 and 9 of the European Convention of Human Rights which deal with loss of liberty and court procedure. This protest group was also joined by former civil rights leaders.
141. Gifford, p. 27 and p. 35.
142. S. Greer and T. Jennings, "Final verdict on supergrass system," *Fortnight* (27 January 1986), p. 8.
143. R. McDonough, letter, *Fortnight* (24 February 1986), p. 14.
144. S. Greer and T. Jennings, "Goodbye to the supergrasses?," *Fortnight* (18 January 1984), p. 6.
145. S. Greer and T. Jennings, "Final verdict on supergrass system," *Fortnight* (27 January 1986), p. 8.
146. R. McDonough, letter, *Fortnight* (24 February 1986), p. 14.

147. See "Anatomy of a frame-up," *An Phoblacht/Republican News* (12 December 1985), p. 8.
148. *Saoirse* (January 2007), p. 2.
149. Skelly, when arrested, had no fixed abode and a long history of giving himself up to the RUC and claiming involvement in crimes. All his claims were proven unfounded. He had been receiving psychiatric treatment since his early teens.
150. *An Phoblacht/Republican News* (15 September 1983), p. 4.
151. *The Irish People* (5 November 1983), p. 7.
152. In 1990 McKeown was targeted by UDA gunmen because it was believed that he was still informing to the RUC. This and other activities meant that he was mistrusted by the UDA. In order to ingratiate himself with Billy Wright, one of the leaders of the organization, McKeown shot McGoldrick as a birthday present for Wright.
153. Gifford, p. 13.
154. Gifford, p. 17.
155. *Ibid.*, pp. 27–29.
156. *Ibid.*, p. 25.
157. Sinn Féin, *The Informers*, no page nos.
158. D. Bonner, "Combating Terrorism: Supergrass Trials in Northern Ireland," *The Modern Law Review*, vol. 51, No.1 (January 1988), p. 31.
159. *Ibid.*, p. 31.
160. Gifford, pp. 29–30.
161. *Ibid.*, p. 36.
162. *Troops Out* (February 1985), p. 5. Their emphasis.
163. Greer, "The Supergrass: A Coda," *Fortnight* (March 1987), p. 8,c.1.
164. Bonner, p. 31.
165. Gilmour, in a radio interview asked about his prospects if he returned to Derry. His answer appeared almost immediately in the form of graffiti on the walls of the Bogside: "Gilmore [sic] don't dare come back." His reaction to this was amazement: "After all that I did for them!" (BBC Radio Foyle, News, 5 February 2007).
166. Collins, p. 291.
167. Danny Morrison, email to author (16 February 2011).
168. BBC News (Northern Ireland), 2 February 2007.
169. Frank Kermode, "Afterword," in Leonardo Sciascia, *The Day of the Owl* (London, 1987).

Conclusion

1. Brigadier Frank Kitson came to Northern Ireland in 1970. This quotation is used frequently in documents about repression. Here it comes from the frontispiece to The Supergrass, published by Concerned Communities Organizations.
2. Bobby Sands, "The Crime of Castlereagh" 1980 (www.bobbysandstrust.com).
3. Jack Hayes, his nephew, tells about having his name queried by a supplier, and his custom or even future entry to the premises refused when he revealed that Stephen Hayes was his uncle.
4. *John Weir's Affidavit*, 03.01.99, from www.seeingred.com, §35.
5. Danny Morrison, email to author (16 February 2011).
6. Gifford, p. 15 and p. 17.
7. Danny Morrison, email to author (16 February 2011).
8. Johnny Gilmour, email to author (7 October 2006).
9. Police Service Northern Ireland, formerly RUC.
10. Christmas is recruitment season for British spooks," Republican News, 25 November 2011.
11. Danny Morrison, "No One's Asking What Really Happened?" Daily Ireland (21 December 2005).

Bibliography

Primary Sources

Archives

NATIONAL LIBRARY OF IRELAND
Benson, Mrs. E., to J. Murphy, 5 January 1924. NLI, MS 44,045/1.
Hayes, S., letter to Máire Comerford, Mountjoy, 21 December 1941, NLI, MSS 44,107/5.
Murphy, J., letter, 4 February 1926. NLI, MS 44,045/2.
O'Connor, Rev. T.J., to R. Mulcahy, 10 February 1922. NLI, MS 44,045/1.
Oglaigh na h-Eireann, *Special Communiqué*, 10 September 1941, NLI, MSS 44,107/2.

NATIONAL ARCHIVES OF IRELAND (NAI)
Bushe, H.G., letter to the Attorney General, 3 February 1939, NAI DO 35/893/6.
Chief Secretary's Office, Minute Sheet, 11 May 1921, NAI CO 904/162.
Foreign Office to the Chief Clerk, Irish Office, 27 April 1921, NAI CO 904/162.
Harding, E.J., Home Office memorandum, 31 January 1939. NAI DO 35/893/6.
Register of Informants, British in Ireland microfilm, NAI CO 904/183.
Witness Statements, NAI:
    Broy, Eamon, W.S. 1280.
    Broy, Colonel Eamon, W.S. 1285.
    Byrne, Vincent, W.S. 423.
    Dalton, Charles, W.S. 434.
    Daly, David, Commandant First Battalion, Athlone, W.S. 1337.
    Dolan, Joseph, W.S. 663.
    Harte, Christopher, W.S. 2.
    Lennon, Patrick, W.S. 1336.
    Leonard, Joe, W.S. 547.
    Mannix, Patrick, W.S. 502.
    Pinkman, Charles, W.S. 1263.
    Saurin, Frank, W.S. 715.
    Stapleton, William, W.S. 822.
    Thornton, Frank, W.S. 615.
    Togher, Joseph, Galway, W.S. 674 and 1729.

IMPERIAL WAR MUSEUM
The Irish Republican Army (from captured documents only), EPS/2/2.

KING'S COLLEGE, LONDON (KCL)
Adjutant of the 1st Cork Brigade to Adjutant General at GHQ, report on Dripsey ambush, "An I.R.A. Ambush," Foulkes, KCL 7/32 (2 February 1921).
Summary of Lindsay case, including text of her letters to Strickland, Foulkes, KCL 7/37, n.d.

Bibliography

WEXFORD COUNTY ARCHIVES (WXCA)

Hayes, Stephen, Extracts from Mountjoy Diary, July 1945–March 1946, Wexford County Archives, WXCA/P 246/1.
Quirke, Billy, "Story of Stephen Hayes," unpublished and incomplete typescript, c.1991–1992, Wexford County Archives, WXCA/P 246/2.

Private Collections

Hayes, Stephen, Letters to B., Mountjoy, various dates 1943–1945, private collection (Browne).

Interviews, Emails, Lectures and Correspondence

Bradley, Denis: "Who are worst at dealing with the past—the British or the Irish?" (lecture, Institute of Irish Studies, University of Liverpool, 31 March 2011).
Browne, Larry (telephone interviews: 24 November 08, 26 January 09, 21 March 2009).
Carlin, Willie.
Gilmour, Johnny (interview, 21 March 2006).
Hayes, Eileen (telephone interviews, 17 September 08, 2 October 08, 20 November 2008).
Long, Des.
McNamara, Dr. Kevin.
Morrison, Danny.
Ó Brádaigh, Ruairí (telephone interview, 15 October 2010).
Rawlinson, Peter.
Ui Suileabhain, Claire (interview: 14 February 2006).

Printed Primary Sources

Amnesty International. "Report on Allegations of Ill-Treatment Made by Persons Arrested Under The Special Powers Act After 8 August, 1971" (London, 1971).
Amnesty International. "Report of an Amnesty International Mission to Northern Ireland" (London, 1978).
Barker, Alan. *Shadows: Inside Northern Ireland's Special Branch* (Edinburgh, 2006).
Bennett, H.G. "Report of The Committee of Inquiry into Police Interrogation Procedures in Northern Ireland" (London, 1979).
Byrne, M. *Memoirs* (Dublin, n.d.), p. 19.
Collins, Eamon. *Killing Rage* (London, 1997).
Compton, Sir Edmund. "Report of the enquiry into allegations against the Security Forces of physical brutality in Northern Ireland arising out of events on the 9th August, 1971" (London, 1971).
Cory, Justice Peter de Carteret. "Collusion Inquiry Report: Patrick Finucane" (London, 2004).
Dáil Éireann Parliamentary Debates: 30 October 1924, vol. 9, col. 6; 28 January 1942, vol. 85, pp. 1453–1454, Emergency Powers (No.139) Order, 1941—Motion to Annul.
Feeney, P.J. *Glory O, Glory O, Ye Bold Fenian Men: A History of the Sixth Battalion Cork First Brigade 1913–1921* (Cork, 1996).
Fulton, Kevin. *Unsung Hero* (London, 2006).
Gilmour, Raymond. *Dead Ground* (London, 1999).
Hansard (Parliamentary Debates): 4 August 1921, vol. 43, cc. 320–2; 16 November 1971, vol. 826, c.220; 16 March 1979, vol. 964, cc. 961–84; 16 March 1979, vol. 964, cc. 961–84; 15 June 1978, cc. 1161–4; 8 January 2003, c.GC28; HL Deb 03 April 1985, vol. 462, cc. 306–35.
Hayes, Stephen. "My Strange Story," part I. *The Bell*, vol. XVII, No. 4 (July 1951).
Hayes, Stephen. "My Strange Story," part II. *The Bell*, vol. XVII, No. 5 (August 1951).
The Jerusalem Bible (London, 1968).
Joyce, William. *Twilight Over England* (Berlin, 1940).
Lewis, Rob. *Fishers of Men* (London, 1999).
McGartland, Martin. *Fifty Dead Men Walking* (London, 1998).

Macready, General Nevil. *Annals of an Active Life*, Vol. II (London, 1924).
Morrison, Danny. *Then the Walls Came Down: A Prison Journal* (Cork, 1999).
Northern Aid and the Association for Legal Justice. "The Record of British Brutality in Ireland" (Dublin, c.1971-72).
O'Donoghue, Florrie. *No Other Law* (Dublin, 1954).
Parker, Judge Hubert Lister (Baron Parker of Waddington). "Report of the Committee of Privy Counsellors appointed to consider authorised procedures for the interrogation of persons suspected of terrorism" (London, 1972).
"Report of the Commission of the European Court of Human Rights, Ireland against The United Kingdom of Great Britain and Northern Ireland" (Strasbourg, 25 January 1976).
Sands, Bobby. *Prison Poems* (Dublin, 1981).
Sands, Bobby. *Writings from Prison* (Cork, 1998).
Sheehan, Tim. *Lady Hostage* (Dripsey, privately printed, n.d.).
Sinn Féin. "An Appalling Vista." *Collusion: British Military Intelligence and Brian Nelson* (n.d., www.cain.ulst.ac.uk).
Sinn Féin. "The Informers" (Dublin, May 1983).
"Sinn Fein Rebellion Handbook." *The Weekly Irish Times* (Dublin, 1917).
Skinnider, Margaret. *Doing My Bit for Ireland* (Edinburgh, 2016).
"Statement by the Police Ombudsman for Northern Ireland on her Investigation of matters relating to the Omagh Bomb on August 15, 1998" (Belfast, 12 December 2001).
Stevens, Sir John. "Stevens Enquiry 3, Overview and Recommendations" (London, 17 April 2003).
Vienna Convention on Consular Relations, 1963 (Vienna, 1963).
Weir, John. *Affidavit*, 3 January 1999.

Newspaper Articles

Breen, Suzanne. "The Tale of Two Martins." *Sunday Tribune* (5 June 2006).
"Callous Conduct." *Freeman's Journal* (12 March 1923).
Clarke, L. "McShane took a hardline on touts." *Sunday Times* (17 February 2008).
Cowan, R. "He did the IRA's dirty work for 25 years." *Daily Telegraph* (12 May 2003).
Cowan, Rosie, and Nick Hopkins. "British Army spy at heart of IRA death squad unmasked." *Daily Telegraph* (12 May 2003).
Harding, T. "I'm no spy, says the man named as Stakeknife." *Daily Telegraph* (14 May 2003).
Harkin, Greg. "Agent was simply a bigot—pal." *Sunday People* (23 June 2002).
_____. "How FRU got IRA to murder top sniper." *Sunday People* (23 June 2002).
_____. "How husband and wife were 'nutted.'" *The People* (18 May 2003).
Hopkins, Nick. "Questions Stevens wants answered by top Army spy." *Guardian* (12 May 2003).
Johnston, P., and T. Harding. "Stakeknife suspect in dramatic TV appearance." *Daily Telegraph* (15 May 2003).
Mac Gabhann, L. "Freedom-fighter on a bicycle." *The Irish Times* (3 August 1968).
Mackay, N. "Rogue British agents name MI5 bosses in video expose." *Sunday Herald* (30 June 2002).
_____. "The Army asked me to make bombs." *Sunday Herald* (23 June 2002).
McCaffrey, B. "Nelson may still be alive—ex-agent." *Irish News* (1 September 2003).
_____. "Former detective says Special Branch protected UVF informer." *Irish News* (28 October 2005).
_____. "Guilty plea meant loyalist's double life remained secret." *Irish News* (15 April 2007).
McInerney, M. "The Stephen Hayes Affair." *Irish Times* (16 October 1968).
McKittrick, David. "Northern Notebook." *Irish Times* (19 March 1977).
Ó hUid, Tarlach. "Stephen Hayes ag cosaint a chlu." *Republican News* (23 November 1962).
"Revulsion over IRA 'execution.'" *Irish Press* (10 September 1985).
Sage, M. "Army Trained Loyalist Death Squads." *PA News* (27 March 2002).
"Somewhere in the Land of Terror." *The Catholic Register*, n.d., vol. xxvix, no. 15.
Ware, John. "It's a deadly business, saving lives." *Guardian* (19 June 2002).

Ware, John, and A. Palmer. "This father of seven claims to be just an ordinary man." *Sunday Telegraph* (18 May 2003).

Newspapers

The American Gael
Andersonstown News
An Phoblacht/Republican News
An Phoblacht
Behind the Wire
Combat
Constabulary Gazette
Cork Examiner
Daily Telegraph
The Echo (Enniscorthy)
The Enniscorthy Guardian
Fingerpost
The Free Press (Wexford)
Fortnight
Freeman's Journal
Galway Observer
The Guardian
Ireland's War
Irish Echo
Irish News
Irish Press
IRIS (Irish Republican Information Service)
Irish Independent
The Irish People
Irish Prisoner of War
Irish Republican News
Irish Times

Leitrim Observer
Manchester Guardian
Mid-Ulster UDA News
National Newsletter
Nenagh Guardian
New York Times
Niacro News
The Northern People
Observer
PA News
The Philadelphia Daily News
The Philadelphia Inquirer
Republican News
Resource
Saoirse
Southern Star
The Shankill Bulletin
Socialist Republic
The Starry Plough
The Straits Times (Singapore)
The Sunday Life
Sunday Times
Sunday Tribune
Sunday World
The Times
Troops Out
Ulster

Secondary Sources

Adams, James, et al. *Ambush: The War Between the SAS and the IRA* (London, 1988).
Anderson, Benedict. *Imagined Communities: Reflections on the Origin and Spread of Nationalism* (London, 1991).
Bardon, Jonathan. *A History of Ulster* (Belfast, 1992).
Bloch, Marc. *Histoire et Historiens* (Paris, 1995).
Borgonovo, John. *Florence and Josephine O'Donoghue's War of Independence* (Dublin, 2006).
_____. *Spies, Informers and the "Anti-Sinn Féin Society"* (Dublin, 2007).
Bowyer Bell, J. *The Secret Army* (Dublin, 1989).
Boyd, A. *The Informers* (Dublin, 1984).
Braudel, Fernand. *Ecrits sur l'Histoire* (Paris, 1999).
Calamati, Silvia. *Women's Stories from the North of Ireland* (Belfast, 2002).
Cole, J.A. *Lord Haw-Haw: The Full Story of William Joyce* (London, 1964).
Coogan, Tim Pat. *The IRA: A History* (Niwot, Colorado, 1994).
_____. *The Troubles* (London, 1996).
Costello, Frank, ed. *Michael Collins: In His Own Words* (Dublin, 1997).
Curtis, Liz. *Ireland: The Propaganda War* (London, 1984).
Dante Alighieri. *La Divina Commedia*, "Inferno" (dates inexact, 1265–1321).
Davies, Nicholas. *Ten Thirty-Three* (Edinburgh, 1999).
Dillon, Martin. *The Trigger Men* (Edinburgh, 2004).
Dolan, Anne. *Commemorating the Irish Civil War: History and Memory, 1923–2000* (Cambridge, 2003).

Elliott, Marianne. *The Catholics of Ulster* (London, 2000).
English, Richard. *Armed Struggle : The History of the IRA* (London, 2003).
Farrell, Michael. *Arming the Protestants* (London, 1983).
Faul, Denis, and Raymond Murray. *The Castlereagh File, Allegations of RUC Brutality 1976-1977* (Dungannon, 1978).
Feldman, Allen. *Formations of Violence: The Narrative of the Body and Political Terror in Northern Ireland* (Chicago, 1991).
Fitzpatrick, W.J. *The Sham Squire, and the Informers of 1798* (London, 1866).
———. *Secret Service under Pitt* (London, 1892).
Foley, Conor. *Legion of the Rearguard* (London, 1992).
Foy, Michael. *Michael Collins's Intelligence War* (Stroud, 2006).
Gallagher, Frank. *The Four Glorious Years 1918-1921* (Dublin, 2005).
Greer, S. *Supergrasses* (Oxford, 1995).
Griffith, Kenneth, and Timothy E. O'Grady. *Curious Journey* (Dublin, 1998).
Hanley, Brian. *The IRA, a Documentary History 1916-2005* (Dublin, 2010).
Hart, Peter. *The I.R.A. and its Enemies: Violence and Community in Cork, 1916-1923* (Oxford, 1999).
Haynes, Alan. *The Elizabethan Secret Services* (Stroud, 2000).
Hopkinson, Michael. *The Irish War of Independence* (Dublin, 2004).
Ingram, Martin and Greg Harkin. *Stakeknife* (Dublin, 2004).
Jackson, Ian T. *The Provincial Press and the Community* (Manchester, 1971).
Kenny, Mary. *Germany Calling* (Dublin, 2003).
Kitson, Frank. *Low Intensity Operations* (Philadelphia, 1971).
Lecky, W. *A History of Ireland in the Eighteenth Century* (London, 1892), p.252.
Lyons, F.S.L. *Ireland Since the Famine* (London, 1971).
MacEoin, Uinseann. *Harry* (Dublin, 1986).
———. *The IRA in the Twilight Years: 1923-1948* (Dublin, 1997).
Madden, R.R. *The United Irishmen; Their Lives and Times* (London, 1842-1846).
Manning, Aidan. *Donegal Poitín: A History* (Donegal, 2003).
Martland, Peter. *Lord Haw Haw* (Kew, 2003).
Matthews, A. *Renegades: Irish Republican Women, 1900-22* (Cork, 2010).
McDonald, Henry, and Jim Cusack. *UDA, Inside the Heart of Loyalist Terror* (Dublin, 2004).
McGee, Owen. *The IRB* (Dublin, 2005).
McMahon, Paul. *British Spies and Irish Rebels: British Intelligence and Ireland, 1916-1945* (Woodbridge, 2008).
McMahon, Timothy G., ed. *Pádraig Ó Fathaigh's War of Independence* (Cork, 2000).
Murphy, Gerard, ed. *"I am Eve": Early Irish Lyrics, Eighth to Twelfth Century* (Oxford, 1956).
Murphy, Gerard. *The Year of Disappearances* (Dublin, 2010).
Murray, Raymond. *The SAS in Ireland* (Cork, 2004).
O'Brien, Justin. *Killing Finucane* (Dublin, 2005).
Ó Broin, Leon. *Dublin Castle and the 1916 Rising* (Dublin, 1966).
O'Callaghan, Sean. *Execution* (London, 1974).
———. *The Informer* (London, 1998).
O'Malley, Cormac, and Anne Dolan, eds. *"No Surrender Here!" The Civil War Papers of Ernie O'Malley, 1922-1924* (Dublin, 2007).
O'Malley, Ernie. *On Another Man's Wound* (Dublin, 1979).
Quinn, R. *A Rebel Voice* (Belfast, 1999).
Ryder, Chris. *The RUC: A Force Under Fire* (London, 1992).
Sciascia, Leonardo. *The Day of the Owl* (London, 1987).
Seldon, Anthony, and J. Pappworth. *By Word of Mouth: Élite Oral History* (London, 1983).
Selwyn, Francis. *Hitler's Englishman* (London, 1987).
Shakespeare, William. *All's Well that Ends Well*, Act III, Scene 6.
Sims, George R. *The Dagonet Ballads* (London, 1879).
Stephan, Enno. *Spies in Ireland* (London, 1963).
Taylor, Peter. *Beating the Terrorists?* (Harmondsworth, 1980).
Taylor, Peter. *Brits: The War Against the IRA* (London, 2001).

Townshend, Charles. *Political Violence in Ireland* (Oxford, 1988).
Townshend, Charles. *Easter 1916* (London, 2005).
Urban, Mark. *Big Boys' Rules* (London, 1992).
Younger, Calton. *Ireland's Civil War* (London, 1970).

Theses

Long, D. "The Provisional IRA in Munster 1969–1974" (unpublished MA thesis, University of Limerick, 2010).
Ni Bheachain, Caoilfhionn. "The Lost Republicans: Sean McCaughey and the disruption of the Free State narrative" (unpublished MA thesis, University College Galway, 1997).

Media

BBC Radio Foyle, News, 5 February 2007.
Clár 2. "Coinsias," *Brathadóiri* [Programme 2, "Conscience," *Informers*]. Series made by Scun Scan Productions for TG4, 2008.
"A Licence to Murder." BBC *Panorama* (19 June 2002).

Online Articles

Carver, Joe. "Love and Stockholm Syndrome: The Mystery of Loving an Abuser." (http://www.drjoecarver.com, 19 November 2011).
Cerulli, S. "Che cosa sta succedendo?" [What's going on?]. *irlandanews* (www.irlandaonline.com, 22 May 2003).
Cobain, I. "Hundreds of Northern Ireland 'Terrorists' Allege Police Torture." *Guardian Unlimited* (11 October 2010).
Cobain, I. "Inside Castlereagh: We Got Confessions by Torture." *Guardian Unlimited* (11 October 2010).
Cowan, Rosie, and Nick Hopkins. "Devastating Report on Omagh Bombing Puts RUC on the Spot." *Guardian Unlimited* (7 December 2001).
Hall, M. "More Questions than Answers." *The Blanket* (August 2003).
Hopkins, Nick, and Rosie Cowan. "IRA Moles Plead for Protection." *Guardian Unlimited* (28 April 2001).
McIntyre, Anthony. "Spooks, Spies and Spoofers," *The Blanket* (5 August 2003).
Thompson, M. "How De Valera Asked UK to Smear IRA Chief Sean Russell." BBC News World (www.bbc.co.uk/news/world, 28 March 2011).
Sergeant "Z," "SECRET." Cryptome (27 December 2001).

Websites

www.theballadeers.com (The Balladeers).
www.bbc.co.uk/archive (BBC Archive online).
news.bbc.co.uk (BBC).
www.birw.org (British Irish Rights Watch)
http://indiamond6.ulib.iupui.edu:81 (*The Blanket*).
www.cain.ulst.ac.uk) (Conflict Archive on the Internet).
www.cryptome.org (Cryptome).
cunamh.org/content/derry_news
www.guardian.co.uk (*Guardian Unlimited*).
www.indymedia.ie (*The Independent*).
www.irelandclick.com (*Andersonstown News*).
www.irlandanews.org (Silvio Cerulli).
www.nuzhound.com (Sinn Féin, newspaper articles).
www.patfinucanecentre.org (Pat Finucane Centre).
www.policeombudsman.org (Police Ombudsman for Northern Ireland).
www.psni.police.uk/ (Police Service of Northern Ireland).

www.thepost.ie (*The Sunday Business Post* Online).
www.relativesforjustice.com (Relatives for Justice).
www.rte.ie (RTE).
www.seeingred.com ("A modern electronic corkboard").
www.timesonline.co.uk (*The Times* and *The Sunday Times*).
www.ywam.org (Youth with a Mission).

Journals

Bonner, D. "Combating Terrorism: Supergrass Trials in Northern Ireland." *The Modern Law Review*, vol. 51, no.1 (January 1988), pp. 23–53.

Chan, Meow Lan E. "Why did you hurt me?" *Review of General Psychology*, vol. 13, no. 3, 2009.

Connolly, J. "The Irish Masses in History." *The Harp* (September 1908).

Costello, F.J. "The Role of Propaganda in the Anglo-Irish War 1919–1921." *The Canadian Journal of Irish Studies*, vol. 14, no. 2 (January 1989).

Doherty, M.A. "Kevin Barry and the Anglo-Irish Propaganda War." *Irish Historical Studies*, vol. 32, no. 126 (November 2000).

Elangovan, A.R., and D.L. Shapiro. "Betrayal of Trust in Organizations." *Academy of Management Review*, vol. 23, no. 3, 1998.

Greer, S. "The Supergrasses: A Coda." *Fortnight* (March 1987).

Greer, S., and T. Jennings. "Final verdict on supergrass system." *Fortnight* (27 January 1986).

Greer, S., and T. Jennings. "Goodbye to the supergrasses?" *Fortnight* (18 January 1984).

Hull, M. "The Irish Interlude: German Intelligence in Ireland, 1939–1943." *The Journal of Military History*, vol. 66, no. 3 (July 2002).

O'Halpin, Eunan. "The Secret Service Vote and Ireland, 1868–1922." *Irish Historical Studies*, vol. 23, no. 92 (November 1983), pp. 348–353.

Rachman, S. "Betrayal: A Psychological Analysis." *Behaviour Research and Therapy*, vol. 48, 2010.

St. Johnston, T.E. "The Judges' Rules and Police Interrogation in England Today." *The Journal of Criminal Law, Criminology, and Police Science*, vol. 57, no. 1 (Chicago, 1966).

Pamphlets

Gifford, T. "Supergrasses: the use of accomplice evidence in Northern Ireland" (London, 1984).

O Tuathail, S. "Torture: The Record of British Brutality in Ireland" (Dublin, 1971).

"Supergrasses," Belfast Bulletin No. 11, Workers' Research Unit (n.d.).

"The Supergrass," Concerned Communities Organisations (Belfast, 1984).

Book Chapters

Bhabha, Homi. "Narrating the Nation," in J. Hutchinson and A. Smith, eds., *Nationalism* (Oxford, 1994).

Dolan, Anne. "The IRA, Intelligence and Bloody Sunday, 1920," in E. O'Halpin, et al., eds., *Intelligence, Statecraft and International Power* (Dublin, 2006).

O'Halpin, Eunan. "Intelligence and Anglo-Irish relations, 1922–73," in E. O'Halpin et al., eds., *Intelligence, Statecraft and International Power* (Dublin, 2006).

Index

Abwehr (German intelligence agency) 60-1, 65, 66
accomplice evidence 160, 175, 188; *see also* supergrass strategy
Adams, Gerry 109, 112, 146, 147, 150, 185
Adams, James 125
Agnew, Kevin 102
Allen, William "Budgie" 183, 186, 187
Allsopp, Jimmy 104
Alton, Professor 38
Amnesty International 88, 93-4, 95, 114, 115, 116, 159, 184
Anderson, Benedict 8
Anglo-Irish Agreement (November 1985) 150, 182
Anglo-Irish War 19, 26; Barry's victory at Kilmichael (November 1920) 30-1, 38, 39; burning of Cork City (December 1920) 31; in Cork 28, 29, 30-5, 38, 39; Dripsey ambush (January 1921) 31-4, 37-9, 41, 48, 54; hanging of Kevin Barry 36-7; as intelligence war 54; pensions for IRA men 59; propaganda during 30-1, 34, 35-8, 50, 54; regional variations in fighting 54-5; and William Joyce 44-7, 49, 54; Witness Statements 13, 22
Anthony, George Watson 115
Anti-Show Trials Campaign 183
"Anti-Sinn Féin Society" 29
Armagh Jail 103, 179, 180, 181
Armstrong, Lilias 125
Asher, Michael 88

"The Badger"(senior Garda officer) 124
Baillie, Harry 90
Ball, Julian "Tony" 124, 130
ballads 3-4, 18, 20, 36-7, 193
Barrett, Jim 32, 34, 35
Barrett, Ken 151, 154
Barry, Kevin 36-7
Barry, Michael 52
Barry, Tom 30-1, 39, 60, 61
Bartlett, Thomas 1, 8

Bedford, Rev. Thomas 7
Belfast: Campbell College raid (1935) 60; Crown Entry raid (1935) 60, 76; Crumlin Road Families Centre 183; Crumlin Road Jail 96-7, 134, 161, 183, 189; Falls Curfew (July 1970) 120; Felons' Club 186; Four Square laundry 122; Gemini massage parlor, Antrim Road 122; IRA Northern Command during Emergency 64, 68, 70, 83; Markets area 143, 173; Nelson as informer in UDA 149, 150, 151; North Queen Street Barracks 104; parades for George V's jubilee 59-60; riots (August 1969) 120; RUC raids (December 1938) 63-4; "Schoolboy Spy-Ring" in (1970s) 105-6; Short Strand area 103, 108, 112; Springfield Road RUC Barracks 116; Townhall Street police station 92; Twinbrook area 104, 109; *see also* Castlereagh Interrogation Center, East Belfast
Bennett, Joe 18, 157, 161, 162-5, 172, 183, 186-7, 193
Bennett Report (March 1979) 93, 94-5, 159
betrayal: Chan's list of types of 10; characteristics common among informers 43, 48, 109, 129-30, 139, 140, 141, 142, 154, 157, 167, 193-4; continuing market for the informer's services 195; Dante's portrayal of 9; as different during Troubles 7-8; E.M. Forster on 26-7; fear as mainspring at Castlereagh 19, 116, 117; and impact on informers' lives 16, 109, 112, 113, 159, 177, 189; of informers 2, 7, 16, 111, 112, 138, 144, 154; Irish nationalist concept of 8, 20, 193; Kevin Fulton 15, 131, 133, 136-7, 138-9, 156, 157, 192, 193; motivations for 9, 14, 35, 41, 48-9, 54, 110-11, 116, 134-6, 157, 166-7, 176-8, 193; motivations for, financial 5, 7, 37, 54, 110-11, 116, 134, 138-9, 166-7, 192, 193; pre-twentieth-century history of 5-7; and psychologists 10, 93-4, 106-8, 192; Rachman's definition of 10; responsibility for 10, 14, 194-5; and serpent in garden of

227

Index

Eden 9–10; and Stephen Hayes 8, 68–85, 192–3, 194; transference of loyalty/dependence 14, 106–8, 169–70, 177, 193
Bettany, Michael 140
Bhabha, Homi 8
Birmingham Trades Council 171–2
Birrell, Augustine 22
Black, Christopher 159, 160–1, 163–4, 171, 183, 187
Black and Tans 24, 31, 42, 44, 45, 46
Bloch, Marc 11, 13
Bloody Sunday (21 November 1920) 26, 28
Bloody Sunday (30 January 1972) 121, 123
Blueshirts 59
Boal, Desmond 171
Boland, Gerry 81, 84
Bonner, D. 187, 188
Border Campaign (1956–62) 19, 85
Borgonovo, John 1, 30
Boundary Commission (1925) 58
Bowyer Bell, J. 73, 76
Boyd, Andrew: *Informers* 15, 16
Bradley, Denis 87
Bradley, Gerard 138
Brady, Hugh 159–60, 173, 189
Brady, Kevin 156
Braudel, Fernand: *Ecrits sur l'Histoire* (1999) 9
Brehon law 8
British Army 24, 25, 31–3, 64, 120, 121, 146; see also military intelligence, British
British government: economic war with Free State 59; intelligence collaboration with Free State 55, 61, 71; knowledge of ill treatment of prisoners 114–15; pre-twentieth-century Irish informers 6, 7, 8; secret service vote 23, 25; use of deathsquads 148; *see also* Dublin Castle
British Irish Rights Watch 116, 155
British Union of Fascists 46, 48
Brodrick, Lady Albina (Gobnait Ní Bhruadair) 49
Brooke, Quentin 42
Brooks, Dave 172
Brophy, Edward 100
Brown, Josephine (later Mrs. Florrie O'Donoghue) ("G") 28–9
Browne, Larry 17, 84
Broy, Eamon 13, 22, 24, 26, 59
Brugha, Cathal 37–8
Bureau of Military History, Dublin 13, 22
Burke, Liam 69
Busteed, Frank 32, 33, 34–5, 38, 39, 40–1
Byrne, Christopher 72, 81
Byrne, Miles 6
Byrne, Vincent 24

Callaghan, James 95
Carey, Hugh 94
Carleton, Francis and John 194
Carlin, Willie 131, 139–42, 156, 157, 192, 193
Carroll, Assistant Superintendent 76
Carron, Owen 174
Carson, Gerard 91
Carson, John 187
Cashel, Archbishop of 6
Castlereagh Interrogation Center, East Belfast: closure (1999) 116; "The Crime of Castlereagh" (Sands) 8, 18, 86, 97, 100, 191–2; death of Brian Maguire 97–101, 117, 146, 192; European Commission Report (1976) 91; ill-treatment of children at 104; ill-treatment of Protestants at 92, 102–3, 115; and Newman's reforms 91; Pearse Kerr case 88, 95–7, 100–1, 117, 146, 192; Ó Brádaigh's detention at 101–2; Palace Barracks as blueprint for 90; and police doctors 91–2, 93, 95, 96–7, 115, 116; recruitment of informers in 19, 92, 102, 103–4, 113, 115, 116; systematic abuse and brutality at 88–9, 90, 91, 92–7, 100–1, 102–4, 114–18, 191; women held 103, 181
Catholicism, Irish 6, 13–14, 50, 60, 70, 81, 89, 111, 157
Ceannt, Eamonn 62
Cecil, William 5–6
censorship 76, 87–8, 170
Cerulli, Silvio 142
Chan, Meow Lan E. 10
Childers, Erskine 26–8, 36
children: executed by IRA 103–4; "Schoolboy Spy-Ring" in Belfast 105–6; targeting of by security forces 103, 104–6, 109, 192
civil rights movement in Northern Ireland 87, 88
Civil War 19, 49–55
Clan na Gael 67
Clarke, James 29, 32, 33, 35, 36
Clarke, Liam 143
Cleary, James 52
Cleary, Peter 128, 131
Coachford, Co. Cork 29–30, 31, 32, 33
Cobden Trust 160
Cohalan, Bishop 31
Cole, J.A. 47
Collins, Eamon 10, 13–14, 106–8, 143–4, 166, 184, 188–9
Collins, Michael 27, 35, 37, 46, 58; agents of in the Castle 13, 24, 25, 53–4; British spying on 25–6; execution of spies and informers 24–5, 26, 35
Comerford, Máire 11, 23, 49–50, 76, 79–80, 83, 85
Compton Report (1971) 88–9, 90, 94
Concerned Community Organizations 184
Connolly, James 6
Connolly, Owen 182
Connors, "Cruxy" 29
Consultative Group on the Past 87
Conway, Grace 33
Coogan, Tim Pat 70, 73, 76, 82
Cooley, W. 53

Index

Cork: ambushes in revolutionary period 29, 31–4, 37–9, 41, 48,54; Barry's victory at Kilmichael (November 1920) 30–1, 38, 39; burning of Cork City (December 1920) 31; as garrison city 30, 191; Protestants in 30, 32; suspected Boy Scout/YMCA spies in 47; Volunteers in 13, 26, 28–9, 30–5, 37–9, 40–1
Cory Inquiry (2004) 131, 132, 152–3, 155
Cosgrave, W.T. 55, 58, 59
Craig, Andrew 174, 175, 177
Craig, Jimmy 151, 154
Crane, Mrs. Geraldine 103
Cranley, Tim 113
Creighton, Carole 154
Crime Investigation Department (CID) 55
Criminal Cases Review Commission (CCRC) 116, 117
Crockard, James 183, 189
Crofton, Jim 73, 80, 83
Cromwell, Oliver 6
Crumley, Cathal 161, 172
Cryptome website 138–9, 143, 144–5, 147
Cuchulain 8
Culvert, Mickey 101
Cumann na mBan 49–50, 59
Curragh internments (1920s) 62
Curtis, Liz 87–8
Cusack, Jim 149, 155

"Daddy, who was Judas?" (untitled amhrán) 18, 158
Dáil Eireann 24, 58, 77–8
Dalton, Charles 25
Daly, David 17, 22
Daly, Prof. Robert 121–2
Dalyell, Tam 142
Dante 9
Davern, Patrick 77, 78
Davitt, Michael 7
De Lacy, Larry 62, 72, 76, 84
Derrig, Thomas 72, 81
Derry: and Angela Whoriskey 179–82; British Army's arrival in (August 1969) 120; Carlin and Sinn Féin 139–40, 141; Civil Rights march (August 1969) 87; Creggan estate 14–15, 104–5, 165, 166, 167, 173; Raymond Gilmour and family 14–15, 165–70, 171, 172–3, 189; Strand Road RUC Barracks 116; Strand Road, Shantallow 179, 180
De Valera, Eamon 23, 27, 37, 58, 59, 60, 61, 71, 83
Devereux, Michael 77–8, 81
Dillon, Denis 171
Dillon, Martin 130, 151
Diplock courts 90, 92, 116, 117, 118, 121, 129, 163–4, 170–2, 180, 182, 184
Dolan, Anne 51
Dolan, Bridget (Croppy Biddy) 6
Dolan, Joseph 24
Donaldson, Denis Martyn 112–14, 165, 193, 195

Donnelly, Liam 156
Doran, William 24–5
Douai, seminary at 6
Dowds, Ernest 173, 174, 177
Downing, Tom 45
Doyle, Eamon 162
"Dripsey Ambush" (amhrán) 18, 21
Dripsey ambush (January 1921) 31–4, 37–9, 41, 48, 54, 191
Drumcree crisis (1996) 186
Dublin 54, 60, 98, 191; British Embassy burned down (1972) 121; Goertz in 65, 66–7; IRA Dublin-Cork link ("G") 28–9; IRA GHQ in 24, 26, 35, 39–40, 61, 63–4, 73, 77, 83; occupation of the Four Courts (April 1922) 50, 55; Ormonde Winter in 26; police G Division 24, 25; Upper Church Street raid (20 September 1920) 36–7; UVF bombings (May 1974) 124, 141; Wicklow Hotel 24
Dublin Castle: Collins' agents at 13, 24, 25, 53–4; espionage resources 7, 23, 24, 25–6, 28, 53–4; and foreign propaganda 12; Ormonde Winter's work at 26; quality of British agents 25; register of Informants at (1880–c.1891) 7; and WWI conscription 22
Dudley, Robert 5–6
Duff, Douglas 44
Duffy, John 108
Dulanty, John W. 71
Dunlop, Charlie 108

Eames, Lord 87
Easter Rising (1916) 13, 17, 19, 22–4, 62
Egan, Barry 32
Eilberg, Joshua 97
Elizabeth I, Queen 5–6
Elliott, Dr. Denis 92, 95
Emergency (WWII): espionage in the South during 65–6, 67, 83, 85; G2 breaking of Nazi ciphers 65, 83; German agents in Ireland 65, 66–8, 82–3; IRA Northern Command during 64, 68, 70, 83; Irish neutrality 19, 61, 71, 72–3; legislation (1939, 1940) 61, 77–8; treaty ports 61
Emergency Powers Act, Irish (July 1940) 61, 77–8
Emergency Provisions Act (EPA, 1973) 95, 108, 121
Emmet's conspiracy (1803) 6, 8
Enniskillen bombing (November 1987) 141
European Commission 91
European Court of Human Rights, Strasbourg 88, 94, 114–15, 184

Fairweather, Clive 125, 126, 127–8, 129
Families for Legal Rights 162, 183
Faul, Fr. Denis 117, 179, 198
Feeney, P.J. 41
Feldman, Allen: *Formations of Violence* 101
Fenians 7, 8, 30

Fenton, Joseph 111
Fianna Fáil 58, 59, 60, 61, 71–3, 83
Finucane, Pat 132, 150–1, 153, 154, 155
Fitt, Gerry 93, 144–5
Fitzpatrick, W.J. 6
Flanagan, Sir James 99, 175
Flanigan, Michael 145
Flood, Paddy 146, 156
Fogarty, Marcus 87
Force Research Unit (FRU): and Brian Nelson 131, 149–55, 157; and Carlin 140, 141–2, 156; collusion and murder allegations 132, 140, 146, 148, 150–5, 156; and Fulton 15, 131, 133–4, 135–7, 141, 156; and Ingram 15, 103, 145, 146–7, 148; Paddy Flood murder 146, 156; Pat Finucane murder 132, 150–1, 153, 154, 155; recruitment methods 131, 133–4, 149–50, 155–6; setting up of (c. 1980) 103, 131; and Stakeknife 143, 144–5, 147–8, 156
Forensic Medical Officers Association 91
Forster, E.M. 26–7
Fouvargue, Vincent 28
Freud, Clement 95
Fulton, Kevin (Peter Keeley) 131, 132–6, 137, 140, 141, 156, 157; financial motivations 15, 138–9, 192, 193; Omagh bomb allegations 137–8; and Stakeknife 138, 144–5; team of informers/blackmail video 138, 141–2, 193; *Unsung Hero* (2006) 13, 15, 134, 137
Furlong, Nicholas 13

G2 (Irish Military Intelligence) 55, 65–7, 83, 85
Gallagher, Frank 23, 28
Galvin, Martin 109
Garda Siochána 58, 61, 71
Germany, Nazi 60–1, 64, 65–8, 82–3
Gibney, Jim 148, 174, 175, 178
Gibson, Lord Justice 129, 187
Gifford, T.: "Supergrasses: the use of accomplice evidence in Northern Ireland" (1984) 16, 107–8, 159, 160, 175, 182, 184, 186–7, 188
Gill, David 106
Gill, Michael 65
Gillman, Mrs. 32
Gilmour, Bridget 169, 171
Gilmour, Johnny 167–9, 171, 172, 173, 189, 194
Gilmour, Lorraine 167, 168, 169, 170, 171, 172
Gilmour, Patrick 166, 167, 168–9
Gilmour, Raymond 159–60, 162, 165–73, 182, 187, 188, 189, 194; *Dead Ground* (1999) 13, 14–15, 112, 165–6
Girdwood Interrogation Center 116, 156, 197–8
Goertz, Hermann 65, 66–8, 73, 82–3
Good Friday Agreement (1998) 142
Goodman, Jackie 186, 187
Gorky, Maxim 195
Gough Barracks, Armagh 92, 115–16

Goulding, Cathal 87
Green, John Francis 124, 130, 141
Green, Roy 144
Greer, Steven 15–16, 182, 184, 188
Griffin, Fr. Michael 44–7, 54
Griffith, Arthur 27
Grimley, Jackie 160, 185, 187

Hadden, Tom 160
Haddock, Mark 144
Hall, Mick 138
Hamill, Felim 98, 100
Hamill, Robert 132
Hanlon, Jimmy 156
Hanna, Joe 60
Harkin, Greg 145, 156
Hart, Peter 27, 30, 54
Harte, Christopher 25
Haughey, Joe "The Hawk" 151
Havers, Sir Michael 164
Hayes, Eileen 17, 84
Hayes, Dr. Maurice 101
Hayes, Dr. Richard 65
Hayes, Stephen 7, 157, 192–3, 194; abduction of (June 1941) 17, 68–71, 82, 83; as Acting Chief of Staff 61, 63, 64; background and character 62–3, 67, 69, 70, 75; Billy Quirke typescript on 13, 68, 69, 82; blamed for Plant and Devereux deaths 78, 81; "confession" document (*Special Communiqué*, August 1941) 18, 62, 71–3, 76–7, 78, 79–80, 81; court-martial of 69–70, 81; escape from Rathmines house 74, 76, 78; and Hermann Goertz 65, 66, 67; IRA discredited by episode 83–4, 192–3; later life of 17, 84–5; "Let Erin Remember" 8, 56–7; letter to Máire Comerford (December 1941) 11, 79–80; McCaughey's dislike of 64, 67, 68, 69, 70; "My Strange Story" (1951) 68; prison sentence 72, 80–1; rise to prominence in IRA 60, 61, 62–3; testimony against McCaughey 74–5, 76, 79, 81; trial (Dublin, 1942) 11, 72, 75, 80–1
Healy, Tim 82
Heatley, Kevin 132–3
Hegarty, Franko 157
Held, Stephen 66, 68
Hempel, Dr. Eduard 82–3
Hermon, Jack 19, 95, 106, 151, 162, 176, 177, 192
Hermon Committee 115, 151
Hess, Bridie (mother of Hayes' son) 17, 69, 73, 84, 85
Higgins, Francis (the Sham Squire) 1, 6
Higgins, Gerry 149
Hogg, Douglas 132, 151
Holroyd, Fred 124, 128
Holywood Barracks, Co. Down 90, 116, 122, 152, 197–8
Hopkinson, Michael: *Green Against Green* 51

Hughes, Brendan 122
Hull, Mark 65
Hume, Cardinal 128
humor and laughter 194
hunger striking: as matter of free will 82; myth of in Ireland 81; 1981 republicans 18, 160; Sean McCaughey 75, 81–2, 83; Terence MacSwiney 28, 31, 36
Hunt report (1969) 120
Hunter, Andrew 142
Hurd, Douglas 172
Hutton, Mr. Justice 180

"The Informer" (cartoon) 18, 119
Ingram, Martin 15, 103, 139, 142, 143, 145, 146–7, 148, 149, 155, 156
internment without trial 88, 121, 179; parallels with supergrass strategy 161–2, 164, 188
Irish Free State: Civil Service 62; Constitution Act (1931) 59; economic and social problems 58, 59, 60; economic war with Britain 59; Eucharistic Congress (1932) 59; intelligence collaboration with Britain 55, 61, 71
Irish Republican Army (IRA): abduction of Hayes (June 1941) 17, 68–71, 82, 83; agents in loyalist paramilitaries 151; autumn 1939 arrests and jailings 64; Black as supergrass 159, 160–1, 163–4, 171, 183, 187; British Army informers in 121, 124, 131–2, 133–41, 156, 157; Campbell College raid (Belfast, 1935) 60; Civil War 51–3; Cork brigades 13, 26, 28–9, 30–5, 37–9, 40–1; discredited by Hayes affair 83–4, 192–3; English campaign (1939) 61, 71; execution of children during Troubles 103–4; execution of informers during Troubles 103–4, 111, 122, 124, 156, 157; execution of informers in Anglo-Irish War 24–5, 26, 28, 29, 30, 35, 44, 48–9; execution of informers in Civil War 52–3; execution of informers in 1930s 60, 76; and Fianna Fáil 59, 60; Galway Brigade 44, 45, 46–7; Gardaí crackdown on (1920s) 58; general amnesty for schoolboys (1975) 105–6; General Orders on death penalty for informers (1920/21) 39–40; General Orders on treatment of civil war spies (1922) 51–2; Grand Hotel Brighton bombing (1984) 109; impact of Stakeknife revelations 156–7; informers against in revolutionary period 23, 24–6, 29, 30; informers at Dublin Castle (1930s) 64–5; informers murdered since 1994 ceasefire 113; murder of Nairac 127, 128–9, 130–1; and Nazi Germany 60–1, 64, 65–8, 82–3; in the North after partition 58, 60, 63–4, 76; Northern Command during Emergency 64, 68, 70, 83; Nutting Squad (security branch) 111, 137, 143–4; proscribed in Free State (1931) 59; publishes *Special Communiqué* 76–7, 78, 79; raid on GHQ in Dublin (1939) 61, 73; restructuring (1980) 159; and ritual of confession 13–14, 111, 157; RUC Belfast raids (December 1938) 63–4; South Leitrim Brigade 28; split of (1969) 87; and suspected Boy Scout/YMCA spies 47; systematic murder of RIC men 24; targeting of ex-soldiers 53; tensions in late 1930s 60, 61; two-week amnesty (1982) 159; violence between Official IRA and Provisionals 123; warnings to informers 48–9, 52, 106, 108–9, 110; in Wexford 62–3, 77–8
Irish Republican Brotherhood (IRB) 7, 22–3
Irish Volunteers 13, 22, 24; *see also* Irish Republican Army (IRA)
Irwin, Dr. Robert 91–2, 93, 95, 115
Irwin, Seán 50, 51
Italy 160

"The Jackal" (Robin Jackson) 124, 130
Jackson, Ian T. 11–12
"Jameson" (British agent) 25–6
Jennings, T. 184
Joyce, Michael 42, 43
Joyce, Patrick 44, 45
Joyce, Queenie (Gertrude Emily) 42, 43, 47–8
Joyce, William 2, 41–4, 47–8, 193; and Anglo-Irish War 44–7, 49, 54; and murder of Fr. Griffin 45–7, 54
Judas 5, 8, 9, 50, 158

"Kate Maloney" (Dagonet ballad) 3–4, 18, 20, 193
Kavanagh, Joseph 24
Kearney, Michael 156
Keating, Captain 46
Keenan, Brian 112
Kelly, Marie 27
Kelly, Paul 105
Kennedy, Edward 94
Kennedy, James 186, 187
Kennedy, Mary 179
Kenny, Mary 45, 47
Kermode, Frank 189
Kerr, Gordon 149, 150, 152–3, 155
Kerr, Pearse Patrick 88, 95–7, 100–1, 117, 146, 192
Kineen, E.L. 41
King, Peter 164
Kinsale, battle of (1602) 1
Kinsella, T. 17
Kirkpatrick, Harry 185, 187
Kitson, Brig. Gen. Frank 120–1, 135, 146, 155, 191
Knight, Maxwell 46, 48
Knight, William 104–5

Land League 7
Larkin, Jim 50, 51, 53
Laverty, Vernon 88

232 Index

Lavery, Tony 60
Lean, Geraldine 185, 186
Lean, Robert 185-6, 187, 188
Lecky, W.A. 6
Leemount House, near Coachford 29, 32, 34
Lennon, Patrick 28
"Let Erin Remember" (amhrán, "My name is Judas Stephen Hayes") 8, 18, 56-7, 58
Lewis, Rob 131, 156
Lindsay, Mrs. Mary 2, 29-30, 32-3, 48, 54; abduction 33-5, 39, 40-1; comparison with Edith Cavell 36, 37; execution 35, 36, 37-8, 41, 49; IRA view of as not Irish 40-1; propagandization of affair 36, 37
Litterick, Tom 95
Llewellyn, Barry 185
Lloyd George, David 27-8, 37
Long, Des 64
Longford, Lord 183
Loughlin, Gerald 183
Loughlin, Roisin 183
Lowry, Lord Chief Justice Robert 171, 172, 173, 175
loyalist paramilitary groups: arms transaction with South Africa 149; Bennett as supergrass 161, 183, 193; execution of informers 155, 157; informers 18, 87, 102, 109, 124, 149-55, 157, 161, 162-5, 172, 183, 186-7, 193; informers murdered since 1994 ceasefire 113; Miami Showband murders (1975) 89, 130; security force collusion with 124-5, 132, 140, 146, 148, 150-5, 156; warnings to informers 87; *see also* entries for individual groups
loyalists: and abolition of B Specials 120; advice to remain silent if interrogated 102-3; and Anglo-Irish Agreement (1985) 182; complaints over RUC informer recruitment 105; endurance esteemed by 8-9; ill-treatment of at Castlereagh 92, 102-3, 115; outrage at Bennett trial 164-5, 183
Lynch, Jack 121
Lynch, Liam 51, 52
Lynch, Sandy 143
Lyons, F.S.L. 51
Lyttle, Tommy "Tucker" 151-2, 154

MacBride, Seán 60, 61, 77, 78
MacCurtain, Tomás 28
MacDermott, Mr. Justice 180
Mac Dómhnaill, Seán Clárach 17
MacEoin, Uinseann 59, 76
Mackay, Neil 141
Macken, Sean 88, 116
Macnally, Leonard 6
Macready, Neville 34, 36
MacSwiney, Mary 49-50
MacSwiney, Terence 28, 31, 36
Madden, R.R. 6
mafiosi trials in Italy 160
Mag Uidhir, Sean 138

Magan, Anthony 84
Magee, John Joe 144
Magee, Pat 140
Maginn, Loughlin 132, 151-2
Maguire, Brian 88, 97-101, 117, 146, 192
Mahon, Catherine 103, 110-12
Mahon, Gerard 109-12, 117
Malins, Julian 125
Mallon, Sean 161, 182
Mannix, Patrick 37
Mannix, Sergeant 26
Martin, Bella 6
Martin, Michael 142
Martindale, Derek 137
Maryborough (Portlaoise) Prison 75, 81-2, 83
Maskey, Alex 116
Mason, Roy 94, 95, 98
Mathers, Joanne 140
Maynard, Joan 98
McAliskey, Bernadette 184
McAllister, Constable Laird Millar 97-8, 100
McCafferty, Nell 171
McCann, Joseph 183
McCann, Mary 103
McCaughey, Sean 60, 63-4, 67, 68, 71, 76, 83, 192; arrest (September 1941) 74, 76; court-martial of Hayes 69-70; hunger and thirst strike and death (1946) 75, 81-2, 83; refuses Hayes' request for priest 70; trial 68, 74-5, 76, 79, 81, 82
McConkey, John 174
McConnell, Robert 124-5
McCormick, Terry 127, 129, 130
McCrory, Maura 186
McCrossan, Alexa 183
McDonald, Henry 149, 155
McDonough, Roisin 165, 184, 185
McDonough, Tom 44, 48
McFerran, Stephen "Inch" 144
McGartland, Martin 109, 112
McGeown, Patrick 151
McGlade, Charlie 63, 64, 68, 76, 83
McGoldrick, Michael 186
McGrady, Kevin 162, 172, 173-8, 187, 192
McGrady, Sean 173, 174, 176, 177-8
McGrath, Mrs. (of Athdown) 6
McGuinness, Martin 112, 139-40, 145-6, 147; and Gilmour family 166, 168, 169-70, 171, 172; on Whoriskey case 180, 182
McGurk, Patrick 188
McHugh, Roger 69, 82
McIntyre, Antony 101, 145
McKearney, Thomas 100
McKee, Elizabeth 179
McKeown, Clifford 161, 183, 186
McKinney, Jack 97
McLaughlin, Mitchell 139, 180
McMahon, Gerard 175
McMahon, P. 51, 55
McMahon, Patrick 175

McMichael, John 150, 154
McNally, Joan 183–4
McNamara, James 24
McNamara, Kevin 95
McVeigh, Columba 124
McWilliams, Stephen 159, 186
Medical Referees Service 91
Mellowes, Liam 62
Melvin, John 52–3
MI 5 19, 103, 114, 122, 148, 149; and Fulton 135, 136; and G2 during WWII 65, 83; gains control of intelligence in North (1993) 147, 152; and William Joyce 43, 44, 46, 48; and Willie Carlin 139–40, 156, 157, 192, 193
Miami Showband murders (1975) 89, 130
Midleton, Earl of 49
military intelligence, British: collusion and murder allegations 124–5, 132, 140, 146, 148, 150–5, 156; and "extreme coercive pressure" 121–2; 14 Int 122, 123–31; informers as expendable 137; and Kitson 120–1, 135, 146, 155, 191; learning of subtle approach to recruitment 19, 156, 157, 192; locally born soldiers as touts/agents 15, 131–2, 133–41, 148–56, 192, 193; MRF 121–2; and Nairac 122, 123–31, 192, 193; rivalry with RUC 103, 121, 123, 147; and RUC Interrogation Centers 90; and Stakeknife 19, 111, 143, 144–5, 147–8, 156; torture methods used by 90, 197–8; see also Force Research Unit (FRU)
Mobile Reconnaissance Force (MRF) 121–2
Molloy, Brian Fergus 25
Molloy, Francie 108
Moloney, Ed 144
Monaghan, UVF bombings (May 1974) 124, 141
Moore, Patricia 181
Moore, Thomas 18
Morgan, John 187
Morley, Eoin 135
Morris, Eamon 102
Morrison, Danny 143, 146, 189, 193, 194, 195
Mountjoy, Lord 1
Moynihan, Daniel 94
Murphy, Denis 34, 35
Murphy, Edmund 127
Murphy, Jer Mickey 34, 38
Murphy, Dr. Lombard 76
Murphy, Patrick 72
Murphy, Simon 77, 78
Murphy, Thomas "Slab" 14
Murray, Fr. 127, 128
Murray, Mr. Justice 163, 164, 186–7

Nairac, Robert 122, 123–31, 192, 193
Nathan, Matthew 20, 22
National Council for Civil Liberties 184
nationalism, Irish: concept of betrayal 8, 20; endurance esteemed by 8–9, 25, 81, 82, 189; rising tide of in post-Rising period 23
Neligan, David 24, 25

Nelson, Brian 2, 112, 131, 132, 148–55, 157
Nelson, Rosemary 132
Newman, Kenneth 90–1, 93, 94, 95, 97, 101
newspapers: and civil war 51, 52, 53; and "Dirty War' 93, 142; government use of D-notices 12; Irish-American 12–13; local 11–12, 52, 53; and Mary Lindsay 33, 36, 38; outing of informers 113, 114, 148, 193; Stakeknife story 143, 144–5, 146, 148; and supergrass system 8–9, 12, 170, 175, 176, 184, 185–6
Northern Ireland: Ballykinlar Army base raid (December 1939) 64; Campbell College raid (1935) 60; Diplock courts 90, 92, 116, 117, 118, 121, 129, 163–4, 170–2, 180, 182, 184; economic and social problems (1930s) 60; local press in 12; RUC Belfast raids (December 1938) 63–4; Special Powers Act (1922) 90; see also Belfast; Royal Ulster Constabulary (RUC); Special Branch, RUC; Troubles
Northern Ireland Assembly 112, 141
Nuremberg war crime trials 15, 116

Ó Beacháin, Donnacha 71
Ó Brádaigh, Ruairí 101–3, 194
Ó hUid, Tarlach 63, 69, 83–4
Ó Nualláin, N.S. 27
Oatley, Michael 141
O'Callaghan, Sean: *Execution* (1974) 32
O'Connor, Joseph 77, 78
O'Doherty, Anthony 186
O'Donnell, Justice 180
O'Donnell, Red Hugh (of Ulster) 1
O'Donoghue, Florrie 13, 26, 29, 34, 53
O'Flaherty, Peadar 61
O'Grady, Seán 76
O'Halpin, Eunan 8, 23, 25, 73
O'Hara, Patsy 187
O'Hara, Sean Seamus 187
O'Hegarty, Seán 28, 29, 31, 35, 37
O'Higgins, Kevin 50
O'Leary, Jackie 31, 32–3, 34, 37, 38, 39, 49
Omagh bomb (15 August 1998) 137–8
O'Malley, Ernie 28, 51, 52
O'Neill, Hugh, Earl of Tyrone 1
O'Neill, Tip 94
O'Rawe, Dr. James 92
O'Rawe, James 185
Ossory, Bishop Collier of 78
O'Sullivan, Jack 31

Pappworth, J. 16
Parker, John: *Secret Hero* 129–30
Parker Report (1972) 94
Pearse, Patrick 8
Penal Code 6
Pinkey, Eugene 175
Pinkey, Thomas 175
Pinkman, Charles 28
Plant, George 77, 81

Index

Plunkett, Count 23
poetry and verse (amhráin) 8, 17–18, 20, 21, 56–7, 86, 97, 101, 119, 158
poitín industry 7
police surgeons 91–2, 93, 95, 96–7, 115, 116
post office clerks 24, 45
Powell, John 52
Powell, Mrs. (sister of Michael Collins) 49
Price, Mary 126
propaganda: during Anglo-Irish War 30–1, 34, 35–8, 50, 54; anti–British in North America 12–13; and Magazine Fort raid (1939) 64; radio transmitters during Emergency 66, 67–8; RUC response to Castlereagh complaints 90, 93, 95; smear campaign against Dr. Irwin 93; during Troubles 87–8, 109, 122, 129, 160, 186, 191
Provisional IRA 87, 91, 123, 135–6, 146
PSNI 194

Quigley, Robert 162, 172, 187, 188
Quinlisk, Harry Timothy 23, 26, 54
Quinn, Lowry 194
Quirke, Billy 13, 68, 69, 82

Rachman, S. 10
Rainbow Portrait, Hatfield House 5
Rawlinson, Chief Superintendent Peter 98, 99–100
Reel, Packy 130–1
Relatives for Justice 184, 185
republicanism, Irish: and de Valera in 1930s 60; endurance esteemed by 8–9, 25, 81, 82, 189; at low ebb in 1920s 58; view of Lindsay as spy 36, 37–8; *see also* Irish Republican Army (IRA); Sinn Féin
Rice, Gerard 106
Rice, Liam 63–4
Riordan, Din Din 29
Roscommon by-election (February 1917) 23
Roy, Wayne 96
Royal Army Medical Corps 91
Royal Irish Constabulary (RIC) 22, 23–4, 59; Auxiliary Cadets 44, 45, 46–7, 54; as basis for RUC 89
Royal Military Police (RMP) 105
Royal Ulster Constabulary (RUC) 8, 14, 15, 88, 89, 146; B Specials 89, 120; Crown Entry raid (1935) 60, 76; raids on republicans in Belfast (December 1938) 63–4; *see also* Special Branch, RUC
Ruddy, Norman 179, 180
Russell, Sean 60, 61, 63, 64, 71, 73
Ryan, Dr. James 71, 72–3, 78, 81

Sagarsky, Israel 52
Sands, Bobby 17, 18, 98, 100, 112; "The Crime of Castlereagh" 8, 18, 86, 97, 100, 191–2; *The H-Block Trilogy* 173; "Weeping Winds" 101

SAS 105, 122, 124, 126, 128, 129
Saville Inquiry (1998) 141
Scappaticci, Fred (Stakeknife) 13–14; denies Stakeknife allegations 145–6, 147–8; as member of Nutting Squad 111, 143–4; Stakeknife accusations against 7, 111, 142–5, 156
SDLP 92
Selborne, Earl of 36
Seldon, Anthony 16
Selwyn, Francis 44
Shakespeare, William: *All's Well That Ends Well* 10
Sheehan, Tim 31, 32
Sheppard, Thomas 144
Shinnick, Fr. Edward 30, 32, 33, 34, 39, 54
Sinn Féin: advice to remain silent if interrogated 101, 102; advice to those approached by Crown Forces 102, 104–5, 106, 108–9, 157; and death of Brian Maguire 98; electoral successes (early 1980s) 106; informer press conferences 104, 105; *The Informers* (booklet,1983) 108–9; post-Rising period 23; and supergrass strategy 160, 161, 180, 185–6, 187; and Willie Carlin 139–40, 141, 156, 157
Skelly, William 185
Skinnider, Margaret: *Doing My Bit for Ireland* 22
Slane, Gerard 150
Smithwick tribunal (opened 2011) 148
sources 11–18, 51
Spanish Civil War (1936–39) 60
Special Branch, Free State 59, 61, 65, 73, 76
Special Branch, RUC: abuse and brutality at interrogation centers 88–9, 90, 91, 92–7, 100–1, 102–4, 114–18, 191; Amnesty International Report (1978) 88, 93–4, 95, 114, 115, 159; collusion with loyalist paramilitaries 124–5, 132, 146, 150–5, 156; and families of supergrasses 161, 167–70, 171, 172, 180, 183–4, 189, 194; "five techniques" 91, 94; "Goon Squad" 101; as independent of main force 90; inducements to supergrasses 159, 187–8; interrogation function 88, 90, 92, 93–5, 159–60; learning of subtle approach to recruitment 19, 106, 159–60, 161, 162, 192; low-level informers as expendable 111; and police doctors 91–2, 93, 95, 96–7, 115, 116; protective custody of supergrasses 15, 168–70; recruitment of supergrasses 2, 14, 161, 166–7; rehearsing/coaching of supergrasses 15, 161, 171, 173, 177, 181, 184, 187; rivalry with British Army 103, 121, 123, 147; and Robert Lean 185–6, 187, 188; "Schoolboy Spy-Ring" in Belfast 105–6; specialized interrogation teams 92; Thames Television documentary (1977) 94; torture methods use by 90, 95–6, 100, 103, 104, 117–18, 197–8; trawling for informers by 12, 19, 87, 92, 102, 103–12, 113, 115, 116, 117

Index

Squires, Martin 123, 125
Stack, Austin 37
Stakeknife 19, 111, 121, 191, 192; accusations against Scappaticci 7, 111, 142–5, 156; alleged separate FRU team for 143, 147; and Cryptome website 143, 144–5; emergence of story 143; Fulton offers to sell name of 138, 144–5; impact on IRA of revelations 156–7
Stapleton, William 24
Stephan, Enno 67
Stephenson, William 174, 175
Stevens Enquiry (1989–2003) 131–2, 143, 151, 152, 153, 155
Stobie, Billy 151, 154
Stockholm Syndrome 106–8, 192
Stop the Show Trials Committee 184, 186
"Stormontgate" (2002) 112, 193
Strickland, General 32–3, 34, 35, 36, 41
Sullivan, Jim 100
supergrass strategy: academic studies 15–16; acquittals on appeal 164, 172, 188; Angela Whoriskey 103, 162, 179–82, 184, 185; Anti-Perjurer Joint Delegation to London (1984) 184; Bill of Indictment 161; Christopher Black 159, 160–1, 163–4, 171, 183, 187; debates over end of system 182, 184–5, 188; Gifford's definition of a supergrass 160; and hunger strike deaths (1981) 160; impact on families 161, 167–70, 171, 172, 180, 183–4, 189, 194; Joe Bennett 18, 157, 161, 162–5, 172, 183, 186–7, 193; Kevin McGrady 162, 172, 173–8, 187; Lean as IRA-plant theory 186; loyalist outrage at 164–5, 183; loyalist supergrasses 18, 102, 161, 162–5, 183, 193; and newspapers 8–9, 12, 170, 175, 176, 184, 185–6; parallels with internment 161–2, 164, 188; protective custody periods 15, 159, 161, 168–70; protest groups/campaigns against 162, 182, 183, 184; rehearsing/coaching of supergrasses 15, 161, 171, 173, 177, 181, 184, 187; reported destruction of documents 185; retraction of statements 108, 161, 184, 185, 186, 188; RUC recruitment process 2, 14, 161, 166–7; RUC's purpose 160–2, 182–3; show trials 15, 16, 19, 102, 163–4, 170–2, 174–6, 183–4, 185, 186–7; and Stockholm Syndrome 106–8, 192; "success" 182–3, 185, 188; *see also* Gilmour, Raymond
Sutton Death List 103–4

Tallon, Laurence 44
Taylor, Peter 95
Teggart, Bernard 103–4
Thatcher, Margaret 103, 141, 153, 160
Thomas, Allan 172
Thomas, Captain (informer for Walsingham) 6
Thomson, Basil 25
Thornton, Frank 25, 26
Togher, Joe 13, 44–5, 46–7

Townson, Liam 127, 129
Treaty, Anglo-Irish 26–8, 50, 51–2
Troubles: Belfast riots (August 1969) 120; British Army's arrival in Derry (August 1969) 120; British Embassy in Dublin burned down (1972) 121; British spread of disinformation 121, 135, 146, 147, 155, 156, 188, 192; child informers 104–6, 109, 192; Civil Rights march in Derry (August 1969) 87; estimated number of paid informers 87; Falls Curfew (July 1970) 120; Kitson's tactics 120–1, 135, 146, 155, 191; loyalist informers 18, 87, 102, 109, 124, 149–55, 157, 161, 162–5, 172, 183, 186–7, 193; northern Ireland Political Collection 1; propaganda during 87–8, 109, 122, 129, 160, 186, 191; Sutton Death List 103–4
Truce (July 1921) 13, 26, 37
Tuite, Matty 61, 73
Turley, Dan 60
Twomey, Moss 58, 60, 76, 83
Tyrie, Andy 150, 151

Ulster Defence Association (UDA) 123, 132, 144, 149, 150, 151–5, 157
Ulster Defence Regiment (UDR) 89, 105
Ulster Freedom Fighters (UFF) 109, 150–1, 152, 155
Ulster Volunteer Force (UVF) 115, 124, 144, 162–3, 164, 183, 187
United Irishman rebellion (1798) 6, 8, 116
United States 12–13, 35–6, 94–5; and Pearse Kerr case 95–7, 100–1, 117, 192

Valentine, Rachael 6

Wall Street Crash (1929) 59
Walsh, James 37
Walsh, Maud 37, 54
Walsh, Michael 77, 78
Walsingham, Francis 5–6
War of Independence *see* Anglo-Irish War
Ware, John 153
Webb, Miles 43, 44, 46
Weir, John 124–5, 130–1
Wexford 6, 62–3, 77–8
White, Harry 60
White, Mrs. (of Athdown) 6
Whoriskey, Angela 103, 162, 179–82, 184, 185
Wimborne, Lord 22
Winter, Colonel Ormonde 26
women: Cumann na mBan 49–50; Eve in garden of Eden 9–10; execution of Catherine Mahon 111; female internees 179; held at Castlereagh 103, 181; ill-treatment of republicans in prison 103, 179, 181; IRA order on dealing with women spies 39–40; IRA policy of not shooting women 35, 37, 39–40, 52; in pre-twentieth-century espionage 6, 7; protests at supergrass system 162, 183,

184, 185; strip searching of 179, 181; Whoriskey as supergrass 162, 179–82, 184, 185
World War I 22, 30
World War II *see* Emergency (Second World War)
Wright, Billy (LVF leader) 132

Wright, John 187
Wright, Seamus 122, 157

Yendall, Catherine 185
Youth with a Mission (YWAM) 174, 176

www.ingramcontent.com/pod-product-compliance
Lightning Source LLC
Chambersburg PA
CBHW051219300426
44116CB00006B/643